THE JOURNAL OF

NEGRO HISTORY

Founded by
CARTER G. WOODSON

Volume 39/1954

UNITED PUBLISHING CORPORATION

New York, Washington, D.C.

Under the auspices of
THE ASSOCIATION FOR THE STUDY OF NEGRO LIFE AND HISTORY

CONTENTS OF VOLUME XXXIX

VOL. XXXIX—JANUARY, 1954—NO. 1

VOL. XXXIX—APRIL, 1954—NO. 2

THE JOURNAL

OF

NEGRO HISTORY

VOL. XXXIX—January, 1954—No. 1

THE THIRTY-EIGHTH ANNUAL MEETING OF THE ASSOCIATION FOR THE STUDY OF NEGRO LIFE AND HISTORY

The Thirty-Eighth Annual Meeting of the Association for the Study of Negro Life and History was held in Nashville, Tennessee, October 23, 24, and 25, 1953, with Tennessee A. and I. State University and Fisk University serving as the host institutions. The state-wide committee on arrangements, led by Dr. J. E. Walker and Mrs. Cora B. Robinson, had done much to lay the foundation for a successful meeting, while the local committee, under the direction of Professor Merl R. Eppse, had ably tended to the innumerable details incident to the comfort of the delegates and participants. The committee on program, believing that the Association was interested in a variety of subjects as well as speakers, made every effort to provide topics of lively interest and participants of unquestioned competence. The enthusiastic support of the members of the committee and the generous cooperation of the participants did much to make the aims of the committee a reality.

The sessions began with a brief program of welcome that had been arranged by the local committee. The chairman of the program was Dr. J. E. Walker, leader of the state-wide

1

committee; and the devotionals were conducted by Dr. Ralph Riley, President of the American Baptist Theological Seminary. Greetings were brought to the Association by Dr. W. L. Crump, Director of Public Relations at Tennessee A. and I. State University, the Honorable Ben West, Mayor of Nashville, Mr. Alf Rutherford, Clerk of the Circuit Court, and Mr. Donald M. McSween, State Commissioner of Employment Security. Music was furnished by the University Choir; and Albert N. D. Brooks, Secretary-Treasurer of the Association, responded for the Association.

Immediately following the close of the welcome program, William F. Butler of Tennessee A. and I. State University called the Association to order to listen to papers under the general topic of "The Negro in Local and Regional History." Alrutheus A. Taylor of Fisk University read a paper on "Fisk University and the Nashville Community, 1866-1900" in which he pointed out the way in which a new institution of higher education, primarily for Negroes, was received by the Nashville Community. Because some white Nashville citizens always believed in the institution, hostility to it was kept to a minimum; and as graduates took their places in the community, the institution grew in public favor. Dewey Grantham of Vanderbilt University devoted his attention to "The Negro and the Progressive Movement," and pointed out how the Progressives never faced the race problem in the way that they faced other pressing questions of the day and indicated that the race question was especially embarrassing to Southern Progressives. William A. Low of Maryland State College led the discussion.

The afternoon session on "Expansion and Conflict" was presided over by Lorenzo J. Greene of Lincoln University (Missouri), due to the late arrival of the train on which Tinsley Spraggins of Virginia Union University was traveling. Raleigh Wilson of Tennessee A. and I. State University read a paper on "Some Aspects of Slavery and Abolitionism Among the Five Civilized Tribes," in which he discussed the extent and nature of slavery among the Indians and the impact of abolitionist sentiment among them. The distinctions which he drew between slavery among the Indians and that among Southern whites were both interesting and convincing. Benjamin Quarles of Morgan State College read a paper on "Ministers Without Portfolio," which centered on the activities of Negroes abroad during the period of intersectional strife and during the Civil War. He described in some detail the way in which Negroes sought to influence official policy in England and other countries so that it would benefit the cause of the Negro and of the United States. Lawrence D. Reddick of Atlanta University led the discussion.

On Friday evening a public meeting was held in the chapel of Tennessee A. and I. State University, and the presiding officer was Dr. Walter S. Davis, President of the University. The topic for discussion was "The Negro's Struggle for Civil Rights, 1900-1953." John Hope Franklin of Howard University traced the struggle from a historical point of view, beginning with the struggle against disfranchisement at the opening of the century and concluding with the fight against segregation at mid-century. Lawrence D. Reddick of Atlanta University described the current struggle of Negroes for civil rights in the Southeast, with particular emphasis on Georgia. F. D. Moon of Oklahoma City told of the fight to secure equal education in Texas and Oklahoma. Lorenzo J. Greene of Lincoln University (Missouri) told of the techniques and successes of Negroes in the area of civil rights in the border states. At the end of this session the University and the committee on arrangements entertained the members and delegates of the Association at a pleasant reception in the foyer of the Administration Building of the University.

The first session on Saturday morning, October 24, was

devoted to a discussion of the problem of "Teaching the
History of the Negro." An overflow audience of delegates,
local teachers, and students at Tennessee State University
listened attentively to two papers. Mrs. Vivian R. Beavers
of the Atlanta University Laboratory School read a paper
on "Teaching the History of the Negro in Secondary
Schools," in which she made a plea for the integration of
the history of the Negro with general American history.
Mrs. Vassie D. Wright of the Author's Study Club of Los
Angeles, California, read a paper on "Teaching Negro
History to Adults, with Emphasis on the History of the
Negro in California." Mrs. Wright described the way in
which her organization had aroused interest among adults
in the study of Negro history and indicated that the results
of the efforts had been most salutary. The presiding officer,
H. C. Savage of Tennessee A. and I. State University, then
called on the leaders of the discussion, Mrs. Lucy Harth
Smith of Lexington, Kentucky, and Mrs. Edna Turner of
Nashville. After these discussants had made comments and
raised significant questions, the discussion was enlivened
by extensive participation on the part of the audience.

The luncheon-business meeting was held in the University cafeteria at 11:30 a.m. The chairman was Dr. Charles H.
Wesley, President of the Association. Dr. Wesley told the
membership of the problems which the Executive Council
had faced during the previous year in connection with operating the Association and the Associated Publishers. Albert
N. D. Brooks, Secretary-Treasurer of the Association and
Editor of the *Negro History Bulletin,* made his report.
William M. Brewer, Editor of the *Journal of Negro History,* then reported on his own editorial activities as well as
those of the members of the editorial board. Some considerable attention was given the problem of the Association's
indebtedness, and several ways of achieving solvency were
discussed. Arnett G. Lindsay reminded the Association of
the forthcoming fortieth anniversary of the organization

and suggested that the occasion could be used both for the promotion of the work of the organization and for raising funds to apply against the indebtedness. Several proposals for raising funds were enthusiastically adopted by the Association.

On Saturday afternoon Herman Dreer of Stowe Teachers College presided over the session on "Race Problems in the Post-Reconstruction Era." In his paper, "Northern Prejudice and the Fifteenth Amendment," Leslie Fishel of the Massachusetts Institute of Technology indicated that sentiment in the North against the enfranchisement of Negroes was strong and that in many instances when Northerners favored it for the South they did not favor it for their own communities. Helen Edmonds of the North Carolina College at Durham read a paper on "The Wilmington Race Riot of 1898," in which she not only identified the causes and consequences of the riot but also gave a vivid description of the city during the course of the riot. Henry L. Swint of Vanderbilt University led the discussion in which the audience participated by making comments and observations and by raising questions.

At the public meeting on Saturday evening the topic for a panel discussion was "Problems of Modern Africa." The chairman of the panel was Preston Valien of Fisk University, who made some remarks regarding the relationship of the problems of Africa to the rest of the world. A. E. Bassey of Atlanta University described some of the pressing economic problems of Africa, with special reference to his own home in Nigeria. Kwasi Siriboe of Central State College described some of the social problems of the continent and made remarks about problems which the people of his own home in the Gold Coast faced. Paul Anene Okoh Mozia of Tennessee A. and I. State University gave attention to the forces underlying the nationalist movements in Africa and told in some detail how nationalism had developed in Nigeria, his own home. H. Alfred Ferrell of Lincoln University

(Pennsylvania) told of Lincoln's historic connection with Africa and described recent efforts, including the Annual African Institute held in collaboration with the Association, to develop even closer ties with Africa.

Sunday morning at 8:30 several hundred persons met in the University cafeteria for the Authors' Breakfast, which had been arranged by the local committee. Thomas E. Poag of Tennessee A. and I. State University served as toastmaster. Among the authors who made remarks about their writings were Benjamin Quarles, Helen Edmonds, Charles H. Wesley, Merl Eppse, Lorenzo Greene, W. Sherman Savage, Virginia Nyabongo, Carl Hill, and John Hope Franklin.

At 10:30 Sunday morning the Association met in the International Student Center of Fisk University for a session on "Negro Music and Poetry," presided over by John W. Work of Fisk University. Frederick Hall of Alabama State College read a paper on "The History of Gospel Music." He traced the evolution of gospel music from Africa, described some of the influences of the New World on it, and pointed up the social and cultural significance of this increasingly popular form of musical expression. Robert Hayden of Fisk University spoke on "Problems of the Negro Poet," and read, to the great satisfaction of the audience, a number of his own poems. Arna Bontemps of Fisk University commented on both papers and led the discussion in which numerous members of the audience participated.

The final session of the Association was held at the Chapel of Fisk University on Sunday afternoon. Dr. Charles S. Johnson, President of Fisk University, presided at this session and made timely remarks regarding the significance of the Association and the wide interest in the history of the Negro which he had observed in various parts of the world. He then introduced Dr. Homer A. Jack of Evanston, Illinois, who spoke on the subject, "Africa Aflame." He told of his recent visit to Africa, his visit with Albert Schweitzer, and his experiences in the Union of South Africa. In considerable detail he described the opposition to apartheid there and of the various signs of unrest which, he believed, would ultimately lead to an immense improvement of conditions. President Charles H. Wesley in "The Association and the Public" described the interest of the Association in the promotion of truth and in the improvement of human relations and indicated that the public itself has a stake in the welfare of the Association. He called on the general public to support the Association and expressed the hope that the intimacy of the Association with the community would continue to increase. The local committee, represented by Mrs. Mabel B. Crooks, presented the Association with a purse containing more than $400. The Department of Music of Fisk University provided music for the occasion.

The author of this report, who was chairman of the committee on program, would be derelict and ungrateful if he did not acknowledge the fact that whatever success the program was can be attributed to the unselfish cooperation and the many wise suggestions made by the members of that committee: Lorenzo Greene of Lincoln University (Missouri), Merl R. Eppse of Tennessee State University, August Meier of Fisk University, and Robert Cureton of the English Avenue School in Atlanta. He wishes to make a public acknowledgment of his gratitude to the members of the committee. On behalf of the committee he wishes to express the appreciation of the group to the participants on the program, whose scholarly papers, wise discussions, and competent conduct of the sessions did more than anything to make the Thirty-Eighth Annual Meeting a fruitful experience for all who attended.

JOHN HOPE FRANKLIN

Howard University

NORTHERN PREJUDICE AND NEGRO SUFFRAGE
1865-1870

A confused and contradictory quiet underlay the frothy excitement which followed Appomattox and Ford's Theater. The victory of Grant and the death of Lincoln in a sense symbolized the mixture of gladness and gloom which marked deeper Northern feeling about the most serious human problem to come out of the war: what to do about the Negro? While the ante-bellum and war years had produced climactic spasms of Negrophilism with some tangible benefits in the form of emancipation and education, the North had not yet loosed itself from the fetters of prejudice and discrimination. Ahead lay real tests. Could the North so conquer its race bias as to eliminate segregation, freely extend its educational opportunities, offer employment without color restriction, and enfranchise its Negro minority? Of these the suffrage question was the first to receive national publicity amid the general clamor over the rights and abilities of the race.

Gladness and gloom indeed characterized the attitude of persons interested in the status of the Negro. Many could proudly proclaim the coming of a new day, as did a white officer with the 32nd United States Colored Troops: "This prejudice that has flourished for a season . . . and has been so strongly grounded in the hearts of our countrymen, is being slowly, but surely abandoned."[1] Exhortations like that of Theodore Tilton were received with attentive good humor:

I ask that the Negro shall receive the respect of the best society. . . . Ask him into your pew at church. Let him ride at your side in the cars. Give him the right hand of Fellowship—as indeed,

---

[1] Letter from Fred S. Eaton, August 9, 1864, *The American Missionary*, VIII (1864), 273-374.

God ordained, for he made the inside of the Negro's hand white, for clasping a white man's hand (laughter).[2]

Lydia Maria Child urged the further use of colored orators so that people could see for themselves the abilities of the race and she cited the statement made by a white person in John D. Gurley's Massachusetts audience: "I tell you what, folks are changing. Some begin to think that a man like Mr. Gurley might as well be trusted to vote as some white folks."[3] From the Bay State to the nation's capital, from New York and Philadelphia to Missouri and Michigan, it looked to many as if "folks are changing."[4]

Less sanguine observers spoke out in tones edged with despair. E. L. Godkin preached "The One Humanity" in an early issue of the *Nation*. The basis of political society, he wrote, lay in "the education and elevation of our humanity." Ancient states failed because they were founded on the principle of race; the Christian idea, the closest approximation to perfection, denies racism and preaches the raising of all peoples. Even so, in the enlightened days of 1865, the dangers which menaced antiquity have cropped up again:

> We are reluctant to concede to the African man what we boast of giving to others . . . presenting no higher claims, apparently, of intellectual or of moral worth. The doubt is openly avowed by some; it lies as an unsatisfied query in the minds of others; it lingers unconsciously, or semi-consciously, with many whose philanthropy or political consistency holds them back from confessing it even to themselves; it haunts the soul as a ghostly prejudice, even when philosophy and religion have made us reject it as a dogma. We do not fully and heartily believe that the Negro is a

[2] Theodore Tilton, *The Negro; A Speech at Cooper Institute*, New York, May 21, 1863 (New York, 1863), 2.

[3] Reprinted in New York Independent, July 27, 1865.

[4] Cf. *Ibid.*, April 28, 1864, June 2, 1864, January 19, 1865, February 9, 1865, April 13, 1865; *Boston Transcript*, May 10, 1865; John A. Andrew to Charles Sumner, November 21, 1865, Andrew Papers, Massachusetts Historical Society; Increase N. Tarbox, "Universal Suffrage," *The New Englander*, XXIV (1865), 165-166; *Freedmen's Bulletin*, I (1865), 89-90.

man. We could not act or reason as we do unless this were the case.[5]
Evidence from all over the North added substance to this
and like charges.[6]

This schizophrenia of fervent hope and foreboding was
transformed into cold fact in the political arena. Here the
Negro had been an issue as a slave since before the Constitutional Convention, as a man since 1863. The fruits of
emancipation tasted bitter to North and South alike. When,
in June, 1864, Senator Waitman Willey of West Virginia
offered an amendment to the Freedman's Bureau bill, authorizing the Bureau head to correspond with Northern
Governors and municipal authorities to find employment
for colored people on farms and in industries in their lo-
calities, Northern Democrats and Republicans alike fought
to reject it. They argued that the publicity involved would
place the local officials in a vulnerable position. An obvious
device for political embarrassment, the amendment was
whittled down and finally disappeared in a joint congressional conference.[7] The next year Senator Lyman Trumbull
of Illinois placed the Negrophobe element on the defensive
with a measure extending the Bureau's jurisdiction to refugees and freedmen all over the country. The opposition
clawed and scratched. "What is office without social rights
and social distinctions?" cried Senator Edgar Cowan of
Pennsylvania afraid that this extension would lead to suffrage and office-holding. "Nothing, nothing," he answered
emphatically, for himself. The black, he asserted, is different, inferior, and cannot be washed white by debates, petitions, and laws.[8]

In both of these cases, the Radical Republicans dis-

[5] I (1865), 520-521.

[6] *New York Independent*, March 24, 1864, February 8, 1866, August 15,
1867; *Boston Herald*, May 10, 1865; *The Liberator*, May 26, 1865; *The Old
Guard*, III (1865), 142.

[7] *Congressional Globe*, 38 Cong., 1 sess., 2934, 3329-3330, 3334, 3335, 3337,
3349, 2 sess., 1348, 1409, Appendix, 141.

[8] *Ibid.*, 39 Cong., 1 sess., 129, 316, 318, 320-321, 334-335, 343, 344.

patched the forces of gloom. Their real passion, however, was the suffrage, their key weapon in reconstructing the former Confederate states. Here was a legal and non-violent means of control which could be dressed in appealing moral clothes. Their effort to seize this all-important tool began in 1865 and encountered Northern opposition from the first.

The Radicals depended to some extent on humanitarian propaganda to whip up sentiment for the Negro voter, and publicists like Theodore Tilton, Increase Tarbox, Gerrit Smith, Frederick Douglass, John Langston, and Lydia Maria Child worked diligently to this end.[9] Behind the scenes, men who engaged in politics scurried about to bring the North into line behind the Radical program. The crucial contest in 1865 came in Connecticut, the only New England state which excluded colored men from the polls. The Legislature passed a bill to submit the question of Negro suffrage to the voters at a special October election. By September, Republicans realized the necessity of carrying the state. Connecticut was one of the few states where the issue squarely faced the voters, and, as the Washington correspondent of the *New York Independent* pointed out, an enthusiastic affirmation there might swing President Andrew Johnson into the Radical fold.[10] By September also, Republicans woke up to the difficulty of winning. "Earnest Republicans," wrote William Grosvenor of New Haven to Charles Sumner, "feel that the influence of a defeat here in retarding the course elsewhere would be disastrous." They

---

[9] Howard K. Beale, *The Critical Year, A Study of Andrew Johnson and Reconstruction* (New York, 1930), 68, 68 n, 73. Beale gives adequate emphasis to the relationship between Northern prejudice and the Radical desire for suffrage in 1865 and 1866 in *ibid.*, 178 ff. For the above propagandists see *New York Independent*, January 19, 1865, April 20, 1865, July 19, 27, 1865; George L. Stearns, comp. *The Equality of All Men Before the Law* (Boston, 1865), 35-39; *Cleveland Leader*, August 17, 1865 in *Annals of Cleveland*, XLVIII, 219.

[10] *American Annual Cyclopaedia and Register of Important Events of the Year, 1864* (New York, 1865), 354; *New York Independent*, September 14, 1865.

could not back out now, despite the gloomy prospects. Prejudice, Grosvenor reported, had even infiltrated the ranks of the politicians:

A great many Republicans flinch, especially in country towns, and curiously enough in abolition districts. Some of our oldest radicals are more weak on this issue than the late converts from Democracy. . . . In some towns the Committees are hostile, One of the State Committee, Agard of Litchfield, is not favorable, absented himself from the meeting, and his name is being used in the hope that he will not have the pluck to disavow it. All this is unpleasant.[11]

The mayor of Norwich expressed the same fears to Governor John Andrew of Massachusetts in a letter asking him to speak for Connecticut Republicans. Negro suffrage must win there, he told Andrew, for the sake of the state and "the influence the vote may have upon the question in other States. . . . Republicans need to be set on fire—will you do it? It's worth $100 to them."[12] As election day approached, the voters received appeals from all sides. A minister flung the Christian argument against prejudice at them: "The unseen Christ will stand by the ballot box watching every vote you deposit," while a Radical editorial blamed all the opposition on a minority of Democrats and pleaded for a Republican vote to support Reconstruction measures in the South.[13] When the smoke had cleared, a substantial majority had decided against the Negro.[14]

The Ohio Democrats tried to make Negro suffrage a campaign issue to embarrass the Republicans, but the latter's convention refused to insert a franchise plank in the platform, realizing, as one orator put it, the "unsettled

[11] September 5, 1865, Sumner Papers, Houghton Library, Harvard University.

[12] James Lloyd Greene to Andrew, September 22, 1865, Andrew Papers, MHS.

[13] *New York Independent*, September 28, 1865.

[14] Edward McPherson, *The Political History of the United States of America during the Period of Reconstruction* . . . (2nd ed., Washington, D. C., 1875), 120.

state of opinion even among Union men.'"[15] Jacob Cox, the Union gubernatorial candidate, had instructed his manager at the convention not to permit his nomination if the party declared for suffrage. Pinned down by Western Reserve radicals after his nomination, Cox walked the equivocal line of separate but equal privileges, proposing a segregated colony on the South Atlantic coast. The problem, he added later, was a national one to be handled on a national basis:

> The few colored men whom we have amongst us at the North may be regarded as the waifs and strays of the great body which is a nation in numbers and in its isolation by mental and physical characteristics. It is as a unit that we must deal with them. . . .

Should the people of the state accept the Negro voter, he admitted still later in the campaign, he would not object.[16] The Union party's evasion of the issue gained them the victory although Cox ran about 1500 votes behind his ticket in the radical Western Reserve area.[17] The state supported the party which had avoided the suffrage issue.

Elsewhere in the North politicians moved cautiously around the controversy. Thaddeus Stevens, in control of the Pennsylvania Radicals, explained to Charles Sumner that the Republican convention at Harrisburg had passed over the question "as heavy and premature."[18] The New York State Republican platform, like its Democratic counterpart, ignored the issue. In New Jersey, Republicans in convention decisively defeated a resolution endorsing it while Democrats went on record opposing it. Indiana's governor, Oliver P. Morton, stated the position of his state organization:

[15] William Cox Cochran, The Political Experiences of Major General Jacob Dolson Cox (Mss. in Oberlin College Library, 1940), II, 808-809, 813-815; Cleveland Leader, June 23, 1865, loc. cit., 217.

[16] Cochran, Cox, II, 803-804, 821-822, 848, 898-899. For comments on Cox's campaign see The Old Guard, III (1865), 431, 481-484; Nation, I (1865), 429-430; Senator Thomas A. Hendricks of Indiana, Cong. Globe, 39 Cong., 1 sess., 369.

[17] Cleveland Leader, November 27, 1865, loc. cit., 132.

[18] Stevens to Sumner, August 26, 1865, Sumner Papers, Houghton Library, Harvard University.

freedmen should wait for fifteen or twenty years before receiving the franchise. In addition to preparing Negroes for political responsibility, this would enable whites to build up majorities in the South with the help of Northern and foreign immigrants. Morton admitted that this proposal relieved Indiana Republicans of the obligation to advocate Negro suffrage at home.[19]

Charles A. Dana, writing to Charles Sumner early in September, warned that only a reading and writing qualification would make Negro suffrage palatable to voters in Illinois, Wisconsin and Michigan.[20] While Illinois had no contest, Wisconsin voters rejected the colored voter and accepted the Republican slate. Michigan's legislature enacted and then repealed a law to submit to a referendum a constitutional amendment enfranchising the race. Instead they laid plans for a convention to rewrite the whole document. In Minnesota, Republicans stumped for manhood suffrage and gained control of the state government. The electorate, however, simultaneously repudiated equal voting privileges by a margin of almost ten per cent of the votes cast.[21]

During the campaigns publicists had made plain the issue's intimate connections with Reconstruction in the South. Horace Greeley had appealed to rational men on both sides of the Mason-Dixon line to work for it as a *sine qua non* of the Radical program. An anonymous Philadelphia correspondent to the *Nation* had asked some "Plain Questions" about the feasibility of requiring of the South that which the North did not grant.[22] After the canvass this

[19] *Cleveland Leader*, September 22, 1865, *loc. cit.*, 133; *New York Independent*, November 2, 16, 1865; Charles P. Smith to John A. Andrew, September 23, 1865, Andrew Papers, MHS; William C. Gerichs, "The Ratification of the Fifteenth Amendment in Indiana," *Indiana Magazine of History*, IX (1913), 132, 137.

[20] September 1, 1865, Sumner Papers, Houghton Library, Harvard University.

[21] *Annual Cyclopaedia* (1865), 823, 577, 566, 598; *Cleveland Leader*, September 19, November 2, 1865, *loc. cit.*, 306; Cochran, Cox, II, 914.

[22] *New York Independent*, May 11, 1865; *Nation*, I (1865), 171.

sensitive spot was further exposed. The *Springfield Republican* twitted Thad Stevens for not pushing his pet project through his home state first.[23] Senators and Congressmen made use of the returns during the debate on suffrage in the District of Columbia.[24] "They who desire the Right of Suffrage for the Blacks of the South," summed up the *New York Tribune,* "oppose the extension of the same right to the Blacks of the North."[25]

In spite of the vicissitudes of suffrage, however, the first session of the Thirty-Ninth Congress began propitiously for the Negro. Boston's *Christian Register* felt that "the interests and best good of this class will be cared for."[26] A group of influential Negroes numbering Frederick Douglass and George Downing among them stated that they were in Washington "charged with the duty to look after the best interests of the recently emancipated."[27] According to the *New York Tribune,* these "outside representatives" were paid for their attentions to Congress, probably the first Negro lobby.[28]

In January, 1866, a civil rights bill came up for action before Congress which eventually passed it twice, the second time over Johnson's veto. Then, to insure that the Southern states should discover no constitutional loopholes to climb through, the legislators started the Fourteenth Amendment on its way. The Civil Rights Act made United States citizens of all native-born persons except untaxed Indians, and guaranteed to all citizens regardless of color, race or previous condition of servitude the right to make and enforce contracts, to sue and be sued, to give evidence, to hold and handle property, to enjoy "full and equal benefit of all

[23] Quoted in *New York Independent,* October 11, 1866.
[24] *Cong. Globe,* 39 Cong., 1 sess., 245-246, 250, 176-177, 201.
[25] December 14, 1865.
[26] December 9, 1865.
[27] "Memorial of a Delegation Representing the Colored People of the Several States. . . .," *Senate Miscellaneous Documents* ⚹56, 39 Cong., 1 sess.
[28] December 13, 1865.

laws and proceedings, as [are] enjoyed by white citizens.''[29]
The first section of the Fourteenth Amendment provided
the same assurances in more general terms.

The opposition to the Civil Rights Act came chiefly from
the Democrats; for the most part they took the constitutional ground that Congress lacked the power to make
citizens of non-citizens. Occasionally the debate turned on
the possible consequences to the North.[30] This type of civil-
rights protection, as contrasted with guarantees of equal
treatment in public vehicles, theatres and restaurants
stripped the issue of emotion. The right to hold property, to
sue or be sued in court can arouse the enthusiasm of a constitutional lawyer; the property owner does not get excited
until the Negro family moves in next door.

Negroes did not accept the Act as the ultimate. A Chicago mass meeting resolved its gratitude to Congress for
the legislation, but they wanted more, they wanted the
elective franchise. The Negro lobby memorialized Congress
to discountenance a proposal of James G. Blaine which
became the second section of the Fourteenth Amendment,
because it extended Congressional approval to the principle
of disfranchisement.[31] The representatives of the colored
people had their eyes on the suffrage in 1866.

The elections that year placed Republicans solidly in
control of Congress. While some Radicals like Horace
Greeley, George Boutwell of Massachusetts, and William D.
Kelley and Thaddeus Stevens of Pennsylvania pressed for
Negro suffrage, the campaign had centered on the Four-
teenth Amendment, accepted by Conservative and Radical
Republicans alike, and the fight between the President and

---

[29] *Cong. Globe,* 39 Cong., 1 sess., Appendix, ch. XXXI, 315, 316.

[30] *Ibid.,* 500, 602, 1156, 1271, 1291.

[31] ''Address of the Colored Citizens of Chicago . . .,'' *House Miscellaneous Documents,* ⚹109, 39 Cong., 1 sess.; ''Memorial of a Delegation Representing the Colored People . . .,'' *loc. cit.*

Congress.[32] Section two of the proposed amendment left the decision on suffrage with the states, its framers fearing the adverse Northern reaction to a direct enactment.[33] "It was our opinion," said Senator Jacob Howard of Michigan, of the Committee of Fifteen where the bill originated, "that three-fourths of the states of this Union could not be induced to vote to grant the right of suffrage, even in any degree or under any restriction to the colored race."[34] Northerners easily met the charge that Section two would decrease Northern Congressional representation by pointing out that there were not enough disfranchised Negroes in any Northern state to affect the representation.[35]

In spite of the outcries of extremists, the politically-wise worked hard to keep the suffrage issue out of the campaign. Former Governor Andrew Curtin of Pennsylvania and Representative Norman Judd of Illinois exerted strenuous efforts to prevent the united Southern Loyalist Convention at Philadelphia from publicizing the issue.[36] The conservative *New York Times* observed that

neither in this state nor in Pennsylvania, nor in Ohio, nor in Indiana, nor in Illinois, has Negro suffrage been generally presented as an article of party faith. On the contrary, in each of these States, the Constitutional Amendment has been approved as an official embodiment of terms presented by the victorious North to the defeated South.[37]

In the state campaigns Iowa Republicans alone came out strongly for enfranchisement. Pennsylvania and Con-

[32] *Annual Cyclopaedia* (1866), 760; *New York Times*, September 11, 26, October 8, 11, November 7, 1866.

[33] Robert Dale Owen, "Political Results from the Varioloid," *Atlantic Monthly*, XXXV (1875), 662-664; Horace Greeley to James R. Lawrence, December 16, 1866, Greeley Papers, New York Public Library.

[34] *New York Independent*, May 31, 1866.

[35] *Cong. Globe*, 39 Cong., 1 sess., 579.

[36] *New York Times*, September 8, October 16, November 3, 1866; Cochran, Cox, II, 1043; Beale, *Critical Year*, 185-187; *New York Independent*, September 13, 1866; *Annual Cyclopaedia*, (1866), 758-759.

[37] October 5, 1866.

necticut Republicans replied vaguely to Democratic attacks on the proposition; the Michigan legislature, which had scheduled a referendum on the question, replaced it with a proposal for a new constitution to be drawn up in convention, a suggestion which the voters overwhelmingly approved.[38] In no other Northern state was the colored vote an issue. The Republican sweep in 1866 grew out of other causes than a popular cause for Negro suffrage.

The flush of victory caused joy and concern. The *Nation* forecast more agitation: no written compact "will ever blind a large body of the Northern people to the outrageous absurdity in a democratic republic, of making the color of a man's skin a reason for denying him anything which he or other men value."[39] Enfranchisement was gladly endorsed by Radicals, some of whom had cautiously avoided it during the campaign. On the other hand, elements in the Republican party worried over the possibility that the suffrage issue would jeopardize their future at the polls.[40] An adjudication of these two points of view would have to await the next Presidential election, but until that time the weather-cock pointed confidently in the direction of compromise.

Influential proponents of Radical strategy showed surface signs of cooling off on Negro suffrage. Schuyler Colfax, soon to be Republican nominee for the Vice-Presidency, told a Detroit audience that "I never believed in Negro equality. I believe God made us, for his own wise purposes, a superior race. . . . But God forgive me if while I think so I would endeavor to grind down lower this oppressed race. Our principle is liberty to all. . . . But I think I can say without any impiety, I wish He had made all these races white, for had he done so, there would not be a Democrat

_____

[38] *Annual Cyclopaedia* (1866), 407-409, 613-615, 254-255, 508.

[39] III (1866), 250-251.

[40] *New York Independent*, January 24, 1867; James A. Doolittle to Oliver H. Browning, November 8, 1866 in Browning, *Diary*, (James G. Randall, ed.) Illinois State Historical Society, *Collections*, XXII, Lincoln Series, III, Springfield, Ill., (1933), II, 107 n. 1.

today.''[41] Such equivocation was more than matched by the illuminating metamorphosis of the *Nation's* editorial policy in the spring of 1867. It gradually abandoned the extremists in favor of a more moderate approach. Its treatment of the Northern suffrage question in April, 1867, combined the condemnatory phrases of the Radicals with the evasions of the party in 1868. Later articles increasingly reflected more caution. By August, the weekly could engage a Radical journal in a quick, spirited debate over Negroes in high office.[42]

By 1867, the franchise issue came before the voters or legislatures of several Northern states. Connecticut again placed a manhood-suffrage clause on the ballot in a special April election and with the same result; a thousand more people voted against than for the Negro and the Radicals became alarmed:

> It is fashionable to criticize the quality of Connecticut Republicanism [wrote the Washington correspondent of the *New York Independent*]; but it will compare favorably with the same article in New York, Pennsylvania, Ohio, Illinois, and other states. If anybody doubt it, let him put manhood suffrage into the canvass, as a prominent issue, in any of the states mentioned. The fact will appear in other states that there is a small class of Republicans who are narrow, mean and low. They need education to bring them upon the platform of manhood suffrage; but they will eventually be compelled to stand upon the side of equality and justice.[43]

Since there was no mistaking the issue here, said Horace Greeley with prophetic, if not informed insight, the answer lay in a federal suffrage measure.[44]

The same conclusions could have been drawn from events in Minnesota and Ohio. In November, 1867, the electors of Minnesota refused by a bare majority to allow its few col-

---

[41] *Boston Evening Transcript*, November 8, 1866.

[42] III (1867), 294-295, IV (1867), 519-520, V (1867), 90-91, 232-233. Cf. *Harper's Weekly*, XI (1867), 483, 531.

[43] April 11, 1867.

[44] *Ibid.*, April 11, 18, 1867.

ored men to vote. Ohio Republicans, split on the question of presenting the issue to the voters for resolution, finally, after two refusals, hesitantly placed the problem on the ballot. Impartial suffrage fell under the majority burden of 38,000 hostile votes and the Democrats swept into office.[45]

New York during this year concentrated its political efforts on writing a new constitution. In the convention, the Republicans controlled the 160 delegates with a majority of 14. The franchise issue, revolving primarily around the Negro, took up roughly three weeks of debate. By and large, the Democrats pinned their hopes of excluding the colored man on a separate submission of the question to the voters. Realizing the dangers implicit in this direct appeal, Republicans fought to include an unqualified franchise in the document, the whole constitution to be placed before the people for acceptance or rejection. In convention, the Radicals were successful but the state senate in 1868 refused its assent to a law placing the constitution before the voters. The following year the Republicans compromised with their opponents and submitted the suffrage clause along with other controversial measures to a referendum. The voters threw a 52,601 majority against the Negro, rejected the whole constitution except for one article and swept the Democrats into office.[46]

In Michigan, where the Republican-controlled constitutional convention of 1867 produced a manhood-suffrage document, the Democrats in the convention adopted tactics similar to those used in New York by calling for a separate submission of this clause. They charged that the Republican victory of 1866 did not indicate popular support for the colored voter, that Republican insistence on its inclusion

[45] McPherson, *Political History*, 257, 354; *New York Independent*, February 21, March 21, April 11, 1867; Cochran, Cox, II, 1088-1089; *Cleveland Leader*, January 1, 1867, *loc. cit.*, 708.

[46] *New York Independent*, April 25, August 1, 1867; *Proceedings and Debates of the Constitutional Convention. . . .* (Albany, 1868), I, 200-263, V, 3560-3586, 3959; *Annual Cyclopaedia* (1868), 544. (1869), 489-490.

smelled like a plot to uphold Radical policy in the South. With foresight they argued that the constitution would not appeal to their constituents with a change in suffrage. Republicans halfheartedly answered these charges as they steam-rolled every attempt to refer the question to the voters separately. The electorate then refused to ratify the convention's handiwork, in part because of the franchise clause.[47]

New Jersey and Pennsylvania did not push very far towards Negro suffrage. In April, 1867, the lower house of the New Jersey legislature refused to strike the word "white" from the state constitution by a 38-20 vote. State Republicans resolved the following fall to work for equal suffrage and assumed their place, as Harper's Weekly put it, among the "advanced guard" who must educate the people by agitation and discussion to the acceptance of the doctrine. State Democrats in convention took a firm stand against this proposal in an address of September 5, 1867, and in the November elections happily welcomed New Jersey back into their fold.[48] Pennsylvania's lawmakers did no more than discuss the proposition during 1867, but the next year they defeated by a vote of 64-14 a motion to amend the constitution. "The Republican majority acted in a base and cowardly manner bringing disgrace upon themselves and their party. Shame on them!" cried the *Independent*.[49]

Of the remaining Northern states, Illinois and Indiana took no action, while in Iowa an act to submit the question to the voters, which had passed the 1866 legislature, was

[47] *New York Independent*, August 15, 1867, March 26, April 16, 1868; Mary Joice Adams, "The History of Suffrage in Michigan," *Publications of the Michigan Political Science Association*, III (1898), 30; *Debates and Proceedings of the Constitutional Convention. . . .* (Lansing, Mich. 1857), II, 712-718, 786-789, 857-858.

[48] *New York Independent*, March 21, April 18, 1867; McPherson, *Political History*, 258; *Harper's Weekly*, XI (1867), 498-499; *Annual Cyclopaedia* (1867), 540.

[49] February 21, 1867, March 12, 1868.

delayed to 1868 in accordance with constitutional procedure. Wisconsin in 1867 prepared for a referendum on the subject, but the Supreme Court intervened with a decision that the Negro had had a legal right to vote since 1849.[50]

In the fall elections of 1867, Democrats captured the New Jersey and Ohio legislatures, one house in New York, and the chief justiceship in Pennsylvania. Observers in and out of Congress joined these results to Republican efforts to obtain equal suffrage,[51] while Horace Greeley noted the peculiar pattern evolving from state elections since the end of the war. The Northern voter, Greeley pointed out, tended first to reject the colored elector when directly faced with him, and then turn around and support the party behind him.[52] Others drew the obvious conclusion to which a few Radical leaders had probably come privately: federal action must replace state inaction in this area. Despite the unpopularity of the issue at the North, Congress must deal with this in 1868. With candor the *New York Independent* warned against those who, looking forward to victory in 1868, sought to equivocate on suffrage as an issue in the Presidential campaign:

We observe, with mingled pain and indignation, that many conservative Republican Journals in various Northern states, are putting forth tentative articles with a view to the framing of a presidential issue in which the Negro shall have no place.[53]

Stick to principles, Editor Tilton urged, and beware of the political enigma Grant, who does not himself know where he stands.

More politic Radicals won this military hero to their

[50] *Ibid.*, April 18, 1867, October 15, 1868; *Annual Cyclopaedia* (1866), 407-409; Carl H. Erbe, ''Constitutional Provisions for the Suffrage in Iowa,'' *The Iowa Journal of History and Politics*, XXII (1924), 208-211.

[51] *Annual Cyclopaedia* (1867), 545-546, 605, 620; *Nation*, V (1867), 396, 414, *New York Times*, September 14, 1867, *Cong. Globe*, 40 Cong., 2 sess., 40-, 49-50.

[52] *New York Independent*, November 21, 1867.

[53] *Ibid.*, November 14, 1867.

cause early in 1868 and they shaped their strategy around him. His nomination on the first ballot at their convention in Chicago manifested the confidence they had in the drawing power of his name.[54] Their platform demonstrated how they intended to tiptoe around the issue of Northern suffrage. The second plank guaranteed equal suffrage at the South but otherwise left it to the "people" of the loyal states.[55]

The campaign of 1868 ignored the problem of Northern Negro suffrage and concentrated on other issues. Questions of currency, debts, and taxes occupied the attention of some campaigners, but the popular subject of the day related to the position of the South in the Union. Republican stump speakers and propagandists did little more than praise the existing policy based on the Thirteenth and Fourteenth Amendments interjecting dire prophecies of the evils of a Democratic victory.[56] While this emphasis satisfied the majority of Northern Republicans, extremists like Tilton raged at the betrayal. The moderates in defense advised the new administration to follow Frederick Douglass' counsel and let the Negro alone as quickly as possible. "The ballot," expostulated the *Nation* early the next year, "is no panacea for political ills."[57]

In two Northern states Negro suffrage received special attention at election time. Iowa Radicals had pushed through the state convention of 1865 a plank committing

[54] G. F. Milton, *The Age of Hate, Andrew Johnson and the Radicals* (New York, 1930), ch. XX; McPherson, *Political History*, 366; Charles Sumner to the Duchess of Argyll, July 28, 1868, in Edward L. Pierce, *Memoir and Letters of Charles Sumner* (Boston, 1893), IV, 359-360.

[55] Adams Sherman Hill, "The Chicago Convention," *North American Review*, CVII (1868), 175.

[56] *New York Times*, September 10, 11, 17, 1868; Charles H. Coleman, *The Election of 1868, the Democratic Effort to Regain Control* (Columbia University, *Studies in History, Economics, and Public Law*, ♯392, (New York, 1933), 286-292, 305-310.

[57] *New York Independent*, November 12, 1868; *Nation*, VII (1868), 386-VIII (1869), 124.

the party majority in the state legislature to support it.
After much hesitancy, the legislature submitted to the pressure in 1866 and two years later the people ratified the
amendment to the constitution. Granted the ballot, however,
colored Iowans were still denied the privilege of running
for Congress. Twice rebuffed in Minnesota on this issue,
Republicans tried again in 1868 and won by a 6,000 vote
majority. They were forced to use deceptive methods on the
ballot, concealing, for example, the nature of the constitutional amendment with the label "revision of Section 1,
Article 7." Undoubtedly these tricks in Minnesota, plus the
excitement of the Presidential canvass in both states, helped
carry equal suffrage.[58]

Horace Greeley perhaps set the tone for Radicals in
interpreting the elections. He asserted that the triumph had
vindicated the Congressional plan of Reconstruction and
paved the way for a suffrage amendment to the Federal
Constitution. Ignoring the obvious fact that Negro suffrage
in the North had not been at stake, that the party had specifically come out against a Federal measure that would
coerce the loyal states, Republican leaders, with the exception of Charles Sumner, turned to the circuitous method of
a constitutional amendment to accomplish what they considered necessary ends in the South. A Congressional statute was liable to invalidation by the judiciary. A new constitutional article needed only the assent of 28 of the 37
states, a simple process since the party controlled the South
by military force and the Northern legislatures by the election. Northern prejudice against the Negro, long the stumbling block to an adequate policy in the rebel states, was
finally to be circumvented.[59]

---

[58] Erbe, "Constitutional Provisions for the Suffrage in Iowa," loc. cit.,
208-211; Annual Cyclopaedia (1866), 407-409, (1868), 504-505; New York
Times, November 7, 1868.

[59] New York Independent, December 3, 1868; Cong. Globe, 40 Cong., 3
sess., 986.

The debate over the proposed Fifteenth Amendment confronted Radicals with the dilemma of the platform they had supported the previous fall. Senator James A. Doolittle of Wisconsin, now in the Democratic fold, denounced it as a two-faced pledge showing a white mask to the North and a black one to the South. Senator Jacob Howard, a Radical from Michigan, tried to amend the proposal to leave the question of Northern equal suffrage to the loyal states. Senator Oliver P. Morton of Indiana defended the platform and Senatorial action by emphasizing that the plank of 1868 referred only to Congressional action, while the Senate was considering a constitutional amendment. With this tortured hairsplitting, Morton could reassure his Radical colleagues against charges of inconsistency and twinges of conscience in voting for it.[60] A year and a month after the two houses of Congress agreed on the form of the amendment, Secretary of State Hamilton Fish notified the legislators that twenty-nine states had ratified it. Of the Northern states involved, New Jersey, Ohio, Rhode Island, Michigan, Indiana, and belatedly New York showed some reluctance to follow the party line.[61] In Illinois, the constitutional convention in session tactfully tabled debate on the suffrage issue until the future of the Fifteenth Amendment had been determined.[62]

By 1870 the Radical Republicans had erected the basic structure of Reconstruction, almost five years after the submission of the architects' blueprints. The key element of the plan, a solid bloc of voting Negroes in the South, had been held up again and again by the refusal of the loyal states to countenance the colored man at their own ballot boxes. As early as 1865, Northern prejudice generally con-

[60] *Ibid.*, 1012, 985-987, 990-991.

[61] McPherson, *Political History*, 545-546, 495-496, 559-560, 562; *New York Independent*, April 22, June 3, 1869; Gerichs, "Ratification in Indiana," *loc. cit.*, 153-163; Adams, "Suffrage in Michigan," *loc. cit.*, 30-31, 31 n.

[62] *Debates and Proceedings of the Constitutional Convention of . . . Illinois . . .* (Springfield, Ill., 1870), I, 157, 159, 160, 855-856, II, 1280-1282.

fronted and surprised politicians, first and most effectively in Connecticut. This reluctance dictated policies of expediency and even deceit. The campaign of 1866 had concentrated on the character of Andrew Johnson, and the Fourteenth Amendment. The party correctly interpreted the victory as endorsing most of the Radical program in the South, adding with less truth that "a majority of the successful party undoubtedly favor universal suffrage but that question has been left by the people to the decision of Congress."[63] The platform of 1868 had specifically promised no Federal action in the loyal states, but the Fifteenth Amendment resulted from that election triumph.

Although race prejudice is infrequently as influential in obstructing national policy as it was in this half-decade, the effort took its toll. Without doubt, the bias against colored voters retreated before the wave of moral and political attacks: Right and Republicanism marching shoulder to shoulder. The tenor of the debates in New York, Michigan, and Illinois and the silent agreement which greeted the final amendment demonstrates that this form of racial prejudice bowed, if slowly, to the inevitable.

This post-war era was the colored man's first real entry into federal politics. Obviously a neophyte, he was to some extent manipulated by the Radicals, but in a large measure he struck out on his own through organization, petition, and lobbying. Alive to all race issues, the Northern Negro placed too much dependence on the ballot. Though a step in the right direction it did not bring with it the equality he sought and deserved. The rewards were slow in coming, and fell short of the desires of the race. Many other manifestations of prejudice remained.

Leslie H. Fishel, Jr.

Massachusetts Institute of Technology

[63] *Nation*, III (1866), 390.

MINISTERS WITHOUT PORTFOLIO

During the two years preceding the outbreak of the Civil War a most eloquent friend of the slave, Sarah Parker Remond of Salem, Massachusetts, lectured in many of the large cities and towns of England, Scotland and Ireland. Her avowed mission was "to extend the active sympathy of the whole British nation toward the cause of abolitionism in America." In pleading the cause of her black brothers, Miss Remond generally avoided the sensational and the sentimental. She might mention that female slaves were "liable to the brutality of the vilest wretches," but the purposeful young miss from Salem was not a four-handkerchief speaker; she did not specialize in heartrending tales of Tom and Topsy. She made her points, wrote one of her admirers, by a "clear elucidation of just principles—no claptrap."

Despite her failure to fire her audience with tales of slave derring-do, or to dissolve them in tears, Miss Remond was a most persuasive advocate. An educated young woman, she had a beguiling air of refinement—a genteel pattern of manners so highly esteemed as an ideal of womanhood in Victoria's England. Her speech was dulcet-toned and quiet, and her fluent vocabulary was pure of unladylike turns of phrase. She had an air of high seriousness, and she conveyed to others her own belief that tomorrow's sun would set upon a better world. For these reasons the Leeds Young Men's Anti-Slavery Society, at its December 1859 meeting, hired her as its agent.

The Society gave her a crowded schedule. On December 23 she spoke at Leeds, followed four days later by an appearance at Wortley, where she addressed an audience composed of "working men and factory operatives." Just before the old year was snuffed out, she went to Bramley where she won all hearts at the "large and commodious"

27

Wesley Chapel. At Hunslet on the fourth day of the new year, her audience ''was enthusiastic and encouraging in the extreme.'' When she appeared at Warrenton in March her address was signed by the mayor, by the rector of the parish, by the member of parliament for the borough and by 3522 inhabitants; no address in Warrenton, wrote a native of the town, had ''ever been more numerously signed.''[1] At Dublin, where she also filled a March engagement, her packed audience included clergymen and university professors. Summing up the worth of her services, the Leeds Society reported that thousands who heard her would never forget the experience, and that the principles which she advocated would find an abiding place in many hearts and ''materially aid in building up the Anti-Slavery sentiments of Great Britain.''[2]

The services of Sarah Remond and other Negro abolitionists in keeping alive the anti-slavery spirit in Leeds and elsewhere throughout the British Isles was a notable contribution to the winning of the Civil War. For in this conflict the South had counted heavily on winning English support; specifically, the Confederacy expected England to recognize her as an independent nation. In turn, so the South hoped, the Continental countries would follow the lead of the British Foreign Office, and the Confederacy would have the moral backing and perhaps the financial assistance of the European concert of nations.

Jefferson Davis and his colleagues had reason to expect British recognition. More than one Englishman in five gained his daily bread from the cotton industry and almost half of England's export trade was in manufactured cotton goods. From Dixie's land came more than 80 per cent of the

---

[1] *Anti-Slavery Advocate* (London), April 1859. For a sketch of Miss Remond see Dorothy Porter, ''Sarah Parker Remond, Abolitionist and Physician,'' *Journal of Negro History*, XX (1935), pp. 287-293.

[2] *Annual Report of the Leeds Young Men's Anti-Slavery Society for Year Ending December 1860* (Leeds, 1861), p. 6.

baled cotton used in English factories on the eve of the war. For years the cry, "Cotton is King," had been echoed throughout the Southern regions, and the South's leaders were confident that her fleecy fields of white would enlist trans-Atlantic support for the Confederacy.[3]

There were other reasons for the South's expectation of diplomatic recognition. She was against high tariffs and so was England. Once John Bull extended the hand of diplomatic fellowship, his cotton mills would find a waiting outlet for their manufactured drygoods in the low-tariff or free-trade markets of the South. Obviously, too, the English ruling class would prefer to deal with two American nations rather than one. The English government was made up of men drawn largely from the aristocracy and, as John Bright informed his American friend, John Bigelow, "it must be hostile to your greatness and the permanence of your institutions."[4] Englishmen whose genealogies were listed in *Burke's Peerage* were congenitally inclined toward the Southern gentlemen-planters as over against the bargain-driving, *nouveau-riche* Yankees, making their money in trade: "London club life was Southern in its sympathies." Moneyed men in England took their cue from the landed aristocracy; so did the military services and the majority of the newspapers.

All this the South's leaders knew. A month before the first shot was fired, Confederate Secretary of State Robert Toombs appointed three commissioners to go abroad and seek diplomatic recognition from the European nations, and then to make treaties of commerce and amity. One of the commissioners, William L. Yancey, described his mission in a bland letter to the London *Daily News*. He sought, wrote he, "simply to obtain a recognition of those states as a

[3] See Frank L. Owsley, *King Cotton Diplomacy* (Chicago, 1931), notably chapter I, "The Foundation of Confederate Diplomacy" (pp. 1-24).

[4] Letter dated Jan. 3, 1863, in R. Barry O'Brien, *John Bright* (London, 1910), p. 144.

government whose people are producers of cotton, tobacco, corn, and naval stores, and who desire to offer manufacturing Europe the benefits of free trade in the peaceful interchange of those valuable products for the woolen, cotton, silk and hardware fabrics of the Old World, unrestricted and unvexed by prohibitory tariffs.''[5]

Despite their sweetness-and-light approach, the Confederate commissioners soon found that they had an uphill fight to secure recognition. As Yancey and his colleagues quickly discovered, there was a deeply rooted hostility to slavery among the day laborers, the middle class element and ''the quiet and religious people.'' In their first dispatch to the Confederate secretary of war, dated May 21, 1861, the commissioners sent word that ''the public mind here is entirely opposed to the Government of the Confederate States of America on the question of slavery and that the sincerity and universality of this feeling'' embarrassed the British Foreign Office ''in dealing with the question of our recognition.''[6]

This British anti-slavery sentiment was in no small measure the product of American Negroes. In the twenty years preceding the Civil War, a procession of colored agitators paraded throughout the British Isles, pleading the cause of the chain-burdened slave. The full extent of their anti-slavery activities in shaping British opinions was to become evident when the North and the South vied to enlist English support.

This impressive roster of visiting blacks began in 1840 with Charles Lenox Remond. Older brother of Sarah, he sailed for England as a delegate to the World's Anti-Slavery Convention, held in London. He remained abroad for two years, lecturing throughout the British Isles. Every-

[5] London *Daily News* in London *Morning Post*, Jan. 27, 1862.

[6] James M. Callahan, *The Diplomatic History of the Southern Confederacy* (Baltimore, 1901), p. 112.

where he was favorably received; he inspired one of his English admirers to express his praise in poetic strain, "On Hearing Mr. C. L. Remond, a Young Man of Talent but Slight Education, Lecture on Prejudice Against Color in the United States."

Remond's influence, as marked as it was, paled before that of the next of the visiting Negroes, the celebrated Frederick Douglass. For nineteen months, beginning in August 1845, the youthful Douglass, not yet turned thirty, created something of a sensation wherever he went. Britishers found their attention rivetted when they caught their first glimpse of this well-built Negro with his white stand-up collar and gleaming white shirt, relieved by a close-fitting stock, and a black broadcloth coat. When he opened his mouth, his listeners heard a deep and melodious voice that hinted of its readiness to shade into wit, irony, invective or pathos.

During Douglass' sojourn in the British Isles, mayors presided over assemblies gathered to hear him, and the large audiences invariably remained attentive during the two and a half hours he spoke. Usually after his address, people crowded forward, eager to shake hands. The demand to hear him was great—in March 1847 he gave an address every night to the month, including Sundays.

Douglass' influence in England was not limited to the spoken word. For he set a widely-copied example by selling his autobiography. His *Narrative of the Life of Frederick Douglass* was a slim volume of 125 pages, published in May 1845, and prefaced by letters from William Lloyd Garrison and Wendell Phillips. During his tour of the British Isles, Douglass sold the book on the spot, suitably autographed, or took orders for it. The *Narrative* sold well; in Bristol alone nearly 200 copies were purchased. Sympathizers who could spare a few shillings bought the book, read it, and then circulated it among prospective converts.

This fugitive slave literature, in which dramatic incidents were mingled with abolitionist argument, was destined to be a powerful lever in the British Isles. "America had the mournful honour of adding a new department to the literature of civilization—the autobiography of escaped slaves," observed the English clergyman, Ephraim Peabody. These slave narratives, however crude from the standpoint of "belles lettres," went right to the hearts of their readers. Often ghost-written, or told by an anonymous collaborator, and always heavy on sermonizing, these stories nonetheless made a lasting impression on British dogooders.

In his travels abroad William Wells Brown, like Douglass, made effective use of both speechmaking and autobiographical writings. Leaving America in July 1849, Wells went to Paris to attend the International Peace Conference. Here he made it a point, as was customary by Negro speakers at international gatherings, to call attention to America's weakness in its aspiration to give moral leadership to the world. The escaped fugitive condemned American slaveholders for prating about peace "while they practiced a form of tyranny which was inevitably driving their country into internecine war." There could be no peace, Brown added, until chattel slavery became a relic of the past.

After the Paris meeting, Brown remained in Europe for five years and two months. Most of his time was spent in the British Isles, where he delivered more than 1,000 addresses, and travelled some 12,000 miles, riding coaches "over nearly every railroad."[7]

During Brown's sojourn abroad, a number of other prominent American Negroes embarked for British shores to bear witness against the sin of slavery. One of these was the scholarly clergyman, J. W. C. Pennington, who spent

[7] *Leeds Anti-Slavery Series*, No. 34 (London, n.d.), p. 12.

several months in Great Britain in 1849 and 1851. Hired as a lecturer by the Glasgow Female New Association for the Abolition of Slavery, Pennington travelled the length and breadth of Scotland. As a result of his eloquence, particularly of his effective use of tearful tales which excited sympathy and sorrow, "the friends of the Slave were much stirred up in many places." Pennington's labors elsewhere in the British Isles were also telling: "The work which he has done in England on behalf of his enslaved brethren," wrote a provincial reporter, "and the interest he aroused on their behalf has been very great."[8]

In May 1851 Pennington was one of a quartette of American Negroes who were guests at a "soiree" given by the British and Foreign Anti-Slavery Society at Freemason's Hall, London. Sharing honors with Pennington were Alexander Crummell, Henry Highland Garnet and Josiah Henson. The last named, soon to win lasting note as the "original Uncle Tom," had come to England to raise funds for a manual labor institute for fugitives at Dawn, Ontario. At the World's Fair, held in London, Henson placed on exhibition four boards of black walnut, seven feet in length and four inches in width, in the hope that the planed and polished lumber, gleaming like a shimmery sea, would induce fair-goers to place sales orders. On one occasion no less a personage than Queen Victoria came to the Crystal Palace Exhibition and moved toward the Henson display. The Negro clergyman bowed to the waist, and as Her Majesty passed, he heard her murmur, "Is he indeed a fugitive slave?"[9]

In England at the same time as Henson, Pennington and Brown, and sometimes speaking from the same platform, was Henry Highland Garnet. Invited to England in 1850 by the "Friends of Free Labor," Garnet first went to Frank-

[8] *Ibid.*, p. 16.
[9] Josiah Henson, *Autobiography* (Boston, 1879), p. 191.

fort to attend the World Peace Conference. Teaming up with Pennington, he addressed two large audiences at the Evangelical Church, urging that free-labor stores be established throughout Germany. The two Negroes spoke through an interpreter, but their addresses were reported to have increased "considerably" the number of friends of the slave.

Garnet remained in Great Britain for three years, speaking and lecturing. His was a potent influence over an audience. Grandson of a Mandingo chieftain and warrior, he was a princely man in appearance, showing little indication that his right leg had been amputated. His head was well-proportioned—a broad nose and a large, firm mouth, flanked by low side-burns. A Presbyterian clergyman, Garnet had a voice of vast compass; once heard, said John Cromwell, it "echoed and re-echoed throughout the chambers of memory."

In 1853, as Garnet returned to America, two other Negro leaders sailed for England. One of these was Samuel Ringgold Ward, formerly a pastor of the Congregational church of South Butler, New York, whose all-white membership stood in sharp color contrast to their pastor whose semicircle of black chin-whiskers could be observed only at close quarters. Ward had subsequently edited two reform weeklies, and had lectured for the Liberty party. As agent of the Anti-Slavery Society of Canada, Ward came to England "to plead in behalf of my crushed countrymen in America, and the freed men of Canada."

Like other Negro visitors, Ward had no dearth of speaking engagements. His public appearances were not confined to the many abolitionist societies that flourished throughout the British Isles; before Ward had been in England a single month he had been, so he related, "on the platforms of the Bible, Tract, Sunday School, missionary, and Peace, as well as Anti-Slavery, societies."

The other Negro notable who came to England in 1853 was the youthful, light-skinned William G. Allen, a graduate of Beriah Green's Oneida Institute, and formerly editor of the *National Watchman,* published at Troy, New York. Allen had left America somewhat in a hurry. He had been teaching languages and literature at Central College, Mc-Grawville, New York, which had two other Negroes on the faculty, George B. Vashon and Charles L. Reason. At Central College, Allen had formed an acquaintanceship, extending over a year and a half, with one of the white students, Mary E. King.

When it became evident that the two were planning to marry, the townspeople thought it advisable to caution the Negro professor. On a Sabbath evening in January 1853, they paid Allen a visit "armed with tar, feathers, poles, and an empty barrel spiked with shingle nails." Miss King's parents removed her to a neighboring county, but she gave her guardians the slip, joined her fiancé in New York, married him, and sailed with him, nine days later, for Liverpool.

Once in England, Allen sketched in a few additional details to the picture of American injustice. He published in 1853 an account of his experiences, *The American Prejudice Against Color: an Authentic Narrative, Showing How Easily the Nation Got into an Uproar.* Priced at one shilling, the book moved quickly from the stalls. At the 1853 meeting of the British and Foreign Anti-Slavery Society, held at Exeter Hall, Allen indicated that he would embark upon a lecture tour "as soon as the season comes around." His reception among British reformers was cordial: "We welcome all refugees from foreign tyrannies," editorialized the *Anti-Slavery Advocate,* "when, like Professor Allen, they are industrious and self-reliant, asking only for a clear stage, and begging no special favor."

Allen never returned to America. In England "he gained

the confidence of all he met." His British friends subsequently raised enough money to purchase control of the Caledonia Training School at Islington, and thereupon they installed him as master, "the first instance in this country of an educational establishment being under the direction of a man of colour."[10]

Like Allen, William and Ellen Craft, who had come to England after the passage of the Fugitive Slave Law of 1850, never returned to the United States. They remained under the Union Jack, moving English audiences to sniffles with the thrilling story of their almost incredible escape from slavery. Their youth, good looks and modesty made them popular in reform circles. In 1854 they began to attend school, assisted financially by the generosity of well-wishers, particularly that of Joseph B. Estlin, a clergyman and physician of Bristol.

On the eve of the war, British anti-slavery sentiment was measurably increased by a visit by Martin R. Delany, fresh from a safari into equatorial Africa. Delany had been in London only a few weeks when he almost precipitated a diplomatic breach between Her Majesty's government and the United States. Because of his explorations he had received a royal commission to attend the sessions of the International Statistical Congress, an organization made up of distinguished scientists and other learned men. At the opening convocation, held on July 16, at Somerset House in London, His Royal Highness, Albert, Prince Consort of England, welcomed the assembled delegates and the invited diplomats.

After Prince Albert had eased himself into the royal crimson chair, Lord Brougham, who was seated on his left, arose to preside. Henry Peter Brougham, excitable and im-

---

[10] *Anti-Slavery Reporter* (London), July 1, 1863.

pulsive, was then over eighty, and for fifty years had been an outspoken foe of slavery. Only a few weeks earlier he had ordered his carriage driven to the suburban home of William and Ellen Craft where he sat for an hour chatting with their house guest, the persuasive Miss Remond. Now, rising to preside at the opening session of the Congress, Brougham caught a glimpse of Martin R. Delany, his black face made more highly visible by the surrounding sea of white skins. Thereupon Brougham made an unscheduled remark, ''I call the attention of Mr. Dallas to the fact that there is a Negro present, and I hope he will have no scruples on that account.''

Seated to the immediate right of the Prince, George Mifflin Dallas, the United States minister to England, could scarcely believe what he heard. A dignified career diplomat of distinguished manners, he had never met a situation like this before, either at the court of the czars or that of St. James. As he combed his mind for precedents in protocol, his habitual calm was further ruffled when Delany ''with all his blackness,'' rose up in full view of the curious gaze of the scientists of the world. With mouths agape, the delegates listened as Delany's voice rang out:

I rise, your Royal Highness, to thank his lordship, the unflinching friend of the Negro, for the remarks which he has made in reference to myself, and to assure your Royal Highness that *I am a man.*

As Delany took his seat, a clapping of hands commenced on the stage, which was quickly echoed from the floor. In a moment, like a barrage of giant firecrackers, peals of loud applause resounded throughout the hall. Seconds later the sound of hand-clapping was completely drowned out by what the London *Times* described as ''the wildest shouts ever manifested in so grave an assemblage.''

Amid the commotion there was one who sat in frozen

disapproval. Mr. Dallas, who had freely confessed that ''my individual opinion as to the races being unequal in intellect is strong,'' debated the advisability of taking a walk. He had no doubt, wrote he in his diary for July 16, that the act ''was a premeditated contrivance to provoke me into some unseemly altercation with the colored personage. I balked that by remaining silent and composed.'' The minister raised a question with himself: ''Is not the government answerable for this insult? Or must it be regarded as purely the personal indecency of Lord Brougham?''

A day later Lord Brougham, realizing that his impulsive act might have international repercussions, sent an American messenger to Dallas, who assured the minister that Brougham had no intention of wounding his feelings. Dallas informed the messenger that ''he would receive nothing from Brougham at second-hand.'' When Brougham himself called, Dallas told his doorman ''to refuse him.'' When Brougham came back later in the day, Dallas made it a point to be at the Kensington Museum, drinking in the Turners and the Hogarths.

Although Brougham finally succeeded in making a personal apology to Dallas, Great Britain sent no word of regret. Secretary of State Lewis Cass favored making an official request for a disclaimer, and he informed Dallas that the President and the cabinet commended him for preserving silence, but that they felt he ''should have taken a walk after the incident,'' as a rebuke.[11]

After his impromptu statement, Delany was a center of attraction at the Congress throughout the remaining five days of meetings. At the closing session the delegates cheered as he made a short speech of thanks and gratitude

---

[11] For this incident see Frank A. Rollin, *Life and Public Services of Martin R. Delany* (Boston, 1883), pp. 99-126; Susan Dallas, ed., Diary of George Mifflin Dallas (Phila., 1892), pp. 407-409; Lewis Einstein, ''Lewis Cass,'' in Samuel F. Bemis, ed., *The American Secretaries of State and Their Diplomacy*, VI (New York, 1928), pp. 309-311.

for the cordial manner in which he had been received. Before leaving London he received a special request from the Royal Geographical Society to read a paper on his African explorations, and his subsequent seven months in England and Scotland were filled with speaking engagements.

From Charles L. Remond's journey to England in 1840 to that of Delany twenty years later, American Negroes had been strengthening the current of anti-slavery sentiment in Great Britain and on the continent. Their audiences were large and sympathetic; their influence was great. Negro agitators had laid their groundwork well; after nearly a quarter of a century of listening to their unsparing condemnation of human bondage, the British public would have found it difficult to conceive of one good argument in favor of slavery.

During the first eighteen months of the war—the critical period in diplomatic relations between the United States and England—American Negroes continued their treks to the land of the sympathizing British and, once there, to stiffen English opinion against the Confederacy. Late in 1861 Henry Highland Garnet, William H. Day and the Boston clergyman, J. Sella Martin, among others, were in England informing all who would listen of the inseparable connection between slavery and the war.[12]

Martin, who had arrived in London in October 1861 and remained abroad for nearly six months, was surprised to see so many Negroes in London. "There is no end," he observed, "to the colored here." Martin travelled in company with the zealous George Thompson, then a salaried agent of the American Anti-Slavery Society, who scheduled meetings "all over the kingdom," as Martin wrote in a letter to a member of his congregation.[13] Self-assured and

[12] *Anti-Slavery Reporter,* Jan. 1, 1862.
[13] J. Sella Martin to unnamed correspondent, Oct. 16, 1861. *MS.* in Moorland Collection, Howard University Library, Washington, D. C.

eloquent, Martin won converts wherever he went. He so moved his English audiences with the story of his sister Caroline and her two children, that they raised over $2,000 to purchase the freedom of these three slaves from the Columbus, Georgia, clergyman whose son was the father of Caroline's young ones.[14]

Perhaps the most influential of the Negroes who came to the British shores in 1862 was Jefferson Davis' escaped coachman, William Andrew Jackson. Arriving at Liverpool on November 5 armed with a letter of introduction from William Lloyd Garrison, the ex-coachman was met by George Thompson, who took him to London and installed him as a house guest.[15] Thompson's wife and daughter tutored the former slave so that he might be "better qualified to serve his brethren than at present."[16]

Thompson found "constant occupation" for Jackson. He took him to Staffordshire for a series of engagements, and at every meeting Jackson delivered "an interesting and telling address." He spoke at "several Sabbath schools" and addressed upwards of 3,000 children. He accompanied Thompson to Manchester and Sheffield and on a tour to "the west of England."[17] Jackson travelled solo to fill engagements in South Wales, Derbyshire and Lancashire. Thompson was highly pleased to send word to Garrison that everywhere that Jackson went, he produced a favorable impression: "I shall," continued Thompson, "be able to obtain for him as much work as he can do for some time."[18]

So busy did Jackson keep, in speaking and in attending meetings, that he felt duty-bound to address a letter to Jefferson Davis, informing him that he could not be with him

[14] *The Liberator*, Oct. 24, 1862.

[15] *Ibid.*, Nov. 28, 1862.

[16] *Ibid.*, Dec. 26, 1862.

[17] Thompson to Garrison, Dec. 12, 1862. *Anti-Slavery Letters to William Lloyd Garrison and Others,* Boston Public Library.

[18] *Ibid.*

in Richmond on December 24, 1862, the day on which Davis had to produce him or "discharge a bond of $1,500" to his former master.[19]

Thompson and Jackson did much of their touring as agents of the two anti-slavery societies that came into existence expressly to prevent England from extending the right hand of political friendship to the Confederacy—the London Emancipation Society and the Union and Emancipation Society of Manchester. The former, born in the closing weeks of 1862, was the lusty offspring of the London Emancipation Committee, which had come into existence in June 1859 at the Bloomsbury residence of Frederick W. Chesson, Thompson's son-in-law. Prominent at this organizational meeting were William Craft and the Baron de Pradine, the Haitian minister to the Court of St. James. Founded to "diffuse information on the slavery question," the group selected Thompson as president and Chesson as secretary.

With the birth late in 1862 of these two influential emancipation societies, there was less need for American Negroes to journey to England to bolster anti-slavery sentiment and thus forestall diplomatic recognition of the Confederacy. Dating from the Emancipation Proclamation the Union trumpet no longer gave forth an uncertain sound. Thenceforth anti-Confederate sentiment in England could be left safely in the hands of native reformers such as Harriet Martineau. Moreover, with the coming of 1863 the agitation of Negro abolitionists would be less needful as Northern successes on the battlefield began to sharpen the military intelligence of Lord John Russell, the perceptive British Foreign Secretary. And, finally, after 1862 the British working classes, already instinctively hostile to slavery, had come to realize that they had a strong personal stake in a Northern victory since the freeing of the American Negro

[19] *Ibid.*

might well bring in its wake an improvement in their own condition in England.[20]

But before 1863, before these things had come to pass, the Negro's role in strengthening British anti-Confederate sentiment had been significant, and that these things had come to pass was in a measure a result of that significant role.

BENJAMIN QUARLES

Morgan State College

---

[20] This point is developed in Frank J. Klingberg, ''Harriet Beecher Stowe and Social Reform in England,'' *American Historical Review*, vol. 43 (1938), pp. 542-552.

THE NEGRO IN CINCINNATI, 1800-1830

The Negro of the first decades of the nineteenth century had two images of Cincinnati. One image presented the city as a refuge from bondage; the other revealed the tough struggle of the free blacks for a respected place in white society. John Malvin caught both of these images in his flight from Virginia to Cincinnati in 1827. "I thought upon coming to a free state like Ohio that I would find every door thrown open to receive me, but from the treatment I received by the people generally, I found it little better than in Virginia."[1] To the Negro, then, Cincinnati was both freedom and struggle—freedom from slavery, and struggle for justice.

The colored population in Cincinnati grew only slowly in the first two decades of the nineteenth century. The first census in 1801 does not mention any Negroes at all,[2] and in 1810 the official total was only 80.[3] Four years later a fire marshal's count added 100 more "free blacks"[4] and by 1816 another listing numbered 247 "blacks and mulattoes" out of a population of 6,493.[5] In 1821 Thomas Dugan's census noted only 135 "people of color," but even the author was not satisfied with its accuracy.[6] Indeed, there is reason to believe that these figures are inexact at almost each instance,[7] but they convey the total picture. Negroes made up about two per cent of Cincinnati's population in 1820.

The next decade, however, found Cincinnati's colored population expanding rapidly. By 1829 the *Cincinnati Di-*

[1] John Malvin, *Autobiography of John Malvin* (Cleveland, 1879), 11.

[2] *Western Spy*, May 6, 1801.

[3] *Western Spy*, November 31, 1810.

[4] *Liberty Hall*, February 15, 1814.

[5] *Liberty Hall*, February 19, 1816.

[6] *Liberty Hall*, January 6, 1821.

[7] There were Negroes in Cincinnati before 1800, but not in large numbers. See *Northwest Centinel*, April 19, 1794.

43

rectory listed 2,258 "blacks and mulattoes" living in the city, comprising almost ten per cent of its people.[8] Though freed Negroes constituted most of this increase, many slaves found sanctuary in Cincinnati. The newspapers complained continually that the local colored community harbored runaways, and even accused Cincinnatians of kidnapping them from ships passing down the Ohio.[9] But escaped slaves accounted for only a small proportion of the city's increasing Negro population, and the question of the rights of free blacks would have been raised even if this problem had not been present.

Not much is known of colored life in early Cincinnati, though enough evidence remains to sketch its outlines. In the twenties most Negroes lived in the first and fourth wards—known as "Little Africa"—where they were cut off, though not segregated, from the white population.[10] Some were well-housed, especially before the great influx.[11] But their increase strained available facilities, and more and more they crowded into wooden shacks and shanties along Columbia Street and Western Row.[12] By 1827 frame tenements ten or twelve feet high covered the entire district creating health and fire hazards. In one instance two families converted a blacksmith's shop into a combined dwelling and grocery store where at least a dozen people lived.[13] In 1830 a fire raged through the area graphically portraying the congestion and warning the town of the consequences of continued neglect.

[8] *The Cincinnati Directory for the Year 1829* (Cincinnati, 1829), n.p.

[9] For example see *Liberty Hall*, May 8, 1815; also Malvin, *Autobiography*, 14-15.

[10] *Cincinnati Advertiser*, August 18, 1830.

[11] *Cincinnati Tax List*, 1818, MSS., (Historical and Philosophical Society of Ohio, Cincinnati). Some Negroes owned land, and Anthony Thampson, John Harrison and others had houses assessed at $100 and $200.

[12] *Cincinnati Centinel*, quoted in the *Western Star* (Lebanon, Ohio), August 29, 1829.

[13] Cincinnati City Council, *Minutes*, August 22, 1827.

Whites owned most of this housing, renting on leases running from three to five years. The property brought good returns and the owners resisted the attempt of the city council to prohibit the further erection of wooden buildings in the center of town. "Heaven preserve the shanties," an editor sarcastically observed, "and supply the proprietors with tenants from whom the rent can be screwed, without respect to color or character."[14] The ordinance finally passed, but it restricted only future construction, and did not disturb existing dwellings.[15] "We cannot drive the black population from the city in the summary way of pulling down the houses over their heads," lamented local officials.[16] Though a few Negroes moved out of this ghetto, most were too poor to escape to the better parts of the city.[17]

Cincinnati's colored people had to take employment where they could find it, since few had the skill that could demand preference, and trade unions denied them membership. They were "generally disciplined to laborious occupations," Daniel Drake observed, finding them "prone to the performance of light and menial drudgery."[18] Some became porters, vendors, shoeblacks and messengers, and women often hired out as domestics.[19] Mostly, however, blacks found employment on the construction of roads and canals, or as laboring hands in the expanding commerce and manufacturing of the city. Bad employment situations tended to aggravate this problem,[20] but opportunities in Cincinnati were

[14] *Daily Gazette*, October 28, 1830.

[15] Cincinnati City Council, *Minutes*, September 19, 1827. For background see also June 8 and June 29, 1825.

[16] Cincinnati City Council, *Minutes*, August 29, 1827.

[17] In 1829 one Negro built a house valued between $200 and $300. *Daily Gazette*, July 28, 1829.

[18] Daniel Drake, *Natural and Statistical View, or Picture of Cincinnati* (Cincinnati, 1815), 172.

[19] *Liberty Hall*, July 9, 1829.

[20] During the depression of 1819 the Overseers of the Poor threatened to invoke the "black laws" to get the Negroes off the pauper lists. *Liberty Hall*, September 3, 1819.

far better than the surrounding country, especially in the twenties. Indeed, the great increase of Negroes in that decade reflected the growing prosperity that followed the depression of 1819.

Irregular employment in legitimate pursuits led some into less useful activity. In fact, underneath Negro life in Cincinnati lay an ugly layer of vice, crime and violence. Of course, this was true of white society in the river town as well, but colored low living was more easily identified and gained greater attention. In 1821 a visitor commented that "the first thing that struck my attention after arriving in this city, was the crowds of negroes, parading the streets after night."[21] Whites lodged constant complaints against gambling houses and the "night walkers, lewd persons, and those who lounge about without any visible means of support."[22] As early as 1808 an ordinance sought to curb "black and mulatto persons of idle lives and vicious habits" and the "Riots, quarrels and disturbances" they created.[23] In the previous year Charles Britton committed the most celebrated crime of the period when, in league with a white, he stole $47,000 from the Receiver of Public Monies.[24] Negroes were responsible for only a small part of the lawlessness in this frontier metropolis, but their enemies never ceased to level every kind of charge against them. Drake observed that though a large portion of the blacks "are reputed" to be petty thieves, "no more than one individual has been punished corporally . . . since the settlement of the town."[25]

[21] *Liberty Hall*, August 8, 1821.

[22] *Liberty Hall*, August 25, 1825.

[23] Town of Cincinnati, *Ordinances*, March 22 and September 20, 1808.

[24] It is interesting to note that Britton was the key witness in the trial, though a state law made it illegal for Negroes to testify against white men. Nicholas Longworth, the defendant's lawyer, tried to keep Britton from testifying but after a long discussion the judge admitted the evidence. "Two Gentlemen of Law Knowledge," *The Trial of Charles Vattier* (Cincinnati, 1807), 30ff., 56-65, 131ff.

[25] Drake, *Natural and Statistical View*, 172.

Fortunately, the growing colored community had stabilizing as well as disorganizing elements. Schools and churches tried to provide the rudiments of learning to the younger generation, while less formalized agencies joined religious organizations to aid adults in finding areas of useful work. Here, however, a pattern of segregation emerged. Though whites often lent support to Negro institutions, they carefully sealed blacks off from participation in nearly all of the town's activities.[26] Since the churches restricted membership, the colored people established two of their own, the African Methodist and Methodist Episcopal. Little is known of their labors until they split over the question of the repeal of the "black laws" of Ohio in 1829.

Schools followed the same exclusive practices, and in 1815 the Cincinnati Lancaster Seminary made the segregation policy official by erecting a separate Negro institution.[27] Fourteen years later, when the city established a common school system, special provision was made for colored children. Religious education embodied the same custom. In 1817 two white ladies, anxious to do something for the "unfortunate children of Africa," founded the first Sunday school for Negroes in the town.[28] Within three years it had between 70 and 80 students instructed by more than a dozen teachers, all of whom were white. By the 1820's the social life of the Queen City sanctioned the increasing separation of the colored community from the rest of society. At just the time when the black population expanded most rapidly, contacts between the two groups lessened markedly.

The response of the white majority in Cincinnati to the growing colored population was a mixture of sympathy, fear and hostility. This ambivalence is nowhere better illus-

[26] The Cincinnati Haytian Union had many white members, though its leadership was colored. It sought to encourage Negro emigration to the new Caribbean republic.

[27] Drake, *Natural and Statistical View*, 157.

[28] *Liberty Hall*, September 30, 1820.

trated than in the constitution adopted by the state of Ohio in 1803. Here the Negro was given his freedom, both from slavery and indenture; but he was also consigned to a clearly inferior status. He could not vote, hold office, or serve in the militia. The convention which drew up these provisions displayed a highly unsettled attitude, and the vote on limitations was close. The Hamilton County (Cincinnati) delegation took a liberal view on questions concerning the status of Negroes, supporting nine to one a motion to extend suffrage to colored citizens, and heavily opposing a move to strip them of all civil rights.[29]

The first session of the Ohio legislature drew the lines tighter, decreeing that no Negro could settle in the state unless he produced a certificate of freedom from some court, and requiring all colored residents to register and pay a fee of 12½ cents. The burden of proof of freedom thus fell on the blacks. In addition, laws prohibited anyone from hiring Negroes without certificates, fining the employer up to $50. Even harsher were the statutes regarding aid to runaway slaves which involved penalties as high as $1,000. All of these regulations embodied provisions which awarded half the fine to the informer, a system which later played into the hands of the unscrupulous.[30]

Three years later the state stiffened these laws. Now a black coming into Ohio had to find two bondsmen to pledge $500 for the "good behaviour of such negro or mulatto" and who agreed to pay for his support if he could not find employment. In addition, the legislature doubled the fine for hiring colored people who did not have the proper papers, and created a new category of discrimination which prohibited Negroes from testifying against whites in court.[31] By 1807, then, the legal system had created a lower order

---

[29] Charles J. Wilson, "The Negro in Early Ohio," *Ohio Archeological and Historical Society, Publications,* XXXIX (1930), 746, 751.

[30] *Acts of the State of Ohio,* 1803, 2nd Session, Ch. II, Sec. 1, 2, 3, 4, 5, 7.

[31] *Acts of the State of Ohio,* 1806, 1st Session, Ch. VII, Sec. 1, 3, 4.

of citizenship for black men. The legislators, at least, considered them a disturbing element, and took care to ring them about with a group of restrictions which came to be known as the "black laws."

This code, however, represented a greater crystallization in attitude than was general in Cincinnati. Many considered the legislation unconstitutional and no attempt was made to register Negroes or require the certificates of freedom.[32] The regulations caused no comment in the newspapers, and the city never raised the issue in the stark form of the state provisions. However, the problem of the runaway remained, and as early as 1803 local officials instructed the constables to watch for slaves who "pass . . . the River Ohio and spend the Sabbath and nights" in the corporation.[33] Five years later the council again took notice of the "many black and mulatto persons . . . who resort to the Town of Cincinnati under the pretext that they are free, and thus impose on the public, to the great damage of town and society."[34] But when, in 1820, five Kentuckians crossed over to capture a Negro who had lived in the city for five years an editor called it an "insulting outrage."[35] Unlike Ohio's state legislators, most Cincinnatians in the first decades of the century had no fixed idea of the place of free colored people in a white society.

However, as the Negro population grew in the twenties signs of hostility appeared. The editor of *Liberty Hall* warned that "the rapid increase of our black population, to say nothing of slavery, is of itself a great evil."[36] The formation in 1826 of the Cincinnati Colonization Society with 120 members, including many prominent citizens, reflected the growing anxiety of some whites.[37] Two years later the city council appointed a committee to look into a

[32] Drake, *Natural and Statistical View*, 171.
[33] Cincinnati, *Ordinances*, March 22, 1803.
[34] Cincinnati, *Ordinances*, September 20, 1808.
[35] *Liberty Hall*, January 28, 1820.
[36] *Liberty Hall*, June 28, 1825.

citizens' petition which asked the city "to take measures to prevent the increase of the negro population within the city."[38] This new concern derived in part from the discussion of the general question of slavery, but its intensity stemmed from the emergence of a significant Negro population in Cincinnati. By 1829 one out of ten people in the city was colored. Some feared that "we shall be overwhelmed by an emigration at once wretched in its character and destructive in its consequences."[39] Hostility fed on this fear—and soon that hostility spilled over into violence.

The "riot of 1829" is well known. A demand grew up in the city in that year to have the "black laws" of 1804-7 enforced; some Negroes fled to Canada, and white sorties into the colored section followed. Carter Woodson wrote of this latter phase, "Bands of ruffians held sway in the city for three days, as the police were unable or unwilling to restore order. Negroes were insulted on the streets, attacked in their homes, and even killed. About a thousand or twelve hundred of them found it advisable to leave for Canada, where they established the settlement known as Wilberforce."[40] Francis Weisenburger pictured the episode in the same dark tones. "Mob rule . . . broke out for three days and nights and resulted in many casualties. . . . Between one and two thousand Negroes . . . left for Canada with the aid of private funds."[41] Other historians have recorded the disorders of 1829 in similar terms.[42]

[37] Cincinnati Colonization Society, *Proceedings* (Cincinnati, 1833), 3.

[38] Cincinnati City Council, *Minutes*, November 19, 1828.

[39] *Daily Gazette*, July 24, 1829.

[40] Carter J. Woodson, "The Negroes of Cincinnati Prior to the Civil War," *The Journal of Negro History*, I (1916), 6-7.

[41] Francis Weisenburger, *Passing of the Frontier, 1825-50* (Columbus, 1941), 42.

[42] For example see John Hope Franklin, *From Slavery to Freedom* (New York, 1947), 231-2; Herbert Aptheker, *A Documentary History of the Negro People in the United States* (New York, 1951), 102; Alvin F. Harlow, *Serene Cincinnatians* (New York, 1950), 207.

Yet a study of contemporary sources fails to disclose any mob rule or three day riot. To be sure there was an effort to drive the Negroes from Cincinnati, sporadic fighting ensued, and over half the black population fled the city in that year. But they left to escape the enforcement of the "black laws" and not in fear of violence. The physical attacks on the colored community were only incidental to the exodus, much of which took place before the outbreaks. The episode is important not so much because of the bloodshed—which was common in western towns—but for the issue it dramatized. The growing Negro population in Cincinnati posed the problem of the place of the free black in white society. For two decades this question had not been raised directly, except as a part of the general argument over slavery and its abolition. But by the late twenties a crisis developed which many people thought required solution. As the black influx increased white anxiety mounted. In the discussion which followed racial fear mingled with a concern for justice, laying bare the deep conflict within this young urban community.

The issue was drawn in July, 1829, when the Trustees of the Township, acting as Overseers of the Poor, announced that they would enforce the "black laws" of 1804-7 which had lain dormant for better than twenty years.[43] All Negroes were directed to register, present their certificates of freedom, and enroll the names of their bondsmen within 30 days or leave the city. Behind this decision was not only the growing uncertainty of many whites, but the results of a ward election which had centered on this proposal.[44] Debate, which had been submerged for many years, immediately came to the surface. The editor of the *Daily Gazette* charged the township officials with hasty action. "Have the Trustees and the citizens who call upon them to act, well considered

---

[43] *Daily Gazette*, July 4, 1829.
[44] *Cincinnati Advertiser*, March 27, 1829.

what they are about to undertake?'' he asked. ''Negroes and mulattoes are men, and have, at least, some of the rights of men under the laws. The proposition to drive fifteen hundred to two thousand persons from their homes, is one that ought not be made or attempted'' without full deliberation.[45] Indeed, many questions were raised. Where could the blacks be sent? Most came from southern states and could not legally return. If they were to be moved elsewhere, who would pay for the mass deportation?[46]

In addition to doubts of expediency, there were also problems of constitutionality and justice. ''Our Constitution was framed and adopted by white people, and for their own benefit,'' ''Wilberforce'' stated bluntly, ''and they of course had a right to say on what terms they would admit black emigrants.'' He further noted that Negroes were streaming into the areas around Cincinnati, and he warned that soon ''we shall be overwhelmed.''[47] ''Blackstone'' countered by declaring the laws to be unconstitutional because they singled out one group and were not for general application. ''We are, by straining the construction of the Constitution, paving the way for the destruction of our own liberties,'' he observed. ''It is just as constitutional to proscribe a man for the size of his head, as for the color of his skin.''[48] Many others joined the debate emphasizing the legal issue raised by either the laws or the trustees' action.

Some grew impatient with the constitutional question. ''I would not wish to complain of the law or presume to judge of its justice,'' wrote one citizen, ''but will call upon humanity to exert her influence in their [the Negroes'] case.''[49] ''Jefferson'' contended that no matter what the legality of ''black laws'' they were so ''odious'' that hu-

[45] *Daily Gazette*, July 4, 1829.
[46] *Daily Gazette*, July 4, 1829.
[47] *Daily Gazette*, July 24, 1829.
[48] *Daily Gazette*, July 27, 1829.
[49] *Daily Gazette*, July 17, 1829.

mane people would never stand for their enforcement."[50] Equally exasperated was the editor of the *Chronicle* who thought the time had come to stop talking and get down to business. "There is but one way—we must remove that population from our territory, while the power is still in our hands."[51] No local issue in Cincinnati had ever received the extended public debate that surrounded the demand to evict the city's colored residents.

While the argument raged the Negroes tried to delay the 30 day deadline. Leading colored citizens called a meeting which drew up a petition to the state legislature asking for the repeal of "those obnoxious black laws."[52] Signatures of many prominent Cincinnatians, including such people as Nicholas Longworth and Wykoff Piatt, gave the document broad support.[53] But the Negroes themselves were split over tactics. The powerful Methodist Episcopal Church disassociated itself with the petition, declaring that "all we ask is a continuation of the smiles of the white people as we have hitherto enjoyed them."[54] Meanwhile, Israel Lewis and Thomas Cressup went to Canada to find a place for resettlement. "If the act is enforced, we, the poor sons of Aethiopia, must take shelter where we can find it. . . . If we cannot find it in America, where we were born and spent all our days, we must beg it elsewhere."[55]

The drive against the colored population continued, however, with support coming from many sources and from every strata in society. Among the most were the town's transients—boatmen, wagoners and adventurers—who had no roots and little interest in Cincinnati, and who could be counted on to join a frolic no matter what its objectives.

[50] *Daily Gazette*, July 28, 1829.
[51] *Cincinnati Chronicle and Literary Gazette*, July 4, 1829.
[52] Malvin, *Autobiography*, 13.
[53] Malvin, *Autobiography*, 13.
[54] *Daily Gazette*, July 4, 1829.
[55] *Cincinnati Advertiser*, March 27, 1829.

They constituted the shock troops of any disorder since no police action frightened or restrained them. In addition, some unskilled workers feared Negro competition on the job, and they hoped that the removal of the blacks would bring higher wages.[56] These groups were leaderless and inarticulate and by themselves could not have acted decisively.

Crucial in the drive against the Negroes was the activity of the Cincinnati Colonization Society. Founded in 1826, this branch of the national association quickly attracted great public attention and recruited for its leaders some of the city's most influential people. Though organizationally weak in the Queen City, its propaganda found many outlets. Newspapers carried long articles on possible homesites for the blacks, and editorials expounded its program. Many churches devoted one Sunday annually to a collection of funds for its support, and ministers lent their name to the idea. Though the Cincinnati group had a membership of only 120 in 1829, its list of officers read like the social register.

The Colonization Society not only sought to solve the slavery question by removing bonded Negroes from the country, but it applied the same doctrine to free blacks. "We consider this class of people a serious evil among us. . . . The only remedy afforded is, to colonize them in their mother country."[57] This notion—that people could be easily moved from one place to another—provided the rationale for the attempt to drive the colored population from Cincinnati. What was cruel was thus made to seem reasonable.[58] In addition to furnishing a philosophical justification to the aggressors, members of the local organization lent respecta-

---

[56] *Western Star* (Lebanon, Ohio), August 29, 1829.

[57] *The African Repository and Colonial Journal*, V (1830), 185.

[58] Alvin Harlow lays the blame for the "riot" on the abolitionists whom he claims darkened counsel and intensified bitterness. *Serene Cincinnatians*, 207. Actually the abolitionists had not become very important in Cincinnati, and their strength was not comparable to the Colonization Society.

bility to the movement. "Now is the time for the Colonization Societies 'to be up and doing,' " wrote one of them in the midst of the crisis.[59]

With this support the tension grew. The exact order of events is hard to establish. The first ultimatum was given the Negroes about July 1st and extensions placed the deadline at the beginning of September. But raids into the colored section took place during the interim, reaching a climax on the weekend of August 22nd when "some two or three hundred of the lowest *canaille*" descended on the blacks bent on terror and pillage. By Saturday evening the Negroes, despairing of official protection, armed to defend themselves. Fighting broke out around mid-night, and in the scuffle that followed Eli Herrick, one of the raiders, was killed and two others were injured. The police rounded up ten blacks and seven whites. After a hearing the Mayor released all the Negroes, declaring they had acted in self defense, and at the same time he fined the others a total of $700.[60]

This was the episode often referred to as the "riot of 1829." Such violence was not unusual in western cities.[61] Indeed, only one of the five daily newspapers reported the event, and memoirs of the period are silent on the incident. There was no mob rule and no reign of terror. Nevertheless, the raids on the colored community were important because

[59] *Hamilton Intelligencer* (Hamilton, Ohio), July 21, 1829.

[60] The best description of the weekend is in the *Western Star* (Lebanon, Ohio), August 19, 1829. Some property damage resulted because shortly afterward C. Foote, "a coloured man," petitioned the city council for damages done "to his house during the late riott." Cincinnati City Council, *Minutes*, September 2, 1829.

[61] Violence of this kind was so frequent that many grew callous. Charles Hammond, the editor of the *Cincinnati Gazette*, wrote to an acquaintance in 1824 that "our friend Sam Richardson has had an affray at Louisville and stabbed a man—it is supposed dangerously—But such things are always expected—If death ensues it is, at best, a case of manslaughter." Charles Hammond to John C. Wright, May 3, 1824, Hammond MSS., (Ohio Archeological and Historical Society, Columbus).

they sharpened the issue and threw into bold relief the grim tendency of events. Public sympathy, for a long time mixed and confused, went out to the Negroes, leading many whites to review the situation and re-examine their position.

Before this re-assessment could take place, however, over half the colored population had fled the city. Lewis and Cressup located some land near York in Canada, later called Wilberforce, where many of the refugees settled. The land "beats all for beauty and fertility," they boasted. "Our rights here as freemen, will be respected. We shall be as free as the atmosphere we breathe."[62] The Quakers donated some money to facilitate the migration, and other large contributions came from New York and Pennsylvania. Some Cincinnatians suggested that public money be used for "the voluntary removal [of the blacks] from the state," but nothing ever came of the idea.[63] Most of the funds, however, were raised among Negroes in the Queen City.

By winter the crisis had passed. Though there is no way of knowing exactly how many colored people left Cincinnati, the number was certainly no less than 1,100 and probably higher. Among these displaced persons were many of the most industrious, stable and prosperous members of the Negro community. They had the financial resources and social energy needed for movement, while the less successful and weaker stayed behind. Some leadership remained in the city, but the cream was skimmed off. The editor of the *Gazette,* who had earlier supported the enforcement of the "black laws," appraised the episode and spoke for a chastened town.

It has driven away the sober, honest, industrious, and useful portion of the colored population. The vagrant is unaffected by it. The effect is to lessen much of the moral restraint, which the presence of respectable persons of their own colour, imposed on the idle and indolent, as well as the profligate. It has exposed employers of coloured persons to suits by common informers, where

[62] *Cincinnati Gazette,* July 30, 1829.
[63] *Cincinnati Gazette,* September 17, 1829.

no good or public motive was perceptible. It has reduced honest individuals to want and beggary, in the midst of plenty and employment; because employers were afraid to employ them. It has subjected men of color who own property to great sacrifices. It has furnished an occasion for the oppressor and the common informer to exhibit themselves, and commence their depredations on the weak and defenceless, under cover of law. It has demonstrated the humiliating fact, that cruelty and injustice, the rank oppression of a devoted people, may be consummated in the midst of us, without exciting either sympathy, or operative indignation.[64]

The attempt to enforce the "black laws" was the critical point in the early life of Cincinnati's Negroes. Success would have removed the Queen City as the central link in the life line which brought so many slaves and free blacks to northern safety. The riots of the thirties, though more spectacular, never carried this same implication, for white abolitionists absorbed as much of the punishment as the colored people. Martyrdom had won friends for the Negroes, and they never again had to stand alone without outside support. By 1830 they had earned the right to live in Cincinnati; the next struggles were over the right to a better life.

RICHARD C. WADE

University of Rochester

[64] *Cincinnati Gazette,* August 17, 1829.

OMAR IBN SEID, A SLAVE WHO WROTE AN AUTOBIOGRAPHY IN ARABIC

Omar ibn Seid is the only known Negro slave in America who wrote his life story in an African language. Written in 1831, it is an account filled with charm and pathos of his capture in Africa, his cruel South Carolina master, and of his escape and recapture while he prayed in a church in North Carolina. With child-like simplicity and innocence Omar tells how he was eventually purchased by kindly "Massa Jim" Owen who converted him to Christianity, and gave him a Bible written in Arabic, the only language he could read.

Omar's autobiography is translated from Arabic exactly as he wrote it. The original manuscript of about 2000 words was first published in full in the *American Historical Review* in 1924.[1] In its original form the autobiography is disjointed and is interspersed with pious expressions and praise of his master, some of which are omitted here. "I have forgotten much of my own, as well as the Arabic language," Omar began. "And so, my brother, I beg you, in God's name, not to blame me. . . .

"My name is Omar ibn Seid. My birthplace was Fut Tur, between the two rivers." Apparently Omar was born about 1770, between the Senegal and the Bounoun, some 250 miles north-east of Dakar. He was a member of the Foula tribe, a tall, straight haired, copper colored people of Berber, Semitic and Negro stock who were scattered from Senegal to Nigeria. According to Omar, his father was a wealthy merchant who owned seventy slaves.[2]

Only five when his father was killed in a tribal war,

---

[1] XXX, 787-795.

[2] Anon., "Uncle Moreau," *North Carolina University Magazine*, III (September, 1854), 307-309.

Omar was taken to live with an uncle who was the tribal chieftain. Here Omar came in contact with Mohammedan missionaries who converted him to that religion, taught him to read Arabic, and to recite Mohammedan prayers. He was extremely pious and returned to his native village to become a missionary and teacher himself. Just before he was captured Omar gave up teaching and became a trader in salt and cotton, but he never lost his piety.[3]

"Before I came to the Christian country, my religion was the religion of Mohammed, the Apostle of God. . . . I walked to the mosque before day-break, washed my face and head and hands and feet. I prayed at noon, prayed in the afternoon, prayed at sunset, and prayed in the evening. . . . I went every year to the holy war against the infidels. I went on a pilgrimage to Mecca. . . ." Omar must have gone on foot the entire 4,000 miles across the African continent.

Omar was brought to Charleston in 1807, the last year that slaves were legally imported into the United States. In 1802 the Foulas began a series of political and holy wars against the Hausas, and probably Omar was captured by them and sold south to the traders.[4] When he was seized Omar was married and had one son. He never saw his family again.

"I reside in this our country by reason of great necessity," he wrote. "There came to our place a large army, who killed many men, and took me, and brought me to the great sea, and sold me into the hands of Christians, who bound me and sent me on board a great ship and we sailed upon the great sea a month and a half, when we came to a

[3] *Ibid.;* see also William S. Plummer, "Moroh, a Native African," *New York Observer,* XLIV (January 8, 1863).

[4] An unidentified writer in a dubious account in the Raleigh *News and Observer,* September 3, 1889, says that Omar was a slave trader, that he was overwhelmed by superior forces when on a slave hunting expedition in the Congo, and that his piety sprang from a belief that his servitude was retribution for his own sin of slave trading.

place called Charleston in the Christian language. There they sold me to a small, weak, and wicked man, called Johnson, a complete infidel, who had no fear of God at all.''

''I was afraid to remain with a man so depraved and who committed so many crimes and I ran away.'' For a month he wandered in the swamps and forests of the sand hills. Perhaps he had learned that far north there was freedom for he went in that direction.

''I fled from the hand of Johnson and after a month came to a place called Fayetteville [North Carolina]. There I saw some great houses (churches). On a new moon I went into a church to pray. A small boy saw me and rode off to the place of his father and informed him that he had seen a black man in the church. A man named Hunter and another with him on horseback, came attended by a troop of dogs. They took me and made me go with them twelve miles ... where they put me in a great house from which I could not go out. I continued in the great house (which in the Christian language, they call *jail*) sixteen days and nights.''

When Omar was arrested as a runaway he had been in America for only about three years, and knew very little English. With the coals from his cell floor he covered the walls with piteous appeals not to be returned to Charleston. To the jailer the straight haired slave who wrote in an unknown language was a ''conjuror,'' and the townspeople flocked to see him.[5]

It happened that James Owen, general in the state militia and brother of John Owen, soon to be elected governor of North Carolina, was visiting Fayetteville. Curious to see the unusual Negro, he went to the jail, and agreed to take the slave until his owner called for him. He took him to his plantation, ''Milton,'' about thirty miles below Fayetteville. ''A man named Jim Owen . . . asked me if I was

[5] Anon., ''Prince Omeroh,'' Raleigh *Farmer and Mechanic*, June 25, 1884.

willing to go to a place called Bladen [County]. I said, Yes, I was willing. I went with him and have remained in the place of Jim Owen until now.''

General Owen liked the intelligent Negro, and Omar worshiped his new master and begged not to be returned. Omar's Charleston owner sent an agent to bring back the slave. "A man by the name of Mitchell came to take me. He asked me if I were willing to go to Charleston City. I said, *No, no, no, no, no, no,* I am not willing to go to Charleston.'' Apparently Omar made quite a disturbance, for General Owen agreed to buy the slave for $900 from his Charleston owner, to the great joy of Omar.[6]

"I continue in the hand of Jim Owen who never beats me nor scolds me. I neither go hungry nor naked, and I have no hard work to do.'' "O ye people of North Carolina, O ye people of South Carolina, O ye people of America all of you, have you among you any two such good men as Jim Owen and John Owen? These men are good men. . . . They permit me to read the gospel of God, our Lord and Savior. . . .''

The Owens procured for Omar an Arabic Bible and an Arabic Koran which the slave called his "richest treasures.'' Omar became a Christian and was baptized in the Presbyterian Church in Fayetteville. For the rest of his life he had a seat by himself in the Church where his master worshiped. He wrote, "When I was a Mohammedan I prayed thus: 'Thanks be to God, Lord of all worlds, the merciful, the gracious, Lord of the day of Judgement, thee we serve. . . .'—But now I pray 'Our Father,' etc., in the words of our Lord Jesus the Messiah.''

Omar's Bible is now preserved in the Davidson College Library, in Davidson, North Carolina. It is a big, worn, dog-eared volume, with about half a dozen homespun covers on it. As one wore out the old slave sewed on another.

[6] MS. in Mrs. W. S. Witherspoon Papers in possession of Rev. E. D. Witherspoon, Wilmington, North Carolina.

With the help of his master, Omar corresponded with the American Bible Society, urging that a new edition of the Bible be translated into Arabic and sent to his people in Africa. Omar apparently wrote his autobiography for the Society to explain his own conversion to Christianity. The Bible was eventually sent to the Foulas, and the chief of the tribe wrote to the Bible Society thanking them for their gift.[7]

Perhaps Omar's actual conversion to Christianity was partly to please his master, however, because when a North Carolina preacher had translated the Twenty-Third Psalm which Omar had written for him in Arabic, the preacher was alarmed to discover that it began "May God have mercy on the Prophet Mohammed," a Mohammedan prayer.[8] Omar's Bible is copiously annotated with both Christian and Mohammedan sentiments.

When the Owens moved to Wilmington, North Carolina, in the 1850's Omar went with them, and he became a member of the Presbyterian Church there. Sincerely devoted to his master, he never expressed a desire to return to Africa. "God doeth no wrong" was the motto of the slave. He lived to be 89 years old, and spent his last years as head butler at "Owen Hill," Governor Owen's plantation, where he would sit on the verandah in a white turban and long black coat and entertain the children with his stories.[9] Although he called himself Omar, or Omero, the family always called him "Uncle Moreau," and after he died one member of the family wrote of "the dear old saint, now gone to his rest."[10]

[7] R. R. Gurley, *African Repository*, XIII (July, 1837), 203-205. Also *Farmer and Mechanic, op. cit.*; Theodore Dwight, "Condition and Character of Negroes in Africa," *Methodist Review*, XL (January, 1864), 77-90.

[8] John F. Foard, *North America and Africa, Their Past, Present and Future* (Statesville, N. C., 1904), p. 67. This account also has a picture of the slave.

[9] MS. in Witherspoon Papers; also Rev. M. B. Grier, *North Carolina Presbyterian* (July 23, 1859).

[10] Cited in Carrie A. Harris, "Omeroh," *South Atlantic Quarterly*, VI (September, 1880), 100.

Omar did not live to be freed by the Civil War. He died in 1859 and was buried on the Owen Hill plantation.

GEORGE H. CALLCOTT

University of North Carolina,
Chapel Hill

BOOK REVIEWS

America Day by Day. By Simone de Beauvoir. Translated by Patrick Dudley. (New York: Grove Press, 1953. Pp. 337. Price $4.00.)

This translation of one of the more interesting recent additions to the voluminous series of books by French visitors to the United States is a difficult work to review, not only because of the impressionistic nature of the diary, but also because of the author's warning in her preface: "I must point out that no isolated passage expresses a definite judgment; besides which, I often never reached a definite point of view, and it is the ensemble of my indecisions, additions and corrections that constitutes my opinion." Indeed, Simone de Beauvoir seems to be groping for an understanding of the United States as she dashes from one end of the country to the other in less than four months. Between January 25 and February 25, 1947, she has "covered" 116 pages, New York, Washington, Lynchburg, Niagara, Rochester, Cleveland, Oberlin, Chicago, and has reached Los Angeles. This hectic pace continues through Nevada, Texas, Louisiana, Georgia, South Carolina, back to Chicago and New York.

To accelerate her comprehension of the country she chats with Americans of different social strata, especially the intellectuals and the underprivileged. Though she dislikes the taste of whiskey, she imbibes frequently "because Scotch is the key to America." (P. 18) Less instructive no doubt are the tequila she drinks in California and the reefers she smokes one evening in Harlem. More solid information comes from the motion picture. "It was through these black and white pictures that I had come to know America, and they still seemed to me to be its real substance." (P. 79) Jazz, which reflects the tempo of our urban life, attracts her night after night, though she can stand but one-half hour of bop, "the breathless, exasperated expression of the fever of New York life." (P. 300) Her lectures at such schools as Vassar, Yale, Harvard, Princeton, Mills, and Oberlin establish contacts with college students who depress her by their docile resignation: "What struck me and what upset me was that they, being neither blind nor unconscious, should be so apathetic: they know and condemn the oppression of thirteen million Negroes in the country, the squalor of the South . . . and they look at race prejudice and reaction increasing in threat day by day, and though they acknowledge their country's responsibility for the future of the world, they feel themselves responsible for nothing. They think they can do nothing in this world. At the age of twenty they are convinced that thought is in vain, that good will towards man is useless and they say, or think, 'America is too vast, too heavy, for one individual to try to shake.' " (P. 101)

As exceptions she cites two white girls who returned to fight race prejudice in their native Louisiana after studying in Boston. This, however, is less exceptional than the author may imagine, for the evidence in numerous colleges, South and North, indicates that the present generation of college youth has a keener sense of racial justice than its elders.

In the midst of debatable generalizations and minute detail (which sometimes becomes boring to this reviewer), there are brilliant passages in this book, as for example the discussions of American literature and some of the analyses of the American and his rôle in the present day world. Especially noteworthy are the numerous references to the Negro for they reveal the importance that our friends abroad attach to American race relations. The book is dedicated to Ellen and Richard Wright, and the Negro novelist is one of her guides around New York City. He takes her to the Savoy and subsequently to the Abyssinia Baptist Church where she hears Adam Powell preach. Despite warnings that her white skin will make her unwelcome in Harlem, she encounters no animosity there and returns on several occasions. She finds that the Harlemites wish ". . . to integrate themselves with America, not to destroy it. These people will not suddenly roll forward in a flood heading for Wall Street; the unreasonable fear they inspire must be the reverse side of some hatred or remorse. Clamped to the heart of New York, Harlem weighs on the good conscience of the white people in the same way that original sin does on that of the Christian.'' (P. 36)

In the South, however, ''from the moment we entered Texas, and everywhere we went, there was hatred in the air, arrogant hatred on the part of the white race and silent hatred on that of the black.'' (P. 224) She saw this hatred in the outward manifestations and concomitants of segregation, in waiting rooms, on buses, or as she walked through the Negro section of Savannah. And she sensed it in the determination of the ex-G.I. to study and practice law as ''about the only concrete means of fighting for the cause of the colored people.'' (P. 225) Unfortunately, she visited no Negro school, but in the French version there is a passing reference to a colored college in Texas in the vicinity of Rice Institute. This incident is not included in the translation.

Also omitted from the translation are several pages in which Mme de Beauvoir discusses Myrdal's *American Dilemma.* Her knowledge of this volume and her close relationship with Richard Wright probably explain in part why she is better informed on the race question than most French commentators. With all due respect to Mr. Wright, he too seems guilty of excessive generalization when he tells her on page 60, ''that there is not a single minute in the life of a Negro that is not penetrated by a social consciousness; from the cradle to the grave, whether working, eating, loving, walking, dancing or praying, he can never forget that he is black; and this makes him conscious every minute of a white man's world whence the word 'black' derives its meaning.''

In short, though *America Day by Day* is a far cry from its illustrious ancestor, *Democracy in America,* it is less ephemeral than the title would suggest. Few contemporary studies offer Americans a better opportunity to see ourselves as others see us.

MERCER COOK

Howard University

The Missouri Controversy 1819-1821. By Glover Moore (Lexington, Ky.: University of Kentucky Press, 1953. Pp. 383. Price $6.00.)

In general, Mr. Moore displays sound scholarship and evidences of careful research in recounting and analyzing the events which produced the famous Missouri Compromise. An examination of his footnotes and bibliography reveals that he has utilized the major primary and secondary sources in relating the story of one of the stormy periods in American history.

The author declares that sectional animosity existed between New England and the South during colonial times. Differences between the two sections were heightened during the era of the Continental Congress when disputes arose over the fisheries, tax apportionment, the western lands, and the navigation of the Missouri River. At this time the Middle states were frequently "a political borderland," although the Eastern and Southern seaboard states were shortly to develop a mutual distrust for each other. Southerners exhibited a certain degree of solidarity in their thinking during the Revolutionary War era, but the Missouri Controversy "made the Solid South more solid."

The efforts made in Congress to prevent Missouri from entering the Union as a slave state were undertaken by a majority of Northern Federalists and Clintonian Democrats, as well as certain other Northern Democrats. This was the first organized attack by Northerners against the extension of slavery into the territories. The Federalist restrictionists saw in the controversy an opportunity to create a new political alignment among Northern voters in which they would play a dominant role. Humanitarian considerations and differences in economic viewpoints between the North and South caused some Northern Congressmen to support restriction in Missouri.

While Missouri petitioned for statehood as early as 1817 and the matter was considered by Congress in the following year, the Tallmadge Amendment of February 13, 1819, brought on the great debate. Little interest was manifested in the North at first, but mass meetings held during the fall and winter of 1819-1820 in a number of northern cities created widespread interest. Southerners who were unaware of the full implications of the contest at first soon united in opposing any restriction on slavery in Missouri. Many people in all sections of the country, however, remained more concerned about other leading issues than the Missouri Controversy.

The Missouri question was considered by the Fifteenth and Sixteenth Congresses. While Senator Jesse B. Thomas of Illinois was the author of the Compromise, it is not known who originated the idea. Maine was admitted to the Union by the Compromise of 1820 and Missouri was authorized to draw up a constitution and form a state government without the requirement that it would prohibit slavery. Slavery was prohibited in the unorganized territory of the Louisiana Purchase north of 36° 30'.

The author discusses at some length the Compromise of 1821 which resulted from Missouri's constitutional provision excluding free Negroes and mulattoes from the state and forbidding the legislature to emancipate slaves without the consent of owners; the rejection of the Missouri constitution by the House of Representatives; the approval of the Clay Compromise by both houses in February 1821, and President Monroe's proclamation of August 10, 1821, whereby Missouri was admitted to the Union.

While this account is generally objective, certain of the writer's conclusions are open to question. The statement that "only a Civil War or the dissolution of the Union could have prevented the creation of a slave state in Missouri" (p. 350) is debatable, as it is the belief that the extension of the 36° 30' line to the Pacific in later decades "would almost certainly have held the nation together until such time as the South, yielding to the humanitarian spirit of the age and the inexorable decree of economic law, should abolish slavery of its own volition." (Pp. 350-351). Mr. Moore regards the introduction of slavery as the greatest tragedy in American history. Some might take issue with him in his assertion that the repeal of the Missouri Compromise in 1854 was the second greatest tragedy in our history.

ROBERT D. REID

Tuskegee Institute

Tobacco Coast: A Maritime History of Chesapeake Bay in the Colonial Era. By Arthur Pierce Middleton. Edited by George Carrington Mason. (Newport News, Va.: The Mariners' Museum. 1953. Pp. xii, 482. Illustrated. Price $5.00.)

It has been asserted that the demand for tobacco in Europe laid the foundation for American commerce. If this assertion is debatable, it can hardly be denied that tobacco during the seventeenth and eighteenth centuries was the dominant factor in the commercial and maritime life of two important British colonies on the Chesapeake Bay—Virginia and Maryland. This commodity was so important that it is easy to imagine that English merchants trading with the Chesapeake Bay region regarded it as the "Tobacco Coast" in much the same way as traders with Africa spoke of the Ivory Coast, Gold Coast, and Slave Coast to designate areas in accordance with their principal exports to Europe or America. In this sense Dr. Arthur Pierce Middleton has coined the expression "Tobacco Coast" as the title of a maritime history of colonial Virginia and Maryland which shows how the Chesapeake Bay and its many tributaries as channels for the tobacco trade greatly affected the historical development of these colonies.

Middleton's interest in the history of the Chesapeake Bay country emanates from several sources. His ancestors for several generations have dwelt on the "Great Bay of Chesapeake's Maryland shore." His doctoral work at Harvard University under Samuel Eliot Morison and his reading of the latter's famous *Maritime History of Massachusetts* stimulated interest in maritime events and influences. War service in the United States Coast Guard increased his nautical knowledge and familiarity with coastal areas. As the director of the Research Department of Colonial Williamsburg, Inc., and a rector in a historic Episcopal parish of Virginia, Middleton has had unusual opportunities to explore the history of the Chesapeake Bay region.

Although the tobacco trade was the dominant enterprise in the maritime life of the Chesapeake colonies, the slave trade was the most profitable enterprise. Middleton relates that participation in this nefarious traffic was eagerly sought by colonial merchants and planters, including some of the leading men of Virginia and Maryland. The slave trade remained profitable despite the mortality hazards of the infamous "middle passage", prejudice against the use of slaving vessels to carry tobacco to Great Britain, and the necessity of extending credit to purchasers of slaves. A few individuals in the Bay region saw that the increased importation of slaves "had a detrimental effect upon the whites, inflating their pride, ruining their industry, and disposing them to idleness" (page 142). Most of the slaves were plantation field workers but some are also shown to have been sawyers, carpenters, smiths, coopers, weavers, and spinners. The author refutes historians who have frequently asserted that New England vessels brought large numbers of Negroes from the West Indies to the Chesapeake Bay colonies. He contends that British vessels rather than American ones obtained the lion's share of the region's commerce in slaves and their owners continually fought colonial measures to restrict it. This situation is shown to be one of the threads in the pattern of alleged imperial abuses that provoked the American Revolution.

This book is a valuable, well-documented factual presentation concerning the maritime and commercial aspects of colonial life in Virginia and Maryland. It properly stresses the importance of tobacco in the economy of these colonies, although it fails to indicate clearly the harmful effects of a nearly single-crop type of agriculture on the soils and on efforts to establish more diversified economic activity. The convincing picture of these tobacco colonies as a physiographic and economic unit and the story of the failure of the British Government to recognize them as a unit are probably the chief contributions of this book. Important also is its explanation of the adverse effect of the Bay and its tributaries on the growth of towns and the development of intellectual pursuits. Indeed Middleton's work contains much information that helps to explain some of the social and economic peculiarities of the Chesapeake Bay region persisting long after tobacco has ceased to be the stimulant of its maritime life and the mainstay of its economy.

HAROLD T. PINKETT

Washington, D. C.

The Historian's Craft. By Marc Bloch. (New York: Alfred A. Knopf. 1953. Pp. 197. Price $3.00.)

This is a description of the historian's art and his methods of craftsmanship in research, evaluation of evidence, and writing. First of all there are accounts of the uses of history and how the historian must proceed in order to reveal the fundamental unification of human experience. The author's central objective is "the study of men in time". He goes directly to sources of information to illustrate how men have lived and worked in time to make history. Not only raw materials but the instruments of the historian and his methods receive careful exploration. Here the intricate nature of evidence and the eminence of error and fraud appear so clearly and concisely that their significance for historical study is evident. The scholar and student as well as the general reader have basic guidance and direction for the critical spirit which underlies every approach in scientific history.

Bloch seals the past and present together and insists that neither can be understood without the other. "This faculty of understanding the living is, in very truth, the master quality of the historian." The author argues that out of present experience the past can best be restored and "men in time" become inseparably linked as one for purposes of historical craftsmanship. The abstruse sifting and evaluation of total evidence emerge in their vital relations to research and systematic organization in writing. Into a kind of mosaic the writer weaves the devious threads of analyses and causation which are indispensable elements in orthodox history. The advocates of teaching history backwards have in this author some sanction, but they will find that his course is not that one-way alone to past actuality. His goal is rather that of strict interdependence of the present and the past for authentic and final historical truth.

The Historian's Craft recommends the study of history as a whole instead of in separate topics and periods. The work visualizes life as "complicated interplay of ideals and realities, conscious innovations and unconscious conservatism." The author was a distinguished medievalist and his two volumes, *La societe féodale*, and *Les caractères originaux de l'histoire rurale française* used many of the devices of the new history in sources. Old maps, places, tools, aviation surveys, legends, and tales illuminate these works. Bloch insists upon the unity of all history and living connections between the present and the past. This sharply suggests the dangers in overemphasis now upon specialized topics and concentration, for example, upon American history too exclusively in schools, colleges, and universities without adequate acquaintance with general history. Indeed, the author's approach becomes especially germane in contemporary international relations where acquaintance with all history is needed as never before. His program of broad comprehensive studies of all history would include also cross fertilizations from the related social and political sciences which are contributing much to the development of the new history.

The divisions of the *Historian's Craft* are: History, Men and

Time, Historical Observation, Historical Analysis, and Historical Causation. Under these titles the author develops what he uniquely interprets as the ''science of men in time'' and suggests that it has possibilities of promoting improved human relations. These he believes would come through comprehensive understanding by the present of the past. His strategy of handling historical evidence is similar to that of law courts which require examination of evidence and testimony. The ideal of the ''whole of historical information'' is Bloch's objective in seeking understanding based upon integration of facts from various sources and fragments. Behind all historical evidence are men whom the author believes are the key for unlocking historical truth and applying it in human affairs as well as to institutions and organizations.

Marc Bloch was a brilliant professor of history at the Sorbonne and the oldest French captain in World War II when he was captured and later executed by the Nazi Gestapo in 1944. This book is an unfinished manuscript which he left and Peter Putnam translated it from the French. Bloch's style is so clear with pertinent illustrations of an autobiographical nature that it affords fascinating reading in the otherwise technical treatment of pure historiography. He wrote out of experience and insisted that the ''historian's first duty is to be sincere'' while pursuing with integrity, truth, and penetration the theme of ''men in time''. To them he subordinated geography, documents, and institutions.

The Historian's Craft will rank high among the increasing publications of its kind and it will serve as an indispensable accompaniment to such works as Nevin's *Gateway to History* and Gottschalk's *Understanding History*. Bloch's work is a timely contribution to current and expanding historiography. Undoubtedly the book will help to make the study and learning of history easier and its general reading a greater pleasure. This is because the author emphasizes ''men in time'' and his interpretations of the relations of the ''present and the past'' offer a somewhat new approach to understanding history.

W. M. Brewer

Franz Boas. By Melville J. Herskovits. (New York: Charles Scribner's Sons, 1953. Pp. 131. Price $2.50.)

Franz Boas sometimes is referred to as ''the father of American anthropology.'' Although he may not be allotted, without equivocation, a position such as this in the development of anthropology as a whole, his influence on that development is quite comparable to that of Jacques Boucher de Crèvecoeur de Perthes, Charles Darwin, Edward B. Tylor, James G. Frazer, or Emile Durkheim—to name only these five—and the scope of his investigations was more inclusive than that of any of them. Thus it is highly appropriate that *The Science of Man in the Making* appears as subtitle of this admirable biographical exposition of Boas' activities and thought.

Herskovits, who obtained his doctorate in anthropology under Boas, shows an intimate acquaintance with and profound understanding of the personal and scientific characteristics of his mentor.

The materials are presented in five chapters, followed by an appendix, which includes a bibliography of Boas' major studies and an indication of the source of his complete bibliography, an index, and a chronological list of the principal events in his life, beginning with his birth on July 9, 1858, at Minden, Westphalia, Germany and ending with his death on December 21, 1952, at a luncheon which he gave at the Columbia Faculty Club for Paul Rivet.

The first chapter relates Boas' change from a physicist and geographer to an anthropologist, following a geographical expedition, in 1883, to Cumberland Sound and Baffin Island, where he became acquainted with the Central Eskimo and came to see them as essentially human, however different in physical type and cultural manifestations they were from the Europeans. This led him to raise questions concerning the interrelations of race and culture and subsequently to contribute more than anyone else to the scientific analysis of the complex problems involved. Here also are reported his first visit to and later permanent residence in the United States, his prolific scientific writings, field work, advocacy of scientific studies, and his positions in museums and universities.

The second, third, and fourth chapters are a penetrating logical synopsis of Boas' studies in physical anthropology and cultural butions were great in number and pioneering in character. His anthropology, including linguistics. In all these fields, his contri-

influence in physical anthropology was stamped especially in three areas (p. 27): "the study of the physical growth and development of the child; the problem of the nature of physical difference between human groups, or that of race, with particular reference to the relation between physical type and behavior; and biometrics, with special regard for the unravelling of those processes which have made for the creation of specific local forms, or ecotypes, . . ." In cultural anthropology, his ethnological monographs and critical guidance in the rectification and development of theory on the basis of concrete data are equally to be esteemed. He expanded linguistics to include the more exotic languages, studied from the point of view of their own structures, amassed an extraordinary quantity of data in this field, and, as in his other work, developed students who themselves have achieved renown.

This scientist's role as citizen is described in chapter five. In Herskovits' words (pp. 104-5), "Two fundamental ideas can be traced throughout the course of his professional life. One was that the scientist must be free to pursue his investigations wherever the data lead him, to reach his conclusions with regard only for the principles of scientific method as they apply to these data, and to publish his conclusions without hindrance, subject only to critical testing by his fellow-scientists. The second concerned the duty of the scientist to ensure that these results would not be irresponsibly used, by sharing his findings with the public that supports him, making them known and understood by his fellow-citizens through the use of every means at his command." These, indeed, are the marks of a great scientist and a truly democratic citizen.

This book is full of intellectual stimulation, inspiration, and encouragement for anyone who may have an interest in the nature of the science of man and its bearings on human problems. It clearly presents the ideas that characterized the useful life with which it is concerned, and it shows the devotion of its author as a student influenced by that life, as well as his objectivity as a scientist and his humanism, resulting from that influence. It is, in addition, enjoyable as literature.

MARK HANNA WATKINS

Howard University

Struggle for Africa. By Vernon Bartlett. (New York: Frederick
A. Praeger. 1953. Pp. 246. Price $3.95.)

Africa, traditionally represented in poetry and in art as asleep,
has awakened and is impatiently and insistently knocking for
entrance to its place among the civilized nations. It is this fierce
trend of the various sections of Africa toward nationalism and
the eagerness of the Native for the education which he believes
will emancipate him from European control that give a unifying
force to this book.

The author presents a challenging problem with sympathetic
treatment of the African's aspirations for self-government and
self-realization, but at the same time he is fair to the European
power in control. In fact one might say that he almost bends over
backwards in presenting the case of the Nationalist Party of the
Union of South Africa. After discussing discriminatory legislation
which disfranchised the Cape Coloreds and the policy of
"apartheid"—separateness or segregation to the nth degree—
Bartlett comments, "The torch of civilization cannot be handed
on to other races until they are more or less prepared to carry it."
He fails to show, however, how this policy of separateness will
aid in achieving the desired preparedness. In spite of the enumera-
tion of services rendered by the government, one finds it difficult
in the face of deplorably crowded Native Reserves and forced
labor at starvation wages or no wages at all to agree with the
author when he states: "It would be a great mistake to suppose
that the Nationalists, within the limits of their racial doctrine,
are inactive in doing good or devoid of a certain remote affection
for the Natives they control."

Struggle for Africa is not confined to a discussion of the prob-
lems of the Union of South Africa. The author takes us to the
Portuguese "overseas provinces" where there is less sense of Color
Bar than in any other European colonial territory in Africa.
Here Africans who can pass a test of means, education, and
European way of life are classed as citizens. We go to the Belgian
Congo, the richest territory in Africa, where 76,000 Europeans
and 12,000,000 Africans enjoy great material comforts but have
no vote. Then we go to Nigeria where a measure of self-government
has already been attained, and many of the civil officials are
Africans. Here there are intense nationalism and much enthusiasm

for education. Here also is the ostentation of the nouveau riche who do not realize that their wealth for a long time to come will be dependent upon the advice, technical help, and capital of the European.

What then is the message of *Struggle for Africa?* That the African's intense ambition for independence, self-expression, and self-respect must be regarded as natural and legitimate aspirations. That these aspirations must be reconciled to his dependency upon the European for advice, capital, technical know-how, and the nuances of democratic culture. That the white man and the African must form a partnership and learn to live together in a state of mutual dependence and respect in order to insure the fullest development of each.

DORA REYNOLDS GEBO

Washington, D. C.

North From Malaya. By William O. Douglas. (New York: Doubleday and Co., 1953. Pp. 352. Price $3.95.)

Along with his other accomplishments, Mr. Justice Douglas doubtlessly has written one of the most significant books of our age. The work, *North From Malaya,* in part is an account of the author's study of the crucial and turbulent Asian fronts in the struggle between Communism and Democracy—Malaya, Indo-China, Burma, the Philippines, Formosa, and Korea. In the work is presented an analysis of the present internal problems with which these several Nation-States are faced—problems which have grown out of World War II and which have been accentuated by an aftermath of Japanese occupation, communistic guerrillas, alien Chinese "middle-men", overlordism, and foreign domination together with poverty, illiteracy and disease. Mr. Douglas interprets the challenge which confronts the United States in helping these Nations achieve national cohesiveness and freedom. Finally, the book presents a broad philosophical and political orientation within which the United States' foreign and economic policy with respect to all Asia may be couched for the extension of the democratic ideals and for the political self-realization of these Nations.

Quite vividly the author indicates that much of the opportunity for the free world particularly in the cases of Vietnam and Malaya has been lost. This situation has developed, the author asserts, primarily as a result of (1) an indecisiveness on the part of the United States in formulating a clear Asia policy at the critical moment towards the end of World War II; (2) as a consequence of what he terms a "temporizing with principle" by the United States in assigning priority to its European policy; and (3) by not standing firmly on the side of the exploited and oppressed Asians when they looked to us for moral guidance in their protests against British and French imperialistic practices which reduced these states to colonial status.

The author suggests that a counter-revolution must be undertaken in these areas at both the "grass-roots" and at the intellectual i.e. "idea" level. Such a counter-revolution must be accomplished by Asians with our assistance "in the Asian way" after a pattern which is proving effective and successful in Burma. The program must strike so vitally at the hearts and minds of men in the improvement of health, in vocational education, land reform, and in improved standards of living through their own efforts that the communists dare not compete or attempt to destroy the work lest suspicions against them be justified. Where the U. S. Point Four and MSA programs have been successful in this area of the world, it has been within an orientation of this kind— where men have been given tangible avenues of hope. Mr. Douglas feels that a Pacific-Asian organization should be created, not on militaristic terms, but on the basis of the interchange of experience, common problems and with a view towards the cementing of the Asiatic Cultural heritage. He asserts that every nation must be given the right to self-determination and that the United States must be strong enough to project its ideas as a way of life out into the crucible with other ideas which are being advanced. Feeling that Red China is first Asiatic and secondly communistic, Mr. Douglas assumes that India will become a greater world force in the unification of the Asiatic world and in the possible dissuasion of Red China from the communistic credo.

In citing the case of Korea towards the end of the work, Mr. Douglas writes "The fight of Korea is symbolic of the struggle going on all over Asia and Africa. It is the struggle for the independence of Nations, for the equality of people regardless of race or color, for the right of every people to their own culture, their own religion, their own way of life. That issue is the foremost political issue in the world today.'' He states further (p. 340) that ''the renaissance of our foreign policy in Asia will be our rededication to the spirit and to the letter of the Bill of Rights. . . . Freedom, Justice, and Equality will then become the fighting faith of millions whose dream of liberty is also the American dream.''

Apart from its dynamic message, the book is written also in an exceptionally beautiful and easily read style. It is replete with verbal descriptions which carry the reader with Mr. Douglas through the jungles, swamps, mountains, paddie fields and guerrilla country. It is an enthralling account of interviews, sometimes at the risk of his life, with persons from all strata of Asian society including the men and women who are presently charting the destinies of these Nations. Above all it is an affirmation of the faith of a great jurist and international statesman who sits in our highest tribunal at a critical time for our free institutions and those of all mankind.

JOSEPH H. DOUGLASS

State College
Fayetteville, North Carolina

The Outsider. By Richard Wright. (New York: Harper & Brothers, 1953. Pp. 405. Price $3.95.)

The Outsider is Richard Wright's first novel since *Native Son,* which was published in 1940. Like *Native Son* it reveals the tragic frustration experienced by one upon whom our society has imposed so many limitations that the development of normal personality-traits is impossible. Unlike Bigger Thomas of *Native Son,* however, whose abnormal traits are due primarily to the handicap of his being an American Negro, the hero of *The Outsider,* even though a Negro, might, with few exceptions, have been a member of almost any ethnic group in the United States. Another difference between the heroes of the two novels is that Cross Damon of *The Outsider* is an intellectual; nevertheless, his frustration is just as thoroughgoing and his life in the United States just as tragic as those of Bigger Thomas, who was denied the opportunity of getting more than an elementary-school education—and that of an inferior quality—and who was a product of one of the worst Negro slums that American city life affords.

The novel is a melodramatic narrative of the experiences of a Negro whose life consists of one tragic incident after another and culminates in his death at the hands of thugs—presumably representatives of the Communist party. His specialties are strong drink, women, and murder. Miraculously escaping from a subway-train accident in Chicago, in which many of the other passengers were killed, he assumes another name, goes into hiding, but remains in Chicago long enough to commit a murder and to see his supposed corpse being carried to church with his mother, wife, and three children following behind. He then flees to New York, carrying the greater portion of eight hundred dollars which his estranged wife had forced him to borrow for herself and the children. In New York he becomes involved with Communist gangsters, receives a permit to carry a gun as protection against a landlord who threatens to kill him because he is a Negro, obtains a birth certificate and a draft card under false pretenses, commits three murders, causes a woman to commit suicide by jumping to the street from the sixth floor of an apartment building, and is himself killed while attempting to leave the city.

Though many of these incidents are not well motivated, they do aid in giving a well-rounded picture of Cross himself and of his strange philosophy. Through District Attorney Houston, who was unable to obtain sufficient evidence to convict Cross for the several murders he had committed, we learn that Cross was well versed in the philosophy of Nietsche, Hegel, Heidegger, Kierkegaard, Dostoevsky, and others, but his friends said that he would not believe anything in the books he read. Pink said: "One time he was all hepped-up over one writer and the next time he was through with 'im and was gone on to another"; and Booker exclaimed: "I went to see 'im one day when he was sick, and I could hardly get in the door! Big books, little books, books piled everywhere! He even had books in bed with 'im. . . . 'Crossy, you better find a gal to sleep with you, 'cause them books can't keep you warm!' Man, in the clothes closet: books. In the bathroom: books. Under the bed: books. I said, 'Crossy, you ain't got no 'flu germs; you got book-worms!' " (P. 6.)

Considering Cross's early upbringing, his varied and extensive reading, and his consciousness of his status in the United States as an outsider (with all that this term connotes), one can understand something of the nature of his frustration. The conception of God that had been created for him as a youth had evoked in him "an aching sense of pleasure by admonishing him to shun pleasure as the tempting doorway opening blackly onto hell; had too early awakened in him a sharp sense of sex by thunderingly denouncing sex as the crime leading to eternal damnation; had posited in him a hunger for the sensual by branding all sensuality as the monstrous death from which there was no resurrection; had made him instinctively choose to love himself over and against all others because he felt himself menaced by a mysterious God whose love seemed somehow like hate." (P. 16.) Cross, like Bigger Thomas, becomes "cold-bloodedly brutal" when caught in situations involving his self-respect. Politically he is not in sympathy with any of the modern ideologies. He belongs to no political party. Fascist and Communist propaganda has no effect on him. The anti-Fascists and anti-Communists likewise, by using the methods of the totalitarians, are making inevitable the surge toward the total and absolute in modern life. "All hands are shoveling clay onto the body of freedom . . . while it lies breathing its last." (P. 337.) Industrial life and an unbridled capitalism have blasted the lives of men in our large cities. The industrialists and politicians who yell about freedom and democracy are the exploiters of the millions caught in the industrial trap. These capitalists not only despise the masses but despise themselves and all mankind. Men today live, dream, and plan on the assumption that there is no God. Since God no longer functions in men's minds and hearts and since the gallant liberals have all died, every event of the modern world feeds the growing movement toward the total and absolute. The future will reveal many "more of these absolutistic systems whose brutality and rigor will make the present-day systems seem like summer outings. . . . Wars will but tear away the last shreds of belief, leaving man's heart more naked and compulsive than ever before." (P. 337.) Our hero sees no real solution to this problem, but he suggests that we look bravely at this "horrible totalitarian reptile," study it coolly, and note down the pertinent facts which should help man to save himself and call the attention of others to the "presence and meaning of this reptile and its multitudinous writhings." (P. 336.) Finally, in commenting on the reason why he chose to live as he

did, Cross Damon says he felt that he was innocent; he merely
wanted to be free: "I wish I had some way to give the meaning
of my life to others. . . . To make a bridge from man to man. . . .
Starting from scratch every time is . . . no good. Men hate themselves and it makes them hate others. . . . We must find some
way of being good to ourselves. . . . We're strangers to ourselves."
(P. 404.)

There are passages and scenes in *The Outsider*, just as in
Native Son and other narratives written by Richard Wright,
which, in telling phrase, concentrated action, and dramatic
suspense, achieve heights seldom equaled in English prose, early
or modern.

LORENZO D. TURNER

Roosevelt College

BIBLIOGRAPHICAL SECTION

COMPILED BY HAROLD T. PINKETT

BOOKS ON THE UNITED STATES

Books dealing mainly or very considerably with Negro life and
history include the following: *The Collected Works of Abraham
Lincoln*, edited by Roy P. Basler (New Brunswick, N. J.: Rutgers
University Press, 1953); *The Growth of Southern Nationalism*,
by Avery O. Craven (Baton Rouge, La.: Louisiana State University Press, 1953); *Negro Segregation in the Methodist Church*,
by Dwight W. Culver (New Haven: Yale University Press, 1953);
The Negro Community within American Protestantism, by Leonard L. Haynes, Jr. (Boston: Christopher Publishing House,
1953); *The Negro Novelist*, by Carl M. Hughes (New York: Cita-
del Press, 1953); *The Cotton Kingdom: A Traveller's Observations on Cotton and Slavery in the American Slave States*, by
Frederick Law Olmsted, edited by Arthur M. Schlesinger (New
York: Alfred A. Knopf, 1953); *A History of the South*, by Francis B. Simkins (New York: Alfred A. Knopf, 1953); *Racial and
Cultural Minorities*, by G. E. Simpson and J. M. Yinger (New
York: Harper and Brothers, 1953); *Steps on My Stairway*, by

Cecil L. R. Spellman (New York: Exposition Press, 1953; and *Fifty-Four Years of African Methodism,* by V. M. Townsend (New York: Exposition Press, 1953).

ARTICLES ON THE UNITED STATES

The following articles relate directly to several aspects of Negro life and history: "Arkansas Slaveholdings and Slaveholders in 1850," by Robert Walz (*Arkansas Historical Quarterly,* Spring, 1953); "Radical Disfranchisement in Arkansas, 1867-1868," by Eugene G. Feistman (*Ibid.,* Summer, 1953); "Toward A Non-segregated South," by E. L. Brook (*Christian Century,* September 9, 1953); "New Jersey Leads in the Struggle for Educational Integration," by Marion Thompson Wright (*Journal of Educational Sociology,* May, 1953); "Kansas Negro Regiments in the Civil War," by Dudley T. Cornish (*Kansas Historical Quarterly,* May, 1953); "The Garner Fugitive Slave Case," by Julius Yanuck (*Mississippi Valley Historical Review,* June, 1953); "Employment and Income of Negro Workers," by Mary S. Bedell (*Monthly Labor Review,* June, 1953); "Eve of Decision," by B. Crick (*Nation,* October 31, 1953); "The Relative Status of the Negro Population in the United States," Yearbook Number (*Journal of Negro Education,* Summer, 1953); "Negro Education in the Alabama Black Belt, 1875-1900," by Glenn N. Sisk (*Ibid.,* Spring, 1953); "Legislation Designed to Control Slavery in Wilmington and Fayetteville," by James H. Brewer (*North Carolina Historical Review,* July, 1953); "Negro Education and the Equal Protection of the Laws," by E. H. Hobbs (*Journal of Politics,* August, 1953); "How Detroit Fights Race Hatred," by Walter White (*Saturday Evening Post,* July 18, 1953); "British Labor Against American Slavery," by Richard Greenleaf (*Science and Society,* Winter, 1953); "The Opposition of French Labor to American Slavery," by Samuel Bernstein (*Ibid.,* Spring, 1953); "Negro Job Status and Education," by Ralph H. Turner (*Social Forces,* October, 1953); "Social Stratification Among an Urban Southern Minority Population," by Charles E. King (*Ibid.,* May, 1953); "Radical Attitudes of Negro Servicemen," by Harry W. Roberts (*Social Problems,* October, 1953); "An Examination of Theories of Race Prejudice," by Isacque Graeber (*Social Research,* Autumn, 1953); "South's Opportunity," by J. M. Dobbs (*South Atlantic Quar-*

terly, April, 1953); and "The American Negro," Special Issue (*United Asia,* Number Three, 1953).

BOOKS ON LATIN AMERICA AND THE WEST INDIES

Miscellaneous books pertaining to Negroes include the following: *Cuadros brasileños,* by Marta Casablanca (Rosario: Ediciones Arbolux, 1952); *Divine Horsemen,* by Maya Deren (London and New York: Thames and Hudson, 1953); *Historia de la esclavitud negra en Puerto Rico, 1493-1890,* by Luis M. Diaz Soler (Ediciones de la Universidad de Puerto Rico, Madrid: Revista de Occidente, 1953); *Les marrons du syllabaire: quelques aspects du problème de l'instruction et de l'éducation des esclaves et affranchis de Saint-Dominque,* by Jean Fouchard (Port-au-Prince, Haiti: Editions Henri Deschamps, 1953); *Foreign Relations of the United States: Diplomatic Papers, 1935, The American Republics* (Department of State, Washington: Government Printing Office, 1953); and *Our Virgin Island,* by Robb White (Garden City, N. Y.: Doubleday, 1953).

ARTICLES ON LATIN AMERICA AND THE WEST INDIES

Articles pertaining directly to Negroes include the following: "Haiti," Special Issue (*Americas,* November, 1953); "Patterns and Problems of Land Tenure in the Lessser Antilles: Antigua, B. W. I.," by John P. Augelli (*Economic Geography,* October, 1953); "The Struggle for Abolition in Gran Colombia," by Harold C. Bierck (*Hispanic American Historical Review,* August, 1953); "The Contributions of Toussaint l'Ouverture to the Independence of the American Republics," by Mary A. Healy (*Americas,* April, 1953); "Semi-responsible Government in the British West Indies," by Colin A. Hughes (*Political Science Quarterly,* September, 1953); "Ethnic Identification in an Indian Mestizo Community," by Bernice A. Kaplan and Gabriel W. Lasker (*Phylon,* Second Quarter, 1953); "The Culture History of a Puerto-Rican Sugar Cane Plantation, 1876-1949," by Sidney W. Mintz (*Hispanic American Historical Review,* May, 1953); "The Colored Castes and American Representation in the Cortes of Cadiz," by James F. King (*Ibid.,* February, 1953); "The Passing of the Coffee Plantation in the Paraíba Valley," by Stanley J. Stein (*Ibid.,* August, 1953); "The Alabama Negro Colony in

Mexico, 1894-1896'' (conclusion), by Alfred W. Reynolds (*Alabama Review,* January, 1953); and ''Political and Constitutional Development in Jamaica,'' by Alex Zeindenfelt (*Journal of Politics,* August, 1953).

BOOKS ON AFRICA

Books containing substantial information concerning Negroes and the race problem include the following: *Color and Culture in South Africa,* by Sheila Patterson (London: Routledge and Kegan Paul, 1953); *This Is Liberia,* by Stanley A. Davis (New York: Wilham-Frederick Press, 1953); *Who Killed Kenya,* by Colin Wills (New York: Roy Publishers, 1953); *Facing Mount Kenya: The Tribal Life of the Gikiyu,* by Jomo Kenyatta (New York: British Book Centre, 1953); *The Gold Coast Revolution: The Struggle of an African People from Slavery to Freedom,* by George Padmore (*Ibid.*); and *Foreign Relations of the United States: Diplomatic Papers, 1935, The Near East and Africa* (Department of State, Washington: Government Printing Office, 1953).

ARTICLES ON AFRICA

The following articles deal directly with Negro life and history: ''Community Development in Uganda,'' by the Secretariat, Uganda (*Journal of African Administration,* April, 1953); ''Politics in the Union of South Africa,'' by Austin F. Macdonald (*Annals,* July, 1953); ''La Fédération de Rhodésie et du Nyasaland'' (*Chronique de Politique Etrangère,* January, 1953); ''Kenya, the Land and the Mau Mau,'' by Derwent Whittlesey (*Foreign Affairs,* October, 1953;) ''Mathew and the Mau Mau,'' by Sandy Sanderson (*Harper's,* August, 1953); ''African Sculpture and Writing,'' by Ladislas Segy (*Journal of Human Relations,* Winter, 1953); ''Crisis in Africa,'' Special Issue (*Journal of International Affairs,* No. 2, 1953); ''The Work of the Christian Church Among the Kikuyu,'' by Canon T. F. C. Bewes (*Ibid.,* July, 1953); ''Industrial Relations in South Africa,'' by J. D. Rheinallt Jones (*Ibid.,* January, 1953); ''The Development of Educational Facilities in the Non-Self-Governing Territories,'' by Robert I. Crane (*Journal of Negro Education,* Spring, 1953); ''An Anthropological Approach to the Mau Mau Problem,'' by Annette Rosenstiel (*Political Science Quarterly,* September, 1953);

"International Information Services in Central Africa," by Leonard W. Doob (*Public Opinion Quarterly*, Spring, 1953); "The Techniques of Ewe Drumming and the Social Importance of Music in Africa," by S. D. Cudjoe (*Phylon*, Third Quarter, 1953); "A Visit to the Africa of Dr. Albert Schweitzer," by Clara Urquhart (*Ibid.*); "British East Africa: Some Economic Aspects," by Merrill K. Bennett (*Rice Institute Pamphlet*, October, 1952); "British East Africa: Some Psychological Aspects," by Robert B. MacLeod (*Ibid.*); "Concepts of Time Among the Tiv of Nigeria," by Paul Bohannon (*Southwestern Journal of Anthropology*, Autumn, 1953); "Africa: Next Goal of Communists," Special Issue (*U. S. News and World Report*, May 1, 1953); "The South African Crisis," by C. W. M. Gell (*Virginia Quarterly Review*, Winter, 1953); "South Africa: A Land Divided Against Itself," by Z. K. Matthews (*Yale Review*, Summer, 1953); and "Notes on the Villages of the Western and Central Provinces of Liberia, West Africa," by G. G. Lill (*Journal of Geography*, May, 1953).

GUIDES AND INVENTORIES

Guides and inventories for archival and manuscript collections containing considerable quantities of material relating to Negro life and history include the following: *Guide to the Manuscript Collections in the William L. Clements Library*, compiled by William S. Ewing (Ann Arbor: Clements Library, 1953); *The Archives of the United States Diplomatic and Consular Posts in Latin America*, by John P. Harrison (National Archives, Washington, D. C., 1953); *Records of the Office of Inter-American Affairs*, compiled by H. Stephen Helton (*Ibid.*, 1952); *Records of the Office of Labor of the War Food Administration*, compiled by Harold T. Pinkett (*Ibid.*, 1953); *Records of the Office of War Information*, compiled by H. Stephen Helton (*Ibid.*); and *Records of the Federal Writers' Project, Work Projects Administration*, compiled by Katherine H. Davidson (*Ibid.*).

HISTORICAL NEWS

John Hope Franklin served as Visiting Lecturer in the Department of History at the University of Toronto December 7-8, 1953. He lectured to the advanced graduate students on research in Southern history and directed attention to Southern travelers in the North during the nineteenth century.

Representative educators and college administrators conducted a symposium November 1, 1953, at Tuskegee Institute in connection with the inauguration of Luther H. Foster as the fourth president.

The National Planning Association released a report in the late fall of 1953 on the employment of Negroes in Kentucky, Virginia, and the Carolinas. Donald Dewey of Duke University prepared the findings which show: 1) exclusion of Negroes from white collar jobs, 2) no Negroes holding supervisory positions, 3) Negroes and whites do not have the same types of work, and 4) racial segregation in employment remains unchanged.

Final arguments on the school segregation cases before the United States Supreme Court were completed December 7, 8, and 9, 1953. Thurgood Marshall, Spottswood Robinson, III, and James Nabrit represented the plaintiffs in these cases which are comparable in several respects to the famous *Dred-Scott* case in 1857.

The Bureau of Records at Tuskegee Institute announced that there was no lynching in 1953. This is progress for which the enlightened leadership of the South merits the highest praise. It must be remembered, however, that lynching of the helpless victims of erstwhile mobs was not the only form of the barbarous practice. Wherever discrimination and disregard for the dignity and sacredness of Negro humanity and personality continue lynching of the mind and spirit still goes on!

The Blue Herron Press, New York has reprinted the *Souls of Black Folk,* by W. E. B. DuBois, after fifty years! This matchless literary and spiritual work will be reviewed in the April, 1954 *Journal of Negro History.*

Negro Slave Songs by Miles Mark Fisher received a prize award from the American Historical Association and was released December 15, 1953 by the Cornell University Press. The author uses the *Negro Spirituals* as unchallengeable evidence in refuting those scholars who have sought during the last half-century to discredit the retention by Negroes in America of any of their African inheritance! This rare and revealing contribution will also be reviewed in the next issue of the *Journal.*

The Columbia University Press published December 15, 1953

Race, Jobs, and Politics, The Story of F.E.P.C., by Louis Ruchames.

Forrester B. Washington has retired from his directorship of the Atlanta University School of Social Work after serving twenty-six years. During this period he became an authority on social work among Negroes and helped to train many workers in this field. His good works will continue in the advisory councils of the Urban League with which he has been associated through the years.

John A. Davis received in September 1953 an associate professorship of government at the College of the City of New York. Previously he served as head of the Department of Political Science at Lincoln University (Pa.); worked on the staff of F.E.P.C.; recently directed preparation of the non-legal historical information requested in 1953 by the United States Supreme Court; and helped as sometime consultant in the State Department at Washington, D. C.

President Horace M. Bond of Lincoln University (Pa.) went to Africa by way of London in early December 1953 for a tour of several points where the institution's distinguished alumni are leaders. Among them are Kwame Nkrumah, Prime Minister of the Gold Coast, and Nnamdi Azikiwe, nationalist leader in Nigeria. Lincoln is celebrating its centenary, 1854-1954, under the title: "Free Persons in a Free World Through Education and Brotherhood."

Fisk University has awarded contracts for two new buildings that will cost $656,000 and be completed by September 1, 1954. Scribner Hall for women will perpetuate the memory and service of Dora Anna Scribner, beloved professor of English, who taught over a generation of Fisk men and women. R. E. Park Hall will house the Social Sciences and honor the sociologist that served Booker T. Washington, taught at Chicago, and closed his career at Fisk.

Johnson C. Smith opened in September 1953 its new power plant which has a special spur-track to the railroad for delivering fuel. The eighty-six year old institution is engaged in a development program and experiencing its greatest period of progress under the able leadership of President Hardy Liston.

W. M. BREWER

THE JOURNAL

OF

NEGRO HISTORY

VOL. XXXIX—April, 1954—No. 2

THE PROSTRATE STATE REVISITED: JAMES S. PIKE AND SOUTH CAROLINA RECONSTRUCTION

Most of his contemporaries, as well as some later historians, have regarded James Shepherd Pike as merely a Northern Republican newspaperman who fortunately happened to visit South Carolina in 1873. The dramatic condemnation of the Negro-Republican government in South Carolina which he published in *The Prostrate State* looked especially impressive in view of Pike's record as an outstanding Republican journalist before and after the Civil War and as Lincoln's minister to the Netherlands during the war. Despite these apparent qualifications, the Maine Republican was far from dispassionate or disinterested in his influential report on Reconstruction.[1]

[1] The author is particularly grateful to Professor Jeter A. Isely of Princeton University for encouragement and criticism in connection with this paper, which was presented to the Trinity College Historical Society, Duke University, on February 5, 1953.

One disqualifying factor arose from the fact that Pike, like some others, had long combined intense hatred for the institution of slavery with pronounced racial antipathy toward the Negro. His scathing journalistic attacks on slaveholders and Democrats had earned him a job as special Washington correspondent for Horace Greeley's New York *Tribune* in 1850, and he soon became an associate editor of that powerful newspaper. Pike's disgust with the Kansas-Nebraska Act impelled him not only to become a Republican but also to espouse the Northern secessionism which was popular among abolitionists like William Lloyd Garrison. Throughout the decade preceding civil conflict he remained in the vanguard of the rising Republican ranks.[2]

Yet from the first his antislavery Republicanism had a strange streak of indifference, even hostility, toward the Negroes as human beings. In 1853, for example, Pike discussed one of the numerous schemes for annexing Latin American territory and referred to the "black, mixed, degraded, and ignorant, or inferior races" which filled Cuba. The "robust and enterprising" North Americans wanted no more "ebony additions to the Republic," he declared, for it would be best for the United States if the "burden and hindrance" of its already fecund black population could be exported to the West Indies.[3] An even more clear-cut revelation of his racial ideas appeared during the campaign of 1860 when Pike asserted in the *Tribune* that "the ignorant and servile race will not and cannot be emancipated and raised to the enjoyment of equal civil rights with the dominant and intelligent race; they will be driven out." Such action might be "cruel and un-

[2] A large number of Pike's *Tribune* articles are published in his *First Blows of the Civil War* (New, York, 1879), but I have used his scrapbooks of original clippings in the Pike MSS, Calais Free Library, Calais, Maine, along with a file of the *Tribune* itself.

[3] *Tribune*, January 10, 1853; *First Blows*, 162-64.

christian'' but, at the same time, it was ''natural'' and the
only available solution in the American dilemma.   Just
so much of North America as possible had to be preserved
for the ''white man'' and for free institutions.[4]

These beliefs were not fundamentally altered during the
war years, when Pike served as President Lincoln's envoy
to The Hague.   While never enthusiastic about the post-war
Republican program for enfranchising the Southern freedmen, he accepted the development as a political necessity if
the Republicans would maintain their politico-economic
program.   Pike returned to America in 1866, renewed his
close contact with Radical Republican leaders like Chief
Justice Salmon P. Chase and Maine Senator William Pitt
Fessenden, and again propagandized for the Republicans in
the *Tribune* as well as in Charles A. Dana's New York *Sun*.
By 1872, however, his loyalty to the Republican administration of General Grant began to be strained.   Greeley and
Dana, among others, directed a swelling chorus of opposition to 'Grantism.'   Reluctantly the Downeaster moved
towards those who soon bolted and met crushing defeat as
the Liberal Republican opposition to the regular Republicans.

The unsettled state of Southern affairs furnished one
convenient club for attacking 'Grantism.'   Pike struck his
blow in March 1872.   He entitled his *Tribune* article concerning South Carolina ''A State in Ruins.''   And strangely
enough, practically every major point he made in his later
book is mentioned in this article, which was written one
year before he even visited the South.   He contrasted

---

[4] *Tribune*, March 12, 1860. The proslavery Southern extremist, George
Fitzhugh, characteristically overstated when he said: ''Hatred to slavery is
very generally little more than hatred of Negroes.'' Cited in U. B. Phillips,
The Course of the South to Secession (New York, 1939), 123. Cf. Albert J.
Beveridge, *Abraham Lincoln, 1809-1858* (New York, 1928), II, 202-05; and
J. G. Randall, *Lincoln, The President: Springfield to Gettysburg* (New York,
1945), II, 181-89.

South Carolina's days of power, when the "dogmatic" but "high-toned" "aristocracy" ruled, with her later days of tribulation. The majority of the Negro legislators he depicted as a "great mass of ignorance and barbarism" who were led by carpetbaggers and "a few intelligent colored people." But these very leaders, he charged, were the miscreants and thieves who fattened on flagrant corruption. The former antislavery spokesman wailed that "300,000 white people, more or less, composing the intelligence and property-holders of the State, are put under the heel of 400,000 pauper blacks, fresh from a state of slavery and ignorance the most dense." His *Tribune* article concluded that the "wild crimes of Ku-Klux youth" might be productive of some good; certainly no Northern state would long bear the "condition of things now existing in South Carolina" without organizing a taxpayers' league and a "court of lynch law."[5]

Since Pike had not yet gone South, the sources of his information in this 1872 article are especially interesting. The newspaper man had several conversations in February, 1872 with important persons who had direct interests in South Carolina. One talk was with William Sprague, millionaire senator from Rhode Island and husband of the chief justice's daughter, Kate Chase. Sprague had invested heavily in South Carolina ventures; through his agent there he gained an impression of the political corruption among the Radicals. Sprague testified to Pike that for $75,000 he could have had his agent named senator from South Carolina but that the transaction was just too disgraceful. Consequently Sprague distrusted the whole batch of carpetbagger senators and furnished Pike with

[5] *Tribune*, March 5, 1872; datelined Washington, February 22, 1872. Clippings in the Pike MSS reveal some approval this article earned in South Carolina.

one opinion which influenced the *Tribune* article.[6]

General Wade Hampton, whom Pike encountered at an agricultural convention in Washington, also furnished information about Carolina conditions. Hampton, who later became outstanding among the "Redeemers" of 1876-77, informed Pike about "oppressive taxation" levied by the Negro-carpetbagger legislature and the thefts perpetrated by unscrupulous "adventurers" who duped the colored voters. The Confederate general described the laborer's disinclination to work for wages and the consequent loss through "idleness and mismanagement" when the freedman share-cropped. Hampton seems to have given the *Tribune* correspondent a valuable insight into the distant situation; needless to say, the insight reflected a conservative, white point of view.[7]

Thus Pike and some of his anti-administration friends looked South in the spring of 1872. The failure of General Grant's Southern program had to be emphasized, for with no economic issues at stake how else could the 'disgraceful' set of office-holders be driven out? But when it came to bolting the party, Pike thought long and mightily before he could brace himself to join Greeley, Dana, Senators Carl Schurz and Charles Sumner, and other prominent Republicans who were ready to organize independently. Finally,

[6] Pike's notebook, No. 28; entry for February 15, 1872. The notebooks or occasional journal which Pike kept from 1861 until his death in 1882 are a valuable part of the Pike MSS, Calais. In connection with Sprague, Charles A. Dana informed Pike during the 1860 presidential campaign that, "Sprague is spending $100,000 mainly in buying voters. The current price is $25. The Spragues regard the election in a mode of advertising their business, and charge the bribery to expense." Dana to Pike, March 26, 1860, Pike MSS.

[7] Notebook No. 28; entry for February 16-23 [?] 1872. Pike also talked with a "Mr. Aiken of S. C. (near Abbeville)" about the reluctance of the freedmen to take their former masters' advice about voting. This was probably D. Wyatt Aiken, prominent agricultural leader and editor. For both Hampton and Aiken, see Francis B. Simkins and Robert H. Woody, *South Carolina During Reconstruction* (Chapel Hill, 1932), *passim*.

after some embarrassing public misgivings about bolting and after Horace Greeley himself had secured the Liberal Republican and Democratic presidential nomination, Pike abandoned the regular Republican party.[8]

Despite, or perhaps because of, his great reluctance in joining the bolt, Pike campaigned feverishly for the Liberal Republican slate. The political situation in his Maine home district lent itself to a party split, and Frederick A. Pike, former Republican congressman and the newspaperman's brother, captured the Liberal Republican nomination for Congress. The Pike brothers, both veteran politicians and ex-officeholders, launched a bitter fight against Republican incumbents.

Just as on the national level, the Liberal Republicans in Maine were badly beaten. The Pikes met defeat with ill grace, however, and James Pike charged in the *Tribune* that his "respectable" hometown of Calais had succumbed to the allurements of vote-buyers and corrupt officeholders. In short, the journalist-politician's excessive charges and rancour only earned him the illwill of his homefolk. After the campaign of 1872 Pike remained politically adrift for the remainder of his life.[9]

A political pariah in Maine, Pike now forgot that he himself had long defended President Grant; the contemporary corruption and government scandals which he had originally ascribed to the "ancient depravity" of men he now increasingly blamed on "Grantism." Earlier doubts and reservations about the attack on Grant's administration changed into fixed hostility. It was in this mood that Pike embarked in January 1873 on his visit to the South and wrote his articles and book on South Carolina's re-

[8] For Pike's misgivings and pro-Grant declaration see *Tribune*, February 27, 28, 1872. Other New York papers, like the pro-Grant *Times*, gleefully noted the confusion within the anti-Grant ranks. Undated clippings, Pike MSS.

[9] Clippings in the Pike MSS; Pike's pamphlet, "Horace Greeley in 1872: His Political Position and Motives in the late Presidential Contest" (New York, 1873); *Calais Advertiser*, October 2, 1872, January 7, 1873.

construction government.[10] Fortunately the journal Pike kept while in the South contains, not only the germ of his published material, but also many long passages which were transferred, after modifications, into print.

The *Tribune* gave enthusiastic editorial support to Pike's articles.[11] Other newspapers across the country also publicized the series, although many of them attacked the *Tribune's* "impartial observer." Frederick Douglass' *National New Era,* for example, assailed the author's tone as "calculated to fire the negro-hating heart to deeds of violence against the black race." "What good THE NEW-YORK TRIBUNE expects to work by its thrusts at the struggling colored people we cannot imagine," the leading Negro spokesman declared. The *Pittsburgh Dispatch* suggested that the *Tribune* "had not yet forgotten the unanimity with which the colored voters supported President Grant through last Autumn's campaign."

From other papers North and South came approval. The *Savannah Republican* emphasized Pike's background in these words: "Years ago, when abolition was a forlorn hope and its open advocates under the ban, Mr. Pike was one of their leaders—he shared in their struggles, he enjoyed their triumphs, and has had no cause, either of interest or ambition, to feel sympathetic toward the Southern people. . . . But he is a man of convictions, and an outspoken one, and the unutterable horror and loathing, surprise and indignation, with which the actual condition of

---

[10] The first article in Pike's series of seven on "South Carolina Prostrate" appeared on the front page of the *Tribune* of March 29, 1873; the last two articles appeared in the issue of April 19. The four other *Tribunes* containing the series appeared on April 8, 10, 11, and 12, 1873. Although the series is datelined from Columbia during late February and early March, the articles were probably written after Pike had returned to the North in late March. The first four pieces correspond exactly to the first four chapters in *The Prostrate State,* the fifth article to the twelfth chapter, the sixth to the thirteenth, and the seventh and last article to the fourteenth chapter.

[11] *Tribune,* March 29, 1873.

misgovernment and oppression at the South have inspired him, cannot be silenced. So he has spoken out and told truths which, from his lips and pen, will be listened to by the Northern people—ignorant accomplices in these crimes. . . .'' Meantime in the North, papers like the *Sun* and *Herald* saw the Pike series as confirmation of their own worst fears and as support for the attacks on Grant.[12]

Perhaps the stir created by his articles impelled Pike to expand his material, pad it a bit here and there, and give it more permanent form in a book. To get his work published, however, he had to underwrite a large part of the costs, which he easily did through loans from New York friends.[13] Since the preface is dated October, 1873, he probably submitted his manuscript about that time. The New York firm of D. Appleton and Company published *The Prostrate State* early in December, 1873, at a price of one dollar. Copies were also on sale at the *Tribune* office, and advertisements proclaimed ''THE BOOK FOR THE DAY'' as a work of ''keen observation, thorough research, and calm judgment.''[14] The total number of sales is not known, but the book received wide publicity and probably sold well. Moreover, a new edition of the book was issued in 1935. Professor Henry Steele Commager wrote the introduction for this edition, in which the text is reprinted from the 1873 version. Commager praises the ''transparent honesty'' and ''thorough documentation'' of Pike's study of South Carolina reconstruction.[15]

[12] These comments along with others reprinted in *Tribune*, April 19, 1873. Also clippings in Pike MSS.

[13] Information in the Whitelaw Reid MSS, courtesy of Professor Jeter Isely.

[14] *Tribune*, December 6, 1873.

[15] Published by Loring and Mussey (New York 1935). A Dutch translation, *Zuid-Carolina Onder Negerbestuur*, was published in Holland in 1875, doubtless because of the author's diplomatic mission at The Hague during the war. According to a letter from Appleton's (October 25, 1951), a fire in 1904 destroyed many of their records, including those concerning *Prostrate State*.

Reviewers in the magazines generally applauded Pike's book. A lengthy notice in *The Literary World* endorsed Pike as one "who, in view of his long and enthusiastic service in the anti-slavery cause, can hardly be accused of color-prejudice."[16] E. L. Godkin's influential *Nation* found "a great deal of valuable information as to the present condition of South Carolina" in the book. A *Nation* editorial, emblazoned "Socialism in South Carolina," borrowed heavily from Pike in showing that the average of intelligence among the vast majority of Negroes was low—"so low that they are slightly above the levels of animals." Godkin, another virtuous critic of the Grant administration, concluded with a query as to how long it would take to transform the "once 'sovereign State' of South Carolina into a truly loyal, truly Republican, truly African San Domingo."[17]

Reports of the bloody rioting at Hamburg, South Carolina, in July 1876 appalled many people all over the country. When discussion of the riot reached the House of Representatives an incident occurred which suggests another aspect of *The Prostrate State's* early repercussions. A Democratic congressman from New York state assailed the "miserably bad government" which Pike had delineated in his book. Using the Maine Republican as his authority, the congressman declared that the book showed how "after the carpet-bag governments had taken nearly all, there was a worse crew of robbers called native Afri-

[16] *The Literary World*, IV (January 1874), 116.

[17] *The Nation*, XVIII (April 16, April 30, 1874), 282, 247-48. This editorial brought a stirring protest from "T. W. H." of Rhode Island, presumably Thomas Wentworth Higginson, an abolitionist and befriender of John Brown. The protest led Godkin to admit that his "assertion was too sweeping" and should have referred only to the coastal or Gullah Negroes. But he again insisted on the point that as a legislator the Negro was "merely a horrible failure." *Ibid.* (April 30, 1874), 282. A reviewer in the *Atlantic Monthly* (February 1874), endorsed *Prostrate State*, as did newspapers like the New York *Express* (January 10, 1874), *St. Louis Republican* (January 20, 1874), New York *Herald* (January 11, 1874); other clippings in Pike MSS.

cans of South Carolina.'' These ''provocations'' the congressman offered not as justification for the killing of Negroes in Carolina but merely as extenuating circumstance. The retort of the Negro congressman from South Carolina, Robert Smalls, to this attack was, ''Have you the book there of the city of New York?''[18]

Aside from its contemporary impact, *The Prostrate State* has been much used by historians of the reconstruction period. A detailed study of the book's place in historiography is hardly necessary, but one or two examples will illuminate this aspect. Claude Bowers extravagantly designates Pike's work ''the 'Uncle Tom's Cabin' of the redemption of the South,'' and he explains: ''Soon thoughtful men throughout the North were reading the truth [about reconstruction] which had been denied them. Democrats had declared it—but here was Republican authority.''[19] James Ford Rhodes, long the dean of American historians and author of what was once the 'standard' study of post-1850 American history, cites *The Prostrate State* no less than seventeen times in one chapter, devotes three full pages to quotes from the book, and describes Pike in the usual reassuring words as a ''strong anti-slavery man before the war and a consistent Republican during it.''[20] Many South Carolina historians have seized upon Pike as chief witness, one stressing the fact that the ''most interesting chronicle of the carpetbag-negro mis-rule'' was

18 *Congressional Record*, 44th Congress, 1st Session, 4707.
19 *The Tragic Era: The Revolution after Lincoln* (Cambridge, Mass., 1929), 417-18.
20 James Ford Rhodes, *History of the United States from the Compromise of 1850 to the Final Restoration of Home Rule at the South in 1877.* (New York, 1906), vol. VII, 149, 152-55. The seventeen citations are in chapter XLII. William A. Dunning, another early authority on the subject, describes *Prostrate State* as one of the ''highly valuable sources of the period'' by travellers. *Reconstruction, Political and Economic, 1865-1877* (New York, 1907), 352. E. Merton Coulter, *The South During Reconstruction, 1865-1877* (Baton Rouge, 1947), 399, describes Pike's book as the ''classic work on the outrages'' of Radical government in South Carolina.

written by a "dyed-in-the-wool Republican abolitionist."[21] From this it is clear how much influence Pike's supposed party orthodoxy and general background have had with most historians, as well as with his own generation.

This, then, is the position occupied by *The Prostrate State*. Fortunately Pike's journal affords the opportunity of a much closer and more instructive look at his visit in the South than does his printed account. By following his movements to some extent, examining the sources of his information, and comparing his own notes and first impressions with what he later published, a new and sharper light is thrown on the book and its author.

Early in the wet, gray morning of January 21, 1873, Pike's train crossed the Potomac. The rolling Virginia countryside he admired, but uncultivated patches of ground and the "old decayed looking town of Fredericksburg" were not so pleasing. Richmond, where he spent several days, offered him his first close look at postwar Southern conditions. The "soft & charming" weather with "no vestiges of ice or snow" probably mellowed the Downeaster; he benignly noted broad shady streets, handsome residences, and "the apparent thrift." He sentimentally sympathized with the "throngs of blacks out after dark" and enjoyed the "jolly countenances of the Negro wenches in the Streets." Even the Richmond newspaper discussions of financial issues struck a happy chord, for Pike detected "a healthy temper in this almost bankrupt State" indicated by the conservative newspapers' exhortations that the people should "carry their burdens like men" and reject the evil temptation to repudiate the vast state debt.[22]

[21] Henry T. Thompson, *Ousting the Carpetbagger from South Carolina* (Columbia, 1927), 33. William W. Ball in his *State that Forgot: South Carolina's Surrender to Democracy* (Indianapolis, 1932), 138, tells a revealing story of the reaction of one adopted Carolinian to *The Prostrate State*.

[22] Notebook No. 28, 33-34; for a discussion of the Virginia financial issues see Charles C. Pearson, *The Readjuster Movement in Virginia* (New Haven 1917); or Nelson M. Blake, *William Mahone of Virginia* (Richmond 1935), 135-55.

During his visit in the lower house of the Virginia Legislature, Pike heard a ''colored member ¾ths black'' make a lengthy, aggressive, and capable speech against a tax proposal then being considered. The Negro was ''listened to with a good deal of interest after it was found he could not be drowned out by rustlings & loud talk,'' although the ''venerable Old Virginia gentlemen on the democratic benches looked on with a mixture of surprize & chagrin at the spectacle of such a successor'' to Jefferson and Madison. The ''self contained, half saucy half intelligent expression'' of a colored senator prompted the observation that the ''race has learned that it is not by modesty that their claims are to be advanced.''[23]

After interviews with several white, Conservative leaders, he left Richmond by train on January 23.[24] Passing into the gently undulating, scrub-pine country around the Virginia border, Pike spent an uncomfortably cool night in the little town of Weldon, North Carolina. The journalist kept the passing scene under close observation. He noted the ''rawboned & stiff'' cows, the ox-pulled cart ''of the purest rural origin,'' and the ''almost inviting'' cabins perched on sand knolls in the midst of pine-fringed corn fields. Such things as the wages paid to the freedmen interested him, and in Weldon he learned that the male, ex-slave cook received fifteen dollars a month while the chambermaids earned only five. En route to Wilmington, he enviously spotted the timber which flourished in the inaccessible swamps, although on higher ground he thought he ''found the Yankee by his tracks.'' Carloads of lumber, a new steam sawmill, and newly built shacks could only denote, he scribbled, the presence of imported, Northern enterprise.[25]

Pike found Wilmington wearing a shabby, ''hopeless

23 Notebook No. 28, 35.
24 Notebook No. 28, 36-40.
25 Notebook No. 29, 1-3.

aspect," with sandy paths for streets and "a perfect
welter of negroes whose nests shockingly disfigure the
outskirts." The giant live oaks which kept their brilliant
foliage in winter could not compensate for the "garbage of
the streets, the wandering swine of the exact wild boar
pattern," or the underfed animals which roamed the roads.
Amid such gloom, the visitor discerned a few hopeful signs:
property had increased in value, finances flourished, and
Wilmington business had doubled since the war. Even
more encouraging to him was the fact that the railroads
had fallen "into the thrifty hands of Northerners & it is
for their interest to exploit the State which they are as-
siduously doing."[26]

Pike believed that even the Negro population in and
around Wilmington had participated in "the general improvement." Some of them, he heard, had bought small
pieces of land on the outskirts of the city, and they soon
found land values upped by high cotton prices. The journalist heard often of "the thrifty & capable darkey," which
led him to predict a "future for the race quite different
from that bred from the old pro slavery idea of universal
inferiority." Politically too, in this early stage of his
journey, Pike approved of what he found; he judged that
the Negro-controlled municipal government was conducted
"with sense & prudence." The much criticized leagues or
clubs which banded the Negroes into an "inexorable parti-
zan association" he credited to the example set by the
whites. If the freedmen failed to vote for party nominees,
"their old enemy" would triumph. The Downeaster concluded that the "darkey . . . is not so much of a fool as he
is of a philosopher in his politics." Such charitable and
even favorable views of the Negro in politics were not repeated in *The Prostrate State*. Pike's description of the
situation in Columbia, and in South Carolina as a whole,

[26] *Ibid.*, 6-9.

presented a vastly different picture.[27]

With his long years of experience as a Washington political correspondent and his numerous visits to sessions of Parliament during his trips to London, he naturally chose the legislative halls as a focus of interest. While he was in Columbia it should be noted that, perhaps unconsciously, he kept the British standard of parliamentary procedure in the back of his mind. If British M. P.'s and peers had made him scornful of Washington senators, how might he regard the members, white or black, of a provincial legislature? Aside from his techniques of observation and independent study, Pike's journal furnishes us with some idea of the sources of his information and impressions. These are impressive neither in their number nor in their character.

Perhaps the best example of this may be found in the use which Pike made of a casual conversation with a "round-headed, young black man" who chanced on one occasion to be standing beside him on the floor of the South Carolina lower-house. In reply to a question from Pike about the white man then speaking, the Negro answered with a reference to the white speaker's scanty brainpower. "My pride of race was incontinently shocked," Pike explains; but he proceeded to converse with his "thick-lipped, wooly-headed" neighbor, pumping him about various members of the legislature. This conversation, with a man apparently unknown and recorded in the journal practically as it appears in the book, forms the larger part of a chapter of *The Prostrate State* which is headed "Sambo as a Critic on [sic] the White Man."[28]   Apparently this is the

[27] Notebook No. 29, 9-10. He arrived in South Carolina during the last week of January 1873 and apparently remained in Columbia, the capital, until February 20, when he began a tour to Charleston, Savannah, and Augusta. Returning briefly to Columbia on March 20, he departed for Washington either the same or the next day. He spent altogether about two months in the South. *Ibid.*, 13; Notebook No. 31, 11-20.

[28] Chapter V, 39-43; Notebook No. 29, 18-21.

only occasion on which Pike gained information from a Negro Carolinian; at least, it is the only one recorded in the journal. But there were a few whites, natives and carpetbaggers, whom he met and talked with.

There are eight instances mentioned in the journal when Pike gained information or opinions from native white Carolinians. A "low-country planter," who also happened to be standing nearby, commented on the shock of seeing the freedmen as legislators. This incident found its way into Pike's book.[29] One of the few Conservative state senators, David R. Duncan from Spartanburg, informed Pike that the Negro legislators learned the methods of legislation and the rules and orders "like a flash." Yet Pike did not use this estimate from a "Bourbon of pure blood" in his book.[30] Another Conservative legislator from Spartanburg, Gabriel Cannon, furnished him with a couple of items,[31] and a white doorkeeper gave him statistics on the composition of the legislature and the origins of some of the Negro members.[32] The four other native white sources, including a "rigid old secessionist," were even more unimportant and need not be listed. The scarcity as well as the conservative nature of his contacts with white Carolinians should be clear.[33]

From carpetbaggers too the journalist learned some things. He omitted from the articles and the book any mention of the female school teacher from Vermont who claimed extensive influence as a lobbyist in Columbia. But then he might well have ruffled many Northern feathers with his journal references to "blatherskyting parasites" and "Northern Amazons & leeches."[34] A fellow Down-

[29] *Prostrate State*, 11; Notebook No. 29, 14.
[30] Notebook No. 30, 17.
[31] Notebook No. 30, 53, 62; for one of these in *Prostrate State*, see the story on page 86 of the Republican congressman, elected by Negro votes, whose pre-war stand on slavery is attacked.
[32] Notebook No. 29, 28; *Prostrate State*, 14-15.
[33] Notebook No. 30, 15-18, 22, 27, 32, 118.
[34] Notebook No. 29, 18.

easter who was employed in the state auditor's office predicted the "Africanization" of the state to Pike;[35] and
Colonel S. A. Pearce, the agent of Rhode Island's millionaire Senator Sprague, who had railway and other business
interests in South Carolina, told the newspaper man the
Sherman version of the burning of Columbia.[36] Two
foreigners, a German ironfounder and an English gardener,
complete the list of individuals whom Pike mentions in his
notebooks.[37]

The inference cannot be drawn that the journalist, who
was generally inquisitive and talkative, spoke with only
those persons mentioned here, for he undoubtedly failed to
give the source for much that he recorded. Still, the failure to seek out either Negro or white Radical leaders suggests an unwillingness even to attempt an impartial survey.
Merely observing the manners of legislators and bewailing
the lack of decorum was a superficial approach to such a
complex problem as "South Carolina under Negro Government."

If Pike was careless or casual in his search for information, were there any preconceived motives or theories which
made his task easier? One factor which probably served
just this purpose was his animus against the Grant administration. The darker the picture of the South Carolina reconstruction government, which was yet controlled
by the Radicals, the greater the discredit to Grant. And,
perhaps unconsciously, the *Tribune* correspondent yielded
to the desire to strike back at the Radicals who had so
recently triumphed over the Liberal Republicans. Strategic omissions as well as alterations seem to corroborate
this explanation.

One clearly developed theme in Pike's original journal

[35] *Ibid.*, 22; *Prostrate State*, 43-44.
[36] Notebook No. 30, 33; *Prostrate State*, 114-15.
[37] Notebook No. 29, 26; *Prostrate State*, 22; and Notebook No. 30, 56;
Prostrate State, 100-01.

relates to quiescence and lethargy on the part of the white Carolinians. Commenting on the problem of inducing white immigrants to come to South Carolina, Pike had this to say in his notebook: "The old proprietors own such an overwhelming proportion of the soil that an intelligent combination among them, such as would be formed in six months by Yankees if the land were in their hands, would lead to [immigration] measures that would restore the just equilibrium of the races and remove the offensive political anomaly that now exists, in a comparatively short period."[38] In the published version, however, there is no invidious comparison of Carolina planters and hustling Yankees. Pike merely declares that the whites have the power, if they would use it, to "remove the offensive political anomaly that now exists."[39]

Concerning this same topic of immigration, Pike commented on the defeat of tax exemption bills designed to attract industry. He privately noted that the legislature, "or at least the white members of it," were not ready for an agitation of the subject. "On this, as on all subjects bearing on the present & future relationships of the races," he wrote, "the whites are now wholly reticent & reserved, and apparently fearful." When this same incident is mentioned in his book the explanation is vastly changed. Referring to the defeat of the tax exemption measures, he declared that it merely illustrated how "the jealousy of the blacks is constant against the white man, and that they do not favor any influential participation by him in the government of the State." The Negroes were "willing to perpetrate the greatest injustices" to prevent white "participation." Participation in this case meant one of the

[38] Notebook No. 30, 49.

[39] *Prostrate State*, 106. Rowland T. Berthoff, "Southern Attitudes Toward Immigration, 1865-1914," *Journal of Southern History*, XVII (August 1951), 328-60, has interesting material on this matter; also Robert H. Woody, "The Labor and Immigration Problem of South Carolina During Reconstruction," *Mississippi Valley Historical Review*, XVIII (Sept. 1931), 195-212.

typical railway subsidy or tax exemption schemes which had encountered opposition.[40]

In another place in his book Pike credited the great majorities which the Negroes and their allies wielded in some counties with producing a feeling of hopelessness among the whites, creating "the depression & inaction which prevails among them in such a striking degree." Yet in the published account this same matter of the counties with a great majority of Negroes is discussed without any reference at all to white "depression & inaction."[41] At one point during his stay in Columbia the visitor noted "an air of mastery among the colored people" and expressed surprise at "how reticent the whites are in their dealings with the blacks, & how entirely self contained & self asserting the blacks appear to be." But the published version contains but one short reference to white reticence or fearfulness.[42]

This estimate of the whites' political inactivity takes on added significance in connection with another of Pike's original theories, namely, that South Carolina was already, in early 1873, in the hands of her own people, white and colored, and that "there really is nothing within the just scope of federal power than can be done to relieve the State from its anomalous condition."[43] He judged that "any federal administration" which performed only "its legitimate duties" could have no influence on internal affairs in the state. If the whites and blacks would only forge some sort of harmonious union in the state government "no federal administration will have any call to practice guardianship or meddle in any way with the States Affairs."[44] According to this line of reasoning, it would be impossible to discredit the Grant administration or the federal gov-

[40] Notebook No. 30, 6-7; *Prostrate State*, 55.
[41] *Ibid.*, 47-48; *Prostrate State*, 56.
[42] Notebook No. 30, 44-45; *Prostrate State*, 110.
[43] Notebook No. 30, 23.
[44] Notebook No. 30, 20-21.

ernment by revealing any anomalous conditions in South Carolina. But in his book Pike largely followed another tact. The Washington government became, accordingly, the main instrument in supporting the Radicals who governed South Carolina.

"Outside forces" accomplished the changes which South Carolina had experienced during reconstruction. This became a major tenet of *The Prostrate State*. The "ignoble and incompetent crowd" ruled the state by means of "an alien and borrowed authority only"; the Negroes were but the humiliating means whereby a "foreign" power forced the native whites to obey. "It is not the rule of intrinsic strength; it is the compulsive power of the Federal authority at Washington. But for that, the forces of civilization would readjust themselves and overturn the present artificial arrangement."[45] He expressed his conviction that the whites had to have their relative weight in public affairs, not only in accordance with their numbers but with "the still weightier claims of property, intelligence, and enterprise." "While the laws of the universe remain," Pike concluded, "these claims must in the end successfully assert themselves. Not even governments can prevent it. And it is about time for the Federal Administration to take this reflection to heart."[46]

The net result of his emphasis on Washington's responsibility for reconstruction in South Carolina was to absolve the local whites; at the same time the local Negroes are pictured as the ignorant dupes, the tools, of Federal power. Pike emphasized the importance of Federal troops and appointments in South Carolina, and he both recorded and published his observations on that aspect of Carolina affairs.[47] But the sweeping manner in which he blamed

[45] *Prostrate State*, 83.
[46] *Prostrate State*, 54, 57; no diary source.
[47] Notebook No .30, 65-67; *Prostrate State*, 85-88. See also Simkins and Woody, *South Carolina during Reconstruction*, 112-13.

Washington for the continuation of Radical rule, and the fact that this had not been so clear and simple in his notebooks, leads to the conclusion that the desire to damn Grant and the Radicals led him to distort his own findings.[48]

Yet Grant was not the only victim of Pike's dramatic indictment of Carolina reconstruction. Even more than the Radicals in Washington, the Negro in Carolina, and by implication the whole race, received the hardest blows and bore the brunt of the Maine journalist's most vitriolic denunciation. The paradox of the antislavery spokesman with a bias against Negroes has already been discussed. He frankly admitted that his "pride of race" was profoundly shocked when the young Negro standing beside him on the floor of the House dared to criticize a white man.[49]

The racist or "white supremacy" note in *The Prostrate State* can hardly be missed, and it appears that the author added or greatly strengthened it, possibly unconsciously, in preparing his material for publication. The examples which could be cited are numerous, but the following comparison shows one type of significant change. Commenting in general terms in his journal on the situation in Carolina, Pike judged: "Looking at its situation & resources, we cannot admit that S. Carolina is going to stop in its progress. . . ." The same sentence, in the published version, became: "Looking at her situation and resources, and the invincible qualities that mark the Anglo-Saxon race, we cannot admit that she is going to be arrested in her progress. . . ."[50] In another published passage, which has no counterpart in the manuscript, Pike exclaimed that

[48] Such would, moreover, suit the general policy of the *Tribune* during 1873 and 1874. Reconstruction in the South furnished the new editor, Whitelaw Reid, with much of his ammunition in the attack on Grant. A series on Louisiana and one on Mississippi paralleled Pike's on South Carolina. For examples see issues of April 9, 1873, January 2, 1874.

[49] See above, p. 14.

[50] Notebook No. 29, 42; *Prostrate State*, 56-57.

to allow South Carolina to remain in the permanent control of her "present rulers" would be "a violent presumption against the manliness, the courage, and the energy of South Carolina white men." "It would be a testimony against the claims of Anglo-Saxon blood, and it would be an emphatic testimony to the decline of public virtue that would be worse than all. These considerations alone should be sufficient to inspire every white man in South Carolina with a resolution to achieve a reform that will bring the State back to its ancient respectability."[51]

Even more damaging to the Negroes than the "Anglo-Saxon" line was the close identity which Pike gave to ignorance and corruption, on the one hand, and Negro blood on the other. The end result of his portrayal of legislative venality and incapacity is to make them seem inveterate racial characteristics. Yet his original, on-the-spot impressions were different. On one occasion while witnessing the legislature in action, Pike observed that the art of legislative robbery was as well understood in Carolina as in any Tammany Hall conclave. As proof for this, in the notebook he cited the example of a certain white legislator, "the adroitest among the strikers," who angled for bribes from a railway company which desired a charter. But his illustration in *Prostrate State* for the Tammany parallel is "the colored Representatives in Congress from South Carolina."[52] Another journal statement is: "Sambo dotes on committees. The white man has shown him their uses & how they can be more profitable." But the revised version reads: "Sambo dotes on legislative committees. The struggle to get on those that pay best is amusing."[53]

In giving a racial slant to Carolina corruption, corruption which admittedly existed, Pike had every reason for

[51] *Prostrate State*, 89.
[52] Notebook No. 30, 62; *Prostrate State*, 46.
[53] Notebook No. 30, 5; *Prostrate State*, 109.

realizing his injustice.[54] The Liberal Republicans of 1872 had raised their loudest cries against the infamous jobbery they professed to see in Washington. And even in Columbia Pike bemoaned "this corrupt perversion of the objects of government" which was rampant "throughout many other parts of the country." Either "society is rotting all the way through," he reasoned, or else "the villains are too much or too many for the honest men." In this broad context, it is clear that corruption had no racial aspect, unless it be a white one.[55]

On the subject of the freedman's "ignorance," or "the blackness of darkness" as he confusingly phrased it, Pike left out a great deal more than he included. Education is treated only briefly on about two pages of his book. The conclusion there is the gloomy one that education of the Negro offers no remedy for Carolina's dilemma. And race is the reason why it does not. "The education they [the Negroes] require is the formation of a race the opposite of the existing race. They have to be taught not to lie, not to steal, not to be unchaste. To educate them properly is to revolutionize their whole moral nature." "Reading and writing" merely lends a cutting edge to their "moral obtuseness" because Negro education really means "the moral enlightenment and regeneration of a whole people debauched and imbruted for ages."[56] A more discouraging estimate could hardly be imagined; the factual basis for it is not to be found in Pike's journal. As far as can be determined from his notes, he gave no attention

---

[54] In his book he borrowed heavily from the "Report of the Joint Select Committee to Inquire into the Condition of Affairs in the late Insurrectionary States, made to the two Houses of Congress, February 10, 1872." *Prostrate State*, chapters XVIII through XXXIII, 122-272. This portion of the book is the least interesting and most unsensational part of his narrative. For a more recent discussion of the frauds, etc., see Simkins and Woody, *South Carolina*, 147-85.

[55] Notebook No. 30, 39.

[56] *Prostrate State*, 62-63.

to educational matters while in the South. The free school system, inaugurated by the Radicals in their constitution of 1868, either escaped the journalist's notice or did not awaken his interest. As a result, in an area where the reconstruction governments' achievement, not only in South Carolina but in most of the Southern states, is most widely recognized and acclaimed, Pike remained not only uninformed but outspokenly prejudiced. Where he did observe the freedmen at work—in the sun-splashed fields—he found the Negro made "the best of workers," men and women alike being "vigorous, quick and athletic." The clear but undrawn moral was that the Negro's place was in the field.[57]

Thus Pike presented the South Carolina situation to the nation. In 1873, and since then, "this prominent Republican Abolitionist" from Maine appeared to offer the outsider's objective view of a controversial and crucial issue.[58] Part of the explanation for the book's weakness seems to lie in a tenuous psychological area; Pike, even as a vehement antislavery spokesman, had revealed lack of understanding or sympathy for the human potential of the Negro. This, however, still leaves unexplained the differences between his journal and his published work. Stylistic improvements and other such changes are to be expected. But discrepancies such as have been mentioned reflect more than mere stylizing.

Pike's animus against the Grant administration may account for part of his abusive treatment of the South Carolina Negroes, Grant's Radical allies. Reworking the material for publication in the *Tribune*, he perhaps wished to have his articles conform to the editorial policy of the leading Liberal Republican organ, as well as to find a

[57] *Prostrate State*, 273; Notebook No. 31, 3-9.

[58] This phrase, typical of many descriptions of *The Prostrate State's* author is found in Robert G. Rhett, *Charleston, An Epic of Carolina* (Richmond, Va., 1940), p. 283.

numerous and receptive audience in the North.

The solution which Pike suggested for the real problems besetting South Carolina, was, in reality, no solution at all. The entire nation, and not merely South Carolina, he asserted, had to study and understand the "Negro question," for "it is a question of the predominance and antagonism of races." If it were true that ours was not "a white man's government," should it be "a black man's government?" Then, perhaps recalling earlier 'moral' crusades of the Republicans, Pike admitted: "We only disposed of one phase of the negro question in abolishing slavery. The great perplexity of establishing just relations between the races in the negro States is yet to be encountered. And it comes upon the country under a cloud of embarrassments. It has to be settled under the growing urgency ... of the question whether the great mass of the black population at the South is not now mentally and morally unfit for self-government, and whether the progress of events will not force a modification of the original reconstruction acts—not based upon race or color or previous condition, but upon other considerations yet to be evolved and elucidated."[59]

The "other considerations" were never found. When Democratic rule in South Carolina was restored in 1876, factors other than the ballot played a part. The Hamburg massacre, "rifle clubs," and "Red Shirts" with their "shotgun policy" were among the answers found to the question Pike had treated three years earlier.[60] While these events shook "the Prostrate State," Pike was quietly pursuing literary labors in his far-away Maine home.

ROBERT F. DURDEN

Duke University

---

[59] *Prostrate State*, 68-69.

[60] Simkins and Woody, *South Carolina*, 474-513. For a less scholarly view, see William A. Sheppard, *Red Shirts Remembered: Southern Brigadiers of the Reconstruction Period* (Atlanta, 1940).

FISK UNIVERSITY AND THE NASHVILLE
COMMUNITY, 1866-1900

The year 1900 marked the thirty-fourth anniversary of the founding of Fisk University.[1] That institution, named at first the Fisk School, was established in 1866, a year of tension for the nation which had then recently solved by recourse to arms several of its persistent problems. One concerned the nature of the American union; another, the fate of American Negro slavery.

The Civil War had brought about the downfall of slavery. The post-war period had ushered in a second revolution which challenged the intelligence and the integrity of the nation. The founding of the Fisk School in this period of upheaval was an incident in the movement which commenced during the war and continued long thereafter, with the view of enabling the American Negro freedmen, approximately 4,000,000 strong, to lay a foundation for the eventual assimilation of their descendants to American culture.

This complex task, because of its supreme importance to the nation, merited the unstinted and sustained cooperation of the American people for its successful issue. The freedmen as a class then occupied the bottom niche in the scale of American civilization. For them, there continued the immediate need for physical relief and remunerative employment. The future demanded the establishment in the South of a comprehensive system of churches, schools and other agencies of social uplift for the purpose of facilitating the religious, moral and mental development of the blacks.

Large segments of the population continued to respond to this need magnificently. These were, in the main, the humanitarian elements located in the North. For a while,

[1] This paper is based upon an unpublished study of the history of Fisk University. Quotations not cited are taken from this study.

at least, the federal government participated in the movement admirably, but not adequately. Eventually some of the Southern states stimulated by funds appropriated by Congress established so-called "land-grant" institutions for the instruction of the Negroes in agriculture and the mechanical trades. Meanwhile, certain institutions established before the war for the education of Negroes continued their efforts.

As a phase of the general movement, the American Missionary Association founded institutions throughout the South, "from the Ohio to the Gulf, and from the Atlantic Ocean to the remotest borders of Texas, intended to break the supremacy of ignorance in the South . . ." During the course of this movement, the Association in cooperation with the Western Freedmen's Aid Commission of Cincinnati founded the Fisk School.

The participating agencies were represented in the founding by men whose experiences gained during the war had convinced them that Nashville offered special advantages for the "planting" of a permanent school for the education of Negroes. That city, they observed, was not only a "point of great business, social and political importance, but also a centre of a large colored population." For the American Missionary Association, these functionaries were the Reverend E. P. Smith, and the Reverend E. M. Cravath. The former, the district secretary located at Cincinnati, had been a field agent for the Christian Commission, with headquarters at Nashville; the latter, the field agent at Nashville, had participated in military campaigns in Tennessee as chaplain of an Ohio regiment. There acted for the Western Freedmen's Aid Commission, Professor John Ogden, educationist, former officer in a Wisconsin regiment and then recently superintendent of education for the Freedmen's Bureau in Tennessee. These men, after experiencing considerable difficulty because of the unfriendliness of some Nashvillians toward Negro uplift, purchased a land site for the school. General Clinton B. Fisk, intrepid leader of men and assistant commissioner of the Freedmen's Bureau for Kentucky and Tennessee, secured housing for the project in federal hospital buildings then about to be abandoned.

On January 9, 1866, the Fisk School was formally dedicated as a high school. Eager thousands assembled to observe the event. The participants on the program included the Honorable W. G. Brownlow, Governor of the State of Tennessee, General Clinton B. Fisk, Dr. J. B. Lindsley, Chancellor of the State University and Superintendent of the Nashville City Schools, the Honorable William Bosson, Chairman of the State Senate Committee on Common Schools, and numerous other officers and civilians. All felicitated the sponsors of the enterprise and Governor Brownlow, a controversial figure in Tennessee politics, warned the schoolmen against antagonizing the local native whites because of the opposition of many to the education of the blacks.

Before the ceremonial had been concluded, the Reverend E. M. Cravath announced that the school would receive pupils the next morning. He thanked all who had assisted in the work and expressed the thought that this event marked the beginning of a great educational institution which should give to the emancipated race the opportunities and advantages which had been so long afforded to more favored peoples in their colleges and universities. Then spoke John Ogden, the administrative principal of the school.

Despite various untoward circumstances surrounding the launching, the Fisk School began "at once to flourish." Under the effective leadership of Principal Ogden, an efficient corps of teachers offered instruction to more than 1000 pupils, the vast majority being residents of Nashville, none of whom were then advanced beyond the fifth reader, rudimentary arithmetic and elementary grammar. In the night school, moreover, elderly men and women learned to read the Bible. "Thus, at the outset, the school met a local need effectively, for although in Nashville several mission schools were doing excellent work, free public education for Negro children did not exist."

In 1867, the city of Nashville, prodded no doubt by this example, opened two free public schools for Negro children. In consequence, the Fisk School raised its status to that of academy and normal school before it secured a charter under the name of Fisk University. Thus legally qualified to receive funds from the Freedmen's Bureau, the institution hitherto known as a school for colored children expressed a new viewpoint. In describing the purposes of the corporation and the rights of the trustees, the articles of incorporation said: "The purposes of the Corporation are the education and training of young men and women irrespective of color and to that end the Trustees shall have the right to prescribe a course or courses of study and have power to confer all such degrees and honors as are conferred by universities in the United States." The first trustees, it may be noted, included several citizens of Nashville, although, perhaps, no natives, who wrought importantly in the business and social life of the city.

The school continued, in the meantime, to meet local needs. In 1867, for example, George L. White, business manager and instructor of music, presented in public concert a school chorus which he had trained. The affair was a success financially. More importantly, however, it tended to prove to some native whites the educability of the Negroes. Expressing this view, a prominent local newspaper "raised the question, whether it was not the duty of the Southern people to take hold of the work of educating the blacks instead of leaving it to persons from the North." In 1868, White presented his chorus in concert again and in 1870, his students rendered the cantata of "Esther", superbly.

Similarly, in 1870, Professor Spence, the new principal of the University, introduced a feature in the work of that year. Thereby he undertook to supplement the enduring work of Professor Bennett who encouraged the Negro pastors of Nashville to study and helped them to organize Sunday Schools and to improve their church services. Referring to this new work as "missionary labors", Spence said: "On Saturdays, in the environs of the campus, the students went from house to house to secure new pupils for the Sunday-School." The result was rewarding, for within a short time the attendance reflected a new increase of 200 pupils. The students distributed tracts among the populace, read the Bible to some, and prayed with others. Consistently, they invited them to attend the church services. Lastly, the "missionary labors" included "street preaching". On this mission the adults went into the streets "to preach Jesus to those who did not go to church, choosing the most destitute parts of the city about them." This work, the Nashville *Republican Banner*[2] endorsed noting that a meeting then recently held, had been "attended by 300 people, both white and colored."

In 1871, the institution admitted its first college class. Its teaching departments, enlarged to four, included the college, the academy, the normal department and the model school. The last named consisted of a teaching staff and a group of children, drawn principally from Nashville and its environs, to serve as a practice school for students of the normal department. The physical plant, improved by an attractive new chapel, had declined in the facilities for teaching and living to a stage of advanced deterioration. The original site did not seem promising for the school's continued growth. The institution was desperately in need of funds. The consistent support of the American Missionary Association, then sole sponsor, was inadequate. The Freedmen's Bureau grants had been wisely used. The

[2] *Op. cit.*, November 13, 1870.

gift of the Peabody Fund supported selected students of the normal department. From other sources, funds came in small amounts. Some thought the day of doom had come.

In this extremity there was conceived a plan as desperate as it was daring. George L. White, ''man of all work'' at Fisk, had, as mentioned above, for several years trained and developed a chorus of music students. Not only in Nashville, but also in Memphis, Gallatin, Chattanooga and Atlanta, he had presented these students in concert. Their performances had been well received. Uniformly, indeed, they had edified as well as entertained the audiences. Partly as a result, certain persons in Nashville suggested that these singers presented before audiences in the North might win for Fisk University the sympathy and the support of many in that section. George L. White sponsored the idea. E. M. Cravath approved and supported it. The American Missionary Association withheld support, because it could not honorably use for so novel an enterprise funds contributed to it for other purposes. The trustees authorized that the experiment should be made.

Thus evolved the movement which gave to the world the famous ''spirituals'' of the American ante-bellum plantation Negro. Throughout a period of seven years the Jubilee Singers appeared before audiences in the United States or in Europe. During the last four, in Europe, they sang before royalty, nobility and commoners. They made the name and the purpose of Fisk University internationally known. For the institution, they won friends, great and small. By their efforts, they earned the sum of $150,-000 which gave to Fisk the earliest impetus to the achievement of its goal as a notable American institution of higher learning. For themselves, the singers won recognition not merely as ''vocalists of so-called plantation melodies,'' but also as ''cultured musicians . . . with ability to maintain good presence in polished society." "They won respect for themselves as persons of human dignity, of essential worth, and of musical talent." As representative American Negroes, they assumed in an international setting the role of ambassadors of good will. They tended to stimulate an interest in the Christianization of Africa, an enterprise which loomed large in the aims of Fisk University. Before the turn of the century that institution had trained more than a half score of students who had gone to Africa as missionaries.

On January 1, 1876, in a famous ceremonial, Fisk dedicated Jubilee Hall, a temple of learning and living, made possible by the work of the Jubilee Singers, and located on the permanent institutional site. The erection of that hall has been called a transcendent event in Southern Negro education. The dedication, "as a symbol of great significance," attracted favorable attention of international scope. Nationally, it marked an advance in "the perilously slow movement toward making the American creed a thing of vitality and of substance."

The new building attracted the attention of a multitude of prospective students of high school and college level. It appealed to their parents, to educators in the South and to Southern state officials and legislators, like some in Nashville, who did not oppose the higher education of Negroes. To many persons, moreover, this event, considered in connection with others, seemed to constitute convincing proof that Fisk University, based upon a sound foundation, had taken high rank as a trail blazer in Negro higher education.

In 1875, Fisk University had graduated its first college class. In that year, too, the trustees had elected its first president and had formally organized the college faculty. During the interval between that year and the year 1900, the institution, although plagued by persistent and imposing problems, reflected, under wise and able leadership, substantial evidence of growth and development as an institution of Christian higher education.

One aspect of this development was the ability of the institution to function with some effect in the promotion of understanding between the white and the black peoples in Nashville and, to some degree, elsewhere in the South. The fact is remarkable, for during this period, especially following the undoing of political reconstruction in the South, the Negroes, in Tennessee as elsewhere, suffered serious abridgement of their rights and various species of cruel persecution which have resulted in a retardation of national development to this day.

The position of Fisk in Nashville was due in no small part to the wise and able leadership of the president and his associates in their relationships with the public, the character of the faculty, the objectives of the teaching and the educability of the students, a majority of whom gave evidence of a creditable interest in learning. Consistent with the fundamental purpose of Fisk, the leaders recognized that an important aim of any effort for the education of the Southern Negro should be to bring about a satisfactory basis of cooperation between the Negro population and the white population of the United States: that the eventual sympathetic cooperation of the intelligent, emancipated white people of the South would be essential to the success of any plan or process for improving the position of the Negro and his relations with the Southern whites generally.

With such ends in view President Cravath and his associates moved among Southern leaders who entertained convictions different from their own, winning the respect and confidence of many and without compromising their own belief in the fundamental equality of individuals before both God and man. The strictly sociable relations between the officers and members of the Fisk faculty and the Southerners were negligible. But the institutional officers maintained good business and professional relations with their neighbors in Nashville, especially with the leaders in business and education. The University and its students spent thousands of dollars with Nashville business houses. Merchants and other proprietors supported projects of Fisk students such as the movement to finance the erection of the gymnasium, and they gave employment of the traditional types to Fisk students. To their credit, it may be said, many of these students did their work well. Among the educators, moreover, professional association extended to the offering of advice, the attendance of Southerners as guests at Fisk ceremonials and concerts and, to a limited extent, of the observation by Fisk students of science and their teachers of demonstrations and experiments in the laboratories of another institution.

In other respects, too, the institution's reputation extended its influence. Before the institution had attained its fifteenth year, the governor of the state and the state superintendent of public instruction had attested the precedence of Fisk as an institution of learning. Consistently, county superintendents of education praised the work of Fisk graduates and students as school teachers and principals. Citizens in the cities and hinterland remarked how the ministerial students trained at Fisk urged the Negroes not merely to prepare for the celestial comforts and joys of heaven but also to seek to live better and more sober lives in this world. Law enforcement officers spoke of the sobriety of the Fisk students. The accessible records of this period fail to reveal the conviction of any graduate or student of Fisk of an infamous crime. The teachers laid stress upon the college years as a period of preparation. They urged students to study and to debate public questions such as the social effects of Tennessee's separate coach law and the social and economic effects of its convicts' lease and prison work systems. But they urged these students to acquire maturity and experience before they should become social actionists, seeking to solve these problems. They emphasized the importance of observing orderly processes in their efforts to effect reform. The students, in the main, accepted this advice. Largely as a result of these several circumstances the people in Nashville[3] and, in other places where the institution had wide contacts, came to regard Fisk as exerting a constructive influence in the community life.

The quarter century ending in 1900 was, therefore, a progressive era in the life of Fisk University. The expansion of the physical plant is a case in point. By 1900, the campus, buildings and apparatus were valued conservatively at $350,000. Yet the physical and the financial needs of the institution were enormous. The University "required 'a great central building' to give unity to its group of buildings and to supply permanent class rooms. With urgency it needed a hall for the department of Music." Its endowment was practically nil. It had created seven professorships, not one of which had been endowed.

Throughout this period, moreover, Northern universities considered the character and the objectives of Fisk's instruction sound. By 1900, its curricula had been greatly expanded and strengthened. Long since had the college department offered both classical and scientific courses of study. The seminary had organized a standard theological course although a majority of its students, consisting in

---

[3] "The substantial leaders among the white people in the city attended the musical concerts held in Fisk Memorial Chapel, participated in the dedicatory programs of such buildings as Livingstone Hall and Fisk Memorial Chapel and directed to Fisk important visitors to the city who were desirous of seeing places in Nashville of compelling interest. Thus in 1895, Mayor Build brought to the Fisk campus the Indiana Editorial Association, 200 strong, on a tour of important places. Again in 1900, the hosts of Admiral Dewey presented that hero before the student body of Fisk. In 1897, moreover, Fisk played a significant part in making the Tennessee Centennial Exposition successful. When President McKinley visited the Exposition he stopped before the Fisk building to hear the Mozart Society sing and to greet its members." (Fisk *Herald*, November, 1895, pp. 11-12; June, 1900, pp. 2-3.)

the main of Nashville Negro ministers, pursued courses conducted wholly in the English language. In consequence of a special grant, the faculty had introduced manual training and domestic science courses, which it considered of subsidiary rather than paramount importance. It had also organized a flexible course of graduate study. The normal course, it had reorganized considerably. Despite the conspicuous role of music in the life of Fisk University, the faculty did not formally organize a department before 1884. Sometime thereafter, Miss Jennie A. Robinson became the director. Under her leadership the work gained a primacy at Fisk which has been achieved only recently by several disciplines.

The faculty of Fisk University, comprising more than thirty-five members, included four of the college faculty elected in 1875. In cooperation with others, these four—Cravath, Spence, Chase and Miss Morgan—constituted a fundamentally important element in the ongoing of Fisk. They were "educators of high intelligence, liberal education, Christian piety and zeal, patience and sympathy." They were consecrated and devoted "to the cause of moulding the youth whom they taught into Christian, American men and women. Deeply religious and superbly moral they sought to infuse into their charges the fundamental tenents of their own code of life."

The characterization of the student body made by President Merrill[4] in 1905 might well apply to that group of many earlier years. "To one attending morning prayers in Livingstone Chapel", said he, "a sight is met alike pathetic and inspiring. The capacious hall is crowded with a company from the Guinea black to the blue-eyed and red-cheeked Saxon, there are black Germans, Irish Negroes, while in the veins of some of the students flows the blood

[4] James G. Merrill, "Fisk University," *From Servitude to Service*, VI, pp. 212-213.

of the far-famed Southern aristocracy. They came from nearly thirty states and territories. . . . Varying motives bring them to Fisk but speedily they find themselves surrounded by an atmosphere of service, to be a factor in the development of a belated race becomes their ambition; not wealth, not place, but ability to lift up their fellows is the goal placed before them and few of those who receive the diploma of Fisk fail to reach this goal.''

The total enrollment of different students at Fisk University before 1900 would surely number a good many thousand. "Primarily as a day school, the institution served approximately 1200 pupils drawn principally from Nashville and its environs during its first year of existence. When in September, 1867, it opened the academic and normal departments the enrollment dropped sharply. In 1867-1868, the enrollment was 412. Thereafter, it varied considerably; increasing on the whole, progressively, but not consistently. In one year, it decreased to 212; in another, it exceeded 504, the enrollment of 1899-1900.''

"With respect to the alumni, the statistics are more specifically informing. At the close of the Commencement of 1900, the grand total of alumni was 433. Of the several departments, the numbers were as follows: theological, 7; college, 201; normal, 210; and music, 13 . . .'' The institution did not classify as alumni those who had completed only courses of study of high school level or below.

In 1900, the graduates of Fisk University were gainfully employed, in the main, in socially useful work. A census of the living graduates of the college and normal departments shows their occupations as of January 1, 1900, as follows:

Occupation	College	Normal	Total
College Professors	7	1	8

High or Normal School

Principals	12	—	12
Teachers	27	18	45

Grammar School

Principals	19	15	34
Teachers	35	85	120
Ministers	17	2	19
Doctors	14	3	17
Lawyers	9	—	9

Students in Professional

Schools	14	2	16
Business	6	7	13
U. S. Government Employment	9	—	9
Wives, not classified above	2	42	44
Miscellaneous	—	—	9
Living at Home	1	12	13

Interest may attach to the individual employment of a few of these graduates as reflected in the following list:

Professor of Anatomy in a Medical College

Special Commissioner for Negro Exhibit at the Paris Exposition

Dean and Professor of Latin and Pedagogy at Howard University

Agent in charge of the Tuskegee Cotton-Raising Experiment Station, at Togo, West Africa, under the German Government

Professor of Physiology and Instructor in Electro-Therapeutics in a Medical School

Departmental Clerk, Pan American Exposition, at Buffalo, New York

Notary Public and U. S. Gauger at Houston, Texas

Professor of Sociology and History at Atlanta University

Court Reporter at Tacoma, Washington

Collector of Internal Revenue at San Antonio, Texas

"Upon the basis of the formal education afforded by Fisk University, several alumni had pursued graduate or professional study in leading American institutions successfully. One, at least, had studied extensively in Europe. Three had earned the degree of doctor of philosophy: one each at Harvard, the Illinois Wesleyan University and the University of Pennsylvania. Eleven had qualified for degrees in theology: two at Yale, three at the Hartford Theological Seminary and six at Oberlin. In law, one had received a degree at Harvard; another, at Yale. Nearly a half score had won degrees in medicine. These included two at Harvard, one at Yale, one at the University of Pennsylvania and others at such institutions as the Chicago Medical College, the College of Physicians and Surgeons of Chicago, the Women's Medical College of Pennsylvania and the Medical School of the Northwestern University. One had taken the Master of Arts degree at Dartmouth College and another had completed a course of study in the Conservatory of Music at Hartford. Of the sixteen then attending graduate or professional schools, one studied engineering at the University of Wisconsin; another, medicine, at the University of Michigan.''

"In 1900, the vast majority of Fisk alumni resided in the South. A census then recently taken shows a sprinkling of graduates living in New England; six or seven in Wisconsin, Minnesota and Michigan; and a number not quite so small in other North Central states. Thirteen, for example, resided in Illinois. Approximately ten were located in Missouri; six in Iowa; eighteen in Kentucky; and fourteen in North Carolina. In Georgia, Alabama and Texas, there lived twenty-six, thirty-four and forty-six, respectively. The largest number, 106, as might be expected, lived in Tennessee.''

Among the notable persons represented in the foregoing statistics, some were nationaly known in 1900. These included Dr. W. E. B. DuBois, scholar; Dr. H. H. Proctor,

Congregational minister who had developed an institutional church in Atlanta; Mrs. Booker T. Washington, feminist and teacher; Dr. Lewis B. Moore, educator; Mr. Richard Morris, lawyer of Minneapolis; Dr. A. A. Wesley, physician and surgeon and the Reverend George W. Moore, Congregational minister, educator and officer of the American Missionary Association.

Of these alumni, too, there lived in Nashville during these years, several men and women of mark. Such were the Burrus brothers: John, James and Preston. John was a lawyer, politician and civic leader; James, a business man; and Preston, a pharmacist. Early in the twentieth century, they bequeathed to Fisk University the residue of their estates, aggregating more than $120,000.00. Dr. Ferdinand A. Stewart, a Harvard medical graduate wrought well as a professor at Meharry Medical School and as a practicing physician and surgeon. John L. Barbour was the proprietor of a furniture business. Samuel A. McElwee, William H. Hodgins, George T. Robinson and William A. Crosthwaite, were lawyers. McElwee, representing a district adjoining Davidson County, served several terms in the State legislature. Frank Gatewood Smith, trained in medicine, became principal of the Colored High School. Numerous alumni, of whom Lena Terrell Jackson, Henry Alvin Cameron and Emma Jane Terry are representative, taught in the city schools.

Some such persons as these President Cravath had in mind when in 1893, he said: "I can take you to graduates who are lawyers and physicians who are the equal of any white men in their professions in Nashville, but they must serve a poor people because of the race line, and they have not the wide field that opens to white men." Similarly, spoke Professor Spence in 1895. "In the city of Nashville," said he, "we have now many most encouraging examples of the new colored South, not only in schools, but in neat and commodious homes, with appointments of modern civilization in which refined manners prevail; libraries and instruments of music are found, and children are growing up like those in the better white families. There are already among the graduates of our colored institutions of learning and others educated in them, able doctors, lawyers, ministers, teachers and men of business who form a society but little known among many, who speak as by authority and say that the case of the Negro is hopeless. There was a club recently formed of men of that race who gather to discuss sociological questions as to health, thrift and general welfare pertaining to their people. It is in these things that the men who think are men who do.''

If, as the president of a great state university once said, the alumni are in a very real sense the university, it may not be amiss to evaluate the Fisk University of the nineteenth century in terms of the performance of its graduates of that time. Some of the foregoing facts have suggested in part, at least, the role which those Fisk alumni have played in Nashville, as elsewhere in American life. ''In their homes of refinement and Christian culture, they demonstrated the merits of religion and education as bases of effective living. In various aspects, they exhibited evidences of aptitude and interest. They exemplified in their daily lives high qualities of citizenship. Participating dynamically in some phases of the affairs of their community, they attempted to resolve, in co-operation with others, problems of major social significance. In these efforts, under the controlling conditions, they wrought with discretion and intelligence.''

A. A. TAYLOR

Fisk University

SHERMAN AT SAVANNAH

Nearly eight weeks before Appomattox, the South, completely demoralized and facing certain defeat, was witnessing a strange and unprecedented event in the city of Savannah, Georgia.[1] On January 11, 1865, the revenue cutter *Spaulding* put in at Savannah with a distinguished cargo, including Secretary of War Edwin M. Stanton, Quartermaster General Montgomery C. Meigs, and other representatives of Washington officialdom. Secretary Stanton went immediately into conference with General Sherman. The meeting took place in a second floor room of the spacious and palatial home of Charles Green on Macon Street where Sherman had established his headquarters.[2] At this conference Secretary Stanton proposed that General Sherman arrange a meeting with the leaders of the local Negro community for the purpose of putting the question: "What do you want for your own people?"[3] Accordingly, a meeting was arranged for the following evening, Thursday, January 12th, at 8:00 p.m. in General Sherman's headquarters.

Exactly one month later a verbatim report of this meeting was given to the Sunday evening congregation of Brooklyn, New York's Plymouth Church by its famed minister, Mr. Henry Ward Beecher. A copy of the minutes of the meeting had been placed in the hands of Mr. Beecher by Secretary Stanton himself.[4] As reported by the *New*

[1] Sherman had entered Savannah on December 20, 1864.

[2] Charles Green, a British subject, and wealthy Savannah cotton broker, offered his home to Gen Sherman for use as his headquarters. Green was sympathetic toward the Confederacy, and as the owner of a fleet of merchant vessels had aided the Confederate cause materially by transporting supplies from Great Britain. He explained his action thus: ". . . by admitting the Northern General to his own house, he, an Englishman, had spared some citizen of the Confederate States, the ignominy of having his house taken as Sherman's headquarters." (Walter C. Hartridge: *The Green-Meldrim House.* Published by the Society for the Preservation of Savannah Landmarks, 1943.)

[3] *New York Daily Tribune*, Monday, Feb. 13, 1865.

[4] *Ibid.*

York Daily Tribune, Monday, February 13, 1865, there were twenty freedmen present:

1. William J. Campbell, 51, native of Savannah, slave until 1849, then liberated by will of his mistress, Mrs. May Maxwell. Pastor of the First Baptist Church of Savannah for ten years. Membership 1800. Church property owned by congregation, valued at $18,000. Church trustees, white.

2. John Cox, 58, born in Savannah, slave until 1849. Purchased own freedom for $1100. Pastor of the Second African Baptist Church. In the ministry fifteen years. Congregation numbered at 1222. Church property valued at $10,000. Owned by the congregation.

3. Ulysses L. Houston, 41, born in Grahamville, S. C. Slave until the Union Army entered Savannah. Owned by Moses Henderson, Savannah. Pastor of the Third African Baptist Church. Congregation 400. Church property owned by congregation, valued at $5,000.

4. William Bentley, 72, born in Savannah and a slave until twenty-five years of age when emancipated by will of his master, John Waters. Pastor of Andrews Chapel Methodist Episcopal Church (only one in Savannah). Congregation 360. Church property owned by congregation and valued at $20,000. In the ministry twenty years, member of the Georgia Conference.

5. Charles Bradwell, 40, born in Liberty County, Georgia. Slave until 1851 when emancipated by will of his master, J. L. Bradwell. Served Methodist Episcopal congregation in absence of regular minister. In the ministry ten years.

6. William Gaines, 41, born in Wills County, Georgia, freed by Union forces. Owned by Robert Toombs, formerly U. S. Senator, and his brother, Gabriel Toombs. Local preacher of Methodist Church (Andrews Chapel). Sixteen years in the ministry.

7. James Hill, 52, born in Bryan County, Georgia. Slave until freed by Union Army. Owned by H. F. Willings of Savannah. In the ministry sixteen years.

8. Glasgon Taylor, 72, born in Wilkes County, Georgia. Slave until freed by Union forces. Owned by A. P. Wetter. Local preacher in Methodist Church (Andrews Chapel). In ministry thirty-five years.

9. Garrison Frazier, 67, born in Granville County, N. C. Slave until 1857, when he purchased freedom for himself and wife for $1000 in gold and silver. Ordained minister in the Baptist Church. Health failing. Not in charge of a congregation. In the ministry thirty-five years.

10. James Mills, 56, free-born in Savannah. A licensed preacher in the Baptist Church. Eight years in the ministry.

11. Abraham Burke, 48, born in Bryan County, Georgia. Slave

until 1845, when he purchased his freedom for $800. Ten years in the ministry.

12. Arthur Wardell, 44, born in Liberty County, Georgia. Slave until freed by Union Army. Owned by A. A. Solomons, Savannah. Licensed minister for six years in the Baptist Church.

13. Alexander Harris, 47, born in Savannah, free-born. Licensed minister of the Third African Church of Savannah.

14. Andrew Neal, 61, born in Savannah. A slave until the Union Army entered the city. A deacon in the Third African Baptist Church for ten years. His former master, Mr. William Gibbons of Savannah.

15. James Porter, 39, born free in Charleston, S. C., his mother having purchased her freedom. A lay preacher, and president of the Board of Wardens and Vestry, St. Stephens Protestant Episcopal Colored Church of Savannah. A communicant for nine years. Congregation about 200. Church owned by the congregation, valued at $10,000.

16. John Johnson, 51, born in Bryan County, Georgia. Slave until freed by Union Army. Owned by W. W. Lincoln of Savannah. A class leader and treasurer of Andrews Chapel for sixteen years.

17. Adolphus Delmotte, 28, free-born in Savannah. A licensed minister of the Missionary Baptist Church, Milledgeville, Ga. Congregation three or four hundred. In ministry two years.

18. Jacob Godfrey, 57, born in Marion, S. C. Slave until freed by Union Army. Owned by James E. Godfrey, a Methodist minister now in the Confederate Army. A class leader and a steward in Andrews Chapel since 1836.

19. Robert N. Taylor, 51, born in Wilkes County, Ga. Slave until freed by Union Army. Owned by Augustus P. Welter, Savannah. A class leader in Andrews Chapel for nine years.

20. James Lynch, 26, free-born in Baltimore, Md. The Presiding Elder of the M. E. Church, and missionary to the Department of the South. Seven years in the ministry. Two years in the South.

Several questions dwelling upon matters relating to the status of the freedmen in the State of Georgia were addressed to the assembled group. Garrison Frazier was chosen by the persons present to express their common sentiments upon the matters of inquiry. His verbatim replies follow:[5]

[5] Letter from the War Department, Adjutant General's Office, Washington, February 1, 1865: "I do hereby certify that the foregoing is a true and faithful report of the questions and answers made by the colored ministers and

1. State what your understanding is in regard to the acts of Congress and President Lincoln's proclamation touching on the condition of the colored people in the Rebel States.

Reply: So far as I understand President Lincoln's proclamation to the Rebellious States, it is, that if they would lay down their arms and submit to the laws of the United States before the first of January, 1863, all would be well, but if they did not, then all the slaves of the Rebel States would be free henceforth and forever. That is what I understand.

2. State what you understand by slavery and the freedom that was to be given by the President's proclamation.

Reply: Slavery is, receiving by *irresistible power* the work of another man, and not by his *consent*. The freedom as I understand it, promised by the proclamation, is taking us from under the yoke of bondage, and placing us where we could reap the fruit of our own labor, take care of ourselves, and assist the Government in maintaining our freedom.

3. State in what manner you think you can take care of yourselves, and how can you best assist the Government in maintaining your freedom.

Reply: The way we can best take care of ourselves is to have land, and turn it and till it by our own labor—that is, by the labor of the women and children and old men; and we can soon maintain ourselves and have something to spare. And to assist the Government, the young men should enlist in the service of the Government, and to serve in such manner as they may be wanted. (The Rebels told us that they piled them up and made batteries of them, and sold them to Cuba; but we don't believe that.) We want to be placed on land until we are able to buy it and make it our own.

4. State in what manner you would rather live—whether scattered among the whites or in colonies by yourselves.

Reply: I would prefer to live by ourselves, for there is a prejudice against us in the South that will take years to get over; but I do not know if I can answer for my brethren. (Mr. Lynch says he thinks they should not be separated, but live together. All

church members of Savannah in my presence and hearing, at the chambers of Major General Sherman, on the evening of Thursday, January 12, 1865. The questions of Gen. Sherman and the Secretary of War were reduced to writing and read to the persons present. The answers were made by the Rev. Garrison Frazier, who was selected by the other ministers and church members to answer them. The answers were written down in his exact words, and read over to the others, who one by one expressed his concurrence or dissent as above set forth.'' (Signed) E. D. Townsend, Asst. Adjt. Gen. (From the Records of the Office of The Adjutant General, R. G. No. 94, War Records Branch, National Archives.)

the other persons present, being questioned one by one, answered that they agree with Brother Frazier).

5. Do you think there is intelligence enough among the slaves of the South to maintain themselves under the Government of the United States and the equal protection of its laws, and maintain good and peaceable relations among yourselves and with your neighbors?

Reply: I think there is sufficient intelligence among us to do so.

6. State what is the feeling of the black population of the South toward the Government of the United States; and what is the understanding in respect to the present war—its causes and object, and their disposition to aid either side. State fully your views.

Reply: I think you will find there are thousands that are willing to make any sacrifice to assist the Government of the United States, while there are also many that are not willing to take up arms. I do not suppose there are a dozen men that are opposed to the Government. I understand, as to the war, that the South is the aggressor. President Lincoln was elected President by a majority of the United States, which guaranteed him the right of holding the office and exercising that right over the whole of the United States. The South, without knowing what he would do, rebelled. The war was commenced by the Rebels before he came into office. The object of the war was not at first to give the slaves their freedom, but the sole object of the war was at first to bring the rebellious States back into the Union and their loyalty to the laws of the United States. Afterward, knowing the value set on the slaves by the Rebels, the President thought that his proclamation would stimulate them to lay down their arms, reduce them to obedience, and help bring back the Rebel States; and their not doing so has now made the freedom of the slaves a part of the war. It is my opinion that there is not a man in this city that could be started to help the Rebels one inch, for that would be suicide. There were two black men left with the Rebels because they had taken an active part for the Rebels, and thought something might befall them if they stayed behind, but there is not another man. If the prayers that have gone up for the Union Army could be read out, you would not get through them these two weeks.

7. State whether the sentiments you now express are those only of the colored people in the city, or do they extend to the colored population throughout the country, and what are your means of knowing the sentiments of those living in the country?

Reply: I think the sentiments are the same among the colored people of the State. My opinion is formed by personal communication in the course of my ministry, and also from the thousands that follow the Union Army, leaving their homes and undergoing much suffering. I did not think there would be so many; the number surpassed my expectation.

8. If the Rebel leaders were to arm the slaves what would be its effect?

Reply: I think they would fight as long as they were before the bayonet, and just as soon as they could get away, they would desert, in my opinion.

9. What, in your opinion, is the feeling of the colored people about enlisting and serving as soldiers of the United States? What kind of military service do they prefer?

Reply: A large number have gone as soldiers to Port Royal to be drilled and put in the service; and I think there are thousands of the young men that would enlist. They have suffered so long from the Rebels that they want to shoulder the musket. Others want to go into the Quartermaster's or Commissary's service.

10. Do you understand the mode of enlistments of colored persons in the Rebel States by State agents under the act of Congress? If yea, state what your understanding is.

Reply: My understanding is that colored persons enlisted by State agents are enlisted as substitutes, and give credit to the States, and do not swell the Army, because every black man enlisted by a State agent leaves a white man at home; and also, that larger bounties are given or promised by the State agents than are given by the States. The great object should be to push through this Rebellion the shortest way, and there seems to be something wanting in the enlistment by State agents, for it don't strengthen the army, but takes one away for every colored man enlisted.

11. State, what, in your opinion, is the best way to enlist colored men for soldiers.

Reply: I think sir, that all compulsory operations should be put a stop to. The ministers would talk to them, and the young men would enlist. It is my opinion that it would be far better for the State agents to stay at home, and the enlistment to be made for the United States under the direction of General Sherman.

In the absence of General Sherman, the following question was asked by Secretary Stanton:

12. State what is the feeling of the colored people in regard to General Sherman, and how far do they regard his sentiments and actions as friendly to their rights and interests, or otherwise?

Reply: We looked upon General Sherman, prior to his arrival as a man in the Providence of God especially set apart to accomplish this work, and we unanimously feel inexpressible gratitude to him, looking upon him as a man that should be honored for the faithful performance of his duty. Some of us called upon him immediately upon his arrival, and it is probable he would not meet the Secretary with more courtesy than he met us. His conduct and deportment toward us characterized him as a friend and a gentlemen. We have confidence in General Sherman, and think that what concerns us could not be under better hands. This is our opinion now from the short acquaintance and interest we have had. (Mr. Lynch states that with his limited acquaintance with General Sherman, he is unwilling to express his opinion. All others present declare their agreement with Mr. Frazier about General Sherman).

To the Secretary's request that Sherman leave the room before he addressed his final question regarding the attitude of the freedmen toward the general, Sherman has recorded the following reaction: "It certainly was a strange fact that the great Secretary should have catechized negroes concerning the character of a general who had commanded a hundred thousand men in battle, had captured cities, conducted sixty-five thousand men successfully across four hundred miles of hostile territory, and had just brought tens of thousands of freedmen to a place of security; but because I had not loaded down my army by the hundreds of thousands of poor negroes, I was construed by others to be hostile to the black race."[6] While there may be some doubt concerning the wisdom of such a question, and the ends to be gained by asking it, there can be little quarrel with the procedure taken by the Secretary of War. In view of the events of the period, a free and uninhibited answer could be expected only in the absence of the general.

Mr. Stanton has also provided us with a record of his reaction to the Savannah meeting. In remarks to Mr. Beecher, Mr. Stanton stated that for the first time in the history of this nation, the representatives of the government had gone to these "poor debased people to ask them what they wanted for themselves."[7]

The immediate result of the Savannah conference was

[6] *Memoirs of General W. T. Sherman*, Vol. II, p. 247.
[7] *New York Daily Tribune*, Monday, February 13, 1865.

Special Field Orders No. 15.[8] This order issued by Sherman, 1. set apart and reserved for settlement of Negroes the islands from Charleston south, the abandoned rice fields along the rivers for thirty miles back from the sea, and the country bordering on the St. Johns River, Florida; 2. provided that at Beaufort, Hilton Head, Savannah, Fernandina, St. Augustine, and Jacksonville, Negroes were to remain in their chosen or accustomed vocations, but in the area set apart (above) they were to be the only settlers, and no whites except authorized military personnel were to reside; that the freedmen were to have sole management of their own affairs, subject only to United States military authority and acts of Congress; that they were not subject to forced military service except by authority of the President or Congress, and domestics and artisans were free to select their own work and residence, but young men were to be encouraged to enlist in the service of the United States to help maintain their freedom, and secure their rights as citizens, those enlisting to be paid, fed, and clothed according to law, the bounties paid upon enlistment, with consent of the recruit, to go to assist his family; 3. stipulated that whenever three heads of families selected a plot on which they desired to settle, the Inspector of Settlements and Plantations was to issue a license and assist in settlement, allowing each head of family a miximum of forty acres of tillable land, and through the use of one or more captured vessels, requisitioned from the Quartermaster as required, the Inspector was to provide for the transportation between the settlement of necessaries for the settlers, and of their marketable produce; 4. provided that Negroes enlisting in the military service of the United States, engaged on gunboats or in fishing, or in navigation of inland waters, could settle their families on any one of

[8] Special Field Orders No. 15, Headquarters, Military Division of the Mississippi. In the field, Savannah, Ga., Jan. 16, 1865.

the settlements at their pleasure without being present in person, but no one else except an actual settler, unless away on government business would be allowed to settle in absentia. Paragraph No. 5 of the order created the office of Inspector of Settlements and Plantations, and Paragraph No. 6 designated Brigadier General R. Saxton as Inspector. The order was effective throughout the Department of the South.

On February 3, 1865, the *Savannah Herald* reported that a huge mass meeting of the freedmen of Savannah and vicinity had been held the previous day, February the 2nd, at the Second Baptist Church, at which time the then Major General R. Saxton, Commanding General, Department of the South, explained the details of the order, and urged all to "enter at once upon the business of locating where they could support themselves and families in comfort and peace, by their own industry, calling no man master, and with none to deprive them of the fruits of their toil".[9]

True the freedmen who participated in the meeting at Savannah were from a single section of the geographical South, but the hopes, dreams, ambitions, and aspirations expressed by them can be regarded as fairly representative of freedmen everywhere. Unfortunately, the restoration of Southern control in the post-Reconstruction period, with its intimidation, violence, and systematic circumvention of all legal safeguards against oppression, served to shatter the brightest dreams, and the vision of "forty acres and a mule" faded in the face of the revival of practical Southern politics.[10]

An examination of the sober, thoughtful replies to the

[9] This meeting was called for the purpose of implementing General Sherman's order. However, the basis of this order, the Confiscation Act of 1862, providing for the confiscation of the property of certain classes of Confederates, was never put into effect.

[10] The Black Codes, voting restrictions, the Ku Klux Klan, etc.

questions put by Secretary Stanton, reveals something of the freedmen's mental processes and their view of a problem vital to the future of Negroes over the entire South. Question No. 4 was prophetic in that it broached a problem which continues in our own day to test the skill and patience of thoughtful Americans throughout the nation. It is interesting to note that even then there was not complete agreement concerning whether it was best for Negroes and whites to live in completely integrated communities, or be separated by rigid barriers imposed by law and custom.

". . . . what is the feeling of the black population of the South toward the Government of the United States; what is the understanding in respect to the war—its causes and object, and their disposition to aid either side. State fully your views." The answer to this question (No. 6) is particularly significant in the light of the myths and romanticism which shrouded the thinking of the first post-slavery generations of Negroes. By replying that the object of the war was not "to give the slaves their freedom", but to bring the rebellious states back into the Union, the spokesman, and those who sanctioned his words, showed incredible insight and comprehension regarding the basic causes of the Rebellion. Such appreciation for the fundamental issues of the great struggle was not always in evidence in later years during which Lincoln and the Republican Party were pictured as saviors and great humanitarians rather than practitioners of the cold and often inhumane art of politics; as great and magnanimous gods who bestowed the gift of freedom upon four million blacks out of the fullness of their hearts. This served to insure Negro support of the Republican Party for many years. In fact, not until the election of Franklin D. Roosevelt in 1932 can it be said that Negroes deserted the Republican Party to any appreciable extent.

The position of Mr. James Lynch, the lone dissenter

in the group, is deserving of special consideration. Being a dissenter he stands out; further, being free-born, from the North, and only two years in the South, and the youngest of the representatives, he was probably regarded as an outsider and a radical. While two years in the South as a missionary had given him an opportunity to observe firsthand the elements of the problems confronting the freedmen, it was hardly enough time to become a part of the total scene with all its passions and emotions. The experience of bondage and sudden liberation, was an experience which had played no part in the development of his basic attitudes and approaches to the problems evolving from such an experience. Therefore, he could sincerely take a position opposed to that of the majority, or reserve his opinion until some future date. Lynch was not necessarily objective, as it may appear at first glance. It is doubtful if he had sufficient information or experience to arrive at an objective view of the situation; but his attitude was to be encountered with increasing frequency over a wider and wider area in the "new Negro"—a more skeptical, and a more aggressive Negro.

JOSEF C. JAMES

The National Archives
Washington, D. C.

THE ATTEMPTED CONVERSION OF JAMES L. ORR

James L. Orr, South Carolina's most powerful representative in the Congress of the United States, had reason to believe that his earthly fortunes had made handsome progress in the year 1856 when he received the following sobering letter from Alfred.[1] As the leader of the National Democrats Orr had seemingly won a permanent victory over those who would have led his state into immediate seces-

[1] Alfred to James L. Orr, June 29, 1856, Orr-Patterson Papers, Southern Historical Collection, University of North Carolina.

sion; he had persuaded South Carolina to send a delegation to the Democratic convention at Cincinnati, a distinct reversal of Calhoun's policy of isolation and the first group from the Palmetto state ever to participate in a national political convention, and as a reward for these nationalistic efforts it was generally understood that he would be the next speaker of the House of Representatives.[2] Even the presidency did not seem beyond the bounds of possibility. Alfred's letter written in a bold, highly legible script washed in on this high tide of Orr's affairs. There can be little doubt that it gave pause to the somewhat worldly Carolinian, for he carefully saved it though little else of his personal correspondence remains.[3]

Alfred's communication has interesting psychological and historical overtones for, though the writer stated that he would "not dare to teach", it is a not entirely unwarranted assumption that he was here asserting his equality and even superiority in a field and in a manner which Orr could not easily resent or reply to with retribution. At once one speculates that religion, beyond its obvious solace, may have offered to many of Alfred's kindred spirits just such avenues of soul satisfying expressions of earthly equality. Historical interest is derived from the fact that Orr, as the governor of South Carolina from 1865 to 1868, was one of the few ante-bellum Southern leaders who earned the respect of both races in those troubled times. In the euphemism of the day he "accepted the situation" and believed that the political and civil equality and co-operation of all men was the only sure foundation in which to rear the future of the region.[4]

[2] Laura A. White, "The National Democrats in South Carolina, 1852 to 1860," South Atlantic Quarterly, October 1929.

[3] Hext M. Perry, ed., Remiscences of Public Men by Ex-Governor B. F. Perry (Philadelphia, 1883), pp. 179-186.

[4] A. K. McClure, undated and untitled newspaper clipping in Jehu Orr Papers, Southern Historical Collection, University of North Carolina; Francis B. Simkins, "James L. Orr," Dictionary of American Biography (New York, 1934) 14, 59-60.

Greenville [S. C.]
29 June, 1856

Dear Master,

You will pardon your servant Alfred, for the liberty . . . in writing to you. You have done me much kindness and I hope that I feel thankful to you for it. But as I owe you all my service I cannot express how much good I wish you unless you allow me to speak of a good that is more precious than any service my hands can render.

I think of you often and I feel concerned for you; not that the world don't show you honor, nor that you are in want of the friendship of man, or the love of kind friends; but this is the thing most concerns me; for you to seek to be honored as a child of God; to have your name witness in the Saintshood of life—that you may take the friendship of God and that you may be a companion of the Saints. Now you know that I would not dare to teach; but I hope you will allow me to remind you that after all the honors and friendships of this world are gone that you will need what God above can give you, even his friendship and love, & you know that these things must be gained before you die, and when I think how much you are engaged for the good of the country & how such things call the mind away from religion, I feel very uneasy about you. Do don't let Jesus miss you. & when I think of the sickness you are exposed to constantly where there are so many people, from every part of the world, & when I think of the dangers that are all around you, from the malice of your enemies, & when I think of the dangers of travelling on water & on land I am uneasy—I am afraid that you might be cut off from this life before you are prepared. Then all your life would be lost to yourself. Let not these things be so—But I desire you 'to seek the Lord where he may be found & to call upon him while he is near'. Let your humble servant beg you to make peace with God, then you will be stronger to serve the country & you will be safe from all harm & you will be helped. I would rather you would be a Christian than to be king & would rather you had the friendship of God if the whole world pressed upon you. Do this 'Seek first the Kingdom of God & his righteousness'. For Christ says 'What shall it profit a man, should he gain the whole world & lose his own soul, & what shall a man give in exchange for his soul?' My Dear Master accept these few words as the sincere love of Alfred for I do want you to be happy in a hereafter.

May God help you with bounteous good wishes & prayer for you. I am your unworthy servant   Alfred
To My Master
    James L. Orr Washington City, District of Columbia
                                            WILLIAM A. FORAN

University of South Carolina

BOOK REVIEWS

The Souls of Black Folk. By W. E. Burghardt DuBois. (New York. The Blue Heron Press. 1953. Pp. 264.)

It is quite fitting that *The Souls of Black Folk* should be reprinted to mark the fiftieth anniversary of its original publication. The work is a landmark in both the literary and social history of the American Negro, and its re-publication will serve a twofold purpose: it will give to this new and much freer generation of Negroes a vivid picture of the social and spiritual handicaps under which their parents labored; and for those of us who grew up in the first decades of the century, it will serve to remind us of the great debt we owe to Dr. DuBois for the intellectual and spiritual leadership he gave us during those "darker" years.

After such a statement, it may seem odd to assert that my first impression of *The Souls of Black Folk* is that the book is surprisingly objective and sane. Viewed from the vantage point of 1954, the work seems almost reactionary. Accustomed as we are to the strident clamorings of present day left wing protest, we are shocked at the "tory" attitude which DuBois takes towards the black peasant, the poor white, and the upper class of both groups. For example, if we saw the following lines (from page 176) printed by themselves, we would scarcely attribute them to the militant Dr. DuBois:

> I should be the last to deny the patent weaknesses and shortcomings of the Negro people; I should be the last to withhold sympathy from the white South in its efforts to solve its intricate social problems. I freely acknowledge that it is possible, and sometimes best, that a partially undeveloped people should be ruled by the best of their stronger and better neighbors for their own good, until such times as they can start and fight the world's battles alone.

How much more "reasonable" could a Negro be without actually putting on a bandana! And yet the above lines are typical. There are many similar statements in the book.

In spite of its basic reasonableness, *The Souls of Black Folk* was anathematized by the white South. The work was branded as

This book with its impressive bibliography and heavy documentation represents a scholarly approach to the solution of a challenging premise. Unfortunately, the promise of its fundamental theory is lost in the unacceptable quality of its conclusions.

Dr. Fisher's premise is predicated on his belief that the folk songs of the slave constitute "oral historical documents"; and, when properly "decoded", they illumine his innermost thoughts on religion, relations with his masters, aspirations for the future, and all the multitudinous problems faced by a people held in crushing bondage. This is interesting because the historical method has not been applied previously to Negro folk songs in the exhaustive manner here attempted. Folk-lorists and musicologists have long recognized that folk music reflects faithfully unique racial characteristics as well as the day to day experiences of a people. They have recognized also that ambiguity often veils the underlying meaning of the text. Dr. Fisher's belief that the Negro was devious, in both talk and act, is doubtlessly true. It was a device, mandatory for survival. The assertion of deviousness in his religion, however, is quite another matter. The evidence presented to prove support for the American Colonization Movement when the slave sang his "yonder" and "wish" songs is not completely convincing. By the same token, one cannot accept as fact that "Jordan", "Deep River", "Moses", "Heaven", and "Home" were representative of linguistic double talk, indicating intense yearning to return to Africa; nor, that the master of the plantation and not his God, was the addressee when he sang "Lord, I want to be a Christian". It is possible that Dr. Fisher does not differentiate carefully enough between the characteristic double talk of secular Negro folk-lore and the intense religious quality of his sacred music. He seems also to mistake superficial resemblance for significant fact. This can happen if enthusiasm for a hypothesis is allowed to cloud the complete objectivity so imperative in this difficult area of speculative scholarship.

The first chapter of the book deals in large measure with African traits and history in the music of Negroes. This lays a ground plan for the theory that "Negro music was the omnibus which carried forward the entire African cult". It explains also "the genesis of the so-called 'secret strain' theory that Negro music was a sort of secret password into the lives of the slaves". The final chapter is devoted to minor considerations of the music itself and its effect on the American scene. The discussions of the remaining seven chapters concern themselves almost entirely with the texts and massive historical data. This seems unfortunate. For, one cannot divorce completely the meaning, beauty, pathos, and moving quality of the music from its text, and hope to arrive at sound conclusions concerning characteristics and essential meanings. Indeed, in terms of the manner in which this book unfolds, it might well have been entitled, "Slave Texts in the Songs of the Negro".

Dr. Fisher limits his study chiefly to the songs of the 18th and 19th centuries and eliminates consideration of earliest slave songs. This makes his task more difficult and his responsibility greater. For in these, convincing demonstration of vestiges of word influence, expression, and African culture is the more difficult. His procedural scheme, by means of word elision and word substitution, is too speculative in his hands, to be acceptable completely as substantive interpretation. His attempts to date songs, their places of origin, their reference to persons and events, their true messages and their expression of intense longing to return to Africa are too often based on insufficient or inconclusive evidence. This is regrettable because Dr. Fisher's book is stimulating, and the idea, as applied to the folksongs of the Negro, is challenging.

WARNER LAWSON

Howard University

The Valley of Democracy, The Frontier Versus The Plantation In The Ohio Valley, 1776-1818, by John D. Barnhart. (Bloomington, Indiana, University Press, 1953, pp. X, 329, $5.00.)

When Frederick Jackson Turner directed attention to the influence of the frontier and free land on the growth of democracy at the American Historical Association in 1892, there opened a new era of historical interpretation and re-writing of American history.

The Valley of Democracy, a social science series publication, at the University of Indiana, by John D. Barnhart, professor of history, is a study of the frontier in the Ohio Valley which adheres to the principles of the Turner thesis. From 1776 to 1818, the line between civilization and the wilderness was being pushed westward from the Alleghenies to the Mississippi River and beyond. Beginning with the movement of the colonizers across the mountains, Professor Barnhart has described the struggle of the frontiersman against the land speculator and planter for control of the government in the new states of the Ohio River watershed. So detailed are his descriptions of routes "o'er the mountains", it is surprising that the writer over-looked the

"Buffalo Trail" through the Greenbrier, New, and Great Kanawha River valleys to the Ohio. Though Kentucky and Tennessee were won by the planter force, contends the writer, the struggle resulted in a radical form of democracy. With the states north of the Ohio River being formed under federal control there was more opportunity for "freer expression of frontier democracy" than in those south of the river where the struggle was against the tidewater states domination. Starting with Kentucky, Professor Barnhart has analyzed the constitutions of each state: Tennessee, Ohio, Indiana and Illinois. In every instance he showed, that while following the general pattern of the previously formed state, an original development in frontier democracy was contributed by each.

Writing on the assumption that all Negroes were slaves, the author failed to realize that Tennessee was the only one of the new states to grant the free Negro suffrage rights. While he does state that the constitution of Tennessee granted "free manhood suffrage" (p. 118), in other chapters he explains that suffrage was restricted to "white males" in Ohio, Indiana and Illinois.

The thirty-two pages of bibliographical notes are indicative of wide and extensive research in preparation for *The Valley of Democracy*. Though much of the material is not new, the writer has drawn upon many newspaper sources of that time for opinion.

Professor Barnhart has attempted to show that "the frontier did not originate democracy, but rather those characteristics which made it western or American." The crux of the idea for this study is best expressed by the author in that "the history of democracy in the Ohio Valley reveals the difference between the civilization of Europe and that of the United States, and gives us an historical basis for the hope that we as a people may continue to have a history of our own, a history that is unique" (p. 234).

In the present world struggle over issues of democracy, *The Valley of Democracy* poses many questions for thought. The book is an analytical treatment of the struggle for control of the government in the states of the Ohio Valley, however, the extent of democracy in that concept may be a matter of opinion.

J. REUBEN SHEELER

Texas Southern University

Race, Jobs and Politics, The Story of FEPC. By Louis Ruchames. (New York: Columbia University Press, 1953. Pp. 255. Price $3.75.)

This writer has made a substantial contribution to the literature which deals with the activities of the President's Fair Employment Practice Committee. In developing the chapter of "Origins" Ruchames discusses the transition by the Negro from an "amorphous" grouping during and following World War I to his mass pressure tactics of the World War II period. These techniques were enhanced by the growing political maturity and strength of the Negro and other minorities whose support was fundamental; by increasing war manpower and selective service demands; and by an international situation which made it more imperative for the United States to seek more allies by virtue of its improved treatment of its minority groups. In addition to these and other factors, it was the threatened march on Washington which was a basic causal factor behind President Franklin D. Roosevelt's issuance of Executive Order 8802 that created the Fair Employment Practice Committee.

This pressure technique represented a distinct departure from the conventional protest methods which the Negro had used. It dismayed some of his friends even though they agreed with his slogan: "We are fighting for the right to work for democracy." As militant Negroes moved to create the National Council for a Permanent FEPC they transcended racial, creedal and nationality lines. By this process they gained adherents and enlarged the movement for economic equality which is a basic ingredient of democracy.

In a technical sense Ruchames differentiated between the activities of what he labeled as "The First Committee" and "The Second Committee." Actually, Executive Order 9346 which lifted FEPC out of the confines and control of the War Manpower Commission did not supersede Executive Order 8802 which originally created FEPC. Senator Richard Russell, a staunch alert foe, recognized the agency's continuous legal existence even (under two executive orders) by introducing an amendment compelling federal executive order agencies over a year old to seek Congressional appropriations instead of being financed out of the President's Emergency Fund. Since Russell's amendment was designed to hamper FEPC, it would not have done so at the time it was introduced if the agency's functional existence had been divided into two segments.

As this study unfolds the author is quite effective in dealing with the investigations of the Smith Committee, "Congress and the FEPC", "The Philadelphia Rapid Transit Case" and the termination of "The Second Committee". Structurally, it seems that it would have been better to have discussed "The Committee in Structure and Function" before dealing with its demise. This reviewer also thinks that the structural arrangement of this study would have been further improved if the final chapter titled "The Movement for Permanent FEPC Legislation" had preceded the one on "FEPC Legislation and American Society".

In order to strengthen his study Ruchames should have given more space to an analysis of the devices which blocked Negroes and other minorities from training for defense jobs; and to the restrictive membership and job allocating techniques of color clause labor unions. Furthermore, it seems apparent that there should have been a more closely knit coverage of FEPC's hearings and a better orientation in terms of a time sequence.

In spite of these reactions Ruchames' book on *Race, Jobs and Politics* helps in an effective way to further reveal the historical importance of the President's Fair Employment Practice Committee. In this respect it will be catalogued with Malcolm Ross' *All Manner of Men*, Sara E. Southall's *Industry's Unfinished Business*, and Louis C. Kesselman's *The Social Politics of FEPC*, which was limited largely to a study of the National Council for a Permanent FEPC.

BRAILSFORD R. BRAZEAL

Morehouse College
Atlanta, Georgia

The Negro in Southern Agriculture. By Victor Perlo. (New York. International Publishers. 1953. Pp. 128. Price $1.00.)

The migration of Negroes from the South has attracted so much attention since 1914 that rural life and labor there have been neglected. Here is an investigation of the Southern agrarian system since World War II and the changes which are seriously affecting Negroes there and their status. The traditional plantation, farms, tenancy, cropping, and patterns of ownership have detailed exploration and analysis. Mechanization and diversification of crops with their concomitant impacts upon rural and urban labor show that, while many outmoded old practices survive, the pressures of local forces and restrictions have become nearly impossible for Negroes to combat. Here are descriptions of the various types of farmers, tenants, ownership, and increasingly rigid controls in which Negroes compete or struggle to exist according to the wills of whites whose authority is supreme. Such fundamental problems as nutrition and the tardy advent of scientific agricultural methods reveal Negroes in the South today with practically no hope for remedying their wretched rural conditions except flight to towns and other regions.

Perlo's investigation is primarily concerned with the plantation South of the Carolinas, Georgia, Alabama, Mississippi, Louisiana, and some sections of Virginia, Tennessee, Arkansas, and Texas. The author compares the system with contemporary forms of feudal land tenure in backward countries abroad to which Point Four aid is too grudgingly being sent. His charge, however, that monopoly capital is deliberately using the agrarian system to exploit labor in general (implies what he mistakenly suspects) is open to challenge as a pure and simple example of Marxist contentions. Obviously, the vast regions are a bastion of reaction which survives from slavery because of ignorance, poverty, and the too meager returns from staple crops of cotton, rice, sugar, and tobacco. Wealth in the rural South now, in contrast to the ante bellum days, has largely shifted to urban centers and more absentee ownership. The masses of Negroes that remain in agriculture and many poor whites have been disfranchised or kept awed and frightened by demagogues and politicians that prefer the smallest possible exercise of the ballot. Hence the author's research shows conclusively that in the plight of agrarianism is the real reason for the South's being the Nation's Economic Problem Number 1!

Mr. Perlo employs the *United States Census of Agriculture, 1950*. Volume I ''State Reports'' with data on the *United States Census of Population 1950*, Chapter B, ''State Multiple Units Operations'', Special reports, Department of Agriculture, Tuskegee Institute findings, and investigations of the regional Experimental Stations. His interpretation of these sources reflects familiarity and acquaintance with economic and human factors which are involved. Moreover, he grasps so comprehensively and accurately the economic forces at work that he is able to interpret their social consequences for the Southern population. The work shows that, contrary to general opinion, the old plantation system is increasing instead of declining. Mechanization is rapidly displacing many rural workers who are drifting to overcrowded towns and cities or migrating to great industrial and other centers of the North. Negroes have gained very little entrance into growing Southern heavy industry beyond unskilled places not wanted by whites. Demands for meeting government grants-in-aid for purchasing lands are too difficult for Negroes in their poverty and oppression to meet. In cropping, tenancy, and co-called wage-tenure control by white operators there is literally peonage in that the Negro agrarian worker seldom sells his crop, and settlements consist of pittancies or the sale to him on credit of wornout jalopies by the absentee town owners of the lands. This means that the Negro agrarian laborers continue year after year in debt repeating the same hopeless routine, move to crowded towns and cities, or trek to the imagined promised lands in the North.

This timely investigation is invaluable in any consideration of life and labor among Negroes in the United States. In the first place, here is a panoramic view of the regrettable ignorance and poverty of ruralism at their worst in the nation for white and Negro. Colored migrants that have scattered in response to labor demands in the North since the cutting off of heavy foreign immigration have carried their Southern burdens of disadvantage with them for other sections and regions unduly to share. The investigation should convince leaders in human relations and the general social welfare that the plight of Negroes in the agrarian South is nationally of vital concern. The author not only sets forth a national responsibility, but he suggests ways of remedying it through improved land tenure, abolition of discrimination, and the ballot which is everyone's shield of protection against exploitation.

W. M. BREWER

Lyman Abbott, Christian Evolutionist. By Ira V. Brown (Cambridge. Harvard University Press. 1953. Pp. 303. Price $5.00.)

This may be considered a definitive biography of the New England Puritan, Lyman Abbott, whose eventful career spanned the crises of Civil War, Reconstruction, and America's participation in World War I. The work vividly portrays the life of a minister who was better known as a journalist although he was prominent as a lecturer and sometime reformer. He carefully selected his reforms, however, and viewed their liberal and subtler aspects through a glass darkly. While not trained in theology, Lyman Abbott appears to have given considerable attention to the higher religious criticism; toyed with labor and many other issues of his times; and included the social gospel to which he gave lip-service. His ministerial services were intermittent and the record reveals his most successful activities in Henry Ward Beecher's Plymouth Church, Brooklyn, New York from 1887-1899. Simultaneously, he edited the *Outlook* which he assumed in 1876 and continued until his death in 1922. The author has mirrored Abbott's many-sided adventures and his influence is described from prodigious research in the writings of this figure and from many other sources. The resulting portrait reflects a blend of narrative, descriptive, and analytical biographical elements assembled with masterly craftsmanship.

The biography originated in A. M. Schlesinger, Sr.'s intellectual and social historical seminars and the book uniquely treats a "critical period in American religion." The author's investigation is in strict historical fashion which veers considerably from the usual biographical approach, and this makes the work significant. It not only shows the devious endeavors of an Olympian Puritan, but at the same time integrates very much of the history with which he was identified. Here are accounts of pressures which made a call to the ministry inevitable; participation in the slavery controversy and Reconstruction very intriguing; and journalism's superb opportunities to treat issues and problems in the public life over nearly a half century. Although the interpretations are historical, they are so comprehensive that the subject seems to live again.

Abbott's approaches to reform are an illustration of the penetration and insight which appear throughout the exploration of his life. For example, the author explains that Abbott always discerned the directions of public opinion and scrupulously followed them. Indian policy, immigration, industrial democracy, immigration, Mahan's imperialism, and popularity of the social gospel are illustrations. Opportunism and adulation of wealth and power are obvious in Abbott's membership in Theodore Roosevelt's "Kitchen Cabinet". Likewise, his dissent against Washington Gladden's challenge of "tainted money" in gifts from Carnegie, Rockefeller, and other millionaires illustrates a preacher willing to walk with devils if they gave generously to causes which he considered worthy! There are accounts also of enthusiastic support for the advance of Northern capital in developing the "New South." Order there rather than real freedom of Negroes was Abbott's ideal as he joined Ogden parties on Southern educational tours. On these trips and through the columns of the *Outlook* he admonished Negroes to meditate not on the *Souls of Black Folk* by DuBois but on Booker Washington's *Future of the American Negro*. Disfranchisement and lynching did not call forth this Puritan's vaunted wrath because they were incidental harsh measures of white supremacy, necessary order, and control! He justified and rationalized war and armaments citing Jesus scourging the money changers from the temple and sending on occasion not peace but a sword. Firing pacifist professors and banning German music in World War I have Abbott's approval as means to noble ends.

The values of this historical evaluation of a minister, so-called reformer, and journalist transcend much of orthodox biography because they afford not only the record of a notable man, but many aspects of the history of the times in which he lived. The author cuts through details and has the subject tell his own story through ingenious interpretations. "He [Abbott] had an unusual faculty for sensing which way the wind was blowing and he generally charted his course accordingly." More accurately, "Never a profound student of any problem, his ideas were often superficial and his judgment hasty." For laymen and historians it is vitally important to have so much of American intellectual and social history interwoven in the biography of a man who lived between 1835 and 1922. The organization and style show that history in biography may attain high literary form. Thus Lyman Abbott's colorful life, shorn of adroit claims, appears in the cold light of history and is found wanting.

W. M. BREWER

Famous American Negroes. By Langston Hughes. (New York: Dodd, Mead and Company, 1954. Pp. 147. Price $2.75.)

Famous American Negroes, Langston Hughes' latest book, is written in the vein of his *The First Book of Negroes* (1952), and like that volume it exhibits a hand-picked assortment of vivid life stories of Negro Americans that spans two hundred years of American history from Phillis Wheatley to Jackie Robinson. Obviously, the book points up Mr. Hughes' versatility as a man of letters, his ability to keep on keeping on, and his ever-expanding concern for the education of the youth population of our time. Since *Famous American Negroes* adds up to the author's fifth piece of creative work addressed to American citizens of tomorrow, it might not be amiss to assume that he has come more and more to recognize the wisdom of attacking the American Negro-white problem by means of educating all American youth to understand and to appreciate all other American youth.

Like *The First Book of Negroes, Famous American Negroes* comes of the thin variety; some have even referred to it as an "in-between book.'' A short chapter has been devoted to each of the seventeen famous Negro Americans our poet-historian has elected to include—four more than one finds in Edwin R. Embree's *Thirteen against the Odds* (1944), and four less than are contained in Benjamin Richardson's *Great American Negroes* (1945). Explaining in the introduction of the book that ''there have been many famous Negro citizens in our country,'' Mr. Hughes, without suggesting the yardstick he employed, proceeded to select a crop of his own, for of his group only Marian Anderson and George Washington Carver are mentioned in either Edwin R. Embree's or in Benjamin Richardson's book. In the area of athletics, for instance, Jackie Robinson gets the nod over Joe Louis or Jessie Owens, and perhaps somewhat strangely, Gwendolyn Brooks, recent Pulitzer Prize winner in poetry comes in second to Phillis Wheatley and Paul Laurence Dunbar. But just the same, each person adequately represents some one aspect of American life.

Now some will perhaps charge that the book contains little or nothing that is new. That is of course contingent upon one's point of view. For the research student in American Literature, the point might conceivably hold, but for the teeming millions of America's growing boys and girls, Harriet Tubman's daring flight to freedom, Joe Louis' exploits in the prize ring, and Ralph Bunche's Nobel Prize winning ingenuity as Secretariat of the United Nations make absorbing reading in the American way of life.

A pronounced evenness, balance, and charm characterize the stories; each is ''full without overflowing'' and exhibits the fine facility of reaching a conclusion while the growing boy still asks for more. And despite the Darwinian note that is implied in their strivings and the added difficulty imposed by a black face, each of Mr. Hughes' heroes and heroines typifies the qualities that have made America great—courage, industry, foresight, integrity, and the gentle art of getting on in the world. In itself, each story is a sort of silent but a powerful *argumentum ad populum*. Implicit also in the totality of the situation is a sense of our gradual movement in the direction of the democratic ideal as set by the Declaration of Independence.

There will probably be none to deny that Langston Hughes' new book, *Famous American Negroes,* like its companion volume, *The First Book of Negroes,* will result in a wider and a fuller understanding of America's tenth man by America's vast youth group.

Fayetteville State College   JOHN W. PARKER

The History of Alpha Phi Alpha: A Development in College Life. By Charles H. Wesley. (Washington, D. C., The Foundation Publishers, 1953. Pp. 526. Price $5.00.)

This is a definitive history, if such a phrase is permissible, of the oldest Negro college fraternity in the United States; and the author has done a Herculean task of amassing every detail great or little. Following an attempt to link the American fraternity movement with the German university Korps, and through them with the guilds of medieval Europe, the writer launches into a discussion of the founding of the society. In its infancy it wavered between a social-literary club and a fraternity. Finally, the fraternity idea won out, not without opposition and a loss of some original members; and the Alpha Phi Alpha Fraternity was launched as a group of Cornell University students in Ithaca, New York, in 1906.

Following the normal development of a college fraternity dedicated to such things as high scholarship, social exclusiveness, secret ritual, handclasps, and initiations designed to strike fear into the heart of the neophyte (every once in a while the arcana had to be revised as the master grips were becoming the common property of *hoi polloi*) the fraternity spread by founding chapters throughout many of the colleges and universities of America. However, the viewpoint of the fraternity was immature —possibly the immaturity characteristic of America of that day. The outbreak of World War I evinced no comment on the part of the brothers assembled in convention in that fateful year of 1914.

A sign of more social and reflective thinking appeared in 1916 with the *Go To High School, Go to College* drive in that year; and by 1921 there was some thinking on the effects of Negro migration. By 1930 the fraternity had set up scholarships and a Foundation.

The 1930's, the decade of the Depression, saw a break with the rah! rah! college boy ideal of the 1920's. The Scottsboro case, the cases of Murray vs. the University of Maryland, and Lloyd Gaines vs. the University of Missouri are not only discussed, but are actively aided. The fraternity had taken official cognizance of the position of the Negro in the socio-political scheme of things. Throughout this decade the issues of the New Deal and social legislation are discussed at the conventions, or written up in the *Sphinx.*

The war decade of the 1940's continued the significant social interest as well as the concern in the part that Negroes were to play in the war effort. The fraternity had grown up enough to become critical of its own goals as we witness in the discussions of "Is Education a Curse to Society" and "Distinguished Negro Educators and Educated Fools". The fraternity also widened its horizon to become international in scope, inviting Norman W. Manley, leader of the People's Party of Jamaica, B. W. I., to be keynote speaker at the Chicago convention in 1945. In the same convention Hilyard Robinson, designer of the buildings for the Liberian Centennial, may be said to represent the African view. Other indications of this social maturity are the banning of brutality in initiation, the alliance of the fraternity with other Negro fraternities and sororities in the Council on Human Rights, and the raising of such questions as: the "Dilemma of Democracies" and "Attitudes on Colonialism".

In evaluating the book, we must remember that it is written by the official historiographer of the fraternity so that many activities and claims are viewed in a most roseate hue. To be realistic, we must remember that other social forces and agencies were working at the same time on the same problems and that Alpha Phi Alpha led, or was dragged by the force of the main current. Occasionally it slips out that all was not sweetness and light within the organization as the constant addresses harping on fraternal loyalty in the yearly conventions would indicate. And from time to time we note that one-third of the chapters were unfinancial, or not represented at the conventions. A large group wanted the fraternity to remain socially exclusive and a badge of educational achievement. Nevertheless, the work does afford a comprehensive account of the oldest Negro college fraternity in America. As such it is a contribution to understanding the intellectual, cultural, and social strivings of young and some mature colored college men during the last half century.

THEODORE G. MILES

Armstrong High School
Washington, D. C.

A BIBLIOGRAPHY OF RECENT PUBLICATIONS ON NEGRO HISTORY[1]

By Harold T. Pinkett

UNITED STATES

BOOKS

FISHER, MILES M. *Negro Slave Songs in the United States.* Foreword by Ray Allen Billington. Ithaca: Cornell University Press. 1953. Pp. 223. $4.00.

GREENWAY, JOHN. *American Folk Songs of Protest.* Philadelphia: University of Pennsylvania Press. 1953. Pp. x, 348. $6.75.

HOLDREDGE, HELEN. *Mammy Pleasant.* New York: Putnam. 1953. Pp. 311. $4.50.

HOPE, JOHN II. *Negro Employment in Three Southern Plants of International Harvester Company.* Washington: National Planning Association. 1953. Pp. 143. $1.75.

LEFLER, HUGH AND NEWSOME, ALBERT. *North Carolina: The History of a Southern State.* Chapel Hill: University of North Carolina Press. 1953. $7.50.

LOGAN, RAYFORD W. *The Negro in American Life and Thought. The Nadir: 1877-1901.* New York: Dial Press. 1954. Pp. 384. $5.00.

MALIN, JAMES C. *The Nebraska Question, 1852-1854.* Lawrence, Kansas: Edward Brothers, Inc. 1953. Pp. ix, 455. $4.00.

MOORE, GLOVER. *The Missouri Controversy, 1819-1821.* Lexington: University of Kentucky Press. 1953. Pp. viii, 383. $6.00.

NICHOLS, LEE. *Breakthrough on the Color Front.* New York: Random House. 1954. Pp. 235. $3.50.

RUCHAMES, LOUIS. *Race, Jobs and Politics.* New York: Columbia University Press. 1953. Pp. 255. $3.75.

SELECTIVE SERVICE SYSTEM. *Special Groups.* Washington: Government Printing Office. 1953. Pp. xv, 212.

SITTERSON, JOSEPH C. *Sugar Country, the Cane Sugar Industry in the South, 1753-1950.* Lexington: University of Kentucky Press. 1953. Pp. 414. $6.00.

ARTICLES

BEAN, WILLIAM G. The Ruffner Pamphlet of 1847: An Antislavery Aspect of Virginia Sectionalism. *Virginia Magazine of History and Biography,* July, 1953.

BOWLES, CHESTER. The Negro—Progress and Challenge. *New York Times Magazine,* Feb. 7, 1954.

COBB, W. MONTAGUE. Daniel Hale Williams. *Journal of the National Medical Association,* Sept., 1953.

DANTE, HARRIS L. Reconstruction History: Recent Interpretations. *Social Education,* Feb., 1954.

[1] This bibliography does not include articles published in the *Journal of Negro History.*

DAVIS, EDWIN A. William Johnson: Free Negro Citizen of Ante-Bellum Mississippi, *Journal of Mississippi History*, Apr., 1953.

DESANTIS, VINCENT P. President Arthur and the Independent Movements in the South in 1882. *Journal of Southern History*, Aug., 1953.

DWYER, ROBERT J. The Negro in the United States Army. *Sociology and Social Research*, Nov.-Dec., 1953.

KAPLAN, SIDNEY. Lewis Temple and the Hunting of the Whale. *Negro History Bulletin*, Oct., 1953.

MANDEL, BERNARD. Slavery and the Southern Workers. *Negro History Bulletin*, Dec., 1953.

——————————. Antislavery and the Southern Workers. *Ibid.*, Feb., 1954.

McNAIR, CECIL E. Reconstruction in Bullock County. *'Alabama Historical Quarterly*, Spring, 1953.

MEIER, AUGUST. Booker T. Washington and the Rise of the NAACP. *Crisis*, Feb., 1954.

PARKER, MARJORIE H. Some Educational Activities of the Freedmen's Bureau. *Journal of Negro Education*, Winter, 1954.

PRICE, EDWARD T. A Geographic Analysis of White-Negro-Indian Racial Mixtures in the Eastern United States. *Annals of the Association of American Geographers*, June, 1953.

REDDICK, L. D. As I Remember Woodson. *Negro History Bulletin*, Nov., 1953.

RUTLAND, ROBERT. Iowans and the Fourteenth Amendment. *Iowa Journal of History*, Oct., 1953.

SISK, GLENN N. Negro Migration in the Alabama Black Belt, 1875-1917. *Negro History Bulletin*, Nov., 1953.

STARR, ISIDORE. Recent Supreme Court Decisions: Racial Discrimination. *Social Education*, Jan., 1954.

TAYLOR, PAUL S. Plantation Laborer Before the Civil War. *Agricultural History*, Jan., 1954.

THORPE, MARGARET N. AND MORTON, RICHARD L. A "Yankee Teacher" in North Carolina. *North Carolina Historical Review*, Oct., 1953.

WESLEY, CHARLES H. The Association [for the Study of Negro Life and History] and the Public. *Negro History Bulletin*, Jan., 1954.

LATIN AMERICA AND THE WEST INDIES

BOOKS

International Bank for Reconstruction and Development. *The Economic Development of British Guiana*. Baltimore: Johns Hopkins Hopkins. 1954. Pp. 366. $6.00.

MARCHANT, ALEXANDER (ed.). *Proceedings of the International Colloquium on Luso-Brazilian Studies*. Nashville: Vanderbilt University Press. 1953. Pp. xii, 332.

VON SCHOEN, WILHELM FREIHERR. *Geschichte Mittel-und Südamerikas*. Munich: Verlag F. Bruckmann. 1953. Pp. 698 DM 27.80.

ARTICLES

ANTOINE, JACQUES C. Haiti and the Louisiana Purchase. *Crisis*, Jan., 1954.

HUGHES, C. A. Semi-Responsible Government in the British West Indies. *Political Science Quarterly*, Sept., 1953.

KING, JAMES F. A Royalist View of the Colored Castes in the Venezuelan War of Independence. *Hispanic American Historical Review*. Nov., 1953.

LANIER, CLÉMENT. La Relâche de Mina en 1816 à Port-au-Prince. *Revue de la societe haitienne, de geographic et de geologie*, Apr., 1953.

LOGAN, RAYFORD W. The United States Mission in Haiti. *Inter-American Economic Affairs*, Spring, 1953.

MASSIO, R. Chronique des sources privées de l'Histoire coloniale dans le Pays de Bigorre (1950-1952). *Revue de la societe haitienne, de geographie et de geologie*, Apr., 1953.

PAUL, EMMANUEL C. Bilan spirituel du Boyérisme (suite). *Ibid.*, Apr., July, 1953.

THOBY, PERCIVAL. Nos crises economiques et financières (suite), *Ibid.*

TROUILLOT, E. Louis Joseph Janvier, le Diplomate, *Ibid.*, July, 1953.

AFRICA

BOOKS

CALPIN, G. H. (ed.). *The South African Way of Life.* New York: Columbia University Press. 1954. Pp. 200. $3.50.

CORY, HANS. *Sukama Law and Custom.* New York and London: Oxford University Press. 1953. Pp. 194.

MILLIN, SARAH G. *The People of South Africa.* New York: Alfred A. Knopf. 1954. Pp. 337. $4.50.

WHITE, AMOS J. *Dawn in Bantuland, an African Experiment.* Boston: Christopher Publishing House. 1953. Pp. 297.

ARTICLES

BELOFF, M. Democracy in Africa. *African Affairs*, Apr., 1953.

BRADLEY, GLADYCE H. Education in Africa—The Problem of the Twentieth Century. *Journal of Negro Education*, Winter, 1954.

CARTER, GWENDOLEN M. Can Apartheid Succeed in South Africa? *Foreign Affairs*, Jan., 1954.

COMHAIRE, JUAN. African Warriors in the Belgian Congo. *Negro History Bulletin*, Dec., 1953.

DAVEY, H. W. The South African Territories. *Contemporary Review*, Jan., 1954.

DAVIES, MALCOM. Mau Mau Activities and the Unrest in Kenya. *Antioch Review*, Summer, 1953.

LITTLE, KENNETH. The Study of Social Change in British West Africa. *Africa*, Oct., 1953.

PADMORE, GEORGE. Behind the Mau Mau. *Phylon*, Fourth Quarter, 1953.

SCOTT, PETER. Migrant Labor in Southern Rhodesia. *Geographical Review*, Jan., 1954.

SHEPHERD, G. W. Mau Mau and Agricultural Development. *Crisis*, Jan., 1954.

GENERAL

INDEXES AND LISTS

ADAMS, JAMES N. *Index to the Transactions of the Illinois State Historical Library.* Springfield: Illinois State Historical Library. 1953. 2 vols. Pp. 663, 654.

FOLSOM, J. C. *Migratory Agricultural Labor in the United States—Annotated Bibliography of Selected References.* Washington: Government Printing Office. 1953. Pp. 64.

Library of Congress. *Negro Newspapers on Microfilm. A Selected List.* Washington. 1953. 15 cents.

National Archives and Records Service. *List of National Archives Microfilm Publications.* Washington. 1953. Pp. 98.

New York Public Library. *The Nation: Indexes of Titles and Contributors.* New York. 1951-53. 2 vols. Pp. 577, 539. $12.50 each.

Randall Albert Carter

On February 6, 1954, passed away Bishop Randall Albert Carter, one of the staunchest supporters of the Association through the years. He was born January 1, 1867, at Fort Valley, Georgia, and his parents were Tobias and Grace (Chivers) Carter. In 1884 he finished Allen University High School, Columbia, South Carolina, and was ordained a minister in the C.M.E. conference of that State in 1887. That year he entered Paine College and became the first and only graduate in the class of 1891. After graduation he married Miss Jane S. Hooks and to them was born one daughter, Grace. She and her mother died several years ago, and Bishop Carter's second marriage was to Mrs. Helen Word, who survives.

Bishop Carter's ministerial career prior to 1914, when he was elected to the bishopric, was spent largely in Georgia where he served several pastorates, but chiefly as presiding elder under Bishop L. H. Holsey. For many years he was behind the scenes "bishop de facto" as advisory aide to Bishop Holsey who early bestowed his blessings. These helped mightily in the election at the general conference of 1914 to the highest office in the church.

The dioceses which Bishop Carter first served were in Texas although he held some conferences in Mississippi. Later there were assignments in the District of Columbia region and several other jurisdictions, including Georgia where his active ministry had previously been. His last assignments were in the Middle West with centers of great interest in Chicago, Detroit, and St. Louis. In 1898 he became the first Secretary of the Epworth League in the C.M.E. church, but he soon resumed the presiding eldership in the Georgia conferences. These were his early parishes and in them he made his home until 1919. On the eve of the Chicago riots that year Bishop Carter moved to Chicago and resided there for the last thirty-four years. With the great migration of colored people from the South during and after World War I, Bishop Carter led in building and purchasing many churches—over 250 are credited to his efforts. In them he successfully provided havens for migrating C.M.E. communicants and others who were recruited as his church's bounds extended.

158

Bishop Carter represented the stalwart leadership of colored people (predominantly ministerial since the Civil War) who chose him and to their vital interests his uncompromising loyalty could never be questioned. His words in tribute to the slaughtered victims of the Chicago riots of 1919 and in support of the heroic defenders who survived are eloquent. He did not serve at any time as "special assistant advisor on Negro affairs" because he loathed opportunists who seek publicity and profit by bartering their people down the river! In distinguished ways he served colored people and his church as fraternal delegate to the M.E. General Conferences at Chicago in 1900, Kansas City in 1928, and Atlantic City in 1932. He was also a delegate from the C.M.E. church to the Ecumenical Conferences of Methodism in London, England, 1901, and Toronto, Canada, in 1921, and served on the Federal Council of the Churches of Christ in America.

While not a scholar in the technical sense or a trained theologian, Bishop Carter assembled his splendid thinking in *Morning Meditations*, 1917, *Feeding Among the Lilies* and *Canned Laughter*, 1923, *Brief Study of the Hebrew Prophets*, 1937, and *Scattered Fragments*, 1939. Among these works are his many addresses, sermons, and sayings which reveal the observations and thought of a leader who comprehended the aspirations and struggles of his people. In these writings are evident also religious statesmanship and ardent zeal for education. He implemented both in the building of Texas College, development of Mississippi College, and in devotion to Paine College, his alma mater, where Carter Hall stands as a memorial.

The Association for the Study of Negro Life and History ranked next in Bishop Carter's allegience to his church and Paine College. To the great founder, Dr. Carter Godwin Woodson, Bishop Carter was ever oak and rock through nearly forty years. When in 1930 philanthropy was drying up and that which remained was cut off from the Association by the clandestine machinations of Thomas Jesse Jones, a white minister, that would never have been known except for his self-appointed obtrusion in Negro education and life, Bishop Carter came to the rescue. He not only gave generously himself, but rallied his ministers who gladly joined him in the effort to sustain this learned society. After President Charles H. Wesley accepted the call to Association leadership in 1951, one of Bishop Carter's last wishes was to join him at the Detroit meeting in 1952. The dates of that meeting, however, conflicted with the dedication of Carter Hall at Paine College and he missed what he feared then might be his last meeting with the Association which regrets his going, but rejoices over his great contributions. Of him and his labors through four score and seven years of services to his church, colored people, and many causes it may be said: ''I have fought a good fight, I have finished my course, I have kept the faith.''

HALEY GEORGE DOUGLASS

Haley George Douglass died in Washington, D. C., January 21, 1954, and was the last surviving grandson of Frederick Douglass. Mr. Douglass's parents were Major Charles and Laura (Haley) Douglass and the son was born in Canandaigua, New York, November 27, 1881. At an early age the family brought him to Washington, D. C., where he was trained in elementary and secondary schools before entering Phillips Exeter Academy from which he graduated in the class of 1901 and entered Harvard that fall. There he participated in football, rowing, and track before finishing in 1905. His experiences at Cambridge were unique in several respects. Stemming out of his grandfather's acquaintance with President Eliot, young Douglass enjoyed the rare privilege of warm personal contact with that great educator. Moreover, his were the afternoon years of Harvard's Golden Age with such giants as James, Munsterberg, Royce, and a galaxy of other notables seldom equaled and never surpassed there. Graduation from the college then, as always, afforded admission to ''Harvard's rarest fellowship.'' Thousands have finished the professional and graduate schools, but the college alone is the gateway to Harvard's genuine fraternity and spirit which an alumnus is never supposed to mention.

Mr. Douglass married Miss Evelyn Dulaney in 1918, and she preceded him in death a little over two years. To them was born one daughter, Jean, who is now a student at Morgan State College. She and a son, Dean Joseph H. Douglass of Fayetteville, North Carolina State College survive. The latter has already distinguished himself, after training at Fisk and Harvard, and served as Fulbright Lecturer in Social Work in the University of Egypt at Cairo, 1952-1953. The father retired two years ago, and he was working on what he hoped would be the definitive life of Frederick Douglass. He had assembled many of the materials (his rare memories and oral traditions, however, may now be lost) and it is hoped that his brilliant son may in time complete the work. This Mr. Douglass fervently wished to be his crowning achievement and it is regrettable that he did not finish it.

Haley Douglass was a ''Harvard man'' and, true to that tradition, did not talk about it. Through fifty years he personified the ideal in Washington, D. C. and neighboring Maryland communities where his record refutes the dictum that a man is not without honor except in his own community. His career was full of activities including forty-six years of high school teaching in Washington, D. C., where he taught hundreds of boys and girls among whom were such men as Charles Drew, Charles Houston, William Hastie, and Ellis Rivers. His special subjects were natural sciences and history in which no student ever missed some of the inspiring tradition of Frederick Douglass which was a legitimate fascination. Mr. Douglass also trained athletic teams and his students universally loved him which is a tribute to any teacher. His instruction went beyond the classroom and laboratory and projected into the community and life. He had a passion of concern about the fortunes and hopes of colored people— an inheritance, no doubt, from his noble lineage.

The town of Highland Beach, Maryland, whose beach-front Mr. Douglass owned, and its development are one of his monuments. This village he served at different times as Mayor a quarter of a century and he was ever vigilant in maintaining its dignity and tone out of reverence for his father who founded the community over sixty years ago. This beautiful little town just below Annapolis, Maryland, was the pride of Haley Douglass's heart and those who have constituted its solid citizenry. The task of keeping established standards has occasionally been difficult with changes in time and points of view. By custom and law the community has remained largely private in so far as obtrusion by outsiders disposed to disregard rules was concerned. This has worked no undue hardships as access to the beach has been possible with conformity and cooperation alone demanded. These, however, have been sometimes resented understandably by some who opposed restrictions which the founders of the town and their successors felt were indispensable.

In public and community relations Mr. Douglass's life was full as he was long a representative survivor of his grandfather. On many occasions he represented the family at honors and tributes to Frederick Douglass, and often spoke giving reminiscences and illustrating in his personal appearance a fitting symbol of con-

siderable resemblance in his long white hair. While he lacked
the heartwarming eloquence of his famous ancestor, there was a sort
of calm quiet dignity of speech, perhaps, acquired in part from observing President Eliot. Mr. Douglass's expression, often with
clasped or folded hands, was always direct and pungent in argument where he never lost his temper. He was at all times and
everywhere God's gentleman indulging no semblance of guile.
This was strikingly evident in relations at Highland Beach where
the waters did not always flow smoothly. No matter how strenu-
ously town ordinances and customs were opposed, Haley Douglass
was never perturbed and his admonitions were generally respected. Here is reflected a type of leadership which is significant
in private and public relations because its persuasive eloquence
was effective nearly a half century. He was a charter member of
the Boule, joined the Fifteenth Street Presbyterian Church under
Francis J. Grimké, and was prominent in the Society of the Oldest Inhabitants. In these and many other affiliations in Washington, D. C., Haley Douglass was one of the community's first citizens. He lived nobly and worthily holding always high the torch
of his inheritance brightly burning and pointing ways for others
to follow.

HISTORICAL NEWS

President Charles H. Wesley lectured in California during
Negro History Week and visited the Los Angeles branch of the
Association. In addition to directing all Association policies, he
has raised since the Nashville meeting $1,025 in the current finan-
cial effort. Indeed, the great founder's mantle appropriately rests
upon the shoulders of this distinguished historian and statesman-
like Dean of Carter Woodson's associates.

The Presidents of colleges in the United Negro College Fund
met in Boston during January 1954 and were addressed by President Pusey of Harvard. Sponsors of the fund in New England
were present and some of the college presidents conferred with
members of their boards of trusts.

Hylan Lewis of Atlanta University is advising on a $400,000,000
project modeled after the T.V.A. for the production of aluminum in
the Gold Coast. Service on the Volta River Commission there
marks the first assignment of an American colored scholar on an
African project of its kind and proportions.

Irene Diggs, who is on leave this year from Morgan State College, is en route on a trip around the world. She is including

sections of Africa on her itinerary and other points of anthropological and sociological interest.

J. Reuben Sheeler formerly head of the history department at West Virginia State College joined the faculty of Texas Southern University at Houston, Texas and began his new duties there the second semester of 1953-1954.

Howard H. Bell for several years a professor of history at Dillard University has accepted a position on the staff of the Library of Congress and is helping in the work of the *Journal* at headquarters.

George Haynes, a life member of the Association and now retired from the Council of the Churches of Christ in America, is lecturing at the City College of New York. His world travels have covered much of the continent of Africa about which his latest book was largely written.

Whitney M. Young, Jr., is the new Director of the School of Social Work at Atlanta University. His previous experience has been in directing Urban Leagues in the Middle West.

Howard K. Beale of the University of Wisconsin opened the series of lectures in Arts and Sciences at Atlanta University October 28, 1953. His subject was: "Freedom is Worth Something if it is Freedom for Dangerous Views."

E. F. Frazier continued the Atlanta University Series in Arts and Science Lectures on February 6, 1954. He emphasized the changing middle class among American Negroes and mentioned the rise of cruder standards of values depending upon "money and status" in contrast to previous ideals of service.

Helen Buckler is completing a biography of Dr. Daniel Williams after doing research on his life and work which carried her in travels to thirty states. This account of the distinguished surgeon's work and career will be an invaluable addition to the records of Negro achievement.

The first issue of *African Affairs* published by the Ruth Sloan Associates, Inc. (4201 Massachusetts Ave., N. W., Washington, D. C.) appeared in January. It is the first newsletter to appear in the United States devoted exclusively to the entire African continent. The purpose of *African News* is to "bring to its readers each month a stimulating collection of news and analysis of developments in Africa, together with a review of recent books." This first issue contains—"Federation in Nigeria: can Western Political Institutions be Transplanted to Africa?"; "Belgian Congo's Watussis Rate 'King Solomon's Mines' a Hit"; news notes covering all parts of Africa and "Some Recent Books on Africa." One year's subscription to *African News* is $4.00.

Archie Alexander, a native of Iowa and bridge-building engineer, has been appointed Governor of the Virgin Islands. He has for some years been residing in Washington, D. C., while working on projects there and serving on the faculty of the Howard University School of Engineering.

President Eisenhower nominated J. Ernest Wilkins, a Chicago lawyer, as an assistant to the Secretary of Labor, March 4, 1954. This is the first appointment of a colored man to a sub-cabinet position since William H. Lewis served as Assistant Attorney General under President Taft.

THE JOURNAL
OF
NEGRO HISTORY

FOUNDED BY

CARTER G. WOODSON

JANUARY 1, 1916

PUBLISHED QUARTERLY BY

THE ASSOCIATION FOR THE STUDY OF
NEGRO LIFE AND HISTORY, INC.

The Association for the Study of Negro Life and History supplies THE JOURNAL OF NEGRO HISTORY to Active Members in good standing; the Executive Council elects the members and determines their duties and privileges. The membership fee is not the same as a subscription. Members may be otherwise assessed. Only persons may become Active Members. THE NEGRO HISTORY BULLETIN goes to Associate Members paying $2.00 a year.

Subscriptions should be sent to the Association for the Study of Negro Life and History, 1538 Ninth Street, N. W., Washington, D. C. The price of a subscription to the JOURNAL is $5.00 a year. Single numbers cost $1.50 each. Volumes I and II bound cost $7.50 each, and the remaining volumes in bound form $5.00 each.

All communications with respect to both editorial and administrative matters should be sent to the address given above.

$30,000 NEEDED

HELP us raise annually the sum of $30,000 to finance the work of collecting and publishing the materials bearing on Negro life and history. Our efforts, at present, are restricted to what we are able to induce interested individuals to undertake in their respective localities. Moving at this slow rate and in such an unsystematic way, the work will proceed so slowly that many valuable documents and the testimonies of the living will be lost to the world, and the story of the Negro will perish with him.

To raise this fund we are appealing to all persons professing an interest in the propagation of the truth. We need

4 persons to contribute annually	$1,000 each
8 persons to contribute annually	500 each
16 persons to contribute annually	250 each
20 persons to contribute annually	100 each
40 persons to contribute annually	50 each
80 persons to contribute annually	25 each
200 persons to contribute annually	10 each

The dual effort of the Association makes its work more expensive than that of other scientific movements. This undertaking differs from most such enterprises in that it unites the efforts of both a learned society and a bureau of research. The Association is concerned with the discussion, publication, and circulation of historical materials, and at the same time it employs investigators to explore fields of Negro history hitherto neglected or unknown. This work cannot be successfully prosecuted with less than $30,000 a year; and, if we hope to develop it in all of its aspects to prevent the Negro from becoming a negligible factor in the thought of the world, the income must be much larger than this amount.

All communications should be sent to the Association for the Study of Negro Life and History, 1538 Ninth Street, Northwest, Washington 1, D. C.

The Association is incorporated and the Secretary-Treasurer is bonded.

THE JOURNAL

OF

NEGRO HISTORY

VOL. XXXIX—July, 1954—No. 3

PITT AND THE ACHIEVEMENT OF ABOLITION

With the death of Pitt the political scene changed. Before consideration of why abolition came so soon after his death, it is necessary to attempt to assess Pitt's contribution to the Abolitionist Cause. It has often been claimed that if Pitt had used the full force of his influence a substantial measure of abolition would have been achieved during his tenure of office. His attitude to abolition, it has been pointed out, was similar to that which he evinced towards parliamentary reform. In this connection Lecky says:

a distinguishing feature of his character was his extreme love of power without any corresponding enthusiasm for particular measures. When it was a question of maintaining his position, no man showed himself more determined and inflexible. When it was a particular line of policy, no one was more sensitive to opposition and more ready to modify his course.[1]

It is therefore claimed that Pitt merely used the force of his eloquence in any parliamentary discussion of abolition but was unwilling to force a measure through Parliament and to risk his reputation and office on its success. Each year he allowed the measure to be defeated by men who

[1] W. E. H. Lecky, *History of England in the Eighteenth Century*, Vol. V, p. 339.

167

would never have dared risk his displeasure. The second James Stephen wrote:

> Had he periled his experience on the issue no man can doubt that an amount of guilt, of misery, and disgrace, and of loss would have been spared to England and to the civilised world, such as no other man had it in his power to arrest.[2]

Many of Pitt's contemporaries shared this view of him. Francis in 1796 bitterly complained that when Pitt had first taken up the Cause he had espoused it with great sincerity and eloquence, but since that early time he had done nothing but descend from his elevated station.[3] Others found it difficult to understand how Pitt could muster a majority on every conceivable occasion but when it came to Abolition seemed so impotent. The explanation seemed simple to James Stephen:

> Mr. Pitt unhappily for himself, his country and mankind, is not zealous enough in the cause of the negroes, to contend for them as decisively as he ought in the Cabinet any more than in Parliament.[4]

More than once Wilberforce felt grieved at his friend's remissness. Pitt's critics could point to the fact that during his tenure of office, despite the fact that he had declared the trade to be immoral and unjust, the trade flourished to such an extent that not only did it continue without restraint but actually increased.[5]

This lack of zeal on the part of Pitt, his general attitude to the trade, and his reversal of opinion after 1792 has elicited an ingenious explanation from a forceful modern writer.[6] This interpreter has claimed that Pitt's interest in

---

[2] Sir James Stephen, 'Essays in Ecclesiastical Biography' (1849) Vol. II, pp. 494-495.

[3] Parliamentary History, Vol. 32, columns 950-51. April 11th 1796.

[4] Wilberforce, op. cit. Vol. II, pp. 224-225. Letter from J. Stephen to W. Wilberforce, undated.

[5] Lecky, op. cit. p. 342; Wilberforce op. cit. Vol. III, p. 29. In 1787 eighty one vessels sailed from Liverpool to engage in the African Trade—P.P. 1789 (633) Vol. XXIV p. 49; whereas in 1804 one hundred and twenty-six vessels cleared out to the coast of Africa from the same port—pp. 1806 (265) Vol. XIII p. 23.

[6] E. Williams, 'Capitalism and Slavery' (Chapel Hill 1944).

abolition was motivated by economic considerations. Faced with intense French competition in the world's sugar market, Pitt's plan in 1787 was twofold: to recapture the European market with the aid of sugar from India and to secure an international abolition of the slave trade. The effect of this would be to ruin St. Domingo, which produced the bulk of the French supply. If international abolition could not be accomplished then British abolition would suffice for the French were so dependent upon British slavers that even an unilateral abolition by England would seriously dislocate the French economy. But by 1793, St. Domingo was effectively ruined by the slave insurrection; moreover Pitt had accepted the French planters' offer of the island. "This," says Williams:

is of more than academic interest. Pitt could not have had St. Domingo and abolition as well. Without its 40,000 slave imports a year St. Domingo might as well have been at the bottom of the sea. The very acceptance of the island meant logically the end of Pitt's interest in Abolition. Naturally he did not say so. He had already committed himself too far in the eyes of the public.[7]

Such is the explanation proferred by an economic determinist of Pitt's original, ardent espousal of the Cause and of his subsequent reversal of opinion after 1792. His humanitarianism was merely a blind to cover the sordity of his base, economic motives.

The transition from Pitt's support of abolition previous to 1792 to the setting of his face to abolition subsequent to that date requires an explanation. It was, after all, Pitt who had suggested to Wilberforce that he should take the matter up in Parliament. Moreover, Pitt had proceeded to show his intense support and advocacy of the matter in the secret negotiations with the French in 1787 and early 1788 in the attempt to conclude a joint abolition previous to the discussion in the British Parliament.[8] Again it was Pitt who gave

[7] Williams, op, cit. pp. 147-148.

[8] Late in 1787 Wilberforce in concert with Pitt wrote to William Eden, at that time negotiating in Paris, requesting him to endeavor to effect an agree-

his word to Wilberforce, when the latter fell ill in 1788, to undertake the cause if his friend should die. The Privy Council Enquiry originated in 1788 to investigate the trade and owed its inception to Pitt's action. Throughout the hearing of evidence by the Commons from 1789 to 1791 Pitt constantly attended the meetings of the Committee; and it was mainly due to his successful intervention that an attempt to close the parliamentary inquiry, before the conclusion of the abolitionist case, was defeated.[9] And the persuasive, eloquent speeches pronounced by Pitt in the Commons in favor of the Cause had shown him to be either an ardent abolitionist or the most consummate liar and hypocrite that the British Parliament had ever seen. As an expression of the intensity and sincerity of his feelings, he stated in April 1791 that from the very first hour of his having had the honor to sit in Parliament down to the present, of all the questions, political or personal, in which it had been his fortune to take a share, there never had been one in which his heart was so deeply interested as abolition of the slave trade.[10] In the following year his attitude was still categorical:

I know of no evil that existed, nor can imagine any evil to exist, worse than the tearing of seventy or eighty thousand persons annually from their native lands by a combination of the most civilised nations inhabiting the most enlightened part of the globe.[11]

Phrases such as this do most to belie the charge that his apparent sincerity and humanitarianism was merely a cloak.

Suddenly his espousal of the cause ended. The first ominous note was in 1792: "Pitt threw out against slave motion on St. Domingo account," notes Wilberforce in his

---

ment with the court of Versailles to abolish the slave trade simultaneously with Great Britain. As Eden could not commit himself on behalf of the government the proposal failed, despite Pitt's private support.

[9] Thomas Clarkson *History of the Abolition of the Slave Trade* (1808) Vol. II. pp. 505-6, footnote.

[10] *Parliamentary History*, Vol. 29, column 335, April 19th 1791.

[11] *Ibid*, column 1149, April 3rd 1792.

diary.[12] Nevertheless, Pitt supported the motion, in what was perhaps the finest speech of his career. Yet the old fire, earnestness and spontaneity had gone and in its place was a dutiful appeal for abolition, perhaps more out of friendship towards Wilberforce than from conviction.

The economic determinist explanation of this volte-face is not satisfactory, for not only does it reveal a total misunderstanding of Pitt's character, but also because it has not the slightest shred of evidence to support it. In refutation of this view it is difficult to see how Pitt could have deceived Wilberforce, with whom he lived on the most intimate terms. Nor did Clarkson ever suspect the existence of such a scheme. It seems strange that Pitt never gave Dundas or Hawkesbury any inkling of such an intention. Moreover the minutes of the West India Committee contain no record of any attempt to import East Indian sugar until 1792 by which time St. Domingo was ruined, and it is significant that Pitt did not enlist the co-operation of the West India Committee in his great plan of ruining their rival.[13] Unilateral abolition of the slave trade would in no way have dislocated the French economy in St. Domingo, for the annual importation of slaves in British ships to that island during the years 1784 to 1787 was less than four thousand annually, whereas according to Williams' own figures forty thousand were needed each year.[14] Furthermore, Pitt's most powerful plea for abolition, which might well have succeeded but for Dundas' amendment, came in April 1792 at a time when St. Domingo was already ruined. If Pitt was scheming to annex St. Domingo and to develop it as a British slave colony it would have been folly to have made such a speech. Lastly it is a wild conjecture to suppose that Pitt desired to annex St. Domingo for economic motives, for as early as October 1791, it was manifest that the island was

---

12 Wilberforce, *op, cit.* Vol. I, p. 341.

13 For an excellent discussion of this point see G. R. Meller, *British Imperial Trusteeship 1783-1850* (1951) pp. 50-53

14 *Ibid*, pp. 76-77 footnote number 87.

crippled as an economic proposition.[15] It would be fruitless to consider the economic determinist case further as it has no firm foundation of evidence.

In my opinion the reason for Pitt's ardent enthusiasm for abolition and his sudden volte-face after 1792 cannot be explained solely in terms of economic or political motives. It rather lies deep in his character. To Pitt abolition was not the intense, emotional, all consuming religious duty that it was to Wilberforce. Pitt considered the slave trade in an intellectual and dispassionate manner, and seen in this light the slave trade was barbaric, unjust and unchristian traffic, which had perpetrated great evil and devastation in Africa. To such a person a postponement of the abolition issue, dictated by what he considered an overwhelming combination of political, economic, military and security reasons was not the unmitigated tragedy that it was to Wilberforce. This not only explains his change of front in 1792-3 but also gives us a clue as to why he betrayed a surprising lack of initiative at all times towards the movement, leaving it to others to provide the motive force in the country and in Parliament. Pitt, in short, lacked the same type of dynamic drive that impelled Wilberforce. Because of this George III can hardly be blamed for remarking to Dundas that Pitt's arguments on the slave trade were not of his own sterling growth but a display of those hatched by others.[16]

The combination of factors, just referred to, which caused Pitt to make a sharp right-turn was most powerful.

[15] "It was computed that, within two months after the revolt first began, upwards of two thousand white persons, of all conditions and ages, had been massacred—that one hundred sugar plantations, and about nine hundred coffee, cotton and indigo settlements had been destroyed. . .and one thousand two hundred families reduced from opulence to abject destitution."—Bryan Edwards, *Historical Survey of the French Colony in the Island of St. Domingo* (1797) pp. 77-78.

[16] *Melville Papers* Add. MSS. 40100 f.169., 6th February 1796. George III to Dundas. George in hoping that the attitude of the Court of Vienna would make those who were eager for peace give up that timid opinion makes a passing reference to Pitt's attitude in this which was similar to that which he had evinced towards abolition.

A majority of the Cabinet was opposed to abolition, and though Grenville replaced Thurlow in 1792 as the chief government supporter in the House of Lords, the Upper House was violently opposed to any measure. Moreover, the Lords could flaunt the resolution gradually to abolish the trade, passed by the Commons in 1792, because the Commons refused to renew their Resolution in the following year. The bill passed by the Commons in 1794 to abolish the slave trade to foreign dominions was so bitterly opposed, and carried by such a slender majority, that the Lords could with justice hold that the Commons did not know its own mind. Opposition in the Lords could safely persist until, as in 1807, an overwhelming desire was manifested by the Commons to abolish the trade. In such a situation opposition could hardly continue in flagrant disavowal of an unanimous Commons decision.

It was popularly known that the King and Court were opposed to abolition. The Duke of Clarence was the foremost protagonist for the trade in the House of Lords. George III, as Pitt well knew, disapproved most strongly of the popular agitation and unrest being stirred up by the abolitionists, and the fact that Wilberforce was elected as a member of the National Convention did not help the cause at a time when the line between sedition and reform was as fine as a razor's edge.[17] Nor did Clarkson's foolish advocacy of Jacobin principles divest the cause of any subversive suspicions.[18] The technique of agitation alienated large sections of the political country. The fact that popular feeling and public sentiment were in favor of abolition was an added reason for not granting it, rather than an inducement to yield. To acknowledge such a demand, and to satisfy the whim of the mob, would set a dangerous precedent and

[17] *Historic Manuscripts Commission* 14th Report, Appendix V, Fortescue MSS II p. 308. George III to Lord Grenville, 3rd September 1792.
[18] Wilberforce *op. cit.* I, p. 343. "You will see Clarkson," wrote Mr. Wilberforce to Lord Muncaster in October 1792. "caution him against talking of the French Revolution; it will be ruin to our cause."

open the flood-gates to popular violence. The tendency to resist abolition on this account was strengthened by fear for the rights of property which underpinned the British constitution. In a time of war when the enemy was identified with everything destructive and anti-British, the British social, political, economic and constitutional structure had to be maintained at all costs. Burke's message was well heeded.

Apart from the political and constitutional dangers inherent in abolition, it was widely held that to abolish the trade in a time of war would be to sacrifice a substantial part of British trade, bound up with British prosperity and contributing a large sum in annual revenue, in return for a dubious advantage to the African. Such a course of action seemed suicidal. The outbreak of the slave insurrection in St. Domingo in 1791, and the spread of revolutionary principles by French agents in the British islands, together with sporadic outbreaks of unrest in Grenada and the other islands, did little to assuage the fear in men's minds that abolition would cause a wild scene of slaughter in the West Indies.

Faced with these considerations Pitt must receive sympathetic judgment. Even if he did discount the dangers inherent in these fears, and there is every reason to believe that he did, it is difficult to see what he could have achieved. Politics is the art of the possible, and measured up against the political situation abolition was impossible. In 1788 Pitt forced through Dolben's bill at the threat of resignation. Whether he thought that this was all that was possible, or all that was desirable, is open to dispute. Perhaps between 1789 and 1792 Pitt could have forced a measure through. It must, however, be pointed out that during those years the trade was still under parliamentary investigation and any precipitate pushing of a measure on Pitt's part might have been regarded as unconstitutional. After 1792 it was too late. Only Pitt and Grenville in the Cabinet favored abolition. Camden (the Lord President), Gower (the Lord Privy

Seal) and Dundas (Home Secretary) were opposed. The inclusion of the Portland Whigs in the Pitt Cabinet in 1794 tipped the balance yet further against abolition, for the Old Whigs were hostile to any measure. In 1792, when their juncture with the government had been first mooted, Pitt had stated to Loughborough that in order to further the formation of a truly national party he was willing to postpone the cause of the slaves and parliamentary reform.[19]

Of the Pitt Cabinet subsequent to 1794 only Pitt and Grenville remained in favor of abolition; Portland, Dundas, Loughborough, Camden and Spencer were opposed; and Windham by 1796 was showing the first signs of his apostasy. Pitt's brother Chatham, the Lord Privy Seal, would probably have supported if pressed by Pitt. The choice before Pitt was: to risk the existence of his Cabinet by proposing abolition; to replace the efficient Dundas and Portland by less efficient men in favor of abolition; or to wait until a more favorable time, and by speaking in favour of Wilberforce's annual motion, keep the issue alive. At the root of Pitt's thinking on the matter was probably the feeling that as Prime Minister he was responsible for government rather than for legislation.[20] He had been entrusted by the King with the task of governing, and after the outbreak of war in 1792, this sense of a duty, of a mission to discharge, became even greater with him. Pitt's duty was to govern and not to break up his Cabinet over one issue. Nor was it his duty to endanger national unity by pressing a measure that would have alienated the commercial and mercantile classes.

When Pitt did attempt to force an issue — Catholic Emancipation, it resulted in his resignation. This illustrates the limits of his power. If he failed over this, it is difficult to see how he could have succeeded with abolition. His sec-

---

[19] *Diaries and Correspondence of James Harris, First Earl of Malmesbury* (1844) (edited by the 3rd Earl) Vol. II pp. 463-4; also pp. 460-1.

[20] I am indebted for this point to Professor Richard Pares, of the University of Edinburgh.

ond Cabinet contained Portland, Eldon, Westmoreland, Melville, Hawkesbury, Castlereagh and Camden, all avowed anti-abolitionists. With the accession of Addington in December 1804 a further opponent of abolition was added. Moreover, Pitt's majority in the Commons was now smaller. Grenville had joined Fox in opposition; Melville was impeached in 1805; and Pitt's plan to admit certain members of the parties of Fox and Grenville into the Cabinet in the same year had been rejected by the King. Pitt's cares had multiplied. He was entrusted with the care of a weak government against a strong opposition, and the years 1804 and 1805 were marked with military disasters and the collapse of the coalition. Trafalgar was more than counterbalanced by the tragedy of Ulm and Austerlitz. And lastly, Pitt's health was failing. Against this background must be set Pitt's procrastination over the issue of the Order in Council in 1804 and 1805, his attempt to prevail upon Wilberforce to postpone the issue in 1805, and his off-hand support of Wilberforce's motion.

Lastly in defense of Pitt it must be stressed that Wilberforce never lost confidence in his friend's advocacy of the Cause. Friction occurred such as in the summer of 1797 at the time when peace negotiations were taking place at Lille. Pitt refused, on that occasion, to introduce the question of abolition into the discussions, either from a fear of complicating them or from the belief that it would be treated better after the conclusion of the peace. The rupture of the Lille negotiations served to justify Pitt for not having weighted it with a contentious proposal.[21] Yet Wilberforce could note, in connection with the refusal of Addington to introduce the subject at the Treaty of Amiens, that if Pitt had been in power the matter would have been discussed.[22] The friction between Wilberforce and Pitt over the latter's procrastination in issuing the Order in Council in 1804-1805

[21] Holland Rose, *William Pitt and the National Revival* (1911) p. 476; also Wilberforce *op. cit.* Vol. III, pp. 224-5.

[22] Wilberforce, *op.cit.* III, pp. 34-5.

has been exaggerated, for Pitt was kept fully informed by Wilberforce of the Opposition maneuverings to force his hand.[23] In short, our judgment of Pitt must be that it is possible for a man to believe firmly in a measure, but feel that the time was not opportune for its introduction.

With Pitt's death the accession of the new Cabinet proved more favorable to Abolition, for ten out of twelve of the ministry were in favor of abolition, with the Prime Minister in the Upper House ready to defend the measure. Moreover, the circumstances were more propitious. Not only was the political opposition to abolition lessened by the accession of a pro-Abolition Cabinet but also the strength of the West India interest pleading on economic grounds had palpably decreased. This was due to the current economic distress in the West Indian Islands, and the discredit cast upon their motives by the failure of their meliorating scheme, which was eventually to have abolished the slave trade.

Those with cap in hand can scarcely claim to dictate policy. Such was the predicament of the West India group in 1806-7. In 1807 sugar was being sold at a loss by the Jamaican planters in the British market. The average loss in that year for the individual grower was £236 sterling.[24] Most sugar estates had yielded 10% during the period of prosperity previous to 1800, but since that period they had gradually diminished to 2½% and 1½% until 1807 when there was no return whatsoever.[25] Between 1799 and 1807 sixty-five plantations in Jamaica had been abandoned, thirty-two had been sold for debts and by 1807 suits were pending against one hundred and fifteen others.[26] Planter distress at that time had become so acute as to have been

[23] R. I. & S. Wilberforce, 'Correspondence of W. Wilberforce' (1840), Vol. II, pp. 14-15. Letter from Wm. Wilberforce to Rt. Hon. Wm. Pitt, March 30th 1805.

[24] Parliamentary Pages. 1808 (178) Vol. IV—Report of a Committee of the House of Jamaica, November 1807. Appendix 42, pp. 215 ff.

[25] P.P. 1807 (65) Vol. III, p. 3.—Report. . .on the Commercial state of the West India Colonies.

the subject of reference for three parliamentary committees during 1806 and 1807, considering measures of relief. Six voluminous reports on the situation were presented.[27]

The West Indian case in Parliament was also weakened by the fact that by 1806 it was obvious that, even where amelioration in the West Indies had been accomplished by the legislatures, no abolition of the slave trade could be expected as a derivative of it. Some islands had even objected to melioration quite apart from abolition. Early in 1805 members of the Commons could read printed extracts of correspondence between Lord Seaforth, Governor of Barbados, and Earl Camden, the Secretary of State, which revealed details of several wanton and inhuman murders which had recently taken place in Barbados. Governor Seaforth regretted that he could see little hope of any bill passing the Assembly to make the murder of slaves a capital offense.[28] Such intractable behavior did much to alienate sympathy for the islands.

A third factor which undermined the West Indian position was that they were not organized as a phalanx. It is true that a Society of West India Planters in Parliament had by concerted action drawn up and carried the amelioration proposals of 1797, and that this group had worked with the support of the Society of West India Planters and Merchants in London. But it would be a mistake to imagine that the West Indians in Parliament were at this period combined into a political block, displaying a regular front in critical moments and ready to vote down any proposal by their concerted efforts. George Hibbert in 1807 declared that if they had possessed such an organization, they would

[26] *P.P.* 1808 (178) Vol. IV.—Report of a Committee of the House of Assembly of Jamaica, November 1807. Appendix 42.

[27] L. J. Ragatz, 'Fall of the Planter Class in the British Caribbean, 1763-1833' (1928) pp. 309-10. The subject of agrarian distress in the West Indies is discussed at length in this book and for its reliability and extensiveness the work is unparalleled.

[28] *P.P.* 1805 (39) Vol. X, p. 7, Lord Seaforth to the Earl of Camden, Barbados, 13th November 1804.

not stand so defenseless as they were then placed.[29] A group of the West Indians looked favorably on abolition as it would check the rise of the acquired territories.

It has been claimed that the West Indies voted en bloc for abolition in order to further a scheme to ruin the newly acquired colonies of Demerara, Berbice and Surinam.[30] At a time when the sugar market was glutted and economic distress prevailed, the planters, it is argued, were in favor of abolition because a cessation of the supply of slaves would strangle the growth of the new colonies and thereby restrict the production of sugar. The number of slaves being imported into Demerara and Surinam was enormous. For the year ending 10th October 1805, 6,630 were imported into Demerara, with none re-exported; Surinam absorbed 6,008, with none re-exported; whilst Jamaica imported only 5,684, of which total 515 were re-exported.[31] Faced with such a situation, it has been claimed, production had to be curtailed.

The answer to the economic determinist explanation of abolition is brief. First, the West Indians did not possess the organization to push such a scheme. Moreover by an Order in Council dated August 15th 1805 the importation of Negroes for the purpose of opening up new territories had been restricted, entries being limited to 3% of the existing number of slaves.[32] An Act of Parliament in 1806[33] superceded the Order in Council, at the same time as preventing foreign dominions being supplied with slaves. Sir William Young strongly contended in favor of this bill.[34]

29 *Parliamentary Debates*, Vol. 8, column 981. February 23rd 1807.

30 Williams, *op. cit.* pp. 149-50. ''It was the same old conflict between 'saturated planters' and 'planters on the make,' '' p. 150.

31 *P.P.* 1806 (265) Vol. XII, p. 27.

32 *P.P.* 1806 (84) Vol. XII.

33 *P.P.* 1806 (124) Vol. I.

34 *Parliamentary Debates*, Vol. 6, column 805. April 18th 1806: ''Sir W. Young approved of the principle of the bill which he considered as a boon to the West Indian merchants, and stated that he had been at a numerous meeting of London merchants, when a majority had agreed with him.''

This is natural enough as it would strike a permanent blow at the new rival colonies and at the same time satisfy the demand of the humanitarians. But when the general abolition bill came up for discussion, the West Indian group was solidly opposed. The reason for this is obvious: the threat of the new islands had vanished, for their supply of slaves had already been eradicated by the previous bill. It cannot, therefore, be claimed that the West Indians allowed abolition to be carried in order to ruin their rivals in Demerara and Surinam.

The West Indians in Parliament all spoke against abolition with the exception of Barham. Sir William Young opposed, as did Fuller, Hibbert and Hughan. The latter declared that the measure was fraught with ruin to the colonies and to the Empire. Hibbert, though arguing in favor of restriction of the slave trade to the old islands, nevertheless voted against the measure.[35]

Outside Parliament the Society of West India Planters and Merchants vigorously opposed abolition. In February 1805 it was unanimously resolved to oppose the progress of any bill for abolition and a committee was appointed to meet the threat.[36] In April 1806 strict attention was directed to the bill then pending in Parliament to abolish the trade to foreign dominions.[37] A General Meeting of the West Indian body in June recommended opposition to the bill for general abolition then pending and voted £500 for the counteracting of writers against the slave trade.[38] A further General Meeting in December 1806 re-affirmed the desire to "employ the most vigorous and incessant exertions in opposing so baneful a project" as abolition.[39] A petition was sent in June 1806 to the Lords protesting against the aboli-

[35] *Ibid*, Vol. 7, colunms 984-5.

[36] *Minutes of the Society of West India Planters and Merchants* February 14th 1805.—MSS in library of the West India Committee in London.

[37] *Ibid*, April 11th 1806.

[38] *Ibid*, June 9th 1806.

[39] *Ibid*, December 10th 1806.

tion resolution sent up from the Commons.[40] Early in 1807 the Standing Committee appointed Mr. Lyon (Agent for Jamaica), Mr. Mitchell, Mr. Wedderburn, George Hibbert (M.P. for Seaford), Beeston Long, Thomas Hughan (M.P. for East Retford) and Mr. Jordan as a special committee to prepare petitions for the House of Lords against the bill for total abolition then pending.[41] A week later General Gascoyne (M.P. for Liverpool), Mr. Dickinson and Mr. Fuller were added to the Committee.[41] A petition was drawn up for the Lords on January 21st;[43] and one for the Commons on February 17th.[44] A general meeting of the Society on March 23rd felt itself called on to represent to the Prime Minister and the Secretary of State for the Colonial Department, the imminent peril to which the British West Indies were exposed. It was also resolved that reinforcements of white troops be sent to the West Indian islands for their defense and to guard against the great dangers of revolt and insurrection with which they were threatened by the adoption of abolition.[45] A further petition was sent to the Lords, after the Commons had returned the bill to the Upper House with amendments.[46] After the bill had passed both Houses the Society of West Indian Planters and Merchants presented an Humble Petition to the King praying for His Majesty "to avert the approaching destruction of their fellow subjects who are inhabitants of these colonies" and to withhold his assent to the bill.[47]

Such was the attitude of the official West India body to abolition. Both the planters in Parliament, out of Parliament and in the West Indies were opposed to abolition. The argument that abolition was engineered by the planters of

[40] *Ibid*, June 17 1806.
[41] *Ibid*, January 14th 1807.
[42] *Ibid*, January 21st 1807.
[43] *Ibid*.
[44] *Ibid*, February 17th 1807.
[45] *Ibid*, March 23rd 1807.
[46] *Ibid*.
[47] *Ibid*, March 24th 1807.

the old islands to cripple the new planters thus falls to the ground . Abolition came when political opportunity, public opinion, the economic distress of the West Indies and the rise of the new colonies coincided. Fear of Jacobinism had declined as the regime in France was transformed into a military despotism and the popular attitude to the trade both inside and outside Parliament had been modified as a result of the abolitionist campaign. In 1788 most contended that the slave trade was legal and just; by 1806 the country's standard of values had been so radically changed that it was considered by a majority of all ranks of society as a travesty of justice and a disgrace to Great Britain.

The actual passage of abolition is not significant. In May 1806 the bill to prevent foreign colonies from being supplied with slaves and to cut off supplies from the newly acquired British territories was passed.[48] Only Hawkesbury, Westmoreland and the Duke of Clarence opposed in the Lords; Sidmouth was prevailed upon to vote for the measure.[49] The temptation to try for a total abolition in that year was resisted as it was held by Grenville that its success would be jeopardized by the fact that the session was nearly at an end.[50] In June, however, Fox moved a resolution in the House of Commons that the House, conceiving the Slave Trade to be contrary to the principles of justice, humanity and sound policy would, with all practicable expedition, proceed to take effectual measures for abolishing the said trade, in such a manner and at such period as it deemed desirable. This passed the Commons by a vote of 114-15;[51] and the Lords by 41-20.[52] Only the Liverpool group opposed in the Commons; and only Fitzwilliam, Hawkesbury, Westmoreland and Sidmouth spoke against in the Lords. It was also voted on June 10th that an Humble Address be pre-

[48] 46 George III c.
[49] Parliamentary Debates, Vol. 7, columns 234-5, May 16th 1806.
[50] Wilberforce op. cit. Vol. III, p. 261.
[51] Parliamentary Debates, Vol. 7, columns 580-603, June 10th 1806.
[52] Ibid, columns 801-9, June 24th 1806.

sented to the King beseeching him to establish by negotiation with foreign powers a concert and agreement for abolishing the slave trade.[53] Before the session ended a bill was passed to prevent any sudden increase in the trade due to the forthcoming abolition.[54]

The death of Fox in September caused no setback to the Cause. Nor did a general election affect the political situation. On January 2nd 1807 Grenville moved the first reading of the bill in the House of Lords.[55] A month's delay ensued in hearing counsel against the bill before it received its second reading by a vote of 100-36.[56] The third reading was carried without a division. Clarence, Westmoreland, Hawkesbury and Sidmouth spoke against the bill, but Grenville was ardent and insistent in his support.[54] Much of the credit for the bill's introduction and successful passage must be given to Lord Grenville. On February 10th the first reading was moved in the Commons by Lord Howick, the Foreign Secretary.[58] Little opposition resulted. Windham voted against; Castlereagh and Rose abstained. The climax of the discussion came on February 23rd when Sir Samuel Romilly (the Solicitor General) pronounced an eulogy of Wilberforce.[59] The second reading was carried 283-16,[60] and the third reading without a division.[61] Fear that the government would fall before the bill received the Royal Assent was dispelled by Perceval promising his support, and his informing Wilberforce that Eldon, Castlereagh and Hawesbury now acquiesced in the decision of the House of Com-

[53] *Ibid*, column 603, June 10th 1806.

[54] 46 George III c 119 See also Wilberforce *op. cit.* Vol. III, p. 263.

[55] *Parliamentary Debates*, Vol. 8, columns 257-9. January 2nd 1807

[56] *Ibid*, columns 657-72, February 5th 1807.

[57] *Ibid*, columns 701-3, February 10th 1807.

[58] *Ibid*, columns 717-22, February 10th 1807.

[59] *Ibid*, columns 977-9, February 23rd 1807.

[60] *Ibid*, Vol. 9, columns 63-6, March 9th 1807,

[61] *Ibid*, columns 114-40, March 16th 1807.

mons.[62] On March 25th the bill received Royal Assent.[63] Grenville's government fell shortly afterwards. Its greatest achievement was abolition of the slave trade.

ALAN M. REES

London and Oxford Universities
Fellow in History, Ohio State University

[62] Wilberforce *op. cit.* we in p. 301.
[63] *House of Lords Journal*, Vol. 46 p. 137; 47 Geo. III c. 36.

THE PRIGG CASE AND FUGITIVE SLAVERY, 1842-1850

In 1832 a colored woman, Margaret Morgan, moved with her husband, a free citizen, from the state of Maryland to Pennsylvania. This woman had lived in virtual freedom even in the slave state of Maryland though neither she nor her parents ever received formal bestowal of freedom by the original owner.[1] The heiress of the original owner of Margaret's parents living in Baltimore sought to recapture the services of this healthy Negress and Edward Prigg, her attorney, was commissioned to recapture this so-called fugitive. In conformity with the procedure established by Pennsylvania's Law of 1826 he obtained a warrant from a Pennsylvania county justice of the peace and took Margaret Morgan before the same magistrate for a hearing. When that justice declined further cognizance of the case Prigg, without further compliance with the law, had Margaret Morgan abducted back to Maryland.[2] Prigg was promptly indicted in Pennsylvania for kidnapping in violation of the Pennsylvania Law of 1826. From these inauspicious events began a chain of events which in a decade culminated in the most famous fugitive slave case before the Supreme Court prior to the Fugitive Slave Law of 1850 and one which highlighted the controversy over the states'-rights vs. central Government's powers current in pre-Civil War America, the case of *Prigg vs. Pennsylvania*. It was agreed between Maryland and Pennsylvania that whatever the decision in the Pennsylvania court, the ultimate arbiter of the case would be the United States Supreme Court.[3] Involved in the full answer to the question why Maryland desired to test the constitutionality of Pennsylvania's 1826 law which regulated the procedure by which a slave owner could recover a

---

[1] The *New York Tribune*, March 14, 1842.

[2] The *New York Herald*, March 4, 1842.

[3] On May 22, 1839 this agreement was formalized by an Act of the Legislature of Pennsylvania. *Laws of the Commonwealth of Pennsylvania*, 1839, pp. 218-220.

fugitive slave in that state were some of the most basic constitutional questions of the political nature of the Republic as well as one of the thorniest problems facing a union of states half free and half slave.

Article IV, Section 3, was the constitutional condescension to the slave owning demands that the owners of slaves have a right to recover their human property whenever it should take flight into any state. It provided: "No person held to service or labor in one state, under the laws thereof, escaping into another, shall in consequences of any law or regulation therein, be discharged from such service or labor, but shall be delivered up on claim of the party to whom such service or labor may be due."[4] From that injunction until the Compromise Acts of 1850 only one national law existed to provide the details of executing its aims, the Fugitive Slave Act of 1793. It permitted the person to whom labor or service was due, his agent or attorney, to seize or arrest his fugitive and to take him or her before any judge of the District or Circuit courts of the United States or before any magistrate of a county, city or incorporated town. The judge or magistrate was thereupon authorized to give the owner or his agent a certificate to remove the fugitive to the territory whence he fled. There was no provision for a trial by jury. The only requirement for the conviction of the person claimed was the testimony of his alleged master or the affidavit of some magistrate in the state from which he came, certifying that such a person had escaped. Hindering arrest or harboring a slave was punishable by a fine of $500.00.[5] Such a law so patently biased to favor the slave owner and designed with so little regard for the protection of the alleged slave as a person was bound to come under attack by the abolitionists. This attack commenced in the second and third decades of the nineteenth century and by the fourth decade rocked the North. Opponents of the law claimed that corrupt justices of the peace unwillingly per-

[4] Art. IV, Sec. 3.
[5] *United States Statutes at Large*, I, 302-305.

mitted the removal of free Negroes and mulattoes claimed as slaves.[6] It is true that under the Act of 1793 nearly all the cases fell into the hands of a few justices of the peace in each particular locality; and these were often men in whom the general community had no confidence.[7] However, because absconding with free Negroes was so hazardous in the free states, kidnapping was limited almost solely to the communities bordering the Southern states. Not only kidnapping but the capture of a genuine fugitive was rare in New England.[8] Until anti-slavery sentiment became common in the North it was the instances of kidnapping and slave hunting which did most to arouse the consciences of abettors of runaways.[9] As the growing conscience of the North found the law less and less palatable the growing anger of the South found the act still less suitable but for opposite reasons. The lack of judges and magistrates to accommodate the slave owners and the uncooperativeness of many were forcing them to recover their property by extra legal direct action, involving either an outright seizure of the Negro by force or some enticement strategem which accomplished the same result with less publicity. Attempts in Congress to achieve a more stringent fugitive slave law were made in 1796,[10] 1801,[11] 1817,[12] and 1822,[13] but all in vain.

[6] Robert C. Smedley, *History of the Underground Railroad* (Lancaster, Pa., 1883), pp. 317-318.

[7] George M. Stroud, *Sketch of the Laws Relating to Slavery* (2 ed., Philadephia, 1856), pp. 111-112.

[8] ''The Action of Congress on the California and Territorial Question'', *North American Review*, LXXI (July, 1850), 254. Marion Gleason McDougall, *Fugitive Slaves* (Fay House Monographs, No. 3; Ginn and Co., Boston, 1891), p. 36.

[9] Smedley, *op. cit.*, p. 26; Marion McDougall describes two typcial cases of kidnapping: the Jones case and the Solomon Northup case. Cf. McDougall, *op. cit.*, pp. 36-37.

[10] McDougall, *op. cit.*, p. 19. Wilbur H. Siebert, *The Underground Railroad from Slavery to Freedom* (New York: The Macmillan Co., 1898), p. 295.

[11] McDougall, *op. cit.*, p. 20; *Annals of Congress*, 7 Cong. 1 Sess., pp. 422-423.

[12] McDougall, *op. cit.*, p. 21.

[13] *Ibid*, p. 24; Siebert, *op. cit.*, pp. 298-299.

Involved in the attack and defense of this law were three legal questions in particular: (1) Did the Constitution and Act of 1793 preclude a trial by jury for the fugitive? (2) To what extent could state legislation supplement the Federal law? (3) Did Congress have the authority to legislate on the subject? The controvery over the meaning of Section III in Article IV of the Constitution and of the constitutionality of the Act of 1793 was a part of the general indistinctness of the legal limits of Congress' power. Even among the judges of the Supreme Court there was no agreement on these matters prior to the year of the Prigg case. One of the principal questions in debate was whether the intent of the Constitution was to clothe Congress with the power of legislation on the question of the surrender of persons held to service and labor in one state who escaped into another; or whether it was intended to leave it to each state to provide a mode for the investigation of claims which might be made, and if found for the claimant, to deliver up the fugitives to him.[14] Anti-slavery men relied upon the constitutional argument that since the fugitive clause was not in the article of the Constitution delegating powers to Congress, any Congressional authority utilized from that clause would be a usurpation. Said a noted spokesman for the fugitives, William Seward, "... the necessity of legislation, under this claim of the Constitution, is *violently* inferred, and then another *violence* is committed by inferring an implied power."[15] A more positive statement of the same idea was that of William Jay:

It [the fugitive clause in the Constitution] was inserted to satisfy the South; and its obvious meaning is, that slaves escaping into States, but confers no power on Congress. . . . As the power of redeemed free by the State authorities, but shall be delivered by those authorities to his master. This clause imposes an obligation on the States, but confers no power on Congress. . . . As the power of recovering these fugitives is not delegated to Congress, it is reserved

---

[14] Stroud, *op. cit.*, p. iii.
[15] William H. Seward, *Works* (George E. Baker, ed. 5 vols.; Boston: Houghton Mifflin Co., 1887), I, 506.

to the several States, who are bound to make such laws as may be deemed proper, to authorize the master to recover his slave.[16]

Another argument branding the Act of 1793 unconstitutional was the claimed contradiction between it and the Fifth Amendment which prohibited the Federal Government from depriving anyone of life, liberty and property, without due process of law. Because the Constitution guaranteed by its Seventh Amendment jury trials in suits at common law where the value exceeded $20.00 it was held that a person in peril of losing his liberty should have the protection of this guarantee. But in no state or national court decisions were these anti-slavery arguments sustained.

Even more than their objections to the congressional fugitive slave law *per se,* the fugitive sympathizers condemned the lack of trial by jury for fugitives.[17] Many people argued that the Act of 1793 did not exclude the possibility of a trial by jury for fugitives. The controversial aspect of this legal possibility was whether the trial would be in the state from which the fugitive fled or the state to which he fled. The Southern contention was that the fugitive should be tried (if at all) in the territory in which the owner would be best able to prove his claim. The necessary witnesses and evidence would most likely be in the slave-owners' home neighborhood. There also, the slave-owner would not have to contend with hostile juries and judges. To him there was nothing humorous about the Vermont judge's answer to the question as to what would constitute sufficient evidence to

[16] William Jay, *View of the Action of the Federal Government in Behalf of Slavery* (New York, 1839), p. 48. This view was maintained by Jay even after he saw how anti-slave legislatures would use the Prigg decision. Said Jay, ''The fugitive slave clause in the Constitution is of course obligatory, but there is a wide distinction between the fugitive slave *clause* and the fugitive slave *law*. The Constitution gives no power to Congress to legislate on the subject, but imposes on the States the obligation of rendition.'' Quoted from a letter by Jay to Josiah Quincy, after 1850, in Bayard Tuckerman, *William Jay and the Constitutional Movement for the Abolition of Slavery* (New York: Dodd Mead and Co., 1893), p. 141.

[17] William G. Goddell, *Slavery and Anti-Slavery* (New York: 1855), p. 568.

prove a claimant's right to a fugitive's service when he replied "a bill of sale from the Almighty God."[18]

Just because so much interpretive controversy did exist about the legal recourses to be had when a slave ran away, Maryland (as probably the slave state most concerned with the problem due to her proximity to free Pennsylvania) was anxious to settle some of the points at issue. Thus when in 1837 Edward Prigg in violation of the Pennsylvania Act of 1826 had Margaret Morgan arrested and returned to Maryland and was accordingly indicted in Pennsylvania for kidnapping, the State of Maryland defended Prigg and in agreement with Pennsylvania decided to have the verdict of the state court appealed to the United States Supreme Court.[19] A better understanding of the Prigg decision involves a knowledge of Pennsylvania's 1826 law and this in turn demands some acquaintance with conditions leading to Pennsylvania's 1820 law on fugitive slavery. Under the National Act of 1793 many fugitives from labor were sought for, arrested and delivered over to their claimants in the State of Pennsylvania.[20] Prior to 1820 the uniform practice in this matter was for the master, his agent or attorney, to seize or arrest the alleged fugitive and to carry him or her forthwith before the nearest judge or magistrate for examination; and if he or they satisfied such judge or magistrate by oral testimony or affidavit as prescribed by the 1793 law that they were entitled to the services and labor of the fugitive, the magistrate granted the necessary certificate, which

[18] E. N. Elliott, *Cotton is King and Pro-Slavery Arguments* (Comprising the writings of Hammond, Harper, Christy, Stringfellow, Hodge, Bledsoe and Cartwright; Augusta, Ga., 1860), pp. 450 ff.

[19] Richard Peters, *Reports of Cases in the Supreme Court*, XVI (Philadelphia: Thomas Cowperthwait and Co., 1846), January, 1842, 539; *Laws of Pennsylvania, 1839*, pp. 218-220; *Letters of Theodore Dwight Weld, Angelina Grimke Weld and Sarah Grimke* (eds., Gilbert H. Barnes and Dwight L. Dumond; 2 vols., New York: D. Appleton-Century Co., 1934), II. 916.

[20] *Report of the Committee on the Judiciary in Relation to the Repeal of an Act to Prevent Kidnapping* (Harrisburg, 1850, hereinafter cited as *Report of the Committee to Repeal an Act,*) p. 4.

was conclusive against the alleged slave.[21] Because of the pro-slave-holding bias of the law it was not too difficult for a master to kidnap free Negroes. And there is record of many such frauds perpetrated by constables and other officials in collusion with certain corrupt justices of the peace and other unscrupulous citizens who lent their aid to transmute undoubtedly free Negroes into fugitives and hence into slaves for the Southern market.[22]

On March 27, 1820, an attempt was made to ameliorate the existing abuses connected with the kidnapping of free Negroes by the passage of an Act to Prevent Kidnapping. The most important of its clauses was that which prohibited aldermen and justices of the peace from assuming jurisdiction over or taking cognizance of "the case of any fugitive from labor from any of the United States or territories, under a certain act of Congress [that of 1793]," and forbidding such officials to grant any certificate or warrant for the removal of a fugitive upon the application or testimony of any persons whatsoever under any laws of the United States. This function was reserved to state and federal judges who were to record any such certificate issued.[23] There was a marked similarity in the language used in this statute to that of the later Personal Liberty acts which denied cognizance not only to the justices and lower state officials but to the judges as well. This Act of 1820 was in accord with the state and national constitutions, since the legislature had full power, at any time, to enlarge or diminish the jurisdiction of the justices and judges of Pennsylvania.[24] Contrary to the general expectations, this act, instead of merely hindering kidnapping went to the other extreme and threw serious obstacles in the way of persons

[21] *Report of the Case of Charles Brown, a Fugitive Slave Owing Labour and Service to William C. Drury* (Pittsburgh, 1835), hereinafter cited as the *Brown Report*), p. 39.

[22] *Report of the Committee to Repeal an Act*, p. 4.

[23] *Ibid.*, pp. 4-5; *Brown Report*, pp. 39ff; John Codman Hurd, *The Law of Freedom and Bondage in the United States* (2 vols.; Boston: Little, Brown and Co., 1862), II, 70-71.

having claims to the service and labor of genuine fugitives
from other states. The difficulty encountered by slave-
owners was due to the small number of state and federal
judges in comparison to the aldermen and justices of the
peace before whom a fugitive slave previously could be
taken for a hearing. As far as Maryland was concerned, the
enactment amounted "almost, in fact, to an act of emancipation itself."[25] Maryland protested to Pennsylvania and
the latter state took heed of Maryland's grievances and
passed in 1826 a new act—the same law which Maryland
condemned in the Prigg case. Why this state's change in
attitude? Basically it was this: she wanted the maximum
legal aid to facilitate recovery of her runaways but she
could not tolerate the guarantees which a free state imposed to protect their free colored citizens. Pennsylvania's
1826 Act outlawed kidnapping of free persons and to help
prevent such kidnapping established a procedure for the
recovery of slaves, viz., any judge, justice of the peace or
alderman could give a claimant the warrant to seize his alleged property, but before the alleged slave could be removed, either the judge issuing the warrant or another
judge (if the warrant were issued by a justice of the peace
or alderman, it had to be returned either to a judge of the
Court of Common Pleas or District Court or Recorder of a
city) had to issue a certificate of removal. Such a certificate
was issued only "... upon proof [of ownership] to the satisfaction of such judge." The evidence usually consisted
of proof that slavery existed in the state from which the
slave fled and the testimony of a witness that the alleged
fugitive belonged to the claimant, providing "that the oath
of the owner or owners or other persons interested shall in
no case be received in evidence."[26]

Prigg neglected to obtain the certificate for removal
against Margaret Morgan and was indicted for contraven-

24 Brown Report, p. 40.

25 Ibid.; Report of the Committee to Repeal an Act, p. 4.

26 Brown Report., pp. 40-41; Hurd, op. cit., II, 71.

ing this act. His defense was the unconstitutionality of this act. The real parties of course were Pennsylvania and Maryland and the real issues were those three questions mentioned above.[27] Justice Story delivered the opinion of the Court, of which the following excerpts embody the most important *dicta:*

> The owner of a fugitive slave has the same right to seize and take him in a state to which he had escaped or fled, that he had in the state from which he escaped. . . . The owner of the slave is clothed with the authority in every state of the Union, to seize and recapture his slave; whenever he can do it without any breach of the peace, or illegal violence. In this sense, and to this extent, this clause in the Constitution may properly be said to execute itself, and to require no aid from legislation, state or national. . . .
>
> A claim to a fugitive slave is a controversy in a case "arising under the Constitution of the United States," under the express delegation of judicial power given by that instrument. Congress, then, may call that power into activity, for the very purpose of giving effect to the right. . . .
> It would seem upon just principles of construction, that the legislation of Congress, if constitutional, must supersede all state legislation upon the same subject; and by necessary implication prohibit it.
>
> The provisions of the Act of 12th February, 1793, relative to fugitive slaves, is clearly constitutional in all its leading provisions; and, indeed, with the exception of that part which confers authority on state magistrates, is free from reasonable doubt or difficulty. As to the authority so conferred on state magistrates, while a difference of opinion exists, and may exist on this point in different states, whether state magistrates are bound to act under it, none is entertained by the court that state magistrates may, if they choose, exercise the authority, unless prohibited by state legislation.
>
> The act of the legislature of Pennsylvania upon which the indictment against Edward Prigg is founded, is unconstitutional and void. It purports to punish as a public offense against the state, the very act of seizing and removing a slave by his master, which the Constitution of the United States was designed to justify and uphold. . . .
>
> The [fugitive slave clause] is found in the national Constitution, and not in that of any state. It does not point out any state functionaries, or any state action to carry its provisions into effect. The states cannot, therefore, be compelled to enforce them; and it might well be deemed an exercise of the power of interpretation, to insist

27 See page 188.

that the states are bound to provide means to carry into effect the duties of the national government, nowhere delegated or intrusted to them by the Constitution.[28]

It will be seen, then, that this decision of the highest court settled two of the three vexing problems prior to the Prigg case. First, it definitely affirmed Congress's right to legislate on the subject. Secondly, it denied to the states the power of legislating on the subject of fugitive slavery since that subject came within exclusive national jurisdiction. The genuinely novel part of the decision was that which gave the state governments the choice between extending or denying to their officials the duty of helping to execute the federal act. That was what marked it an important decision in the history of fugitive slavery before 1850. Clearly the decision was a pro-slavery document. Yet, it must have been realized that withholding the aid of state officers would prove a boon to sympathizers of fugitives. Whether or not this result was intended is only a matter of speculation. William Story in his biography of his father, Justice Joseph Story, claims that he was hostile to slavery and would have preferred not to deliver the majority opinion in the Prigg case.[29] The venerable justice even considered the decision a "triumph of freedom" because it localized slavery. It was, says Justice Story's son, a triumph of freedom because it would in effect practically nullify the act of Congress because fugitive slaves could hardly be reclaimed from a free state except with the aid of its law and officials.[30] This was fully realized by Chief Justice Taney and Justices Daniel, Thompson, and McLean, all of whom dissented against Story's denial of a state's authority and responsibility.[31]

---

[28] Peters, op. cit., pp. 540-543, 615-616.

[29] William W. Story, Life and Letters of Joseph Story (2 vols., Charles C. Little and James Brown, Boston, 1841), II, 391.

[30] Ibid., 392.

[31] Peters, op. cit., pp. 627, 630-631, 634, 652, 665. Niles' Register, March 5, 1842.

II THE PRIGG CASE AND ITS CONSEQUENCES

Horace Greeley commenting on the Prigg decision said editorially, "A decision of the Supreme Court of the United States is to us the end of controversy, so far as the question concerns what *is*—not what should be."[32] Neither he nor the anti-slavery men of the North who condemned the decision nor the Southern slave owners praising it were able to foretell the consequences of this case either in terms of the Personal Liberty laws that followed or the practical effects it had upon the ability of fugitive slaves to escape.

Story's decision challenged the constitutionality of the laws of Massachusetts and New York and other northern states which had lately been passed granting a trial by jury to alleged fugitives.[33] To this anti-slavery men reacted violently. William Lloyd Garrison proposed immediate withdrawal from the Union for "by a recent decision of the Supreme Court of the United States, the right of trial by jury is denied to such of the people of the free States as shall be claimed as goods and chattels by Southern taskmasters. . . ."[34] And N. P. Rogers at a meeting of the Massachusetts Anti-Slavery Society in 1844 resolved:

That the United States Constitution providing for the recapture of fugitive slaves in the free states, no abolitionist, if he is a politician, can consistently take any political action under it, either by holding office or voting, and that the only consistent anti-slavery political action, if there could be any, would be to go for the radical amendment or overthrow of the Constitution and the government.[35]

Though the question of the power of the national government over fugitive slavery had been settled by the decision, legal thought in the free states continued to maintain

[32] *New York Tribune*, March 9, 1842.

[33] See letter from Theodore Weld to Angelina Weld, February 8, 1842. Weld, *Letters*, p. 916.

[34] Proposed at a meeting of the anti-slavery society in 1842. Wendell Phillips Garrison and Francis Jackson Garrison, *William Lloyd Garrison* (3 vols.; New York: The Century Co., 1889) III, 59.

[35] Twelfth Annual Report, *Massachusetts Anti-Slavery Society* (Boston, 1844), p. 90.

that Article IV, Section III, was directed toward the states and therefore conferred no power on the central government.[36] William H. Seward, as counsel for the defendant in the famous Van Zandt case argued the erroneousness of the Prigg decision in his pleading:

> We have read, with profound respect, the opinions of this Court delivered in the case of Prigg vs. Pennsylvania, in which it was argued that Congress might exercise the power manifested in the Act of 1793, from a supposed analogy to many cases in which the National Legislature necessarily exercises inferential legislative authority, to carry into effect, constitutional provisions. But this reasoning fails to satisfy us. . . .[37]

His viewpoint was that a state could pass laws and regulations as long as they did not free a slave. This he insisted was the early understanding of the Constitution and the basis of much early state legislation. In fact, representatives of such diverse centers of thought as Virginia and Massachusetts both continued to believe that it devolved upon the states to provide for the capture and delivery of fugitives. Daniel Webster of Massachusetts spoke contrary to the beliefs of many in the state he represented but, nevertheless, so argued.[38] For Virginia Senator James Y. Mason (author of most of the fugitive Act of 1850) asserted, "I advance the confident opinion that it devolves upon the states the duty of providing by law both for their [fugitive slaves'] capture and delivery."[39] When it came to reconciling this view with the Prigg decision, which all southerners accepted, he argued much in the way Stephen Douglas

[36] *Annual Report, 1850, American and Foreign Anti-Slavery Society* (New York, 1850). Robert Rantoul in a speech delivered April 3, 1851, argued the unconstitutionality of the fugitive act on the basis that the fugitive clause of the Constitution was directed to states and not the national government and therefore conferred no powers on Congress. Robert Rontoul, Jr., *Memoirs* (ed. Luther Hamilton; Boston: John P. Jewett and Co., 1854), p. 742.

[37] William Seward, *Works*, II, 506.

[38] *Annual Report, 1850*, American and Foreign Anti-Slavery Society (New York, 1850), p. 5. See also his 7th of March speech entitled, "The Constitution and the Union", *The Writings, and Speeches of Daniel Webster* (18 vols.; Boston; Little, Brown and Co., 1903. X, p. 56.

later reconciled Squatter Sovereignty and the Dred Scott decision. As he expressed it:

> I do not understand the Supreme Court to have decided . . . that there is no obligation on the states to provide, by their laws, for the surrender of fugitives from labor. . . . The Supreme Court has only said . . . that there were no means under the Constitution of coercing the states to provide by law for the delivery of this class of fugitives. I am very far from understanding that it has ever been said by the Supreme Court, or by any of its justices, that it was not the *duty* of the states so to provide by law, although they cannot be coerced. The Court has only said, that any provision in the state laws in contravention (not in support) of this clause of the Constitution is unconstitutional and void.[40]

Subsequent legal study of the decision did not fail, in fact, to reveal something of its inconsistency. In Story's opinion it was admitted that the claimant may be interrupted by a civil suit in trespass or of replevin and must suffer damages if he failed to prove his claim on trial. The court would not probably have denied that he might be indicted for kidnapping and found guilty, if the person carried off by him was not a fugitive within the meaning of the provision. These remedies, it was pointed out, against unlawful seizure and removal are given by the state law—common or unwritten as the case may be—but state law in origin and authority every bit as much as statute law. Why, then, could not the state express its will in a statute![41]

The dynamic ferment in the North which in the 1840's changed from the religious fervor of abolition to the more secularized anti-slavery was not to be denied; and if Story's decision precluded the opportunity for a trial by jury for fugitives, anti-slavery men seized upon the principle of the same decision that state magistrates could be withheld from executing the fugitive act. Thus resulted the Personal Liberty laws of the 1840's. The term "Personal Liberty Law" is a generic one which covers a set of laws passed by the states between the years 1824 (Indiana) and 1858 (Ver-

[39] *Cong. Globe, 31 Cong., 1 Sess.*, p. 233.
[40] *Ibid.*, pp. 234-235.
[41] Hurd, *op. cit.*, II, 764.

mont). It is a somewhat misleading term because it gives the impression that all the laws were the same, that they were designed toward the same end, and that they were prompted by the same spirit. None of these things is true. Actually, without resort to artificial distinctions there were at least four different types of Personal Liberty laws: (1) That passed by Connecticut in 1838. It provided that on appeal fugitives from labor might have a trial by jury. As indicated by its title the purpose of the act was primarily to assist in the rendition of slaves. It was entitled ''An Act for the fulfilment of the obligation of this State, imposed by the Constitution of the United States, in regard to persons held to service or labor in one State escaping into another, and to secure the right of trial by jury in the cases therein mentioned.''[42] (2) The laws passed by New York and Vermont in 1840 entitled acts ''to extend the right of trial by jury.'' Provisions were included in these laws for the state to provide attornies to defend the fugitives. These were the first real Personal Liberty laws in that their purpose was primarily to help free Negroes and alleged fugitive slaves by assuring them a trial by jury. (3) The acts passed as a result of the Prigg decision between 1842 and the Fugitive Slave Act of 1850. States passing them included, Massachusetts (1843), Vermont (1843), Connecticut (1844), New Hampshire (1846), Pennsylvania (1847) and Rhode Island (1848). These statutes forbade state officers from performing the duties required of them by the Act of 1793 as well as prohibiting the use of state jails in fugitive slave cases. While ostensibly in some cases to protect the free Negroes from kidnappers, the animus prompting the passage of these laws was a determination to interfere with the execution of the national statute. (4) Those laws which were passed in several of the states after the Fugitive Slave Act of 1850 went into effect. Since the law of 1850 avoided the employment of state officers, this class of state legislation

42 Hurd, *op. cit.*, II, 46-47.

differed but slightly from that preceding it. Generally it prohibited the use of state jails, forbade state judges and officers from issuing writs or giving assistance to the claimant and punished severely the seizure of a free person with the intent to make a slave of him.

Type three, only, those laws passed between 1842 and 1850, will be considered in detail because they alone were directly related to the Prigg decision. Massachusetts was the first state to make use of the anti-slave loophole in Prigg's case. Its law of March 24, 1843, was popularly known as "Latimer's Law" after the well-known fugitive, George Latimer. Latimer was a fugitive slave seized in Boston against the furious objection of many of the townsfolk. By law he would have been returned to Virginia had not a large crowd in Boston collected $400.00 and forced the owner to accept this in lieu of the man. Public dissatisfaction with the Prigg decision was expressed in a report of the state legislature dated February 1843, and this report added significantly:

> Luckily the decision [in the Prigg case] . . . furnished in one portion of it a clue. . . . Thus the very weapon that inflicted the wound may be made to furnish some matter with which partially to heal it. For whilst, on the one hand, the majority of the judges rigidly insist upon the right of the general government to execute the provisions of the law of Congress of 1793, for the better recovery of fugitive slaves on "Claim" made by their owners, through officers of its own creation, on the other hand, it leaves the States perfectly free to refuse the cooperation of their magistry whenever they shall think it right to do so.[43]

"Latimer's Law" provided: (Section I) Judges of the State courts and justices of the peace were forbidden to take cognizance or grant any certificate in cases that arose under the Act of 1793. (Section II) State officers were forbidden to arrest or detain in public buildings any person claimed as a fugitive slave. (Section III) Penalty for dis-

[43] "House No. 41," *Anti-Slavery Pamphlets* at the Boston Public Library. pp. 25-26.

obeying this statute was a fine not to exceed $1,000.00 or imprisonment for not over a year.[44]

That same year Vermont repealed her Personal Liberty law of 1840 establishing a trial by jury for fugitives and passed in its place a Personal Liberty law to hinder the recovery of fugitives. Its provisions were similar to Massachusetts', though the penalty for violation was a fine of not more than $1,000.00 or five years in prison.[45]

Connecticut in 1844 became the third northeastern state to adopt the type of Personal Liberty law sanctioned by the Prigg decision. This decision was alluded to in the Preamble which began:

> Whereas, it has been decided by the Supreme Court . . . that both the duty and the power of legislation . . . pertain exclusively to the National Government . . . [it continued]
> No judge, justice of the peace, or other officer appointed under the authority of this state shall be authorized, as such, to make, issue, or serve any warrant or process for the arrest or detention of any person claimed to be a fugitive for labor or service. . . .[46]

It was substantially the same as Massachusetts' and Vermont's.

For some unknown reason all the authorities on the Personal Liberty laws have neglected to mention New Hampshire's law of 1846.[47] It was very much like its predecessors though Section II more comprehensively excluded "sheriff, deputy sheriff, coroner, constable, jailer, or other officer of the state, or citizen, not holding a commission from the United States Government" from arresting or detaining any claimed fugitive.[48]

Although held invalid by the Supreme Court in the Prigg case, Pennsylvania's law of 1826 remained on the statute books until 1847 when it was replaced by that state's

[44] *Acts and Resolves* passed by the Legislature of Massachusetts, 1843, p. 261.

[45] *Acts and Resolves* of Vermont, 1842-1850.

[46] *Public Acts of Connecticut, May Session*, 1844, pp. 33-34.

[47] Siebert, *op. cit.*, p. 286; McDougall, *op. cit.*, p. 67, err by asserting that New Hampshire had no such law, and Hurd, *op. cit.*, II, 35 in his collection of state laws on the subject omits this act completely.

Personal Liberty law. While the former act was enacted in a spirit of compromise and cooperation, the law of March 3, 1847, was definitely animated by hostile feeling. It was "most probably" a consequence of the Prigg decision that the new law was passed in 1847.[49] The Act of March 3, 1847, was entitled "An act to prevent kidnapping, preserve the public peace, prohibit the exercise of certain powers heretofore exercised by judges, justices of the peace, aldermen and jailors . . . and to repeal certain slave laws." No element of compromise here. Its eight parts were as follows: (Section I) The kidnapping of free Negroes or mulattoes for the purpose of taking them into slavery was made a misdemeanor punishable by a fine of between $500.00 and $2,000.00 and a prison term of between 5 to 12 years at hard labor. (Section II) The transfer of any free Negro fraudulently for purposes of reducing him to slavery was made a high misdemeanor. (Section III) No judge, alderman, or justice of the peace could take cognizance of any fugitive slave case under the Act of 1793; nor could they issue any certificate of removal. (Section IV) Fugitives from labor could not be violently carried off. This was to prevent disturbances of the public peace; in practice it made seizure of genuine fugitives almost impossible. (Section V) Judges were given the power to issue the writ of habeas corpus to anyone seized and claimed as a fugitive slave. (Section VI) The use of state or city jails to detain fugitives was prohibited. (Section VII) The abolition of slavery in Pennsylvania was reaffirmed and the few slaves in the state were accorded the privilege of being witnesses in court cases. (Section VIII) The Act of 1826 was repealed.[50]

Rhode Island was the last state to pass a Personal Liberty law prior to the Act of 1850. Her law of 1848 forbidding judicial and executive officers from assisting in the re-

[48] *Laws of New Hampshire*, 1846, p. 295.

[49] *Report of the Committee to Repeal an Act*, p. 7.

[50] *Laws of the Commonwealth of Pennsylvania, 1847*, p. 206; Hurd, *op. cit.*, II, 73-79.

capture of fugitives and forbidding detention in public jails differed from the others only in the leniency of the punishment for offenders, which was a fine up to $500.00 and imprisonment for 6 months or less.[51] It passed in the state lower House by a 39 to 16 vote and a unanimous vote in the Senate.[52]

Between 1842 and 1850 fugitive slavery in the northeastern states was characterized by two conditions: (1) number of fugitives increased greatly and (2) Southern slave owners made almost no use of the federal machinery to recover their runaways. It was becoming increasingly difficult to secure the recapture and return of the increasing number of fugitives.[53] Those states—Massachusetts, Vermont, Connecticut, New Hampshire, Pennsylvania, and Rhode Island—which had prohibited their state authorities from abetting slave catchers made legal recover of runaways almost impossible.[54] By 1850 the law of 1793 was a dead letter and Southern leaders knew it. As Senator Mason of Virginia said, "...you may as well go down into the sea, and endeavor to recover from his native element a fish which had escaped from you as to expect to recover [a] fugitive."[55]. In more prosaic terms a committee report of Congress protested that:

... the laws now in force are inadequate to remedy the evil ... the non-slaveholding states will not recognize and enforce them ...

What remedy have the slaveholding States now left for the enforcement of their constitutional right to the delivery of their property escaping into non-slaveholding communities? They have the *parchment guarantee of the constitution*, without ability to enforce it themselves, and with the hostile legislation of the non-slaveholding States to defeat them.

... A single clause of the act of 1793 is all that is left, and is a

[51] *Acts and Resolves of the State of Rhode Island*, January, 1848, p. 12.

[52] *Seventeenth Annual Report*, Massachusetts Anti-Slavery, January 24, 1849 (Boston, 1949), p. 33.

[53] Henry Wilson, *History of the Rise and Fall of the Slave Power in America* (3 vols.; Houghton, Mifflin and Co., 1874), I, 473.

[54] Siebert, *op. cit.*, p. 309.

[55] *Congressional Globe, 31 Cong., 1 sess., Appendix, p. 1584.*

dead letter, so far as it regards the power of giving it practical efficacy. All that is left of it is the right to bring an action against those in the non-slaveholding States who may conceal, or protect from seizure, a runaway slave. The right to sue a mob of irresponsible persons, without the power of procuring witnesses, and before a tribunal administering justice in a hostile community: Who would venture a such litigation?[56]

How much of this situation was actually due to the Prigg decision? The standard assumption in nearly all texts is that as a result of the decision the northeastern states passed their Personal Liberty laws and thereby succeeded, by depriving the slave-owners of the use of state officials, in frustrating their attempts to recapture fugitives. This idea is well exemplified in a popular work as follows:

> The Prigg case, in 1842, also served the Underground Railroad as well as a phalanx of new adherents. . . . The effect of this ruling was tremendous. The danger of the law had always hung over the heads of the runaway's friends, but now, although the Federal Law was no less stringent, they could offset it by a fresh crop of new personal liberty laws prohibiting the state authorities from joining in the man hunt.[57]

That such was the effect of this decision was generally accepted at the time, both among pro and anti-slavery men. A succinct statement from one of each group will show this. Said Butler of South Carolina in Congress, "I concur with. . .this: That since the decision in the case of the Commonwealth of Pennsylvania vs. Prigg, there has been less security for slave property escaping into free States, than there was before."[58] That same year (1850) William Jay said in a speech before an antislave gathering, "This decision has practically proved inconvenient to the slave-catcher by depriving him of the aid formerly granted by State laws and State officers. . ."[59]

It is worthwhile to note that almost without exception

[56] *Senate Reports, 31 Cong. 1 sess., No. 12.* pp. 5, 13.

[57] Henrietta Buckmaster, *Let My People Go* (New York: Harper and Bros., 1941), p. 124.

[58] *Congressional Globe. 31 Cong. 1 sess.,* Appendix, p. 1588.

[59] *Annual Report,* American and Foreign Anti-Slavery Society, 1850 (New York), pp. 3-4.

the memoirs and writings of those people most closely associated with the fugitive, i.e., the Underground Railroad workers, in describing their efforts between 1842 and 1850, never even mention the Prigg decision. As little deference is paid by them to the existence of the Personal Liberty laws. This, of course, is attributed to the fact that these workers carried on their illegal efforts with little consideration of the law, favorable or unfavorable. Some Underground Railroad workers who left memoirs or writings with not so much as a comment on the Prigg case include: Austin Bearse, Levi Coffin, Elizabeth Chace, William Cockrum, Daniel Drayton, Benjamin Drew, Calvin Fairbank, Laura Haviland, William Hawkins, H. U. Johnson, W. M. Mitchell, Eber Pettit, Nathaniel P. Roger, Alexander Ross, Robert Smedley, Peter Still, and William Still. A few of the fugitive slaves who described their experiences during this period but made no mention of the Prigg case are Henry "Box" Brown, Frederick Douglass, Josiah Henson, and Henry Watson. The only reference that the writer found to the Prigg case among such writings was a statement by William Whipper, who in 1871 recalling his career from memory wrote, "You are perfectly cognizant of the fact, that after the decision in York, Pa., of the celebrated Prigg case, Pennsylvania was regarded as free territory, which Canada afterwards proved to be, and that the Susquehanna River was the recognized northern boundary of the slave holding empire."[60]

The conclusion is therefore warranted, although admittedly it depends upon an "argument from silence", that whatever effect the Prigg decision may have had in facilitating fugitive escapes, those who aided them were hardly aware of that fact at the time. It is likewise true, however, that the decision in the Prigg case did enable Northern antislavery men more easily to frustrate Southern slaveholders in their attempts to recapture their runaway property. In

[60] Quoted in William Still, *The Underground Railroad* (Philadelphia: Porter and Coates, 1872) p. 735.

short, the effect of the decision should be limited to this: that it encouraged the spread of the old idea of withholding state officials from helping administer the Act of 1793. Prior to 1850 six of the nine northeastern states had already embodied this idea into law. Even if there had been no Prigg decision, there would have been no difference in the number and stringency of the impediments created by northern states to foil the slave hunters in pursuit of their quarry, although these impediments might have been created somewhat less quickly after 1842. The Prigg *dicta* merely furnished a welcome peg upon which to hang a growing public determination to give no aid to slave catchers. Had there been no Prigg decision this determination would probably have turned to trial by jury as its means of success.[61] Evidence in support of this is the fact that prior to the decision, six of the nine northeastern states, including the big three of Pennsylvania, New York and Massachusetts, had assured fugitives a jury trial. Furthermore, it is not inconceivable that even if Justice Story had never delivered his opinion in the Prigg case, some legislatures would have forbidden state officials from assisting Southerners in search of their slaves. In fact, Pennsylvania had done so unintentionally but nevertheless effectively in the early 1820's. Nothing said by the Supreme Court in the Prigg case was really new; it merely gave a solemn sanction of a highly revered tribunal to what had been done or was about to be done in the Northern states. The fundamental fact to remember is that by the beginning of the 1840's more and more Northerners were ready to express their hatred of slavery by action. As compared with this fact in its importance for the fugitive slave, the Prigg decision shrivels almost into insignificance.

JOSEPH NOGEE

University of Chicago

---

[61] This is what some Anti-Slavery men like William Jay believed would have been the proper course of action.

NEGRO CONCEPTS OF AMERICANISM

In his pioneer study of American patriotism, *The Roots of America Loyalty,* Merle Curti noted that in certain basic respects, the American Negro was an alien.[1] Dragged from an alien culture, set apart by his color, and associated with slavery in the minds of the whites, what did the Negro think of the United States and of his prospects there? How did his loyalty to and identification with the United States, i.e., his "Americanism", resemble or differ from that of the white American?

These questions have been of particular concern to the Negro intellectual throughout the course of American history. They became of special concern to whites during the two world wars of the twentieth century, when the question of Negro loyalty was widely discussed. They are of fundamental interest today as the United States moves toward a realization of democratic ideals as respects the Negro and as the United Nations seeks ratification of an international charter of human rights.

Early Americanism took it for granted that the hand of God was guiding the destiny of a favored people. After the Revolution, America was visualized as a stronghold of humane republicanism, an example to the rest of the world. However, Negro opinions of America's role in the world have generally revealed a natural preoccupation with race relationships.

Such concern with matters of race likewise characterizes Negro thinking about domestic affairs. Despite discrimination, most articulate Negros have been quick to consider themselves as Americans. In identifying himself with America, the Negro usually has asserted his claim to citizenship, which meant at first, citizenship of a particular state. As early as 1791, free Negroes in Charleston, claiming South Carolina citizenship, petitioned the legislature to remove legal restrictions upon the courtroom testimony of Negroes.

[1] M. Curti, *The Roots of American Loyalty,* New York, 1946, 87.

Having paid taxes since American independence, they wished to be treated as freemen but cautiously renounced hopes for a strictly "equal footing" with the whites of South Carolina.[2]

Upon what basis have Negroes claimed *American* citizenship? Birth on American soil and a share in the development of the country always were essential elements. Negroes had provided the necessary bone and sinew to make America what it was.[3] Also, as many writers pointed out, Negroes had aided and fought for the United States.[4]

For more than a century intelligent American Negroes have compared their situation with the European immigrants'. In 1837, when colored citizens of New York State with property worth less than $250, could not vote, a group of Negroes petitioned the legislature to extend the franchise to *all* male citizens. "Strangers to our institutions are permitted to flock to this land", they complained, "but we *native* Americans, the children of the soil are most of us shut out."[5] A half century later, Negroes as well as whites were identifying immigrants with radicalism or dual loyalty. They contrasted America's injustice to the Negro with her hospitality to numerious foreigners who, it was said, created disorder and anarchy.[6] During World War II

---

[2] Herbert Aptheker (ed.) *A Documentary History of the Negro People in the United States*. New York, 1951, 26-28.

[3] E.g., Martin R. Delany, *The Condition, Elevation, Emigration and Destiny of the Colored People of the United States*, Philadelphia, 1852, 66.

[4] Ibid., 67-85; P. S. Foner (ed.) *Frederick Douglass, Selections from His Writings*, N. Y. 1945, 53-54; William C. Nell, *The Services of Colored Americans in the Wars of 1776 and 1812*, 2nd ed., Boston, 1852. See also his "Colored American Patriots," *Anglo-African Magazine*, I, No. 1, Jan. 1859, 30-31; cf. James McCune Smith, "Citizenship," *ibid.*, No. 5, May 1859, 144-150. Cf. Carter G. Woodson, *Negro Orators and Their Orations*, Washington, 1925, 669.

[5] New York *Weekly Advocate* (extra ed.), February 22, 1837.

[6] E.g., D. Augustus Straker, *The New South Investigated*, Detroit, 1888, 67-68; Coffeyville, Kansas, *Afro-American Advocate*, September 29, 1892.

Horace M. Bond considered the Negro's lack of any separate national existence as a guarantee of his patriotism.[7]

Negroes were not nativists, yet some nineteenth century Negroes sounded an anti-Catholic note. James McCune Smith and Frederick Douglass believed that the Romanism of the Irish and the Germans threatened the integrity of American institutions.[8] But Smith was also concerned with the uniqueness of the American people, themselves largely the products of immigration. It was necessary, therefore, to educate the immigrants to the evil of slavery and the meaning of liberty.[9]

Slavery and the disabilities of the free Negroes led to doubts that equality was possible in the United States. Colonization or "expatriation" projects dominated much Negro thinking in the nineteenth century, and more recently the only Negro mass movement involved a nationalism centered about an empire in Africa. In the repudiation of these proposals lay vital ideas of Americanism. The earliest recorded instance occurred in 1789, when a society of free Negroes in Philadelphia failed to support the idea of a return to Africa.[10]

The founding of the American Colonization Society in 1817 evoked immediate opposition and many protest meetings were called. Some three thousand colored people in Philadelphia proclaimed: "Whereas our ancestors (not of choice) were the first successful cultivators of the wilds of America, we their descendants feel ourselves entitled to participate in the blessings of her luxuriant soil, which their blood and sweat manured; and that any measure or

[7] Horace Mann Bond, "Should the Negro Care Who Wins the War?" *Annals* of the American Academy of Political and Social Science, CCXXIII, Sept. 1942, 82.

[8] *Anglo-African Magazine*, I, No. 3, March 1859, 86; *New National Era*, Dec. 22, 1870, Jan. 5, 1871.

[9] *Anglo-African Magazine, loc. cit.*, 86.

[10] The opposition is implicit in the Philadelphians' reply, which was mildly worded. Charles H. Wesley, *Richard Allen, Apostle of Freedom*, Washington, 1935, 66-67.

system of measures, having a tendency to banish us from her bosom, would not only be cruel, but in direct violation of those principles, which have been the boast of this republic.''[11]

When John B. Russwurm, editor of the *Freedom's Journal*, announced in 1829 his support of the Colonization Society, he admitted that a majority of his readers would oppose him.[12] David Walker's *Appeal*, an exceptionally dramatic document, not only rejected colonization but scored the white Americans as brutal overlords who punished the Negroes for their own enrichment. Using the term "Americans" to mean whites only, Walker warned: "I tell you Americans!. . .that unless you speedily alter your course, *you* and your *Country* are gone! ! ! ! ! !" Yet he asserted: "America is more our country, than it is the whites'—we have enriched it with our *blood and tears.* . . Treat us like men, and there is no danger but we will all live in peace and happiness together."[13] A quarter century later, Samuel Ringgold Ward regarded the terms "American" and "Negro-hater" as almost synonymous. But Ward, too, never completely lost faith: the Negroes would advance, they knew American history, and their wrongs were violations of American principles.[14]

Throughout the resolution of Negro protest conventions run a few simple themes: The United States is our country, not Africa; we are content to remain where we are. All attempts to send us to Africa are uncalled for. It is our duty to resist all inducements to forsake our native soil for a strange land.[15] Some meetings went even further, and

[11] Samuel E. Cornish and Theodore S. Wright, *The Colonization Scheme Considered, in its Rejection by the Colored People.* . . Newark, 1840, 4. W. L. Garrison, *Thoughts on African Colonization*, Boston 1832, Part II, 9.

[12] *African Repository*, XXVII, December 1851, 357. Within a year Russwurm emigrated to Liberia.

[13] David Walker, *Appeal*, Boston, 1830, 24-25, 51, 56, 76, 80.

[14] Samuel R. Ward, *Autobiography of a Fugitive Negro*, London, 1855, 39, 51, 97.

[15] Garrison, *op. cit.*, 30-31, cf. 17, 25, 33, 37.

considered any colored émigré as a traitor to his race or an enemy to his country.[16] In several gatherings the Colonization Society was branded as selfish rather than benevolent, or a wicked device of slaveholders to get rid of troublesome free Negroes.[17] Whereas some of the conventions resisted *all* emigration projects, others looked favorably on a Negro colony in Canada, or suggested a possible haven within the western territories of the United States.[18]

We cannot determine how many free Negroes thought colonization undesirable or of dubious value. Many of the meetings took place in Quaker or abolitionist strongholds. The interest and influence of white abolitionists is apparent in most of the Negro conventions, and some of the more able and vocal colored spokesmen like Frederick Douglass were abolitionist leaders. Perhaps, therefore, the Negro conventions gave a false impression of strength and unanimity. Nevertheless the American Colonization Society itself admitted considerable free Negro opposition to emigration, even after the Fugitive Slave Law of 1850.[19]

The passage of that law contributed to a growing despair, however, and the colonization movement tended to drain off talented Negroes, some of whom, like Russwurm and Garnett, devoted their lives to Africa.[20] Perhaps Augustus Washington of Hartford, Conn., best expressed the colonizationist view. In 1851 he wrote that American politics

[16] *Ibid.*, 31, 35; Cornish and Wright, *op. cit.*, 5

[17] Garrison, *op. cit.*, 22, 32-33.

[18] Ibid., 35, 42, 46, 49. As one meeting expressed it: ''We see nothing contrary to the Constitution, to Christianity, justice, reason, or humanity, in granting us a portion of the Western territory''.

[19] *African Repository*, XXVII, October 1851, 290. Carter G. Woodson, *The Mind of the Negro as Reflected in Letters Written during the Crisis, 1800-1860*, Washington, 1926, 116.

[20] *African Repository*, XXVII, November 1851, 322; Woodson, *Mind of the Negro*, 42, 104, 116. In 1851 a Negro society was founded in New York City to advocate emigration to Africa, a course suggested by individuals as far apart as Philadelphia and St. Louis. In Richmond, Va., a Negro whose wife was sold and his children scattered, lamented: ''I do not weep to stay in any part of America, But to go home to my forefathers Land!''

had always victimized the Negro; this was to be expected when the Constitution guaranteed protection to both slavery and free institutions, securing liberties of one class at the expense of the other. Since it was impossible for Negroes to develop in America their "moral and intellectual qualities as a distinct people," Washington advocated the friendly separation of the races and the creation of another republic for the Negro.[21]

Martin R. Delany and J. T. Holly were among those who, sharing this despair, advocated colonizing Central America, Haiti, Trinidad, or Canada.[22] Delany suggested Central America.[23] Holly was interested in Haiti, which had been proposed as an asylum by Prince Saunders as early as 1818.[24] If those favoring Africa were snubbed by those who stressed asylum in the New World, the advocates of Africa held their own meetings.[25]

After the Civil War, with slavery in the United States no longer an issue, Negro thinking about America emphasized the problems of the present and the tasks of the future. Negro utterances of the Reconstruction period were optimistic and generally linked patriotism with Negro freedom. A convention of Kentucky Negroes asserted: "We are part and parcel of the great American body politic, we love our country and her institutions; we are proud of her greatness, and glory in her might; we are *intensely American*. . . Here we wish to remain. . .our destiny shall be that of earnest and faithful Americans. . .".[26] Expatriation was no longer

[21] Letter to N. Y. *Tribune*, July 3, 1851, as reprinted in *African Repository*, XXVII, September 1851, 259-265.

[22] Woodson, *Negro Orators*, 192.

[23] Delany, *op. cit.*, 171, 178 ff.

[24] J. T. Holly, "Thoughts on Hayti," *Anglo-African Magazine*, I, No. 11, November 1859, 363-367; Prince Saunders, *A Memoir presented to the American Convention for Promoitng the Abolition of Slavery, and Improving the Condition of the African Race*, Philadelphia, 1818.

[25] *Weekly Anglo-African*, April 28, 1860; see also the issues of March 31, April 7, 21, 1860.

[26] *The* (Nashville) *Tennessean*, July 18, 1866. See also the poems of

necessary, for emancipation had made America the Negroes' own country.[27] In the verse of Elijah Smith:

> We have a country now, and a bright guidon,
> Studded with stars on our pathway to shine. . . .[28]

Optimism was not the only theme. Hopes were voiced that the new gains would be safeguarded. Negro congressmen argued that a civil rights bill would relieve the colored man of anxiety about his status and encourage him to enter non-political fields.[29] He would then *want* to do his best "to advance the interests of a common country."[30] Negro conventions also stressed the obligation of meriting equal rights through self-education, honest achievement, and acquisition of property.[31] In 1867, for instance, a National Colored Labor Convention resolved to encourage industrious habits, education, and participation in the material and spiritual development of the country.[32]

As the period of Reconstruction receded into the background, once bright hopes faded away. The Negro's failure to achieve civil rights led to a renewal of the emigration

George Moses Horton, especially "To the Fourth," "My Native Home," "Assassination of Lincoln," and "The Obstructions of Genius," in his *Naked Genius*, Raleigh, N. C., 1865.

[27] Woodson, *Negro Orators*, 439, 440.

[28] *New Era*, April 28, 1870.

[29] E.g., John R. Lynch of Mississippi and J. T. Rapier of Alabama, in Woodson, *Negro Orators*, 356, 369.

[30] *Ibid.*, 356, cf. John M. Langston's views, *ibid.*, 444.

[31] E.g., resolutions of the convention of colored men of Kentucky, *The Tennessean.* July 18, 1866, and of the National Colored Labor Convention, Washington, D. C., *New Era*, January 13, 1870.

Supporting Congressional Reconstruction, the *Weekly Loyal Georgian*, August 10, 1867, urged a state common school system, "the elevation of labor and the passage of such laws as will protect the toiling masses of society in their just and legal rights." The words of the *Anglo-African Magazine*, September 1859 (p. 298), seem to have anticipated this era: Negroes should be the most worthy citizens in the country, adopt the ideal of upright, thrifty, self-reliant manhood, teach this ideal to the young, teach them even to excel the whites "in all that is noble, and prudent, and upright."

[32] *New Era*, January 13, 1870.

controversy. Booker T. Washington was *optimistic* about advancement in America, and Frederick Douglass held that the American Negro owed no more to the Negroes of Africa than he owed to the Negroes in the United States. "All this native land talk is nonsense", he exclaimed, "The native land of the American Negro is America.[33]

Opposing views represented the growth of Negro nationalism and the Pan-Negro ideologies at the turn of the century. As early as 1859, however, J. T. Holly had complained that the lack of a powerful and enlightened Negro nationality lay behind all the wrongs suffered by Negroes throughout the world.[34]

Almost forty years later, in 1897, W. E. B. DuBois asserted that if the Negro ever were to be a factor in the world's history, it would be through a Pan-Negro movement. The destiny of American Negroes was to reject a servile imitation of white Anglo-Saxon culture, to lead the Pan-Negro forces, and to insist on a stalwart Negro originality.[35]

No Negro who had thought about the problem in America, continued DuBois, had failed to ask himself: "Am I an American or am I a Negro? Can I be both?" "We are Americans", DuBois decided, "not only by birth and by citizenship, but by our political ideals, our language, our religion. . .Farther than that our Americanism does not go. At that point we are Negroes. . .that people whose subtle sense of song has given America its only American music, its only American fairy tales, its only touch of pathos and humor amid its mad money-getting plutocracy. . .as a race

---

[33] Booker T. Washington, *Up From Slavery*, Garden City, 1925, 282, 285; Frederick Douglass, *The Lessons of the Hour*, address delivered January 9, 1894, Baltimore, 1894. Douglass criticized colonization as encouraging the absurd belief that the Negro ultimately could be driven from the country.

[34] This, Holly believed, would lead to the extirpation of slavery and the slave trade. "Thoughts on Hayti," *Anglo-African Magazine*, I, No. 11, November 1859, 364-367.

[35] W. E. B. DuBois, "The Conservation of Races," American Negro Academy occasional papers, No. 2, Washington, 1897, 10.

we must strive by race organization, by race solidarity, by race unity to the realization of that broader humanity which freely recognizes differences in men, but sternly deprecates inequality in their opportunities of development.''[36]

The Pan-Africanism of DuBois never had mass appeal. It remained for Marcus Garvey, a Jamaican Negro, to develop the first mass movement, the only truly nationalist movement among American Negroes. During the first world war, Garvey preached the complete repudiation of white standards. America, said Garvey, was a white man's country. The one real hope for the Negro lay in the founding of an independent nation, which must be in Africa, the true home of the Negro.[37] Garvey's Universal Negro Improvement Association appealed to group-consciousness and pride; it gave the individual a psychological release from his social burdens and a chance to display himself through an elaborate ritual, gaudy uniforms, and parades which heightened the emotional appeal.[38]

Garveyism made a virtue of blackness. It transformed what traditionally was a thing of shame into a symbol of strength and superiority. ''We shall march out'', Garvey announced, ''as black American citizens, as black British subjects, as black French citizens, as black Italians or as black Spaniards, but we shall march out with a greater loyalty, the loyalty of race. . . To win Africa we will give up America. . .''[39]

The Garvey movement reached its height about 1920-21.

[36] *Ibid.*, 11-12.

[37] Ralph J. Bunche, ''Conceptions and Ideologies of the Negro Problem,'' unpublished manuscript prepared as a part of the preliminary researches (1940) for Gunnar Myrdal's *An American Dilemma*, 152 ff; Ralph J. Bunche, ''Programs, Ideologies, Tactics and Achievements of Negro Betterment and Interacial Organizations,'' part of preliminary researches for Myrdal's *An American Dilemma*, II, 393-394, 396, 397.

[38] *Ibid.*, 398; E. F. Frazier, ''Garvey, a Mass Leader,'' *Nation*, August 18, 1926, 147-148; Bunche, ''Conceptions and Ideologies . . .'' *loc. cit.*, 153.

[39] Amy Jacques Garvey, comp., *Philosophy and Opinions of Marcus Garvey*, New York, 1923-26, II, 96, 100, 107.

Its membership never has been exactly ascertained, but Garvey's estimate of six million, no doubt, is exaggerated. One of his enemies denied that it reached even a million. Kelly Miller thought four million nearer the truth.[40] With the imprisonment of Garvey for mail fraud, his deportation in 1927, and in the face of strong opposition from other Negro organizations and individuals, the movement disintegrated. Garveyism has been noted here primarily because it did *not* stress Americanism, which is at least *one* reason for its failure.

Later Pan-Negro movements had relatively little popular support. Among these was a "National Movement for the Establishment of the Forty-Ninth State," launched in 1934. The movement for a Negro state made no headway, however, despite support of the idea by the Communist Party.[41]

Politically, American Negroes have been conservative. The Socialist Party welcomed colored members, but never won many to its cause. Negroes had grown skeptical of reformers seeking their aid and, as Wilson Record has put it, "were too preoccupied with staying alive and praising God (in that order) to give time to the building of the new society."[42] Moreover, the race stigma was enough; why invite the stigma of radicalism?

Unlike the Socialists, the Communist Party saw Negroes not simply as workers but as an exploited minority whose support might be gained through specially directed propaganda. The Communist failure to capture the Negroes resulted largely from the Party's adherence to the Kremlin line, to which the Negro question was subordinated. Behind this failure lay the Party's inability to appreciate the Amer-

[40] Bunche, "Programs . . .", *loc. cit.*, II, 398, 402.

[41] *Ibid.*, III, 437-443.

[42] Wilson Record, *The Negro and the Communist Party*, Chapel Hill, 1951, 11.

[43] *Ibid.*, 213. Colored members of the Communist Party probably never exceeded 8,000 at any one time. *Ibid.*, 299.

icanism and lack of class solidarity among colored Americans.[43] This is illustrated by the anti-radical stand of the well known Negro betterment organizations.[44]

The world wars brought out the dominant patriotism of American Negroes. Coupled with strong protestations of loyalty, however, were complaints about segregation and unequal treatment.[45] While in 1918 Francis J. Grimké refused to buy liberty bonds and while socialists A. Phillip Randolph and Chandler Owen proclaimed that patriotism meant nothing to them, R. R. Moton, Booker Washington's successor at Tuskegee, was assuring President Wilson of the loyalty of American Negroes.[46] Significantly, Moton called Wilson's attention to an unprecedented Negro restlessness and dissatisfaction.[47] After the war Negro editorials took the position that since the colored man fought to make the world safe for democracy the United States should now be made safe for him.[48]

Wartime and postwar conditions led to further interest in race solidarity. The growth of a Negro middle class, a Negro press, reform organizations, and above all, the mass migrations from the South to the industrial centers of the North fostered an increased race-consciousness. In the nineteen twenties the concept of the "New Negro", as advanced by Alain Locke, emphasized the Negro's creativeness and wholesome contribution to the country. Let the Negro avoid colorless conformity to American life, but let him also avoid

[44] For discussion of replies to questionnaires distributed among N.A.A.C.P. branches, as well as branches of the National Urban League and various independent groups, see Bunche, "programs . . .", loc. cit., I, 192-194; II, 292-293; IV, 662, and Bunche, "Conceptions and Ideologies . . .", loc. cit., 150.

[45] Robert T. Kerlin, The Voice of the Negro, 1919, New York, 1920, 28, 33, 34.

[46] Francis J. Grimké, Works (Woodson ed.) III, 72; Randolph and Owen are quoted in Charles S. Johnson's "The Rise of the Negro Magazine," Journal of Negro History, XIII, No. 1, January 1928, 17; Moton to Wilson, June 15, 1918, in Grimké, Works, IV, 216-217.

[47] R. R. Moton, Finding a Way Out, Garden City, N. Y., 1921, 236-237; Moton to Wilson, loc. cit.

[48] Kerlin, op. cit., 34.

narrow Negro nationalism. His choice, Locke explained, was "not between one way for the Negro and another way for the rest, but between American institutions frustrated on the one hand and American ideals progressively fulfilled and realized on the other".[49]

Another indication of race consciousness during the last thirty years has been the stress upon American Negro history. Its foremost advocate, Carter Woodson, the guiding spirit of the Association for the Study of Negro Life and History, edited for many years the *Journal of Negro History* and wrote caustic reviews of books which slighted the Negro. Muzzey's *American History,* he objected, made "no mention whatever of what the Negroes. . .have thought and felt and done", and Oberholtzer's second volume had "very little to say about Negroes except to refer to them as an ignorant, illiterate mass of thieves and rascals".[50] Woodson's leadership led to the inauguration of Negro History Week in 1926 and to the demand that Negro history be taught in all the schools.[51] In a book with the significant title, *The Negro, Too, in American History,* Merl R. Eppse asserted that American Negro achievements would "convince the most critical mind that the Negro is an integral part of American culture",[52] and Charles H. Wesley proposed that historians treat Negroes not merely as receivers of liberty but as winners of it, not simply as slaves or an alien part of the population but as Americans.[53]

[49] Alain Locke, *The New Negro*, New York, 1925, 12.

[50] *Journal of Negro History*, VI, No. 3, July 1921, 376-377; VIII, No. 4, October 1923, 460. Of F. L. Paxson's *Recent History of the United States*, Woodson wrote that a foreigner upon reading it might wonder whether, after the success of the Bourbon Democrats, the Negroes had been exterminated or had emigrated from the country. *Ibid.*, VII, No. 4, October 1922, 452. *Cf.* L. D. Reddick, "Racial Attitudes in American History Textbooks of the South." *ibid.*, XIX, No. 3, July 1934, 224-265.

[51] E.g., J. W. Bell, "The Teaching of Negro History," *ibid.*, VIII, No. 2, April 1923, 123-127.

[52] Merl R. Eppse, *The Negro, Too, in American History*, enlarged ed., Nashville, 1949, XII, 363, 364.

[53] Charles H. Wesley, "The Reconstruction of History," *Journal of Ne-*

During World War II Negroes remembered earlier disappointments. Segregation in the armed forces and discrimination in defense industries led to Negro criticisms of the war effort. In his article, "Fighting for White Folks?", Horace Cayton quoted a young Negro as saying, "Just carve on my tombstone, 'Here lies a black man killed fighting a yellow man for the protection of a white man.' "[54] Cayton predicted that with appropriate demagogic leadership the Negro would join another Garvey movement.

Nevertheless Negroes generally remained loyal. In an article, "Should the Negro Care Who Wins the War?" Horace Bond called it nonsense to ask if *Americans* should care.[55] Although loyal to the nation at war, Negroes were unwilling to halt their effort to achieve equality. "It is a wicked notion," declared one group at Durham, N. C., "that the struggle of the Negro for citizenship is a struggle against the best interests of the Nation."[56] Similarly, Ralph Bunche considered it defeatist to accept the status quo. . . "The practical essence of a democratic society," he insisted, "is in the mechanisms it affords for the solution of its problems. This is precisely why democracy is worth fighting for. . ."[57]

---

gro History, XX, No. 4, October 1935, 422-427. This journal carried a review (XVI, No. 3, July 1931, 341) of Spero and Harris' *The Black Worker*, praising it for considering the Negro worker as an integral part of the American laboring community.

[54] *Nation*, September 26, 1942.

[55] Horace M. Bond, "Should the Negro Care Who Wins the War?" *Annals* of the American Academy of Political and Social Science, CCXXIII, September 1942, 81. Cf. Walter White, "It's Our Country, Too," *Saturday Evening Post*, December 14, 1940; "The Negro's War," Fortune, June 1942, 77; B. Schrieke, *Alien Americans*, New York, 1936, 151-153.

[56] Charles S. Johnson and others, *Into the Main Stream*, Chapel Hill, 1947, 7-8.

[57] Ralph J. Bunche, "The Negro in the Political Life of the United States," *Journal of Negro Education*, X, No. 3, July 1941, 583-584; Bunche's statement is remarkable, for only two years earlier he had written: "The Negro is an American citizen, but his thinking is often more Negro than American. The white American may look with subjective interest upon Munich,

The effect of the second world war was to broaden Negro horizons. Wartime and postwar developments seemed to vindicate the faith in democratic ideals now universalized in the United Nations charter.[58] Not only did American Negroes evidence interest in the charter, but several well known Negroes participated in the San Francisco conference which gave birth to the United Nations.[59] As Negroes have shown increased sympathy for the aspirations of other non-white people, the Negro press has emphasized the protests of the African colored and Indian population against the racial policies of the Union of South Africa.[60]

While American Negroes have tended more and more to identify themselves with the darker people of the world, their basic American loyalty remains unquestioned. The more chauvinistic Negro efforts in America have failed, but the more moderate programs have sought to equate racial pride with national pride by fuller emphasis on the positive contributions of the Negro. This call to develop inner resources is consistent with historic Negro concepts of Americanism, which have interpreted literally the Declaration of Independence and proclaimed the ideal of full equality for all peoples in the United States.

ROBERT ERNST

Adelphi College

but the American Negro regards the latest lynching as infinitely more important to him." (Bunche, "Programs," *loc. cit.*, IV, 766, quoting from an article he wrote for the *Journal of Negro Education*, July 1939.)

[58] Mary M. Bethune, "The Negro in Retrospect and Prospect," *Journal of Negro History*, XXXV, No. 1, January 1950, 19; cf. Charles H. Wesley, "Racial Historical Societies and the American Heritage," *ibid.*, XXXVII, No. 1, January 1952, 34-35. Johnson and others, *op. cit.*, 8.

[59] John Hope Franklin, *From Slavery to Freedom*, New York, 1948, 583; chapter XXX presents the theme of growing international interests of American Negroes.

[60] *Ibid.*, 580-585; Edwin R. Embree, *Brown Americans*, New York, 1943, 233. Cf. Rayford W. Logan, *The Negro and the Post-war World, A Primer*, Washington, D. C., 1945, and Merze Tate, "The War Aims of World War I and World War II and their Relations to the Darker Peoples of the World," *Journal of Negro Education*, XII, Summer 1943.

BOOK REVIEWS

Out of Confusion. By Manmatha Nath Chatterjee. (Yellow Springs, Ohio. The Antioch Press, 1954, pp. 165. Price $3.00.)

Dr. Manmatha Nath Chatterjee has distilled his Brahman background, European education, three decades of teaching in an American college, and a lifetime of learning into this book. The result is a mixture of autobiography, personal philosophy, and social theory in a summation that weds the thought of two cultures in an attempt to reach a synthesis greater than either.

The author was raised in the intellectual and social aristocracy of the Brahman Indian, but he knows the other side of Eastern life too, the India of the illiterate and depressed masses. A friend and confidant of Mahatma Gandhi and other Indian leaders, he is well acquainted with the social philosophy and ancient culture of the entire Far East—its enduring strengths as well as its problems in meeting the challenges of the present. His knowledge of the Western world is equally wide and deep. Completing his higher education in Scotland, Germany, and the United States, he prepared for a career in engineering, thus gaining a first-hand acquaintance with Western achievements in material culture. His observations of the two ways of life, however, convinced him that his own greatest contributions to both could best be made through teaching and instilling in students the bases for a well rounded social philosophy.

This contribution was made during thirty-one years of teaching social sciences at Antioch College. Shortly before his retirement in 1953 a poll of Antioch alumni overwhelmingly named Professor Chatterjee as the teacher who had most profoundly influenced their thought and lives.

Out of Confusion amounts to a collection of essays on such subjects as "Man and Society," "Laws of Living," "Standard of Value," "Competition and Man," "Wealth and Welfare," "Race and Civilization," "The National State," "Behavior in Democracy," "God and Man," "Education in an Ancient Society," and "Education for Our Time." In his treatment of these subjects Dr. Chatterjee brings the serenity of the East to bear upon his long experience with the life and problems of the Western World. In his penetrating discussion of the problems of war and peace, economic life, and the responsibility of democratic citizenship, "he always keeps before his readers the basic consideration that human life is

220

an indivisible whole and that sound, civilized values must be worked out and deliberately infused through all our life.''

''Race and Civilization'' and ''Education in Our Time'' are, no doubt, the two chapters of greatest concern and interest to readers of *The Journal of Negro History*. In the former Dr. Chatterjee compares the race issue in Anglo-American countries, which means ''no intermarriage with the out groups,'' with the Hindu method of preventing inter-caste meeting and marriage. By following a strict code and guarding it with fanatic zeal, the Brahmans have kept their unique position in society without legal or police help in guarding their women. No cases of race or lynching are on record. When inter-caste meeting takes place, the only punishment is ostracism. Both parties become ''out-caste,'' Brahman and lower caste members alike. No double standard is condoned, as in the case of inter-mating (in distinction to marriage) of a white man and Negro woman in America. In this way India has escaped the kind of race controversy that plagues the United States.

Professor Chatterjee observes that neither solution is the right one; both are based on misconceptions about race. And these misconceptions are charged with emotions that make them difficult to overcome. The race question still divides mankind, and does not seem to be solvable by intellectual means.

In the last chapter of his book the author emphasizes that the main obligation of education in a democratic society is to make provision for the individual to develop himself so that he can *exercise his own judgment*. Dr. Chatterjee, as an American, is naturally interested in a people in search of a Free Society and believes that a solution of the world's problems will have to originate in this land. Therefore, we must pay very careful attention to the kind of education that is offered here. ''If the American people with their relative freedom, spirit of free enterprise, initiative, and resources fail to rise to the occasion, the future of humanity seems very dark indeed.''

MERZE TATE

Howard University

The People of South Africa. By Sarah Gertrude Millin. (New York: Alfred A. Knopf, 1954. Pp. 337, xii. Price $4.50.)

This book continues and elaborates further the presentation of a body of subject matter which Mrs. Millin brought together in a book entitled *The South Africans,* published in 1926 and revised in 1934.

There is good evidence—much of it repeated in this volume—which indicates that the *Weltanschauung* of the European-derived South African people, especially with reference to the aborigines, has not been altered basically since the seventeenth century, but over the decades, and most particularly the recent ones, the country has felt the shock of accelerated social changes. First the colonies and Dutch republics and later the Union, always seeking for self-contained isolation, have been engulfed by movements which they were unable to avoid. Hence, although the general theme with which Mrs. Millin was concerned in 1926 remains, the consideration of new events in the South African scene has caused this book to be "half again as long as the book of 1926. Four fifths of it is new. Not many pages are unaltered." Yet "the beginning and the end are more or less as in 1934," for the South African problem is essentially not different, though much intensified by the more recent occurrences.

"Today," she says (page 7), "all understand that South Africa can no longer ignore its native question, can no longer depend on it to solve itself. The black man and the white man are irking one another; the Indian is troubling both; and whether it is to be eventually a black man's country or a white man's country or an Asian's country is not the only question. There is the question of the present as well as the future.

"Here we all are, a heterogeneous collection of Europeans; an imported and established population of Indians; a man- rather than a God-created nation of half-castes; a ghosthood of yellow aboriginals and a flood—a strong and spreading flood—of dark-skinned peoples. And, since we are not alone on the planet, and, so small as we are, cannot control our own destinies, the problem that chiefly concerns us is how, being here together, we may live and grow with the least unhappiness and enmity."

This is the problem. Briefly, it is that of maintaining a pluralistic order, with the white population dominant and having symbiotic relations with the non-whites, and with every safeguard against social and biological mingling. Everything that Mrs. Millin says—and she speaks of a great number of persons and events—is related to this problem, and it is so complicated that one easily may share her feelings when she says (page 171), "South Africa faces a question beyond solution, that is all."

The book is in two parts, the first of which is historical and begins with a sketch of the origins of the population, including the Hottentots and Bushmen, who already were there, the migrations and settlements from Europe, the coming of the Bantu from farther north, and the importations of oriental slaves and coolie laborers. This is followed by chapters describing developments resulting from the discovery of diamonds and gold, one which gives a generalized portrait of the social life of the whites, conditioned primarily by the position of the Bantu, and a final and longer chapter on South African politics, with the native again being a determining element. The second part consists of six chapters which characterize in succession the Africaners, English, Jews, Indians, the Cape Coloured, and the Bantu.

Perhaps the chief distinction of this book among the considerable number of writings about South Africa is the relative absence of polemics; rather, it describes and discusses the issues, and it does so with appreciable objectivity.

MARK HANNA WATKINS

Howard University

The Growth of Southern Nationalism 1848-1861. By Avery O. Craven. (Baton Rouge, Louisiana: Louisiana State University Press, 1953. Pp. 433. Price $6.50.)

This is the sixth published volume in a ten-volume series entitled "A History of the South." The entire project is sponsored by Louisiana State University and the Trustees of the Littlefield Fund for Southern History at The University of Texas.

Mr. Craven has examined the major primary sources and secondary materials which deal with his subject. He has placed particular emphasis upon the conflicting points of view among Southerners in regard to the Mexican War; the abstract right of slaveholders to enter territories; the Compromise of 1850; the Kansas-Nebraska Act; the political estrangement between the South and the Northwest; party realignment; the wisdom of secession itself. While the study deals largely with the South's position in political matters, some attention has been given to the interest or lack of interest among articulate Southerners in humanitarian reforms, education, and economic matters.

In his study the author has relied heavily upon the opinions expressed by contemporary Southern newspaper editors who represented a cross section of the varying shades of political opinion. This dependence upon newspapers was not only due to the fact that they expressed and molded public opinion, as Mr. Craven has said, but also to the relative paucity of information dealing with the crystallization of Southern opinion in regard to slavery and secession.

Mr. Craven asserts that the sectional conflict which resulted in the Civil War stemmed largely from ''slavery as a thing in itself and then as a symbol of all differences and conflicts.'' He states that neither section could modify its position ''because slavery had come to symbolize values in each of their social-economic structures for which men fight and die but which they do not give up or compromise.'' Attitudes toward other issues of the times were colored by the majority feeling in the South on slavery. The most aggressive sentiment was manifested in South Carolina and Mississippi. However, in all of the Southern states opinions tended to wax and wane until the fatal steps leading to secession and Civil War were taken. By this time aggressive leaders had gained the upper hand and ''the masses had become numb and helpless before the onrush of events.'' Following the election of Lincoln many Southerners were still not favorable to secession, although few endorsed complete submission.

The statements that ''the South in the 1840's was only vaguely conscious of itself as a section'' (p. 6) and that this section ''was ready to consider secession seriously as a practical remedy for grievances'' for the first time in the winter of 1847-1848 and in the Presidential campaign of the following summer (p. 41) seem to be in conflict. It is doubtful that John Brown's Raid ''served a purpose in demonstrating to the North and South alike the loyalty and contentment of the slave'' (p. 308). The photograph of a Negro cabin in Louisiana (facing page 262) is certainly not ''typical of former slave quarters throughout the Deep South.''

The author gives the impression that not only was Southern reaction which culminated in secession and Civil War slow in developing, but that it was aroused by the Northern press and leading public figures from that section. He is correct in asserting that slavery was an anachronism in a nation in which vast socio-economic changes were taking place and which, in addition, professed Christianity and Democracy. While this volume reveals little concerning the period that is not already known, it is well written and generally exemplifies sound scholarship. It is a valuable addition to the long list of studies which deal with the sectional conflict that led to civil strife in the United States.

ROBERT D. REID

Tuskegee Institute

Americans Interpret Their Civil War. By Thomas J. Pressly. (Princeton, N. J.: Princeton University Press, 1954. Pp. xiii, 347. Price $5.00.)

To contemporaries and to successive generations, what was the meaning of the Civil War? To describe and analyze the changing interpretations of that conflict: this is the task which Pressly lays upon himself. A three-pronged work, this volume is a profile of American historiography, a sidelight on our social and intellectual ordering, and an exercise in historical relativism — the manner in which writers of history can read into the past their own ideas.

As a sketch-book of historiography, herein are contained illuminating vignettes of more than a score of the figures who have shaped our thinking about the past, including such worthies as Von Holst, Rhodes, Turner, Channing, McMaster, Beard, Parrington, Phillips, Randall, and Nevins. These writers fall into rather well-defined schools of historical interpretation, states Pressly. During the two decades following Appomattox, the typical Northern historian viewed the conflict as a "war of the rebellion," whereas the prevailing Southern attitude was reflected in the title, "the war between the states." At the turn of the century, James Ford Rhodes and the professionally trained historians viewed the war as an "irrepressible conflict," and infused their writings with sentiments of nationalism and sectional reconciliation.

Some two decades later Charles A. Beard held that the war was primarily a life-and-death struggle between two power aggregates, the industrial North and the cotton-culture South. The views of Beard and Vernon Parrington as to the primacy of economic factors were naturally also reflected in the pages of the Marxists, notably James S. Allen and Richard Enmale. Concurrently with the economic-emphasis vogue was the "new vindication of the South" school, cued by the commanding figure of U. B. Phillips. This sympathetic view of the South had much in common with the "revision-ist" attitude of the Craven-Randall wing, which pronounced the war as a repressible conflict brought about by a "blundering gen-eration" of sectional extremists, the Garrisonian abolitionists in the vanguard. Entering the lists relatively recently, the redoubtable Allan Nevins gave to the war an interpretation that apparently sought to combine the ideas of failure-of-American-leadership and inevitability, an uneasy dualism that did not lack for critics.

While disclaiming any deterministic bent, geographical or other-wise, Pressly nonetheless establishes his biographies in space and time. Thus, for example, the Rhodes generation of historians is viewed in relation to the "road to reunion" spirit which charac-terized America at the turn of the century; Beard is projected against reform movements of the early 1900's, and the Phillips-Ramsdell-Owsley school of Southern sympathizers is viewed in re-lation to the reaction in the South to criticism of its treatment of the Negro. In like manner the exponents of the "needless war" theory are portrayed in the light of contemporary disillusionment concerning armed conflict as a solution to human problems. In thus furnishing a backdrop for the major historians, Pressly gives some-thing of a running history of ideas in post-Civil War America.

Pressly's study is finally a case history in relativism—the man-ner in which a memorable event may be interpreted so as to subserve a multiplicity of interests. To Civil War writers the objectivist goal of history for history's sake has not seemed challenging. Indeed the forthright opinions that the Civil War has evoked among the technicians would seem to indicate that they have reacted no less compulsively to their times and manners than have lay writers of history or radio newscasters with tomorrow morning's headlines.

A student of the problem of objectivity, Pressly's own approach is balanced and well-rounded. He thought it advisable to tell a little of his own background (born in Tennessee of Confederate for-bears, schooled at Harvard, teaching appointments at the University of Washington and Princeton) and perhaps it is just as well—otherwise detection would not have been easy. If the author's pages are without partisanship, they are not without stylistic sparkle. The footnoting is abundant; if it is almost exclusively gleaned from readily available printed materials, the nature of the study is ample explanation. The appendix, "Note on the Sources," is a helpful introductory statement both to Civil War historiography and to the general problem of "relativism" in historical studies.

If some criticism of this admirable work must be voiced, it is the unfamiliar internal arrangement of the chapters. Each sub-topic in a chapter begins on a separate page with its own title; thus seeing a "4" or a "5" at the top of a fresh page, followed by a title, one has to remind himself that this is a continuation of the current chapter rather than the beginning of a new one.

BENJAMIN QUARLES

Morgan State College

A History of the Southern Confederacy. By Clement Eaton. (New York: The McMillan Co., 1954. pp. 351. Price $5.50.)

After nearly ninety years since its establishment, here is another history of the Southern Confederacy. The work is a comprehensive interpretation of the intellectual, political, and social factors and forces which were responsible for launching Southern independence. The resulting Civil War is inseparable in the investigation and appears to have been inevitably provoked by a generation of intensified emotionalism rather than dispassionate consideration of fundamental economics on which the South was undoubtedly in error. The author maintains superb historical detachment in assessing the evidence on both sides in arriving at what may well be considered the most definitive history of the Confederacy that has yet been written. His coverage of causes of the conflict and the war itself leaves no doubt of his dispassionate historical judgment and capacity to handle explosive human and political issues with judicial calm. For example, futile diplomacy, conflicts in sectional loyalties, military strategy in logistics, bitter personal rivalries among incompetent Confederate civilian officials, and fumbling in conducting of the war effort pass in review.

The prosecution of the war on both sides is given appropriate examination with accounts of land and naval maneuvers. Here the high quality of Confederate military leaders is treated with pertinent comments on the strength and weaknesses of other leaders. President Davis's shortcomings are not overlooked as they often conflicted in war councils where policies of momentous decision had to be determined. Especially enlightening is the revelation of Confederate failure to coordinate civil and military procedures which proved so effective in World Wars I and II. Civilian morale was sadly neglected as well as the vital war economy which often caused soldiers to suffer hunger and almost starvation when there was abundant available food! While the Confederacy lacked many of the vital sinews of war, some which slipped through the blockade were often improperly handled. Likewise, the author shows that Southern foreign relations were nearly a complete failure due in a large measure to incompetence of diplomats as well as to the insuperable difficulties of recognition. The mistaken hopes of cotton's indispensability, on which the South staked so much, however, in foreign relations are generally omitted although they were fundamental. Treatment of cotton would have involved, perhaps, the discussion of more urgent demands, abroad for grain from the Middle West and ideational issues on slavery which space limits precluded.

The author's equipment in preparing this history of the Confederacy is possibly without precedent. His birth in the western North Carolina Piedmont and training at Chapel Hill as well as Harvard were unusual in opportunity to study issues in the Confederacy from Northern as well as Southern points of view. These advantages were enriched and enlarged by contacts in teaching and research at Princeton, Wisconsin, and Kentucky universities and in Manchester, England university where he explored the British interest in the struggle. To these should be added sources in vast numbers of books, collections of manuscript materials, and previously untouched personal memoirs and letters. His problems here required discerning selections rather than exhaustive inclusion of all relevant information which would possibly have required at least two additional volumes! For this task Dr. Eaton had also a background in his *Freedom of Thought in the Old South* (1940) and *A History of the Old South* (1949) that no historian of the Southern Confederacy has possessed.

In handling the innate difficulties of the Civil War the author maintains similar balance and rare discretion to that which he employs in evaluating the subtle causes leading to the conflict. The sheer differences in fighting resources both material and human are analyzed and evaluated. Such puzzling problems as manpower, presence of slaves, intransigeance of some Southern Governors, disintegration and deterioration of fighting potentialities accompanying reverses and, most of all, loss of the Southern "will to fight" receive interpretation that is as enlightening as it is revealing. To these vital issues confronting the Confederacy the author adds such equally relevant centrifugal and peripheral distractions as: absence of a united Southern front in the contest, sectional diversity and hostility of social classes, and impacts of war upon the "mind and heart" of the South. While the consequences of these factors for Southern fortunes and hopes are fully assessed, it should be remembered that there were also handicaps to the North in the "Copperheads" and other distractions. Since the records of the Confederacy constitute the central theme of the work, it is not strictly germane to include or compare essentially similar deflections in the North. Under the circumstances, Dr. Eaton seems correctly to be dubious as to whether the South could have possibly won, but he presents the record so clearly that the reader, scholar or layman, may speculate about possibilities (if the outcome had been different) which are out of the bounds of the historian.

The values of *A History of the Southern Confederacy* are significant because it reveals neglected aspects of logistics, morale of Southern people under the most trying circumstances, the roles of Negroes in the South and in the Union armies, Western Confederate campaigns, women in the conflict, cultural and literary life, and changes. Throughout the treatment there is splendid proportion between military history and economic, cultural, political, and social history. The truth about both sides in the Civil War has been the author's goal which the work abundantly proves that he has attained. The style and craftsmanship of the work attain the heights achieved in his books previously mentioned. Finally, here is fascinating history of the nation's greatest and most bitter crisis. While the work is a result of the most rigorous and thorough research, the author has written so pungently and understandably that reading his findings on the Confederacy and the Civil War will undoubtedly afford pleasure. A bibliography similar to that in *A History of the Old South* should be appended for teaching purposes and further explorations.

W. M. Brewer

The Negro People in American History. By William Z. Foster. (New York: International Publishers, 1954. pp. 608. $6.00.)

If the historian expects to find in this volume a scholarly contribution to the already sizeable body of literature of Negro history he will be disappointed. The author, long time leader of the Communist party in the United States, approaches this study from the "standpoint of Marxism-Leninism" and the result is less a "history" of the Negro people in the United States than an apologia for left-wing groups in general, and the Communists in particular, in their devious relationships with Negroes in America. The volume, in that sense is polemic, rather than historical. The author belabors throughout the book Marxism, with its stresses on equality and the good of the toiling and oppressed masses which would be achieved by cooperative action. This theme he develops in something less than the restrained diction and lucid exposition usually employed by the meticulous, trained historian.

The work faithfully treats the Marxist theme in such movements as the "Early Negro Liberation Movement"; activities of the abolitionists, which it describes as "the most radical section and vanguard of the Northern capitalist class"; and the Civil War, "the Second American Revolution." The book devotes six chapters to the problem of Reconstruction and discusses it as the second stage of the second American Revolution. The decade beginning in 1866 refers to one of "the broadest democratic experiences for the South" which ended when "the Northern bourgeoisie . . . betrayed the Negro people by making a bargain with Southern reaction." Three separate chapters examine labor unionism in which the author pays a great deal of attention to what he characterizes as continuing efforts of Marxists to integrate Negroes into organized labor despite "white chauvinist prejudices among the white workers and their leaders." He explores also the Negro's role in the Populist movement and links American "imperialism" with disfranchisement of the Negro as "monopolists" intensified their attacks upon "Negro rights." Using Lenin's definition of imperialism, Foster sees Negro disfranchisement resulting from an "unholy alliance between big planters of the South and big monopolists of the North."

Among the Negro leaders, Frederick Douglass and W. E. B. DuBois receive the most sympathetic treatment, while Booker T. Washington and Marcus Garvey are severely criticized. The author characterizes Washington's program as one of "Organized surrender to the big planter and industrialist exploiters," and says that Garvey "actually became an enemy of all struggle for Negro rights in the United States.'' As to race leaders of a more recent date, Foster castigates them as ''conciliators'' and ''betrayers of the Negro people.'' He devotes an entire chapter to the National Association for the Advancement of Colored People with one section dealing with the National Urban League as a ''social service organization.''

The author's solution of the pervasive and ubiquitous problem of race relations lies in the building of an ''alliance of Negro and white democratic and progressive forces'' within the all-embracing framework of the Communist Party, which will culminate in the millenium of a ''People's Front Government'' operating under the benign auspices of a ''People's Democracy.''

Aside from being highly controversial, the volume contains much with which the reader will disagree. The author erroneously lists ''Thomas E. Watson of North Carolina'' and ''Ben Tillman of Georgia'' (p. 381). It will surprise some to learn that President Wilson ''cynically declared war on Germany'' (p. 431), and they will not find general acceptance for the statement that ''all the capitalist countries were guilty of having started the [first world] war.'' Congress did not in the first instance ''authorize'' Lincoln to suspend the writ of *habeas corpus* (p. 262). In the opinion of this reviewer Negroes in the United States do not consider themselves a ''young and undeveloped nation,'' but an integral part of the American nation. There will be question of the assertion that ''the Communists took an active part in building the Republican party'' unsupported by documentary evidence. The services which Karl Marx rendered to the Union cause, and to the Negro cause in particular, during the Civil War are certainly open to challenge. Excellent studies of the free Negro in the ante-bellum period show that no general work on the Negro in this country can afford to dismiss this element in the pre-war society, yet the author gives him only passing notice as ''proletariat'' and ''petty bourgeoisie,'' with occasional reference to this group during colonial times.

The author writes in turgid style which borders on propaganda. One may question the relevance to a history of the Negro in the United States of excerpts from the Constitution of the Soviet Union (p. 496), and excerpts from the Constitution of the Communist Party of the U.S.A. (pp. 544-545). These criticisms, however, should not be taken to mean that this is not a book of some significance. With the subject as large and as complicated as the history and present status of the Negro in the United States, there is room for differing points of view in seeking the truth. Here we have an approach that is distinctly different from that of our standard historians. All serious students of the Negro in this country should examine this volume objectively and critically to see if it offers any new insights into what has been, and still remains, a big question for scholars, as well as the laymen and the makers of public policy. The work presents a point of view which offers "solutions" to domestic discriminations which have to be recognized, if not accepted.

EDWARD F. SWEAT

Clark College
Atlanta, Ga.

Breakthrough On The Color Line. By Lee Nichols. (New York: Random House, 1954. Pp. 235. Price $3.50.)

This book is a picture of the integration of the Negro into the Armed Forces of the United States as seen through the eyes of a newspaper reporter. Mr. Nichols is at present a staff member of the United Press. His information was secured from formerly secret military documents and interviews with high officials. The long struggle of the Negro to gain recognition and status as a soldier of combat rather than a member of the labor battalion is told from Crispus Attucks to the soldiers of World War II and the Korean War.

How was this "integration" accomplished? Ex-President Truman in 1948 issued his Executive Order 9981 stating that there was to be no segregation in the Armed Forces. The Navy was the first to try integration, and the Army was the last to war on segregation. Kenneth Royal, Army Secretary in 1948, stated that the Army was "not an instrument for social evolution—Negro troops were less qualified than whites for service in combat." Was the Negro soldier inferior because he was a Negro, or did he fail to equal the white soldier because of factors inherent in segregated forces? Studies by the Army showed that Negroes in integrated squads showed the "same frequencies of desirable and undesirable combat behavior as white soldiers; the similarities outweighed the differences."

Integration did not move swiftly throughout the Armed Forces.

It met much opposition. Its slowness was perhaps due to the prejudice within the military structure rather than social pressure exerted from the outside. Chicanery was practiced by underlings of high officials in an effort to circumvent true integration.

Has integration been achieved in the Armed Forces? Because certain military documents were given to the author in secrecy, one doubts that he had access to all pertinent information. Could the author achieve objectivity? Is his account colored by information military sources only desired to give him? Were his interviews with servicemen wide and varied enough to constitute a good sampling? Are the lesser officials still practicing chicanery? These questions can only be answered when all information concerning the "integration" is open to scrutiny. Perhaps, Mr. Nichols was a little too anxious to prove his thesis. Integration is not yet a "fait accompli."

The military has done much to dispel the cloud of segregation by power of example and exchange of experiences. This book is valuable in that it shows that integration is workable and that there is no essential difference between Negroes and whites when both are accorded "first class citizenship."

ALBERT O. LEWIS

Washington, D. C.

Out of These Roots. By Agnes E. Meyer. (Boston: Little, Brown and Company. 1953. Pp. 374. Price $4.00.)

With considerable skill Agnes Meyer makes being the servant of the people in a democratic society an existence exciting, purposeful and rewarding enough to lure even the wariest and most battle-scarred conservative to return to the fight. This is, however, the end product of her autobiography.

Beginning with "a delightfully democratic childhood in a rural American community of our halcyon era which ended with the devastating impact of the First World War," stalking through her college and maturing years as a "priggish, introverted, and not uncommon type of self-centered girl," she reveals how she develops, through trying experiences, into today's forceful liberal.

A review of chapter titles gives just as good a bird's-eye view of the material as any. "Childhood," "Adolescence," "College Days," "New Horizons," "Europe," and "The Female Egotist Gets Married" give the first portion of this odyssey of the "intellectual" woman, perfectly adjusted to her childhood of German discipline, overly sensitive, introspective, and misunderstood during her college days, and brought to grips with reality only when she marries stabilizing Eugene Meyer, owner of the Washington *Post-Times Herald.*

Vigorously hurling herself into the world of work, Mrs. Meyer embraces politics, describes her adventures in Westchester County, N. Y., in "Boss Ward—The Last of the Barons," and summarizes her thinking and experiences on diversified and crucial problems in "Commissioner of Recreation," "World War in Britain," "America's Home Front," "The Battle To Improve Public Education," and "Health for All Americans." The chapters "Women Aren't Men" and "Out of These Roots" conclude her wonderfully optimistic life story and leave the reader with a sense of gratification that the contemporary scene may not be so muddled after all: it has had the surging force of Mrs. Meyer.

Of the Negro she writes, "The Negro is far less eager to associate with us socially than a lot of fearful whites can imagine. Most white people are too poor in the milk of human kindness, in spontaneous humor and joyousness to be a treat to the Negro. It is my conviction that we whites have far more subtle things to learn from the Negro than he has to learn from us, among others, his sense of rhythm, his appreciation of the poetry of life, his deep aversion to regimentation. Let us hope that in the process of integration in our society, which fortunately is now well under way, the Negro will not allow the American steam roller of conformity to destroy his creative gifts."

Despite many discussions of the major influences of her life, her own family background and her home life, her devotion to Chinese art, her friendships with Paul Claudel, Thomas Mann, and John Dewey, the heart of her book lies in eight features for "the spread of justice and freedom and human happiness." In brief, they are public schools worthy of the new democracy; federal aid to schools only in areas with inadequate tax resources; local health units coordinated with public and private school systems and acting as referral centers to the community hospital and the large medical centers.

Slums will be eliminated and public housing will grow; hospitals will be integrated and free medical care for the indigent and insurance available to all, Federal security programs re-evaluated, all voluntary welfare programs integrated where possible, and the Negro given equal opportunities as an American. Utopian, yes, but Mrs. Meyer knows of what she speaks.

Limitations of the book are few. Much of the material is familiar to the close observer of the American scene. Mrs. Meyer never lets us forget her position as privileged public servant, devoted wife and mother. And the story of her evolution can be applied in so many respects to every aggressive college woman who is working to fulfill herself beyond the home as well as within it.

Mrs. Meyer, however, has had many times over a quantity and quality of supremely rich experiences. And she cheerfully admits, when she is discouraged and questions the good she has done in the world, she has at least prevented much evil. But she has done infinite good.   MARJORIE FELTON

A BIBLIOGRAPHY OF RECENT PUBLICATIONS ON NEGRO HISTORY[1]

BY HAROLD T. PINKETT

UNITED STATES

BOOKS

Durham, Frank. *Dubose Heyward: The Man Who Wrote Porgy*. Columbia: University of South Carolina Press. Illustrated. 1954. Pp. 152. $4.50.

Foley, Albert S. *Bishop Healy: Beloved Outcaste*. New York: Farrar, Straus and Young. 1954. Pp. viii, 243. $3.50.

Fremantle, J. A. L. *The Fremantle Diary*. Edited by Walter Lord. Boston: Little, Brown and Company. 1954. Pp. 304. $4.00.

Ickes, Harold L. *The Secret Diary of Harold L. Ickes*. Volume II, *The Inside Struggle, 1936-1939*. New York: Simon and Schuster. 1954. Pp. 759. $6.00.

Polk, William T. *Southern Accent: From Uncle Remus to Oak Ridge*. New York: William Morrow and Company. 1954. Pp. 264. $4.00.

Street, James. *The Civil War: An Unvarnished Account of the Late but Still Lively Hostilities*. New York: Dial Press. 1953. Pp. 144. $3.00.

[1] This bibliography does not include articles published in the *Journal of Negro History*.

ARTICLES

Abramowitz, Jack. Crossroads of Negro Thought: 1890-1895. *Social Education*, Mar., 1954.

Ader, E. B. Why the Dixiecrats Failed. *Journal of Politics*, Aug., 1953.

Anderson, C. A., and Bowman, M. J. Vanishing Servant and the Contemporary Status System of the American South. *American Journal of Sociology*, Nov., 1953.

Bean, W. G. John Letcher and the Slavery Issue in Virginia's Gubernatorial Contest of 1858-1859. *Journal of Southern History*, Feb., 1954.

Clark, E. R. Negro Composer: A Mid-Century Review. *Negro History Bulletin*, Mar., 1954.

Conlin, Katherine E. Dinah and the Slave Question in Vermont. *Vermont Quarterly*, Oct., 1953.

Cox, John and LaWanda. General Howard and the "Misrepresented [Freedmen's] Bureau." *Journal of Southern History*, Nov., 1953.

Davis, George L. Pittsburgh's Negro Troops in the Civil War. *Western Pennsylvania Historical Magazine*, June, 1953.

Ducoff, Louis J., and Motheral, Joe R. The Manpower Situation in Southern Agriculture. *Journal of Farm Economics*, Feb., 1954.

Garrett, Romeo B. The Negro in Peoria, 1773-1905. *Negro History Bulletin*, Apr., 1954.

Gordon, Milton M., and Roche, John P. Segregation—Two-Edged Sword. *New York Times Magazine*, Apr. 25, 1954.

Hall, Andy. The Ku Klux Klan in Southern Illinois in 1875. *Journal of the Illinois State Historical Society*, Winter, 1953.

Leflar, R. A., and Davis, W. H. Segregation in the Public Schools— 1953. *Harvard Law Review*, Jan., 1954.

Miller, A. F. Southern Youth and Non-Segregation. *Nation*, Mar. 13, 1954.

Morsch, J. S., and Smith, M. E. Judgment of Prejudice, before, during, and after World War II. *Journal of Social Psychology*, Aug., 1953.

Morton, R. L., "Contrabands" and Quakers in the Virginia Peninsula, 1862-1869. *Virginia Magazine of History and Biography*, Oct., 1953.

Nash, Philleo. Races: USA. *New Republic*, Mar. 22, 1954.

Robock, Stephen H., and Peterson, John M. Fact and Fiction about Southern Labor. *Harvard Business Review,* Mar.-Apr., 1954.

Stephenson, Richard. Race in the Cactus State. *Crisis,* Apr., 1954.

Suthon, Walter J., Jr. The Dubious Origin of the Fourteenth Amendment. *Tulane Law Review,* Dec., 1953.

United States Department of Labor. International Harvester's Non-discrimination Policy. *Monthly Labor Review,* Jan., 1954.

Vance, Joseph C. Freedmen's Schools in Albemarle County during Reconstruction. *Virginia Magazine of History and Biography,* Oct., 1953.

White, Walter. How Washington's Color Line Looks to Me. *Saturday Evening Post,* Apr. 3, 1954.

MICROFILM

United States. National Archives and Records Service. *State Department Territorial Papers: Kansas, 1854-61.* Microcopy No. 218. Washington: National Archives and Records Service. 1954. 2 rolls.

BIBLIOGRAPHICAL AIDS

Biggert, Elizabeth C. *Guide to the Manuscript Collections in the Library of the Ohio State Archaeological and Historical Society.* Columbus: Ohio State Archaeological and Historical Society. 1953. Pp. x, 153. Paper, $1.50; cloth, $2.50.

Handlin, Oscar; Schlesinger, Arthur Meir; Morison, Samuel Eliot; Merk, Frederick; Schlesinger, Arthur Meir, Jr.; and Buck, Paul Herman. *Harvard Guide to American History.* Cambridge: The Belknap Press of Harvard University Press. 1954. Pp. xxiv, 689. $10.00.

United States. Library of Congress. *Writings on American History, 1949.* Edited by James R. Masterson. Washington: Government Printing Office. 1954. Pp. xi, 636. $2.75.

—————. *A List of American Folksongs Currently Available on Records.* Washington: Library of Congress. 1953. Pp. 176.

LATIN AMERICA AND THE WEST INDIES

BOOKS

Bröndsted, Johannes (ed.). *Vore Gamle Tropekolonier.* Volume II, *Dansk Vestindien.* By Jens Bro-Jörgensen, Jens Viboek, Fridlev Skrubbeltrang, and Georg Nörregaard. Copenhagen: Westermann. 1953. Pp. 577.

Marias, B. J. *Colour: Unsolved Problem of the West.* London:

George Allen and Unwin. 1953. Pp. 322. 18s.

Ortiz, Fernando. *Los Instrumentos de la Música Afrocubana.* Habana: Ministerio de Educación. 1952. Volume I, pp. 304. Volume II, pp. 341. $10.00.

United States Library of Congress. *Handbook of Latin American Studies.* Gainesville: University of Florida Press. 1953. Pp. 332. $7.50.

Wilgus, A. Curtis. *The Caribbean: Contemporary Trends.* Gainesville: University of Florida Press. 1953. Pp. xxvi, 292. $4.00.

ARTICLES

Alba, Guillermo Ribon. Las cartas inéditas de Bolívar al Presidente de Haitá [Petión]. *Repertorio boyacense* (Tunja), Mar.-June, 1953.

Erasmus, C. J. Agricultural Changes in Haiti: Patterns of Resistance and Acceptance. *Human Organization,* Winter, 1952.

Frank, Waldo D. Puerto Rico and Psychosis. *Nation,* Mar. 13, 1954.

Levey, S. Puerto Rico, Problem Island. *New York Times Magazine,* Mar. 7, 1954.

Ratekin, Mervyn. The Early Sugar Industry in Española. *Hispanic American Historical Review,* Feb., 1954.

Roucek, J. S. Puerto Rico. *Contemporary Review,* Nov., 1953.

AFRICA

BOOKS

Brookes, Edgar H. *An Appreciation of the Life of John David Rheinallt Jones.* Johannesburg: South African Institute of Race Relations. Pp. vi, 43. 21½cm.

Brooks, E. H. *South Africa in a Changing World.* Cape Town: Oxford University Press. 1953. Pp. 151. 12s 6d.

Clark, F. Le Gros. *The New West Africa.* New York: Macmillan. 1954. Pp. 184. $3.50.

Great Britain. Colonial Office. *Some Aspects of the Development of Kenya Government Services for the Benefit of Africans from 1946 onwards.* Nairobi: Government Printer. 1953. Pp. 24. 1s.

Hailey, William M. H. *Native Administration in the British African Territories.* London: H. M. Stationery Office. 1950-53. 5 volumes.

Kamil, Murad. *Das Land des Negus.* Innsbruck: Inn-Verlag. 1953. Pp. 116. Öst. S. 45.

United Nations. Educational, Scientific, and Cultural Organization. *African Languages and English in Education.* Paris. 1953. Pp. 91.

ARTICLES

Beloff, Max. Race Relations and the Colonial Question. *Confluence,* June, 1953.

Bing, H. F. United Nations and Human Rights. *Contemporary Review,* Dec., 1953.

Buchanan, Keith. Northern Region of Nigeria: The Geographical Background of Its Political Duality. *Geographical Review.* Oct., 1953.

Cartwright, Marguerite. Progress in the Congo. *Negro History Bulletin,* Mar., 1954.

Cuvelier, J. Note sur la documentation de l'histoire du Congo *Bulletin de l'Institut Royal Colonial Belge,* XXIV, No. 2, 1953.

Gelber, L. M. Commonwealth and World Order. *Virginia Quarterly Review,* First Quarter, 1954.

Hance, William A. Economic Potentialities of the Central African Federation. *Political Science Quarterly,* Mar., 1954.

Horoth, V. L. Why Belgium Succeeded and French-British Policies Failed. *Magazine of Wall Street,* Oct. 31, 1953.

Jeffreys, M. D. W. Pre-Columbian Maize in Africa. *Nature,* Nov. 21, 1953.

Kyagambiddwa, Joseph. The Blessed Martyrs of Uganda. *Interracial Review,* Sept., 1953.

Little, Kenneth. A Study of "Social Change" in British West Africa. *Africa,* Oct., 1953.

McCann, Owen J. Race Relations in South Africa. *Interracial Review,* Mar., 1954.

Neame, L. E., and Carew-Slater, H. J. South African Tensions. *Fortnightly,* Dec., 1953.

Sears, Mason. Progress toward Selfrule in African Territories. *United States Department of State Bulletin,* Feb. 22, 1954.

————. Progress in the Cameroons. *Ibid.,* Mar. 1, 1954.

————. Administration of Tanganyika. *Ibid.,* Mar. 22, 1954.

Swanzy, Henry. Quarterly Notes. *African Affairs,* Oct., 1953.

Wilson, Monica. Nyakyusa Ritual and Symbolism. *American Anthropologist,* Apr., 1954.

PERSONAL
Alrutheus Ambush Taylor

Alrutheus Ambush Taylor, Research Professor of American History and former Dean of the College at Fisk University, died in Nashville, Tennessee, June 4 in his sixty-second year. A native Washingtonian, Professor Taylor attended the public schools in the District of Columbia and was graduated from Armstrong High School. At the University of Michigan he majored in mathematics and received the degree of Bachelor of Arts in 1916. Already, however, he was developing a major interest in the field of historical studies; and at the first opportunity he went to Harvard University, where he studied with such scholars as Channing, Haskins, Merk, Schlesinger, Sr., and Morison. In 1923 he received the degree of Master of Arts from Harvard. In 1935 the same institution conferred on him the degree of Doctor of Philosophy.

Professor Taylor's long and distinguished teaching career began with a one-year assignment at Tuskegee Institute in 1914. The following year he returned to Michigan to complete the work for his baccalaureate degree. Although he did not see action with the armed forces during World War I, he worked with the National Urban League in 1917-1918, when that organization was seeking new employment opportunities for Negroes and attempting to facilitate the adjustment of the several hundred thousand Negroes who left the South and settled in Northern cities. In 1919 he went to West Virginia Collegiate Institute. It was there that he became closely associated with Carter G. Woodson, whose writings were already winning for him an important place in American historiography. When Dr. Woodson returned to Washington in 1923 to devote more time to historical studies, Professor Taylor became the first full-time investigator for the Association for the Study of Negro Life and History, a position he held for two years.

It was during his tenure with the Association that he did much of the research that became the basis for several significant works on the Reconstruction. In 1924 the Association published his *The Negro in South Carolina during Reconstruction;* and two years later his *The Negro in the Reconstruction of Virginia* appeared. These publications were the first extensive attempts to challenge the writings of the Dunning school of Reconstruction historiography, which had almost succeeded in establishing the point that

Reconstruction was a complete failure and that Negroes not only showed no talent for government but contributed greatly to the corruption that characterized the period. Taylor's writings pointed up the benefits of Reconstruction and proved conclusively that some Negroes possessed political morality and a keen sense of responsibility in the public service.

When Fisk University underwent extensive reorganization in 1926 for the purpose of strengthening its curriculum and faculty, Taylor accepted an invitation to become professor of history and chairman of the department. Four years later he became Dean of the college of Liberal Arts, a position which he held until 1951 at which time he returned to full-time research and teaching. During Professor Taylor's tenure as Dean of the College Fisk University became the first Negro institution to receive an "A" rating by the Southern Association of Secondary Schools and Colleges and to be placed on the approved list of the Association of American Uni-versities. But his administrative duties were never too great to prevent him from writing and teaching. In 1941 he published *The Negro in Tennessee, 1865-1880*. At the last meeting of the Association for the Study of Negro Life and History he read a paper, "Fisk University and the Nashville Community, 1866-1900," which was published in the April, 1954, issue of the *Journal of Negro History*. At the time of his death he had just completed his "History of Fisk University," on which he had been working for many years.

In addition to his teachers at Michigan and Harvard and his contact with Carter G. Woodson, two factors seemed to influence the historical scholarship of Alrutheus A. Taylor. One was his early training in mathematics which induced him to seek the precision in historical writing that was the attainable goal of the skilled mathematician. The other was his determination not to engage in the polemical writing that had filled the pages of the historical works he undertook to refute. Invariably he was governed by the maxim, "Let the facts speak for themselves." He adhered to the view that truth needed no rhetorical flourishes, didactic digressions, or picturesque metaphors. Thus, his books and numerous articles are straightforward, logical, and unemotional. Since 1924, when Taylor published his first work on the Reconstruction, numerous historians have written from a point of view that has contributed greatly toward illuminating the period to which he gave so much attention. He was an influential pioneer in rewriting Reconstruction

history and, to that extent, he contributed much to a clearer understanding of that turbulent period in the nation's history.

JOHN HOPE FRANKLIN

WILLIAM PICKENS

William Pickens died April 6, 1954 while cruising with Mrs.
Pickens aboard the Mauretania off the coast of South America. He
was born January 15, 1881 in Anderson County, South Carolina.
His parents were Jacob and Fannie (Porter) Pickens who migrated
when the son was a small boy to Arkansas which was a frequent
trek from the Cotton-Piedmont before the great exoduses of Negroes
North. Young Pickens worked in cotton fields and sawmills during
his youth before he entered Talledega College where he graduated
in the class of 1902 and became the institution's most distinguished
graduate of all time. Immediately that year he entered Yale whose
bachelor's degree then required two years of additional residence
for graduates of the best colored colleges. During this short period
Picken's record was so brilliant that he was elected to Phi Beta
Kappa and won the Henry James Ten Eyck Prize over thirty-seven
Yale competitors in 1903. Languages were Picken's specialty and,
in spite of his Southern background, he mastered the intricacies of
"New England" English pronunciation, astounding his fellow
students and others.

Mr. Pickens married Miss Minnie Cooper McAlpine August 10,
1905 and to them were born three children, William, Harriet, and
Ruby (Mrs. Holbrook), who with Mrs. Pickens survive and reside
in New York City. The father's devotion and loyalty to them
spanned a joyous journey of nearly fifty years during which Mrs.
Pickens often shared his adventures including observation of burial
at sea—perhaps a fitting grave for the remains of a spirit as coura-
geous, vigilant, and crusading as that of William Pickens. In life he
feared no man and risked more than once death in behalf of justice
and opportunity for Negroes whose status had reached the nadir
of hopelessness when Pickens left Yale in 1904 to teach at Talladega.

William Pickens's life was dedicated in three great contributions
to the improvement and progress of colored people. With a few exceptions the most brilliant colored college men a half century ago
almost invariably entered teaching often because there were few or
no other openings for employment. Many of them went into this
field through deliberate choice because they felt more than some do

today the idealistic urge to help in the common cause of raising the curtain of ignorance that enshrouded the masses of American Negroes. Mr. Pickens returned, therefore, to Talladega in 1904 where he taught foreign languages ten years. From there he went to Wiley in Marshall, Texas where he served as professor, dean, and vice president until 1918 when he accepted a call to Morgan in Baltimore, Maryland to labor until 1920 in his last teaching assignment as such in the classroom although he taught in other ways all of his life. Like DuBois, Pickens could not refuse the irresistible challenge to help remove the slough of despond in which colored people were shackled and passing their darkest days of oppression since Emancipation. In 1920 he began the second period of his great work with the *National Association for the Advancement of Colored People* where for twenty-two years he was an outstanding militant advocate in that organization which has been responsible for the major advances in civil and human rights for Negroes over forty years. Through travels, that involved many grave risks, Pickens continued to teach with his pungent eloquence, wit, and devastating logic in conferences and on the lecture platform. In this role he equaled or surpassed Frederick Douglass as the most powerful Negro spokesman that has appeared in America. Pickens's training and freedom from opportunism, politics, and appeasement enabled him to arouse colored people from the lethargy which hovered over them during the early decades of the twentieth century. From 1942-1950 he worked with the Treasury Department of the United States in the promotion and sale of bonds among Negroes where he was very successful. If he, on assuming this work, veered briefly in a sort of apostasy from his previous faith and ardent crusades for Negro rights, this may now be forgiven! Yet, it must be noted that Ralph Bunche, in contrast, has suffered no loss in continuing at all times and everywhere to defend the righteous causes of colored people. The situations of these two great leaders did not differ fundamentally; but Bunche came from different experiences that tempered his steel more thoroughly for combatting wrongs inflicted upon his people than some of those from which Pickens emerged.

Pickens's best known book is an autobiography, *Bursting Bonds,* 1923. His other published writings consisted of lectures which were frequently repeated to far-flung audiences. Their titles are: ''Abraham Lincoln, Man and Statesman'', 1909; ''The Heir of Slaves'',

1919; "Frederick Douglass and the Spirit of Freedom", 1912; "Fifty Years of Emancipation", 1913; "The Ultimate Effects of Segregation and Discrimination", 1915; "The New Negro", 1916; "The Negro in the Light of the Great War", 1919; "The Vengeance of the Gods", 1923; and "American Aesop", 1926. That he could have produced other solid and scholarly works there is no doubt, but William Pickens chose what he and several other brilliant Negroes considered the more urgent demands of colored people bogged down and trudging through the kith and kin of almost hopeless struggle. Through his innate and matchless eloquence he presented the case of Negroes to America and in many travels abroad to the world in an era when present means of appeal and protest were unavailable and commanded little or no power of implementation . How much he and lesser lights contributed to recent legal triumphs is unpredictable, but let no one ever presume that it was not mightly and for this there should be eternal gratitude because greater courage and caution were required in 1910 or 1920 than in 1954!

William Pickens finally was a natural leader of colored people who rose through the strength of his rare ability and deep allegiance to the fortunes of Negroes whose defense a generation ago was precarious. He did not have to be chosen but, like a Moses of old, sighted the Promised Land afar and urged his people forward. While he would have been overjoyed May 17, 1954, at the Supreme Court decision, no one should forget that he helped tremendously through many years of preparation for that memorable day. Perhaps it was appropriate that death, which he never feared, came while he was cruising on the deep ocean under whose waves his mortal remains found their last resting place. His good works and great leadership need no bronze or marble markers as many yet unborn will read and remember that William Pickens lived dangerously and sacrificially in his times that American colored people might live more freely.   W. M. BREWER

HISTORICAL NEWS

The General Conference of the C.M.E. Church at Memphis, Tennessee May 5-17, 1954 voted to change *Colored* to *Christian* since a religious body, the delegates decided, should not have in its title racial connotation or denotation.

Ralph Bunche spoke at the eighty-first annual forum at the National Conference of Social Work at Atlantic City, New Jersey May 14, 1954. He emphasized that "peaceful and friendly relations among nations and peoples" depend upon world-wide economic and social progress.

Merze Tate was awarded the Radcliffe College Graduate Chapter Medal June 12, 1954 for distinguished post graduate professional service.

Howard University held its second Phi Beta Kappa initiation April 12, 1954. Judge William Hastie of the third district of the United States Circuit Court of Appeals was the speaker as sixteen members were inducted.

John Hope Franklin will be Fulbright Lecturer on American Studies at Cambridge University, England July 12-August 14, 1954. The subject of his lectures is *Regional and Ethnic Influences in American History.*

Ernest A. Hooton, a world renowned anthropologist and chairman of the department at Harvard, died May 3, 1954. He, like Franz Boas, did very much to repudiate the "mythical claims of racists", and he also served briefly on the Executive Council of the Association for the Study of Negro Life and History.

Arthur M. Schlesinger, Sr. has become Henry Lee Higginson Professor Emeritus of History at Harvard. He has been a member of the Association's Executive Council many years. His most eminent disciple, Merle Curti, currently President of the American Historical Association, has granted the addition of his name to those of other learned sponsors of the *Journal of Negro History.*

Chief Justice Warren presented the unanimous decision of the United States Supreme Court in the School Segregation Cases on May 17, 1954. This opinion reverses the dicta of that court in the *Civil Rights Cases of 1883* and *Plessey vs. Ferguson* in 1896. Thus the late Mr. Justice Harlan's noble and prophetic dissents in those cases are at long last vindicated.

The Southern Bapist Convention at St. Louis, Missouri on May 28, 1954 and the Southern Presbyterian General Assembly at Montreat, North Carolina the same day approved adherence to the United States Supreme Court decision on school segregation. Both actions are illustrations of Christian and Democratic progress in the advancing South. ,

The Baltimore, Maryland Public School Board of Education unanimously voted June 3, 1954 to integrate schools there September 1, 1954. Hence this great Southern City blazed the way for Washington, D. C. and other cities, sections, and regions of the South to follow.

Majorie Felton, an alumna of Smith and Columbia and teacher of English in Spingarn High School, Washington, D. C. is continuing her third year of assistance to the Editorial Board of the *Journal of Negro History.*

The Ford Foundation has made a grant of $250,000 to the work of the Southern Regional Council. This body consists of representative leaders and thinkers of the South that have been steadily developing programs and plans there for the advance of civil and human rights.

Lincoln University (Pennsylvania) celebrated its centennial April 29, 1954 with representatives from over 300 colleges in America and foreign countries. Dr. Milton S. Eisenhower was the principal speaker, and honorary degrees were conferred upon six men that have distinguished themselves in different fields.

Haile Selassie, the Emperor of Ethiopia, visited Washington, D. C. and was honored at a special convocation May 28, 1954 by Howard University with an honorary degree. The Ethiopian ruler made a gift to the institution's art collection on Africa.

Alain L. Locke, the first and only colored American Rhodes Scholar, died in New York City June 9, 1954. He was trained at Harvard, Oxford, and Berlin Universities and taught at Howard University forty years prior to his retirement in 1953. A biographical sketch of him and his scholarly career will appear in the October 1954 *Journal.*

The Annual Meeting of the Association for the Study of Negro Life and History will be held in St. Louis, Missouri October 22-24 1954. The Program Committee under the direction of President Charles H. Wesley and in cooperation with the local committee of arrangements is making preparations.

The Theme for NEGRO HISTORY WEEK February 13-20, 1955 is: NEGRO HISTORY—A CONTRIBUTION TO AMERICA'S INTERCULTURAL LIFE.

Leslie H. Fishel, Jr.'s *Northern Prejudice and Negro Suffrage 1865-1870* has been Reprinted as *Publication In The Humanities No. 4* by the Department of Humanities of Massachusetts Institute of Technology.

W. M. BREWER

THREE STEPS IN NEGRO HISTORY

By Carter G. Woodson

I. The First Book of Negro History, Adapted to Pupils Beginning this Phase of History

Negro Makers of History

This is a textbook for children of the sixth and seventh grades or of the junior high school. It is an introductory work in simple language. The book omits no essentials, but it avoids tiresome details which interest only advanced students.

The very make-up of the book is so worked out as to make it attractive and useful for children. It has one hundred and eighty-five illustrations portraying almost every aspect of the life and history of the Negro. The type is large and readable. No chapter covers more than about six or seven pages. At the end of each chapter is a summary of the facts, and this is followed by hints and questions.

362 pages   Illustrated $2.65 by mail

II. The Second Book of Negro History, Adapted to High School Work

The Story of the Negro Retold

This is an intermediate textbook of Negro-American History. It is intended to bridge the gap between the first textbook of this series entitled *Negro Makers of History* and the author's advanced work, *The Negro in Our History*. *The Story of the Negro Retold* introduces the study of the Negro in the 11th or the 12th grade. The book is copiously illustrated and planned in conformity to the requirements of the schoolroom in the light of recent educational methods. The language, too, is simplified to adapt it to the capacity of those to be taught.

369 pages   Adequately illustrated $2.65 by mail

III. The Third Book of Negro History, Adapted to College Work

The Negro in Our History

Ninth Edition, Revised and Enlarged

In this work the author has endeavored to meet the long-felt want for a suitable textbook adapted to the capacity of college students desirous of knowing the leading facts of Negro life and history. The numerous references for more extensive treatment of the various topics considered, moreover, render it useful for advanced classes in universities. It is now being used as a textbook in colleges and universities in twenty-three states, and its popularity is increasing as it passes into its sixth edition. The author discusses the African background, the enslavement of the race, colonization, abolition, freedom, and citizenship.

700 pages   Well illustrated $5.25 by mail

THE ASSOCIATED PUBLISHERS, Inc.

1538 Ninth Street, N. W.   Washington, D. C.

THE JOURNAL

OF

NEGRO HISTORY

FOUNDED BY

CARTER G. WOODSON

JANUARY 1, 1916

PUBLISHED QUARTERLY BY

THE ASSOCIATION FOR THE STUDY OF NEGRO LIFE AND HISTORY, INC.

The Association for the Study of Negro Life and History supplies THE JOURNAL OF NEGRO HISTORY to Active Members in good standing; the Executive Council elects the members and determines their duties and privileges. The membership fee is not the same as a subscription. Members may be otherwise assessed. Only persons may become Active Members. THE NEGRO HISTORY BULLETIN goes to Associate Members paying $2.00 a year.

Subscriptions should be sent to the Association for the Study of Negro Life and History, 1538 Ninth Street, N. W., Washington, D. C. The price of a subscription to the JOURNAL is $5.00 a year. Single numbers cost $1.50 each. Volumes I and II bound cost $7.50 each, and the remaining volumes in bound form $5.00 each.

All communications with respect to both editorial and administrative matters should be sent to the address given above.

$30,000 NEEDED

HELP us raise annually the sum of $30,000 to finance the work of collecting and publishing the materials bearing on Negro life and history. Our efforts, at present, are restricted to what we are able to induce interested individuals to undertake in their respective localities. Moving at this slow rate and in such an unsystematic way, the work will proceed so slowly that many valuable documents and the testimonies of the living will be lost to the world, and the story of the Negro will perish with him.

To raise this fund we are appealing to all persons professing an interest in the propagation of the truth. We need

4 persons to contribute annually	$1,000 each
8 persons to contribute annually	500 each
16 persons to contribute annually	250 each
20 persons to contribute annually	100 each
40 persons to contribute annually	50 each
80 persons to contribute annually	25 each
200 persons to contribute annually	10 each

The dual effort of the Association makes its work more expensive than that of other scientific movements. This undertaking differs from most such enterprises in that it unites the efforts of both a learned society and a bureau of research. The Association is concerned with the discussion, publication, and circulation of historical materials, and at the same time it employs investigators to explore fields of Negro history hitherto neglected or unknown. This work cannot be successfully prosecuted with less than $30,000 a year; and, if we hope to develop it in all of its aspects to prevent the Negro from becoming a negligible factor in the thought of the world, the income must be much larger than this amount.

All communications should be sent to the Association for the Study of Negro Life and History, 1538 Ninth Street, North west, Washington 1, D. C.

The Association is incorporated and the Secretary-Treasurer is bonded.

THE JOURNAL

OF

NEGRO HISTORY

Vol. XXXIX—October, 1954—No. 4

ANNUAL REPORT

The Association for the Study of Negro Life and History operated during the last year on a balanced-budget the first time since the passing of the founder April 3, 1950. This was accomplished through several administrative and promotional departures by the Executve Council, sub-committees of that body, and especially the program of the new Secretary-Treasurer, Albert N. D. Brooks. While his arduous labors and carefully designed financial plans have been fruitful, several other changes have also been effective. Closer surveillance of the Associated Publishers by the Executive Council removed difficulties which had unfortunately existed three years. In implementing the actions of the Nashville meeting of 1953, many members, friends, and supporters of the cause succeeded in raising contributions although the vast majority was understandably small though significant and encouraging. Among individuals the following were the highest: Charles H. Wesley, $1,386.50; Frederick D. Moon, $1,017.20; J. Rupert

Picott, $666.43; Merle R. Eppse, $478.20; and H. Council
Trenholm, $240.67. Likewise, communities reported well:
Washington, D. C., $2,157.09; New York City, $330.95;
Maryland, $292.00; Texas Southern University, $262.16;
and California, $181.80.

While the Secretary-Treasurer will modestly hardly
admit credit for the performance in the District of Columbia, this should quite legitimately be credited to him. He
originated the "Carter Woodson Clubs," which have just
begun with encouraging possibilities, and sponsored the
organization of several with a view primarily to promoting
the dissemination of Negro History information and incidentally the solicitation of funds to support the effort. The
results reveal potentialities which justify extension to far-
flung communities. Most important, however, have been the
small contributions from many people—rural and urban
teachers, men and women who are learning of the Association for the first time, pupils and college students, and the
historians. It is hoped that the last group will catch the
spirit of the others and report more satisfactorily hereafter.

A system of cost-accounting has operated this year
which enables officials of the Association, members, and
supporters to see at a glance the income and disbursements.
This represents progress over the past three years in keeping with orthodox administrative procedures for handling
finances of any going concern. Space precludes the detailed
breakdowns, but the totals show that the Association was
operated not only within available financial resources from
July 1, 1953-July 1, 1954, but that the outstanding debt was
reduced from received income in the payment of $2,406.92!
Totals only appear from the Secretary-Treasurer's detailed report which members of the Executive Council received during the summer of 1954 and a few copies are
available on request from headquarters for anyone who
may be interested to see them.

FINANCIAL STATEMENT OF THE ASSOCIATION FOR
THE STUDY OF NEGRO LIFE AND HISTORY
JULY, 1, 1953-JULY 1, 1954

(1) *Journal of Negro History*

	Income	Disbursements	Surplus
Total	$4,902.52	$4,892.10	$10.42

(2) *Negro History Bulletin*

	Income	Disbursements	Surplus
Total	$4,713.12	$4,621.55	$91.57

(3) *Negro History Week Kits*

	Income	Disbursements	Surplus
Total	$1,318.29	$1,139.21	$179.08

(4) *Association*

	Income	Disbursements	Surplus
Total	$8,096.11	$6,034.85	$2,061.26
Total	$19,030.04	$16,687.71	$2,346.33
Brought forward 7/1/1953	$1,155.63		
Applied to debt		$2,406.92	
Balance on hand 6/30/1954		$1,091.04	
Grand Total	$20,185.67	$20,185.67	

RESEARCH

Research under the auspices and direction of the Association continues partially suspended primarily for financial reasons, but more largely because of the absence of a Director-Editor. Book manuscripts are not being accepted for publication, which is unfortunate, as competitors are entering the field where Dr. Woodson was outstanding. Interest of historians in research on the Negro is proceeding, nevertheless, if manuscripts submitted to the JOURNAL OF NEGRO HISTORY and articles appearing in learned publications may be considered evidence. Nearly forty years of the Association's efforts can claim some credit for the interest in investigating the records of Negroes in civilization and history. Yet, this achievement may now be challenged by other more active but less competent competitors who are entering the Association's former nearly exclusive vineyards. This, of course, marks a trend over which there should be alertness among those who sponsor and support investigation in the still neglected fields of Negro accomplishment. The purpose of this reporting is to emphasize the necessity for the Association to resume its

former more active role in research and publication. There
is every reason to urge the advisability of resumption because the Associated Publishers under the new management and control is going well, but its continued growth
demands sensitivity to business demands. Integration, for
example, has increased the requests for all kinds of information about Negroes, and publishers are generally seeing
and beginning to exploit the growing markets.

EDUCATIONAL WORK

This phase of Association activity continues with less
modification understandably than research and publication.
Offerings in courses about Negroes in colleges are now
rather generally operating in colored institutions. These
mean that teachers are receiving training for systematic
instruction on the Negro in elementary and secondary
schools. Of greater significance is the interest in more advanced investigations. The African institutes at North
Western University, Boston University, and the conference
on "Contemporary Africa" by the Johns Hopkins University School of Advanced Studies in August of 1954 show
a trend in response to world demands. Moreover, Howard
University is inaugurating a venture in this field which
brings together its top-flight scholars in anthropology,
geography, history, and political science in a similar institute with support from the Ford Foundation.

Branches of the Association are still operating in several communities and through them it is hoped that "Carter Woodson Clubs" will be organized to function in extending the effort educationally and financially. To facilitate this new departure shelves were installed in the three
floors above the basement book-storage area of the headquarters building during the summer of 1954. The vast
files of periodicals and other materials have been systematically arranged to supply with dispatch requests for
information. Dorothy Porter of the Howard University

Library is continuing her invaluable advice in the Association's information service. This still operates in America and extends occasionally abroad where information and materials are sent in response to requests. The Executive Council has approved expansion of the Association's information service and some volunteer helpers have agreed to assist as they do during Negro History Week.

An important item in the cause's educational efforts this year is the revision of *The Child's Story of the Negro* which has served a vital need for several years. Under the direction of the Association's president, the writer outlined the format and pattern of revising this splendid and indispensible little book. The suggestions were approved by the author, Jane D. Shackelford of Terre Haute, Indiana who wrote the beautiful *My Happy Days,* which has been outstanding among books for small children. She is not only adding chapters on such notables as Carter G. Woodson and Mary Church Terrell, but refining the vocabularies and including teaching devices and directions. She aims in the revision in all essential respects to bring the book into accord with the demands and requirements of integration which will be a contribution to be expected from this author and pioneer in writing books for the instruction of youngsters in the history of the Negro. The Associated Publishers will publish the revised edition.

NEGRO HISTORY WEEK

Negro History Week in 1954 was based upon the theme: *Negro History—A Foundation for Integration.* Organization followed the patterns of the last two years in which specific suggestions were given for the arrangement of programs to suit the needs of elementary grades, secondary schools, colleges, and public meetings. Integration and the advance of interest in civil and human rights increased the demands upon the too limited headquarters staff. Cooperation, however, of interested and highly competent volunteer helpers in the Washington, D. C. community and elsewhere enabled the celebration to function effectively as usual. High praise is due these workers, many of whom were closely associated with Dr. Woodson, and their continued sacrificial devotion and loyalty deserve and have the deepest gratitude of the official staff at headquarters and the Executive Council.

Regrettably, it is pertinent again to report that the celebration in 1954 was exploited in some instances where individuals and organizations used the occasion to serve their purposes rather than the goals of the Negro History Movement. It is gratifying to observe that the occasions are on the wane. The aims of Negro history, like those of all scientific history, are so clear and specific that the propagandists cannot exploit them before any intelligent audience. The subject for 1955, which will be organized along lines similar to those of last year, is: *Negro History—A Contribution to America's Intercultural Life*. The truths of Negro progress and achievement will be modestly but emphatically mentioned in the light of scientific history as they have been through the years. Paramount in the celebration next year will be, as in previous years, the presentation of historical facts in the conviction that these will speak for themselves in revealing the still untold records of Negroes. That these are now indispensable is quite evident in the requests for information which come constantly to headquarters.

THE NEGRO HISTORY BULLETIN

This periodical remains the voice of the Association and its most vital link of connection in public relations and promotional activities. The eight monthly issues keep the cause publicized and its programs before those who contribute the principal financial support of the Association. The columns of the *Bulletin* aim to present the records of Negro life and history in such form as to inspire interest among children, adolescents, and adults. How well this medium of publicity is succeeding is best attested by the increases in circulation and the demands which it receives for services which it is endeavoring to render. History materials and information about methods of teaching are presented with a variety of brief articles by scholars of distinction in America and abroad. Circulation has reached an all-time high and is steadily increasing at home and in foreign countries.

THE JOURNAL OF NEGRO HISTORY

The *Journal* has been reduced in length this year as a part of retrenching expenses to meet outstanding financial obligations. This has been accomplished without sacrifice of quality or the standing of this periodical among learned publications. The task has been difficult because the lengths of manuscripts do not easily fit in the more limited spaces. It is hoped that the former space limits may be resumed as early as possible in view of excellent manuscripts which continue frequently to be submitted. How well the Editorial Board is succeeding in the tentative departure may be observed in the following quotation from a letter of July 9, 1954 by one of America's most distinguished historians: "I think that the *Journal* has been excellent under your direction. . . ." This opinion is heartening and the Association will be interested to learn that the *Journal,* like the *Bulletin,* has reached the largest circulation of record and is increasing. Subscriptions now extend to Africa, Asia, Australia, Canada, England, Europe, Latin American countries, and nearly all outstanding college and public libraries in the United States. The *Journal* remains the principal medium of publishing scholarly historical research on the Negro in America. Scholars in fields other than history continue their gracious cooperation with the Editorial Board.

PROMOTIONAL ACTIVITIES AND THE FUTURE

The new Secretary-Treasurer of the Association inherited July 1, 1953 obligations which had accumulated through the interlude of three years. During this period promotional efforts declined, systematic payments on outstanding obligations were regrettably neglected, and Association debts allowed to accumulate. The Secretary-Treasurer courageously assumed leadership, installed one of the latest types of addressograph machines, and had the files of the *Bulletin* and *Journal* processed and screened in strict periodical fashion. The results were highly satisfactory, and they explain many of the financial increases previously mentioned in this report. If the records of accomplishment by volunteer and uncompensated helpers could produce what they did last year, there is every reason for reassurance. While the outstanding financial obligations remain heavy and must be liquidated, the demands for the work of the Association have promise of remaining urgent for the predictable future. This points up the vital need now for the full-time services at headquarters of a Director-Editor. His absence is causing publication and research under the auspices of the Association to lag and pursuit of the great founder's goals to slow down. The time is overdue and opportune for one of the historians whom Carter Woodson inspired to assume the nestor's mantle. There are several historians of stature in the Association and it is now *imperative* that one of them should no longer decline the call to leadership.

W. M. BREWER

THE RE-ENFRANCHISEMENT OF NEGROES IN FLORIDA

Most students of the American electoral process are familiar with the main outlines of the movement to disfranchise Southern Negroes. By about 1900, the concentrated actions of Southern whites had substantially eliminated most Negroes from public political life in the states of the old Confederacy. In the course of the movement, the whites used disfranchising techniques that were "informal"—intimidation, violence, and fraud—as well as "constitutional" and "legal"—the gerrymander, a highly centralized election code, "centralization of local government, poll tax requirements, elaborate and confusing registration schemes, and devious complications of the balloting process."[1]

Before Florida Democrats completed the disfranchisement of Negroes in that state they had used most of the informal techniques. As late as 1888 and 1892, for example, the platform of the state Republican party contained planks condemning "lynch law", fraudulent elections, and intimidation of Negro voters in certain counties.[2] But it was the legal methods of disfranchisement that set the pattern which prevailed until 1946.

In Florida, these methods took four principal forms: (1) a poll tax; (2) the temporary adoption of a multiple ballot box requirement, followed by the compulsory use of the Australian ballot; (3) the radical subversion of traditional practices of local self-government[3] in order to assure white control in "black" counties or cities; and (4) the adoption of a "white primary" for partisans of the Democracy.

[1] Paul Lewinson, *Race, Class, & Party:* A History of Negro Suffrage and White Politics in the South (London: Oxford University Press, 1932), p. 65. On the disfranchising movement, see Lewinson, *op. cit.*, and V. O. Key, Jr., *Southern Politics in State and Nation* (New York: Knopf, 1949), chap. 25.

[2] *Appleton's Annual Cyclopedia and Register of Important Events*, 42 vols. (New York: D. Appleton & Co., 1862-1903), *1888*, p. 343; *1892*, p. 279.

[3] This phrase describing the phenomenon is Key's. *Op. cit.*, p. 541.

In the constitutional convention that produced the Florida Constitution of 1885, the state's present organic law, the struggles over the earliest of these measures began.[4] Perhaps the sharpest occurred over the poll tax question. The disfranchising Democrats were not strong enough to impose a heavy cumulative feature on the tax, or to write the tax as a suffrage requirement into the Constitution itself. They were strong enough, however, to defeat a proposal to submit the Constitution's poll tax provisions to the electorate as a separate proposition, and to push through a section *authorizing* the Legislature to impose the tax, with a cumulation period of only two years.[5]

The new Constitution's legislative apportionment did not take effect until the elections of 1888. In consequence, the "un-reapportioned" Legislature of 1887, the first to meet after the ratification of the new Constitution still contained enough Republicans and insurgent Democrats in the House to defeat the disfranchisers' poll tax bill. The anti-poll tax coalition failed, however, to get the House to propose a constitutional amendment divesting the Legislature of its power to pass a poll tax statute. In 1889, finally, the newly apportioned Legislature, by large majorities in each House, put the poll tax act on the books.[6]

Also emerging from the session of 1889 was a multiple ballot box law, the most severe of several "devious complications of the balloting process." Aimed at the illiterate voter, either white or Negro, who would have difficulty in reading the labels on the ballot boxes indicating the "correct" boxes in which to deposit his various ballots, the bill met a determined but ineffectual opposition. It stayed on the books until 1895, when the Legislature, in a general re-

[4] For a more detailed account of the events to be described, see Charles D. Farris, ''Effects of Negro Voting upon the Politics of a Southern City: An Intensive Study, 1946-48'' (Unpublished Ph.D. dissertation, Dept. of Political Science, University of Chicago, 1953), pp. 33-54.

[5] *Ibid.*, pp. 39-41.

[6] *Ibid.*, pp. 41-43.

vision of the election laws, adopted the Australian ballot. The new ballot form, devoid of party symbols or names, using the "office block" system of grouping candidates' names, and making no provision for straight ticket voting, was all that a ballot reformer's heart could desire. Like the multiple ballot box provisions which it replaced, the Australian ballot reform also struck heavily at illiterate voters.[7]

Statewide returns in elections for members of the U. S. House of Representatives in 1878, 1882, 1886, and 1890—all of them non-Presidential years—dramatically illustrate the effect of the two disfranchising measures of 1889. A straight-line projection of the trend in the two-party vote at the first three of these elections suggests that an unrestricted electorate in 1890 "would" have cast about 39,100 Democratic votes and 26,100 Republican votes. The actual vote in 1890 was 29,090 for the Democrats (largely from white voters, it is assumed) and only 15,045 for the Republicans (largely from Negro voters, it is assumed). The Democratic loss was about 26 per cent of what the vote "should" have been, while the Republican loss was 43 per cent of what might reasonably have been expected to be the total Republican vote in 1890. Since the percentage of adult Negro males in the state who were illiterate in 1890 was 45 per cent, a connection between the disfranchising measures and the drop in Republican (that is, mainly Negro) voting seems plausible.[8]

The third disfranchising method, the subversion of local self-government, was not entirely a product of the movement to drive Negroes from politics. Under the Reconstruction Constitution of 1868, the Governor had power to appoint all county officials except constables. In the convention of 1885, the anti-disfranchisers were able to return the choice of county officials to the electorate, with one ex-

7 *Ibid.*, pp. 44, 51.
8 *Ibid.*, pp. 47-49.

ception: the disfranchisers were able to retain for the Governor the power to appoint county commissioners, and by doing so, to leave control of election machinery largely in the hands of gubernatorial appointees.[9]

Even more extreme was the Legislature's tinkering with city government, although this tinkering also had precedent. By 1889, the city government of Pensacola, one of the three largest cities in the state, was already in the hands of a board appointed by the Governor. In 1889, the Legislature abolished elective local government in Jacksonville and Key West, the two other major cities in the state, and gave the Governor power to appoint city councilmen. The latter chose the rest of the city officials.[10]

This extreme state of affairs did not last long. In 1893, the Legislature restored elective government to Jacksonville and Pensacola, and in 1897 to Key West. Finally, in 1900, the state's shrunken electorate ratified a constitutional amendment making the office of county commissioner elective. Since governors had already been appointing white Democratic primary nominees to that post, the effect of the amendment was largely formal.[11]

Of the major disfranchising techniques already mentioned, the white primary was probably the most restrictive. Although it did not become fully established in Florida until 1902, its beginnings can be discerned at an earlier date. The Democratic state platform in 1892, for example, resolved that "the purity and integrity of the party" ought to be maintained, and that only those persons could vote

[9] *Ibid.*, pp. 35-36, 39.

[10] *Ibid.*, pp. 45-47. Both Republicans and Democrats were guilty of sharp practice in the Jacksonville situation. In 1887, the all-Republican legislative delegation from Duval County (Jacksonville) got the Legislature to pass a "ripper" charter, abolishing the existing city government of Jacksonville, annexing two large Negro suburbs to the city, and calling new elections. In the latter, the local Republicans won the Mayor's office and 13 of 18 seats on the City Council. It was this government that the "ripper" legislation of 1889 unseated.

[11] *Ibid.*, p. 53.

in Democratic primaries (then "private", or conducted by the party) who had the qualifications "necessary to qualify an elector for Democratic nomination, or to admit them to the full confidence and counsels of the Democratic party." Since the party was not then nominating Negro candidates, the reference of the resolution is obvious.[12]

Five years later, when the Legislature enacted the first Florida statute regulating primary elections—it applied only to county primaries—, it gave to the county executive committees of political parties the power to regulate the admission of voters to primaries. In 1900, the Democratic state convention pledged the party to enact legislation requiring "the nomination of all candidates for office . . . and of United States Senators, by a majority in white primary elections, held under the provisions of law. . . ." The Democratic Legislature of 1901 thereupon applied to state-wide primaries most of the features of the 1897 statute, including the provision on party membership. When the Democratic state committee issued its call for the first state-wide primary in 1902, it restricted participation to white persons only. This action marked the virtual completion of the legalistic process of disfranchisement that had begun 13 years earlier.[13]

The poll tax, the multiple ballot box law, the Australian ballot, and the temporary subversion of local self-government contributed greatly to the destruction of the Republican party as a significant force in state and local politics. The party having become a nullity, Negroes lost what had been the traditional vehicle for the expression of their political demands, and general elections become ritualistic formalities.

In the course of this development, the Democratic primary became the forum in which the bulk of "effective"

[12] *Ibid.*, pp. 50-51.
[13] *Ibid.*, p. 52.

and "significant" electoral decisions, at both state and local levels, were made. The all-white rule barred Negroes from participation in the making of these decisions.

THE STATUS OF DISFRANCHISEMENT, 1902-37

Between 1902 and 1937, a politically conscious Negro in Florida might have found his way to effective participation in politics cut off by any one of three legal barriers. To attack the Australian ballot, either on the hustings or in the courts, was extremely difficult. Ballot reform swept over the United States as a reaction to "corrupt elections and government,"[14] and opposing it on the stump would have been like defending sin. Attacking it in the courts yielded no success,[15] although in no case was it alleged that the ballot denied an illiterate voter his freedom of choice.

To attack the poll tax, the second of the barriers, in the courts was equally difficult. Most agitation against the tax was political rather than litigious, and the Florida Legislature had repealed the requirement before the United States Supreme Court held that a Georgia poll tax requirement did not violate the Fourteenth Amendment.[16]

The remaining legal barrier to a Negro's effective participation in politics, the white primary, gave rise to a considerable body of litigation. Although most of the major white primary cases arose outside Florida, some of them were not without effect on the Florida situation. The first

---

[14] Cf. Eldon Cobb Evans, *A History of the Australian Ballot System in the United States* (Chicago: University of Chicago Press, 1917); John H. Wigmore, *The Australian Ballot System*, 2d ed. (Boston: Boston Book Co., 1889).

[15] *State* ex rel. *Lamar* v. *Dillon*, 32 Fla. 545, 14 So. 383, 22 L.R.A. 124 (1893); *State* ex rel. *Harris* v. *Belote*, 106 Fla. 938, 143 So. 881 (1932).

[16] *Florida Laws, 1937*, chap. 18061: *Breedlove* v. *Suttles*, 302 U. S. 277, 58 S.Ct. 205, 82 L.Ed. 252 (1937). The case actually turned on a rather narrow question: whether the Georgia poll tax statute, in exempting men over 60 and all women, unfairly discriminated against men under 60. The *dicta* suggest that the Court found no objection to the tax as a suffrage test.

major case, *Nixon* v. *Herndon*,[17] was irrelevant, but the
next, *Nixon* v. *Condon*,[18] was not. In the latter, the U. S.
Supreme Court held a Texas statute invalid which granted
to the state committees of political parties the power to
prescribe tests of party membership. When the Texas
Democratic committee used this grant of power to prescribe a white primary rule, it acted as an agency of the
state, and its rule fell within the purview of the equal protection clause of the Fourteenth Amendment.

The Court's decision in the *Condon* case left three major
questions unanswered: (1) does a *political party* have "inherent powers" to determine who may be its members?
(2) what agency of the party can exercise such powers, if
the party has them? and (3) are there circumstances in
which parties are agencies of government, rather than
"voluntary private associations"? As further white primary cases arose, one or another of these questions was to
come into controversy again.

At the time of the *Condon* decision, Florida primaries
were held under the mandatory direct primary statute of
1913, which had replaced the optional law of 1901. Under
the mandatory statute, state and county governments were
heavily concerned with the financing and regulation of primaries. The two "major" parties were required to nomi-
nate almost all candidates in primaries. Party executive
committees for the state, Congressional districts, and counties were chosen biennially by voters in the respective party
primaries. State committees had statutory power to prescribe the terms upon which otherwise qualified electors
would be permitted to enroll as registrants in their respective parties, and only party registrants could vote in primaries.[19]

[17] 273 U. S. 536, 47 S.Ct. 446, 71 L.Ed. 759 (1927): state statute pre-
scribing white primary denied Negroes equal protection of the laws.

[18] 286 U. S. 73, 52 S.Ct. 484, 76 L.Ed. 984, 88 A.L.R. 458 (1932).

[19] *Florida Laws, 1913*, chap 6469, as amended; *Compiled General Laws of
Florida, 1937*, secs. 355-424, 8169, 8175, 8179, 8182, 8183, 8197-99.

The primary law did not mention party conventions. The Democrats had held their last state convention in 1900. Since 1902, the Democratic state committee had always had a white primary rule.[20]

It was that rule whose validity a Jacksonville Negro, Sylvanus H. Hart, attacked in the Duval County Circuit Court early in 1934. Hart asked the Court to compel the Duval County Supervisor of Registration to register him as a Democrat. He argued that the state committee's white primary rule, passed under its statutory power to exclude, was invalid according to *Nixon* v. *Condon*.[21]

The Court decided against Hart. It held that the Democratic party in Florida was not an agency of government but a voluntary private association, with "inherent power to determine the qualifications of its own membership." The party's, and thus the committee's, power to exclude "derived not from the statute but from . . . the electors of the party. The statute . . . [was] but the recognition by the State of the powers inherent in the . . . Committee" and the party.[22] The state committee in Florida was the proper agency to exercise the powers of the party, because the Florida situation differed from that in Texas at the time of *Nixon* v. *Condon:* Florida had no Democratic convention, while Texas did; the Florida committee was elected by the Democratic voters, while the Texas committee had been chosen by the convention; "therefore," the Florida committee had powers analogous to those of the Texas convention.[23]

---

[20] *State* ex rel. *Hart* v. *Price*, Case No. 12842L, Circuit Court, Duval County, Florida (1934); William T. Cash, *History of the Democratic Party in Florida* (Tallahassee, Florida: Florida Democratic Historical Foundation, 1936), p. 178.

[21] *State* ex rel. *Hart* v. *Price*, Case No. 12842L, Circuit Court, Duval County, Florida (1934).

[22] *Ibid.; Florida Times-Union*, May 25, 1934; Duval County Circuit Court Minute Book, LV, 357.

[23] This line of argument was necessary if the Duval County Circuit Court were to defer at all to Justice Cardozo's *dictum* in the *Condon* case: "what-

The following year, substantially similar conclusions became the law of the land. In *Grovey* v. *Townsend*,[24] the United States Supreme Court held that the Democratic party and its convention in Texas were not agencies of the state, and that when primary managers followed the convention's white primary rule, they were not state agents either. Since neither the convention's rule nor the managers' obedience of it was state action, the equal protection clause of the Fourteenth Amendment could not come into operation.

THE REPEAL OF THE POLL TAX

By the end of 1936, a politically conscious Florida Negro could hardly have regarded his prospects as bright. The Republican party continued a nullity in state and local politics, and the poll tax presumably continued to make voting in general elections—if they were genuine contests —rather difficult. After two defeats before the U. S. Supreme Court, the white Democratic primary at last seemed constitutionally unassailable. Within a year, however, the first step toward re-enfranchisement became a reality: in 1937, the Florida Legislature repealed the poll tax requirement that another Legislature had imposed almost 50 years earlier.

From a newspaper man's point of view, the biggest story about the abolition of the poll tax in Florida was that there was no story to it.[25] Repeal had been a minor legislative issue since 1931: bills embodying it regularly expired in the State Senate. Into the House of what some observers refer to as the "amazingly liberal" Legislature of

---

ever inherent power a State political party has to determine the content of its membership resides in the State convention."

24 295 U. S. 45, 55 S.Ct. 351, 79 L.Ed. 1236, 97 A.L.R. 680 (1935).

25 The account that follows is based largely on Frederic D. Ogden, "The Poll Tax in the South" (Unpublished Ph.D. dissertation, Dept. of Political Science, The Johns Hopkins University, 1951), pp. 372-77.

1937, several members introduced bills for repeal. Although one measure was killed before the successful one passed, the whole atmosphere of the debate was calm.

Not that there were no conflicts of interest. Some professional politicians, allied with gambling and racing interests, had built up blocs of voters by paying poll taxes for them, and these politicians opposed repeal. Other professionals, including Senator Claude Pepper's wing of the Democratic party, supported it. In opposition was the school lobby: repeal would hurt poll tax collections, earmarked for school uses.

HB 95, the first repealer that came to the House's attention, met its death at the hands of the school lobby. An agreement to increase state grants-in-aid for teachers' salaries soothed the school people. HB 159, another repealer which Representative Hodges had introduced at the request of a labor leader in his county, then readily passed the House, 69 to 21 (5 not voting). Fear of Negro voting had little to do with Representatives' responses on either roll call. The vote on HB 95 bore no statistically significant relationship to the percentage of Negroes in the population of the counties from which the Representatives came. On HB 159, there was a statistically significant tendency for "No" votes to come from counties with the highest percentages of Negroes, but the proportion of anti-repeal votes in the whole House was hardly politically significant. By 1937 the number of Black Belt counties in Florida was too small to give their spokesmen much influence.[26]

As a freshman member of the House, Representative Hodges did not feel it appropriate for him to lobby for his bill's passage in the Senate. There, Senator Graham of Miami, by a clever use of "pet bill" procedure, succeeded in getting HB 159 regarded as "non-controversial," and it passed the Senate, 32 to 4 (2 not voting), without

[26] For the statistical analysis, see Farris, *op. cit.*, p. 74.

the question of Negro voting being raised. Senator Graham's motives in supporting the bill did not, apparently, coincide with those of Representative Hodges in introducing it.[27]

In this aimless fashion, with this lack of large-scale organization, with Negro voting hardly in question, the poll tax payment as a qualification for voting ceased to exist in Florida.

The End of the "Public" White Primary

Negro voting was not involved in the case of *U. S.* v. *Classic*,[28] either, although as later events proved, it was this case that turned the tide against the white primary. Although the U. S. Supreme Court refused to hold that political parties had ceased to be voluntary private associations, the majority of the Court was impressed by the particularity with which the state's statutes (Louisiana's, in this instance) regulated the primary election involved in the case. "Where the state law," wrote Justice Stone,

> has made the primary an integral part of the procedure of choice, or where in fact the primary effectively controls the choice, the right of the elector to have his ballot counted at the primary is . . . included in the right [to vote] protected by Article I, [section] 2 [of the Constitution].[29]

What the *Classic* decision suggested was that where primaries, as in the Southern states, were an "integral part" of the procedure of choosing public officials, the right to vote in them was a federal right. What the decision left in doubt was whether this federal right was a right to vote only in primaries for nominating Congressional candidates,[30] or a right to vote in other sorts of primaries as well.

[27] Cf. Ogden, *op. cit.*, pp. 373 *et seq.*

[28] 35 F. Supp. 66 (1940); 313 U. S. 299, 61 S.Ct. 1031, 95 L.Ed. 1368 (1941).

[29] *Ibid.*

[30] The constitutional basis for the decision was Article I of the Constitution, rather than the Fourteenth or Fifteenth Amendment. The government

Three years after *Classic*, the United States Supreme Court decided *Smith* v. *Allwright*,[31] the fourth and (at this writing) last of the Texas white primary cases. Again at issue was the Texas Democratic convention's white primary rule. "We think," wrote Justice Stone for an almost unanimous Court,

> that this statutory system for the selection of party nominees for inclusion on the general election ballot makes the party which is required to follow these legislative directions an agency of the State insofar as it determines the participants in a primary election. . . . If a State requires a certain electoral procedure. prescribes a general election ballot made up of party nominees so chosen and limits the choice of the electorate in general elections for State offices, practically speaking, to those whose names appear on such a ballot, it [that is, "a State"] endorses, adopts and enforces the discrimination against Negroes, practiced by . . . [the] party . . . . This is state action within the meaning of the Fifteenth Amendment.[32]

The *Smith* decision issued during the 1944 Democratic primary campaign in Florida, too late to allow Negroes in most counties to try to qualify under existing primary law. Its applicability to future primaries excited considerable comment. Only one public official, R. A. Gray, the Secretary of State, was willing to recognize a *fait accompli*. "I think the circumstances in the two states [Texas and Florida] are the same," he said.[33]

Thomas Conely, chairman of the Democratic state committee, spoke of the possibility of getting around the decision. He took comfort from the fact that the Florida Legislature, in 1943, had repealed its statutory grant of power to party committees to set rules governing party

---

had neglected, in the trial court, to allege the equal protection of the laws as one of the rights infringed by Classic's activities, and the Supreme Court did not discuss the question when the government raised it on appeal.

31 321 U. S. 649, 64 S.Ct. 757, 88 L.Ed. 987, 151 A.L.R. 1110 (1944).

32 *Ibid.*

33 *Florida Times-Union,* April 7, 20, 1944.

membership,[34] although just why this should have comforted any one is hard to see: the Texas convention's rule, controverted in the Smith case, also "lacked" a statutory basis.

It was Senator Claude Pepper, then in the middle of a heated primary campaign for re-nomination, who made the most vigorous defense of the Florida white primary. Southerners would not, he said,

> allow matters peculiar to us to be determined by those who do not know and understand our problems.[35] The South will allow nothing to impair white supremacy. I think the Florida law is different from the Texas law . . . , and therefore the Supreme Court decision should not affect Democratic primaries in Florida.[36] In the Florida not the State but the Democratic party determines the qualifications of members of the party.[37] If . . . there is any question about . . . our statute, it can be altered and the matter left exclusively in the hands of the party of determining who may vote in the Democratic primary.[38] This can be done and the Democratic primaries kept white under the decision of the Supreme Court.[39]

The "Private" White Primary and Its Defeat

In point of fact, the legal right of Negroes to vote in Florida's Democratic primaries was not definitely established until three years after the *Smith* decision. The three-

[34] *Ibid.; Florida Laws, 1943,* chap. 21958.

[35] Justice Reed, who wrote the majority opinion in the Smith case, was from Kentucky, and Justice Black, who was with the majority, was from Alabama. The only dissenter, Justice Roberts, was not a Southerner.

[36] In *Davis* v. *State* ex rel. *Cromwell,* 156 Fla. 181, 23 So. 2d 85 (1945), the Florida Supreme Court "overruled" Senator Pepper on this point.

[37] This is what Allwright and his lawyers had thought about the Texas situation.

[38] This is what South Carolina Democrats tried—without success. *Elmore* v. *Rice,* 72 F. Supp 516 (1947); *Rice* v. *Elmore,* 165 F. 2d 387 (1947); certiorari denied, *Rice* v. *Elmore,* 333 U. S. 875, 68 S.Ct. 905, 92 L.Ed. 759 (1948).

[39] *Florida Times-Union,* April 5, 1944. For a sympathetic account of Senator Pepper's difficulties with this question, see Francis P. Locke, "Claude D. Pepper," *Public Men in and out of Office,* ed. by J. T. Salter (Chapel Hill, North Carolina: University of North Carolina Press, 1946), pp. 257-76.

year period included litigation on the subject before the
state courts, two unsuccessful attempts to repeal the Florida statutes regulating primary elections, and more litigation in the federal courts.

Florida registration officials seemed to be dragging
their feet in complying with the new rule. It took R. A.
Cromwell, a Pensacola Negro man, eight months to get the
Escambia County Supervisor of Registration to register
him as a Democrat for the forthcoming state and county
primaries. When the trial court ordered the Supervisor to
register Cromwell, the Supervisor appealed to the Florida
Supreme Court, which confirmed the trial court's order:
the *Smith* case controlled, and the Democratic state committee's white primary rule was no basis for the Supervisor's refusal to register.[40]

In Jacksonville, while the *Cromwell* case was on appeal,
a Negro man named Dallas J. Graham sought to register
as a Democrat for the approaching municipal primary.
The Supervisor refused to register Graham, because of a
resolution of the Jacksonville Democratic committee re-
stricting participation in the municipal primary to white
persons. Graham then asked the Duval County Circuit
Court to compel the Supervisor to register him. The day
before the primary, the Court reluctantly held the instant
case to be controlled by *Smith* v. *Allwright*, and issued the
peremptory writ.[41]

When Graham took his mandamus to the Supervisor's
office, a deputy refused to register him on the grounds that
the time for registration for the next day's primary had

[40] *Davis* v. *State* ex rel. *Cromwell*, 156 Fla. 181, 23 So. 2d 85 (1945).

[41] *State* ex rel. *Graham* v. *Bowden*, Case No. 16237L, Circuit Court, Duval
County, Florida (1945); Duval County Circuit Court Minute Book, LXXXIX,
212. In an earlier order denying the Supervisor's motion to quash the alterna-
tive writ, the judge expressed personal agreement with the Roberts dissent
in *Smith* v. *Allwright* and his own dissatisfaciton with the overruling of *Grovey* v. *Townsend*. Nevertheless, he held himself bound, he said, to follow the
latest decision of the U. S. Supreme Court. For the printed text of the order,
see *Florida Times-Union*, April 4, 1945.

already expired. Graham then sued the Supervisor in the U. S. District Court for $50,000 damages and asked an injunction restraining the Supervisor from refusing to register him. Several days later, he asked the Duval County Circuit Court to hold the Supervisor in contempt for refusal to obey the mandamus. Thus facilitated, negotiations between attorneys for Graham and the Supervisor resulted in Graham's registration as a Democrat. The contempt proceedings and federal court suit were then dropped.[42]

While settlement of the *Cromwell* and *Graham* cases was pending, the 1945 Florida Legislature was considering a "private" primary bill, which would repeal specified statutes and "all others relating . . ." to primary elections. Introduced by State Senators John E. Mathews of Duval County and G. Warren Sanchez of Suwannee County, the measure was similar in objective to a series of some 140 South Carolina statutes passed in 1944.[43]

What the proponents of such acts of expunction assumed was that if primary election laws were repealed, primaries would no longer be an "integral part" of the procedure for choosing public officials. They further believed that the decision in both the *Classic* and the *Smith* cases had turned on the "integral part" criterion, and that when the Court spoke in those cases of primaries "effectively controlling" the choice of public officials, the Court was uttering mere *dicta*, not law. If primaries were not an "integral part" of the procedure of choice, parties would be in no sense agencies of the state, but would be volun-

---

[42] *State* ex rel. *Graham* v. *Bowden*, Case No. 16237L, Circuit Court, Duval County, Florida (1945); *Graham* v. *Bowden*, Case No. 833-J-Civ, U. S. District Court, Southern District of Florida (Jacksonville) (1945). Graham did not get to vote in the municipal Democratic primary of 1945. When the registration books closed for the municipal general election of 1945, 157 Negroes had registered as Democrats in Jacksonville (*Florida Times-Union*, May 24, 1945). The election was a formality, since all Democratic candidates were unopposed.

[43] Florida Senate, *Journal, 1945*, p. 15; *South Carolina Laws, 1944*, nos. 688-828.

tary private associations with inherent power to exclude Negroes.

Before a joint committee of the Legislature of 1945, Senators Mathews and Sanchez defended their bill. The former warned of Negro bloc voting which, he said, would place the "balance of power" in close primary contests in the "hands of a few thousand negroes." In the "classical" tradition, Senator Sanchez ceremonially resorted to symbols of violence, shouting that the bill would "determine whether our people are going to survive or whether we're going to have bloodshed."[44]

For over a month after the hearings, the Senate's committee sat on the bill, which Senator Mathews was finally able to have calendared. A few days later, during his absence, the Senate by an anonymous voice vote recommitted the bill. The committee then adversely reported the bill, and it was tabled for the rest of the session.[45] Just why the committee decided to kill the bill is hard to say, but the Secretary of State, R. A. Gray, is commonly credited with having convinced most members of the joint committee that complete repeal of primary laws would result in large-scale frauds in the conduct of private primaries.

Meantime, a federal court case in Georgia apparently upheld the private primary proponents' views of the Constitution. Primus E. King, a Negro in Muscogee County (Columbus), sued several election officials who had refused to allow him to vote in the Democratic primaries. Relying on the *Classic* and the *Smith* cases, the trial court awarded damages to King. When the election officials appealed, the Circuit Court of Appeals upheld the decision, but not the reasoning, of the trial court. The statutory situation in Georgia, different from that in Texas and Louisiana, made

---

[44] *Miami Herald,* April 13, 1945. The joint committee also considered the dubiously constitutional "affiliate" plan of J. Tom Watson, the Attorney General of Florida. *Ibid.; Florida Times-Union,* April 13, May 18, 1945.

[45] Florida Senate, *Journal, 1945,* pp. 404, 501, 505; *Florida Times-Union,* May 17, 18, 22, 1945.

it incorrect to rely on *Classic* and *Smith*. It was the existence of the Georgia statutes regulating primaries that brought the instant case within the purview of the Fifteenth Amendment.[46] The clear implication was that a "private" white primary, unregulated by statute, would not violate the Fifteenth Amendment.

By the time the Court had enunciated this rule, the Florida state Democratic committee had already rescinded its white primary rule, and over 32,000 Negroes eventually registered for the Florida primaries of 1946. Except in Jacksonville and Duval County, the voting passed off quietly, and the Negro press reported no "incidents" in the areas of large Negro registrations.[47]

In the Jacksonville-Duval County area, State Senator John E. Mathews, co-author of the 1945 white primary bill, won a close run-off primary campaign against an opponent who was heavily supported by Negro voters. The Senator made white supremacy and the white primary the issues in the run-off, and pledged the voters that he would work for the maintenance of both if he were returned to the Senate.[48]

For almost a year, the private primary proposal competed with other political issues for the attention of Florida voters and politicians. As the vote on its adoption in 1947 suggests, it was an issue in only a few areas, but there was a state campaign against the bill, as well as a vigorous discussion, in the Jacksonville-Duval County area, of its merits and demerits.

[46] *King* v. *Chapman*, 62 F. Supp. 639 (1945); *Chapman* v. *King*, 154 F. 2d 460 (1946); certiorari denied, *Chapman* v. *King*, 327 U.S. 800, 66 S.Ct. 905, 90 L.Ed. 1025 (1946).

[47] *Jacksonville Journal*, January 21, 22, 30, February 8, 1946; Florida Secretary of State, *Report, 1945-1946*, pp. 97-98. There were 12 counties with 4 or fewer Negro Democratic registrants. On the balloting, the Florida edition of the *Pittsburgh Courier* spoke of the "cordial relationship" that prevailed between white and Negroes at the polls, and of "harmony and a noticeable lack of friction." Cf. *ibid.*, May 11, 18, 25, 1946.

[48] For a detailed account of the Duval County campaigns, see Farris, *op. cit.*, chap. V.

As the time approached for the 1947 Legislature to convene, the entrance of a Negro Democratic candidate into the Jacksonville municipal primaries aroused additional interest in the Mathews proposal. The Senator refused to say "I told you so," he stated to the press, because that would be "in bad taste." Before he left for the session, he spoke briefly at a public meeting, where he described the white Democratic party as "a time-honored tradition of the South—in favor of segregation and opposed to comingling of the races."[49]

As the Legislature convened, Jacksonville opponents got in their last blows at the measure. The League of Women Voters began circulating petitions to the delegation and to the Governor, urging that they oppose "any proposal to set up a private primary system in this city, county or state." The Jacksonville Ministerial Alliance passed a strongly-worded resolution in which it made clear its "unreserved disapproval" of the Mathews measure. And as a final touch, one of the local newspapers disclosed that Senator Mathews had been instrumental in abolishing a private municipal Democratic primary system in Jacksonville ten years before.[50]

At the state level, the white primary controversy proceeded somewhat less vigorously than in the home of its sponsor. In June, 1946, the Democratic state committee, by unanimous vote of the 98 members present, asked the 1947 Legislature to repeal all election laws "which prevent the Democratic Party from remaining an exclusively white party."[51]

Four months later, the newly formed Florida State Association of Supervisors of Registration heard Secretary

---

[49] *Jacksonville Journal*, March 19, 20, 1947. He had earlier debated the question with Secretary of State R. A. Gray, a vigorous opponent of the private primary. *Ibid.*, February 18, 20-22, 1947.

[50] *Ibid.*, April 1, 7, 1947.

[51] *Miami Herald*, June 6, 1946. The full committee consists of 134 members.

of State Gray speak against the private primary bill, and passed a resolution opposing any attempt to repeal acts governing primaries.[52] A month later, Governor Caldwell gave oblique approval to the private primary. He saw no reason, he said,

> why a party shouldn't be able to govern itself. South Carolina appears to have worked out the idea very well and without any disruption. There is nothing in ethics to prevent any group of people from forming any organization they may want to form. Whether it's a wise thing to do, I don't know. I don't know what the answer is till I've seen the bill.[53]

Late in March, 1947, the Committee to Defend Democracy in Florida met to oppose the Mathews bill. The assembled members urged the Legislature to retain the existing primary system and "to erect no barriers to participation in primaries because of race, color, creed or economic status."[54]

The bill did not seem to be gaining much support. Incomplete returns to a poll of legislators by the Associated Press revealed only two, Senators Mathews and Johns, who would publicly commit themselves to the measure. As the Legislature convened, a Tallahassee correspondent was able to assert that "the real fight over the white primary was settled weeks ago." Members from the panhandle counties, where the issue (Jacksonville aside) had been most agitated, had already agreed that "they didn't think Mathews had the right answer." According to the correspondent, the Speaker-designate of the House, T. D. Beasley, expressed the pre-session consensus of the legislators: few Negroes would vote if Negroes were "quietly" accepted into the Democratic party; if whites made an issue of the question, Negroes might register as Republicans in

---

[52] *Jacksonville Journal*, October 6, 7, 1946.
[53] *Ibid.*, November 8, 9, 1946.
[54] *Ibid.*, March 24, 1947.

such numbers that, in some counties, they could overwhelm white Democrats at the general election.[55]

On April 10, two days after the Legislature convened, Senator Mathews introduced the private primary bill, one of five measures that embodied his program of electoral "reform."[56] Senator Sanchez, Senator Mathews' coadjutor in 1945, co-sponsored the white primary bill and thus became the third Senator to go on record in favor ot it.[57]

The Senate Committee on Privileges and Elections took two weeks to arrange what turned out to be a "tumultuous" hearing on the measure. The audience included a large delegation of students from the Florida State College for Women (now Florida State University), "who cheered witnesses against the bill and laughed noisily" as Senator Mathews spoke in favor of it.[58]

Two members of the Democratic state committee presented the committee's pro-white-primary resolution. A Jacksonville attorney discussed the constitutionality of the repealer. Senators Mathews and Sanchez, in their comments, both expressed the belief that "outside agitators" would be able to "stir up" Florida Negroes if the latter were allowed to vote in Democratic primaries. In closing, Senator Mathews said that, if necessary, he would run for "high office" to accomplish the purpose of his white primary bill.[59]

Leo Sheiner, representing the Committee to Defend Democracy in Florida, denounced the Mathews bill as un-

---

[55] *Florida Times-Union*, March 9, 1947; Allen Morris in *Jacksonville Journal*, April 1, 1947.

[56] The others dealt with fraud in the conduct of affairs of *all* voluntary private associations, a petition procedure for getting candidates' names on general election ballots, the choice of candidates for offices having multiple incumbents and identical titles, and a literacy test amendment to the state Constitution.

[57] *Florida Times-Union*, April 11, 1947; *Jacksonville Journal*, April 10, 1947.

[58] *Ibid.*, April 25, 1947.

[59] *Ibid.*

constitutional, immoral, unChristian, and undemocratic. DeWitt Upthegrove, president of the Florida State Association of Supervisors of Registration, said that the Association wanted "good, honest and square elections," which the Mathews bill would make it impossible to achieve. Sheiner, he went on, "expressed my sentiments exactly." It remained for Senator Walter G. Walker to make the most vigorous attack on the Mathews proposal. Under that measure, the Senator said, it would be possible to deny Roman Catholics, or Jews, or trade union members, as well as Negroes, the opportunity to vote in Democratic primaries. "If we deny the negro the right to vote in the party of his choice," he asserted, "we must exempt him from the payment of taxes and from military service." In conclusion, he labeled the measure as "the most vicious bill" that he had encountered during his four terms in the Legislature.[60]

Opponents of the bill unsuccessfully tried to report it unfavorably, but Senator Mathews, with the aid of proxies from two absent members, was able to secure a report without recommendation. The Senate was in no hurry to take up the proposal until Senator Mathews' delaying tactics—he spoke daily and at length on "points of personal privilege"—forced a special order of business for his bill.[61]

On May 8, before packed galleries and jammed doorways and aisles, the debate began. Senator Sanchez led off the speaking. "There would be no necessity for this bill," he said, "had the people of the Southern states not been bothered by outside agitators." Until recently, he continued, it had been possible "to work out the problems of the people of the Southern states to the satisfaction and best interest of all [sic] involved." He warned that a third party, Communist-inspired, was on the way, a party that would promise "the same thing for all." The white pri-

[60] Ibid.
[61] Ibid., April 25, May 8, 9, 1947.

mary bill, he concluded, would prevent "a mass of uneducated people from being misled" by the Communist third party.[62]

Senator Mathews' garb and the introduction to his speech conformed with the regional traditions appropriate to the occasion. Clad in a white suit, he began his hourlong discourse by establishing the antiquity and the patriotism of his Southern ancestry: one of his Georgian forebears had signed the Declaration of Independence, and another had fought for the Confederacy during the Civil War. The family tradition of patriotism extended to one of his sons, who had served with heroism during World War II.

In his own opinion, Senator Mathews went on, "Southern civilization, ideals and institutions are at stake. So far as I am concerned, I've taken my stand. As long as I live, I will expound my views." Florida was faced with a problem that arose, he said, from allowing Negroes to register as Democrats. So registered, he charged, they would be under the domination of outside agitators—"the Communists, the CIO, the PAC and the Eleanor Clubs," who would thus control state politics. He denied that he was a Negro hater. "No man in this senate," he continued, "has any more love for the negro race that I have." As evidence of his affection, he cited his votes in favor of making appropriations for the state college for Negroes. In conclusion, he rehearsed his unhappy experiences with Negro voters in the Duval County primaries of 1946, and repeated his charge that Negroes there had been urged to register as Democrats in order to control the balance of power in the Democratic party.[63]

Senators Walker and Gray made the principal speeches against the bill. Obtaining the floor on a point of personal privilege, Senator Walker denied that he had ever said Senator Mathews was "un-American." He *had* said, Walker

[62] *Ibid.*
[63] *Ibid.*

went on, "That these bills, which I think are the biggest bunch of trash ever presented here, were un-American and vicious," and those remarks he had no desire to withdraw. If passed, he concluded, the Mathews bills would destroy free elections in Florida.[64]

Closing the attack on the white primary bill was Senator Carl Gray, from the "hog and hominy" belt of Northwest Florida. He was careful to match his Southern ancestry with that of Senator Mathews and to establish his status as a three-year veteran of the recent war. That war, Senator Gray declared, grew out of racial hatreds. He avowed his belief that it was fought to preserve democracy. The Mathews bill, Senator Gray continued,

> is not based upon my concept of democracy. It is class legislation aimed at a minority group. It would destroy every gain that we have made for clean elections in the last 100 years.[65]

Senator Gray went on to argue that legislation directed against one minority group might broaden into legislation directed against other minorities. Even though there were no Negroes in Florida, he declared, he would still oppose the Mathews bill. He discounted the fears of Communism in Florida expressed by Senators Mathews and Sanchez, and defended the right of trade unions to be politically active. He disparaged Senator Mathews' charge that Florida Negroes had to be urged to give up Republicanism by pointing out that they had not been allowed to register as Democrats until recently. "Mr. President and Senators," he declared in peroration, "I hope that this bill will be defeated, because it is one of the most damnable pieces of legislation I have ever seen."[66]

Senator Gray sat down amid a burst of applause from the galleries. A few minutes later, his hope was realized

---

[64] Ibid.

[65] Editorial from Tallahassee Democrat, reprinted in Gainesville Sun, May 14, 1947.

[66] Ibid.; Jacksonville Journal, May 9, 1947.

when the Senate defeated the bill, 30 votes to 4 (4 not voting). Senator Mathews had a few more remarks to make. "You have voted me down here," he said.

> It is very likely you have made me a candidate for governor. I will take this issue into the highways, the byways and the crossroads and tell the people about it. *If somebody gets hurt, that will be just too bad.*[67]

There is no simple explanation of the Senate's refusal to pass the white primary bill. The geographical distribution, by state senatorial districts, of adult Negro population, of Negro Democratic registrants in 1946, and of all Negro registrants—all three distributions bore little discernible relationship to the roll call vote on the defeat of measure. In the absence of other evidence, it can only be suggested that, in addition to their attitudes toward Negroes, the voting of individual Senators was influenced by their feelings on one or more of the arguments of the anti-white primary people: (1) the private primary led to fraud and clique control; (2) the white primary violated some of the moral imperatives of Christianity and the democratic credo; and (3) the white primary was unnecessary: its objectives could be substantially achieved under the system of statutory primaries.

Only the third argument requires comment. Speaker Beasley expressed it as the session convened: few Negroes would try to register as Democrats if those who did try were "quietly" accepted into the party. The validity of this argument depends upon the assumption of at least one of three conditions: (1) widespread political apathy among unregistered Negroes; (2) the absence of vigorous Negro leaders to stimulate registration; and (3) the availability of intimidation as a deterrent to registration. An examination of the "registration map" of Florida since 1947 shows

---

[67] *Ibid.* (italics supplied). At the last minute, and in spite of the civil rights agitation, Senator Mathews decided not to run for Governor in 1948. He turned up in the camp of the winning candidate, however, who later appointed him to State Supreme Court.

wide county-to-county variations in the proportions of Negroes registered, but short of a study beyond the scope of this article, the existence of any one of these three conditions cannot be shown.

CONCLUSION

With the defeat of the Mathews bill in 1947, the legal right of Florida Negroes to become Democrats was finally established—three years after the decision in *Smith* v. *Allwright*. Accordingly, the action of the federal courts on the private white primary in South Carolina had no effect on the Florida situation except to emphasize that Floridian white primary supporters had guessed wrong about the effect of *Classic* and *Smith* upon a "statuteless" Democratic primary.[68]

It is a truism, of course, that legal "rights" are not always "real" rights. Where and under what circumstances, in Florida and in the South, legality becomes reality should be the subject of continuing studies of the political behavior of Negro Democrats.[69]

This is not to say that the battle over legality is a sham battle. Certainly it is to Negroes' advantage that, in Florida as a whole, there is now no very considerable disposition to resort to "legal," state-wide disfranchising techniques. A severe economic crisis and consequent sharp declines in the level of employment and personal economic security may conceivably produce new anti-Negro-suffrage movements. But national economic policy might so mitigate the effects of a depression as to check or destroy such movements.

CHARLES D. FARRIS

University of Alabama

[68] See *Elmore* v. *Rice*, 72 F. Supp. 516 (1947); *Rice* v. *Elmore*, 165 F. 2d 387 (1947); certiorari denied, *Rice* v. *Elmore*, 333 U.S. 875, 68 S.Ct. 905, 92 L.Ed. 1151 (1948).

[69] For one such study, see Farris, *op. cit.*

FURTHER NOTES ON NEGROES AND MULATTOES
IN EIGHTEENTH-CENTURY FRANCE

This material reveals that the Negro residents of eighteenth-century France, relatively few though they were, represented to some degree a cross-section of society, certain of them possessing wealth and aristocratic blood but the vastly greater number coming from the servant class, some disreputable but most of them loyal and honorable. A few rare individuals created for themselves reputations as military and political leaders, yet the great mass lived in obscurity. None is mentioned as a priest, a merchant, or a financier. The information on them usually is of the most fragmentary sort, interspersed in side remarks on other topics. From an accumulation of such material, however, historians in time may acquire a very good picture of the part that Negroes and mulattoes have played in the history of European nations since the nautical discoveries and slave raids of the 1400's.

In this article therefore I shall relate a series of anecdotes and episodes rather than attempt to give a general history of Negroes in France during the eighteenth century. I have already pointed out that not infrequently Negro and mulatto youths were brought to France to study. Some were the sons of African chieftains, others the natural sons of French Caribbean planters. An example of the former was Abram Hannibal, son of the king of Ethiopia who was captured in war, sold in the slave market of Constantinople at the age of eight to a Russian nobleman, and given as a present to Peter the Great. Peter was very fond of him. He had him christened in the Orthodox faith in 1707 under the name of "Abram Hannibal," and took him in his entourage to various regions. At length in 1716 he decided to send him to Paris to study military engineering, desiring that he should serve in the Russian army on his return. In Paris he spent several years, was shown attention by the Duke of Orleans then regent, and served

284

as an officer in the French army. In 1723 he returned to Russia and entered the Russian military service as an engineering officer in the Czar's private regiment. He declined an invitation from his older brother to return to Ethiopia, saying that he had thrown in his lot with Russia. But shortly afterwards Peter died and Abram Hannibal experienced diverse fortunes under the subsequent rulers, falling into disfavor with Catherine I, being exiled to Siberia by Peter II, and at length being restored to imperial favor and honors by Elizabeth I. Marrying a German girl, he became the father of five sons. Descended from one of them was the great Russian poet Alexander Pushkin.[1]

The Marquis D'Argenson in his journal entry for June 25, 1752 reports that a Negro prince from Guinea was being educated at the Jesuit college in Paris (Collège de Louis-le-Grand), at the expense of the French government. It amounted to 100 francs a day, which was a handsome allowance, for later in the century Napoleon and other students attending the French military schools at government expense received only 700 francs per year and found the allowance sufficient. D'Argenson reports having seen the young prince at the opera. The French government had signed a treaty with the boy's father, evidently in regard to the slave trade, and was holding him as a hostage.[2]

One African chieftain sent his daughter, aged fourteen, to France for education. For this purpose he confided her to a sea captain in 1784, as the latter set out with a cargo of slaves for Le Cap, Santo Domingo. On his return journey the captain set her ashore at Honfleurs and engaged for her a tutor, who was to take her to Paris and see to her education. The girl created exceptional attention be-

[1] More details are given by Beatrice F. Fleming and Marion J. Pryde, *Distinguished Negroes Abroad* (Washington [1946]), pp. 166-70.

[2] *Journal et mémoires du Marquis d'Argenson, publiés pour la première fois* . . . par E. J. B. Rathery (Paris, 1859-65, 9 v.), VII, 257. The boy's father is designated as ''the king of Anamabon'' (Anamaboe). Today Anamaboe is a fort on the Gold Coast.

cause of the fact that she was an albino. Her skin and hair were white or relatively so, the iris of her eyes was red, and her nose was less repressed than common with her race. It was reported by a journalist of the day that among her brothers and sisters only one brother was albinal like herself, the others being dark in complexion. At the time of her arrival she knew only a few words of French, but happily her custodian, Captain Herblin, was well-versed in her language. Further details on her residence in France are not given.[3]

In 1744 another albino Negro had visited Paris and been seen by Voltaire, but it is not indicated whether he was a student there. He was only four or five years old.[4]

In 1788 the Chevalier de Boufflers, governor of Senegal, contemplated sending to France for a commercial education four or five Senegalese youths, in the hope that they might return to their country as exponents of French culture and inspire an exodus of other youths to France for training. Evidently he did not get to carry through his idea, but in 1796 the French Directory did institute in Paris a special school for colonials, entitled Institut National des Colonies. From the outset its doors were open to the youth of all colors, white, brown, or black.[5] Earlier governments of the Revolution had established primary schools for Negro and mulatto children in the colonies, where prior to 1789 none existed save for the whites.[6]

Sometimes rich planters in the Americas sent their natural sons of mixed blood to Paris for education. One

[3] *Mercure de France*, March 22, 1788, pp. 183-85.

[4] Mercer Cook, ''Jean-Jacques Rousseau and the Negro,'' *The Journal of Negro History*, XXI (1936), 295; Nicolas Le Cat, *Traité de la couleur de la peau humaine en général, de celle des nègres en particulier* . . . (Amsterdam, 1765), pp. 102-03. Le Cat was greatly interested in the cause of color and to study it he made an autopsy in 1757 on a Negro youth who had died at Rouen. He also studied the brain and blood of Negroes. *Ibid.*, pp. 53-4, 77.

[5] Paul Roussier, ''L'application des lois de la Révolution aux colonies,'' *Cahiers de la Révolution française*, III [Paris, 1935], 65-6.

[6] *Ibid.*, p. 64.

such youth was the Chevalier de Saint-George (1745-99), native of Guadeloupe, where his father, Jean Nicholas de Boulogne, was controller general of the treasury and a royal councillor. On a trip to France the father took the youth for training, and during subsequent years spent partly in France and partly in England, provided him adequately with money for his needs. Already before the Revolution he had acquired a reputation as a skilled swordsman, a violinist, a musical composer, and a playwright. Stirred by the events of the Revolution, he enlisted in the national guard in 1791 with the rank of captain, and set about the next year to recruit a regiment composed wholly of Negroes and mulattoes. Among the recruits was Alexandre Dumas, later distinguished as a general. In this regiment were seven hundred men, who were designated variously as the Legion of Saint-George and the Legion of Americans of the South. A British author who visited the French camp in Belgium in December 1792 and January 1793 described it as the best dressed and most prim unit of the French army. It was "dressed and accoutred in the richest and most brilliant manner."[7]

In May 1793 the minister of war ordered the company to be transported to Santo Domingo. This aroused the indignation of the Jacobins, who considered it humiliating that a body of soldiers who had distinguished themselves in Belgium fighting under the banner of freedom for their adopted country should be relegated to obscurity in a distant colony. The committee of war in the National Convention on May 16 called on that body to revoke the minister's order, saying that these men must not be "plunged again in fetters." It was so ordered.[8]

They were kept in France and in January 1794 were

[7] Beatrice J. Fleming and Marion Pride, *Distinguished Negroes Abroad* (Washington [1946]), pp. 63-8; J. M. Thompson, *English Witnesses of the French Revolution* (Oxford, 1938), p. 220.

[8] *Réimpression de l'ancien Moniteur* ... (Paris, 1858-63, 32 v.), XVI, 400.

employed as execution squads for exterminating the aristocrats at Nantes. This they did with "a total indifference and an instinctive brutality." Those whom they failed to kill with bullets they finished off with the saber. "It was with extreme reluctance that they agreed to bury their victims," and even then they covered them with so little dirt that the foul odor resulting "rendered neighboring quarters [of the city] uninhabitable." Dogs despoiled the graves, and a cholera epidemic was avoided with difficulty.[9]

Another natural son whose life in some respects paralleled that of Saint-George was Julien Raymond (or Raimond). Born in Martinique about 1743, he came to France in 1784, enjoying an income of 55,000 livres a year, but lived quietly in southeastern France until the outbreak of the Revolution when he went to Paris to assume leadership of a small group of mulattoes (*gens du couleur*) who fought first for the representation of their group in the National Assembly and afterwards for the rights of citizenship to mulattoes both in France and the colonies. He appeared more than once before the National Assembly as spokesman for his body and engaged heavily in pamphleteering and other propagandistic activity. Reportedly he spent his entire fortune on his cause, and in 1793 served a short period as a political prisoner in Paris, at the time of Brissot's arrest. He lived to see his cause triumph, and afterwards, during the era of the Directory, was sent as commissioner by the government to the Antilles or Windward Islands.[10]

There were even instances where slaves were sent to France for education. The Abbé Grégoire records the story of the naturalist Michaud who bought in Philadelphia a young Negro from Africa and took him to France and

[9] Gaston Martin, *Carrier et sa mission à Nantes* [Paris, 1924], pp. 336-37.

[10] A Brette, ''Les gens de couleur libres et leurs députés en 1789,'' *La Révolution française*, XXIX (1895), 402 n. 1; *Réimpression de l'ancien Moniteur*, VIII, 399-400, XIII, 643; Mitchell B. Garrett, *The French Colonial Question, 1789-91* (Ann Arbor, 1916), pp. 134-35.

there educated him. Later he took him to Madagascar to engage in exploratory activity, but Michaud there died and his plans went awry. The Negro was again sold, this time into abject servitude.[11]

Not only was kindness sometimes shown by master to slave, there were some remarkable instances of kindness shown by slaves to their masters. Grégoire reproduces the story of such a slave, whose name he does not even mention, who belonged to a colonial planter named Du Colombier. Colombier brought him to France and settled at Nantes. The Negro became free since he had been brought to free soil and gradually acquired some means. Hearing that his former master had become destitute, he came to him with money. Later he tilled a garden and sold its products for the maintenance of his old master. Still later when Colombier became sick the Negro came to his bedside and waited on him. For twenty years this good former slave maintained his master and then predeceased him, in 1776.[12]

There was another loyal Negro who fought for his master, an aristocrat named Guillin, at the latter's estate at Poleymieux, near Lyons, in early July 1791. According to a royalist newspaper of the time, Guillin was "attacked by a considerable number of national guards and peasants, with their mayors at their head." For five hours Guillin, aided only by his faithful Negro servant, fought them off, until he was killed and frightfully mutilated and his home burned. A subsequent issue of the journal charged the attackers with cutting the body to bits and with outright cannibalism. The fate of the brave servant, alas, is unrecorded.[13]

[11] Henri Grégoire, *De la littérature des nègres* . . . (Paris, 1808), pp. 180-81.

[12] *Ibid.*, pp. 122-23. Variants of this story are *given by* Pahin de la Blancherie, *Extrait du journal de mes voyages* . . . (Paris, 1775, 2 v.), I, 352-58, and by Hilliard d'Auberteuil, *Considérations sur l'état présent de la colonie Française de Saint-Domingue* . . . (Paris, 1776-77, 2 v.), I, 142 n.1.

[13] *Journal de la cour et de la ville* for July 8 and 13, 1791, pp. 62, 101.

Another instance of loyalty and kindness was displayed during the Reign of Terror of the Revolution by the Negro turnkey Théodore, employed at the Prison du Plessis in Paris. Formerly he had been a valet for a certain French family of means. When in 1794 Madame de Vassy, a friend of this family, and certain of her female friends were arrested as aristocrats and brought to Paris, they were first imprisoned at the Château de Chantilly (near Paris) and afterwards at the Du Plessis. The little band of women was placed in the custody of this Negro immediately on their arrival. Madame de Vassy recognizing him found opportunity to call him by name and to give him some money. From that moment her friend and protector, he cautioned her to hide her money lest it be taken from her by the other prison custodians. He brought her a number of old newspapers to read, stepped forward to assist her and a friend when they were summoned before the concierge, favored her in the assignment of cells, brought her at night a lighted lamp, and in other ways aided her. Toward the aristocrats he revealed no resentment; on the contrary, according to Madame de Vassy, he was animated to show favors out of sentiment for his former master. One of the jailors, however, did not regard him as favorably as did Madame de Vassy, calling him under muttered breath "This cursed black!" and expressing delight at the thought that soon the women would have no more money to tip him.[14]

Not every Negro, however, was loyal toward his former master. The chief agent in the arrest and conviction of Madame du Barry during the Terror, according to Helen Maria Williams, was a Negro whom she had reared from childhood and of whom she was fond. Miss Williams, who calls him "this viper," tells of his having been given a

[14] Albert Savine (ed.), *Les géôles de province sous le Terreur* (*Récits de prisonniers*) (Paris [1911]), pp. 46-53.

pension of 600 livres a year by Louis XV and asserts that he still at the time of her writing enjoyed it.[15]

Negroes and mulattoes are mentioned much more in records of the Revolutionary period than previously, partly no doubt because there were more of them then, but even more so because they were greatly excited by the issues of the Revolution and for the first time had an opportunity to participate in the molding of national destiny. Perhaps another factor was the greater interest of the French in the lot of the Negro. Gaston Martin, the great authority on the history of French slavery, states that of more than twelve hundred *cahiers de doléances* of 1789 conserved in the *Archives parlementaires* "at least fifty" asked the Estates General to do something to remedy the evils of slavery or the slave trade. None asked for complete abolition of slavery.[16] Not all the *cahiers,* however, are reproduced in the *Archives parlementaires,* and the little town of Bagnères, in Bigorre, can be cited as one that did ask in its *cahier* for complete suppression of slavery, as inconsistent with justice and humanity. It was item no. 5 in the *cahier,* high on the list. How the people of that little mountain town in the Pyrenees became interested in the welfare of Negroes is a mystery, for it would not be at all unlikely that such a secluded community had never seen a Negro, but their interest illustrates the attention that all the French now had come to manifest in this unfortunate race.[17]

---

[15] *Letters Containing a Sketch of the Politics of France . . . and Scenes which have passed in the Prisons of France* (Philadelphia, 1796), p. 154. Inasmuch as the National Assembly in 1790-91 made a drastic revision of the pension system in France and excerpted all or virtualy pensions granted sheerly out of royal favor, it may be doubted that the pension was paid after 1791. The author of the biographical sketch of Miss Williams in the *Dictionary of National Biography* asserts that she is often inaccurate.

[16] *Histoire de l'esclavage et les colonies françaises* (Paris, 1948), p. 171.

[17] *Département des Hautes-Pyrénées, Cahiers de doléances de la sénéchaussée de Bigorre pour les Estats-généraux de 1789 publiés par Gaston Balencié . . .* (Tarbes, 1925), p. 120.

Not only did Negroes and mulattoes display interest in the Revolution by enlistment in the national guard, but also by joining the political clubs. Two mulatto women enrolled in the Jacobin Club of Paris and showed themselves to be such ardent and rash members in connection with the Champs de Mars Affair of July 16-17, 1791, that other members recommended their expulsion. On the morning of July 16 there had been a meeting of the members of the various political clubs at the hall of the Cordeliers, and these two Jacobin members proposed that they all go and knock the statues of the kings from their pedestals throughout the city. Even the president of the radical Cordeliers did not care to engage in so rash an enterprise at that time, and some member of the Jacobins afterwards protested against their conduct as members and asked for their expulsion as troublemakers. The two women thereupon were called before a committee of twenty-four members, of both sexes, to justify their conduct. One, Madame Corbin, was quiet and orderly on this occasion; the other Madame Maillard, came with a child and made an unsatisfactory defense. She was sent with her child into an adjoining room to await the committee's decision. There she fell into despair and made ready to commit suicide by climbing into a window and preparing to jump from it. Her actions however attracted members of the commtitee, who rushed in and seized her. This maneuver instead of softening the attitude of the committee toward her antagonized it, and the members voted to expel both women. It ordered two of its members to report the expulsion to the Jacobin officials.[18]

On July 14, 1791, two days prior to their proposal that got them into trouble, they were among a hundred or more signers (forty-one of them women) of a petition at the Champs de Mars, addressed to the National Assembly, re-

[18] Isabelle Bourdin, *Les Sociétés populaires à Paris pendant la Révolution* (Paris, 1937), pp. 37-8, 278.

questing that body not to take action on the king's recent
flight to Varennes without considering also the perfidy of
"their enemies" who had thrown France into civil war. It
is readily seen therefore that they were extreme left-wing-
ers and out for trouble.[19]

On April 15, 1792 a Negro was chosen among some honored citizens to welcome back to Paris the mutineers of
Nancy who eighteen months previously had been sentenced
to the galleys at Brest. It was a fete of patriotic nature,
first suggested by Marat and organized by Tallien, Palloy,
and Santerre. Pétion, the mayor of Paris, gave it his support. There was a big parade and the mutineers were welcomed on the spot where previously the Bastille has stood.[20]

Curiously enough a Negro was among those guillotined
during the Revolution, but probably not as a reactionary.
He was one of those guillotined for participating in the riot
of May 20, 1795. These rioters, the tools of malcontent leaders who wanted the Convention brought to an end, stormed
the Convention hall, killed a deputy, placed his head on a
pike, and threatened to do likewise to the president, Boissy
d'Anglas, unless he acceded to their demands. Not until
midnight was quiet fully restored. Though some royalists
were among the participants, the most were Jacobins, and
it may be assumed that the Negro was of the latter group.[21]

The troubles of the time produced some Negro prison-
ers. One such was a Negro domestic or orderly named
John Joachim, who was among a group of British and
Spanish prisoners taken at Toulon on 10 frimaire an II
(November 30, 1793) and imprisoned at the Luxembourg
in Paris.[22] Later, in November 1796, the deputy Bourdon

---

[19] *Ibid.*, p. 275 n.

[20] J. M. Thompson, *The French Revolution* (4th ed., New York, 1950),
p. 264.

[21] R. R. Palmer, *A History of the Modern World* (New York, 1950), p.
373; *The Cambridge Modern History*, ed. by A. W. Ward *et al* (13 v., Cambridge and New York, 1902-12), VIII, 388.

[22] *Réimpression de l'ancien Moniteur*, XIX, 172.

reported on the floor of the Corps Legislatif that "more than forty mulattoes" were being illegally "detained" at Rochefort and Bayonne.[23]

Here and there was a Negro or mulatto in a less honorable role. A mulatto woman named Bersi is described as one of the twelve most noted prostitutes of Paris during the Revolution. These twelve lived in well furnished second-floor apartments around the Jardin Egalité (the former Palais Royal), set lavish tables, and possessed servants. Their expenditures approximated 50,000 livres a year. They attended the opera and the theatres. Each had a small Negro boy to accompany her, in fashion similar to the aristocratic women prior to the Revolution.[24]

Another fashionable prostitute of the period was Madame Hamelin, a quadroon, who along with Josephine was among "a bevy of frail and lovely ladies" that Madame Tallien assembled in a salon, in a home given her by Barras. The salon "was frequented by all the celebrities of the day." There Barras brought Napoleon and introduced him to Madame Tallien and Josephine. At the first Madame Tallien was more interested in Napoleon than was Josephine.[25]

Throughout the period of the Revolution the Negroes and mulattoes in France took an active part in military service, more especially in the national guards, which one entered through voluntary enlistment. Thomas Clarkson, the English abolitionist, spent the last six months of 1789 in France endeavoring with Lafayette's help to influence the National Assembly to make legislation in behalf of the Negroes. He found at Lafayette's table, at that early period, two mulattoes from Santo Domingo in the uniform

[23] Ibid., XXVIII, 481.
[24] Edmond and Jules de Goncourt, Histoire de la société française pendant la Révolution (Paris, n. d.), p. 225.
[25] F. M. Kircheisen, Napoleon, tr. by Henry S. Lawrence (New York, 1932), p. 65.

of the national guard of that island.[26] The total number that served during the decade cannot be, or at least has not been, determined, but it ran into the hundreds. There were some hundreds even in the Legion of Saint-George. Even in June 1798 there were enough Negro and mulatto soldiers on the Isle of Aix, off the mouth of the Charente near Rochefort, to constitute a company, under the command of Marin-Pèdre, Negro captain.[27]

Even more important than their military service was their activity in political affairs inasmuch as this helped pave the way for the recognition of the mulattoes as citizens in 1791 and for the abolition of slavery in 1794 and the consequent recognition of Negroes too as citizens. Under the Old Regime no opportunity existed for political activity by mulattoes or Negroes; the Revolution brought a great change. Thomas Clarkson at the time of his visit to Paris in 1789 witnessed six of them from Santo Domingo sitting as guests of the National Assembly. One was the mulatto Ogé, whom Clarkson advised to move slowly but without success.[28] On March 30, 1792 a deputation of mulattoes, composed of Raymond Dusouchet, Saint-Réal, Poizet, Fleury, Lamotte, Colon, and Honoré Saint-Albert, was permitted to appear before the Legislative Assembly, and Raymond as spokesman pledged to France the allegiance of all the mulattoes in the colonies.[29] On February 4, 1794 a report on conditions reigning on the island of Santo Domingo was made to the Convention by one of three delegates newly arrived in France (a Negro, a mulatto, and a white) and so impressive was the report and so charged was the atmosphere that their abolitionist

[26]*Mémoires, correspondance et manuscrits du général Lafayette, publiés par sa famille* (Paris and London, 1837-38, 6 v.), II, 290-91. In October 1789 Lafayette accepted the position of honorary commander of a mulatto national guard unit in Paris. *Ibid.*, III, 71 n.1.

[27] *Réimpression de l'ancien Moniteur*, XXIX, 285.

[28] Earl Leslie Griggs, *Thomas Clarkson, the Friend of Slaves* (Ann Arbor, 1938), p. 56.

[29] *Réimpression de l'ancien Moniteur*, XX, 3.

friends proposed an immediate vote on Negro freedom and without a dissenting voice freedom was then and there decreed. Slavery was abolished in all French possessions.[30] After the decree of independence a group of mulattoes went before the Convention and afterwards the Jacobin party to express their gratitude. The three deputies from Sanot Domingo called on the General Council of the Commune of Paris and thanked it likewise.[31] Shortly afterwards, on March 8, 1794, a deputation from Bordeaux, containing in their number three mulattoes, appeared befor the Convention to express gratitude for the emancipation edict.[32] At length on June 28, 1795 still another deputation, consisting of Negroes and mulattoes, came before the Convention to testify their loyalty to France. Their loyalty they stated had been questioned, but wrongfully. Their appearance, however, aroused the ire of a deputy named Grouly from Ile de France, near Madagascar, who protested their repeated appearances before the Convention to swear allegiance. If they were accused unjustly, he added, why did they not get redress in the courts?[33] This evidently was the last colored delegation to appear before the Convention, but colored delegates from the colonies, it appears, sat both in this body and in the Corps Législatif of the Directory that followed it.

In summarizing this material it will be seen that sidelights are thrown on Negroes and mulattoes in various walks and roles of life in France during the 1700's. It is extravagant to say that all facets of French life were here represented. Many however were. Paris was the chief scene of their activity, as it was the place of enchantment

[30] *Ibid.*, XIX, 389-95, 615. The names of the colored representatives from Santo Domingo on this occasion were Bellay and Mills. Cee C. L. R. James, *The Black Jacobins* (New York, n.d.), pp. 112-13.

[31] *Ibid.*, XIX, 429 475 615; *Mercure français, historique, politique et littéraire,* February 15, 1794, pp. 306-07.

[32] *Mercure français, historique, politique et littéraire,* March 15, 1794, p. 128.

[33] *Réimpression de l'ancien Moniteur,* XXV, 103.

for all foreigners visiting France. They were so few in number as to be a curiosity to the French, and many of these were employed as pages or butlers in wealthy households. From them the French came to form a more intimate and a kindlier opinion of the slaves that were working on the plantations of the Caribbean planters and of the cargo that French slave ships (*négriers*) were transporting from Africa to the American colonies. Their presence in France was thus a great aid in building up humanitarian sentiment in favor of suppressing the slave trade and slavery. Though in the colonies they were subjected to the role of an inferior race, in France, unless slaves, they were treated relatively as equals. Prior to the Revolution the slave came to be free after a month's residence if brought into France proper; he could be retained by his master only by being shipped back to the colonies or by being kept in confinement in a seaport at the master's expense.[34] The Revolution tolled the bells of freedom not only for the French, but, as pointed out, eventually (in 1794) for the Negro also; and he was entrusted with citizenship, which lasted down to the outset of the nineteenth century when Napoleon again restored slavery, to continue until 1848. The Negroes and mulattoes in France, more especially the latter, were tremendously stirred by the Revolution and participated in military and political activity, with the result that they had a faint but proud part to play in the cause of Liberty, Equality, and Fraternity, and in laying the foundations of the modern "Free World."

SHELBY T. McCOY

University of Kentucky

[34] For the laws on the rights of Negroes in France, see my former article in *The Journal of Negro History*, XXX, 288-90.

WILLIAM WELLS BROWN IN BUFFALO

In January, 1834, William Wells Brown, a mulatto youth about nineteen years of age, escaped from slavery in Missouri and settled in Cleveland, Ohio. There he began working, educating himself, and reading anti-slavery newspapers. During the following summer he became a workman on a Lake Erie steamboat and continued as such for nine years. By the end of the summer he had met, wooed, and married Elizabeth Schooner, whom he affectionately called Betsey; and by the end of the year he had established a home in the city and had begun to bring up a family.[1]

At the end of the summer of 1836 Brown moved his family to Buffalo, New York, for several reasons. Because Buffalo was a terminus of the lake steamboat lines, it was more convenient for a steamboat workman to reside there than in Cleveland. In addition to being then three times as large as Cleveland, it had a much larger Negro population—a fact which seemed to indicate that opportunities for employment for Negroes were more numerous there.[2] Brown was interested in this fact, of course, for every year after the navigation season he would need to find other work, as he had had to do during the two preceding winters. Another fact which Brown could not have overlooked was that it was comparatively easy to move quickly from Buffalo to Canada—whither he might find it necessary to move he knew not how soon. There was also a circumstance

[1] For sketches of Brown's life see the *Dictionary of American Biography*, Vol. III, New York, 1929, p. 161, and also my ''William Wells Brown, America's First Negro Man of Letters'', *Phylon, The Atlanta University Review of Race and Culture*, First Quarter, 1948, pp. 13-23, ''William Wells Brown, Social Reformer'', *The Journal of Negro Education*, Winter, 1949, pp. 29-39, and ''A Flight Across Ohio: The Escape of William Wells Brown from Slavery'', *The Ohio State Archaeological and Historical Quarterly*, July, 1952, pp. 272-282.

[2] In 1835, according to a state census the population of Buffalo was 15,661. See H. Perry Smith (Editor), *History of the City of Buffalo and Erie County*, Syracuse, 1884, I, 211, and II, 149.

of which Brown was unaware at the time but which began within the next decade to determine the course of his life for many years. Removal to Buffalo brought him into a little closer contact with Garrisonian abolitionism, which was soon to develop in western New York. Many years were to pass, however, before he was to know William Lloyd Garrison personally and to be directly influenced by him.

When Brown moved to Buffalo, presumably he found a house somewhere in the area east of Michigan Avenue and between Exchange Street and Broadway, for that was where the majority of the Negroes in the city were living when he settled there. I have searched the city directories of Buffalo for the period beginning with 1836 and ending with 1844; and in these directories, which listed residents by race, I found no Negro named Brown listed for any year earlier than 1841. In the directories for this year and the next William Brown, "cook," was listed as a householder on North Division Street, and in the directory for 1844 William W. Brown, "lecturer," was listed as a house-holder at 13 Pine Street.[3] Both of these addresses are in the area designated above. The first two listings might or might not have referred to Brown. Inasmuch as the name *William Brown* was common then, as it still is, and Negro cooks were relatively numerous, as they still are, there might have been in Buffalo at the time another Negro who had this name and who was a cook—which William Wells Brown is not known to have been. The third listing almost certainly referred to Brown, for before 1844 he had become a lecturer for the Western New York Anti-Slavery Society, and lecturing of any kind was not a common occupation among Negroes.

[3] *Crary's Directory for the City of Buffalo*, Buffalo, 1841, p. 17 [p. 193]; *Walker's Buffalo City Directory*, Buffalo, 1842, p. 94; *ibid.*, Buffalo, 1844, p. 65.

For access to the Buffalo directories and newspapers referred to in this article, I am indebted to the librarian of the Buffalo Historical Society

No directories of Buffalo seem to have been published for either 1843 or 1845. Early in the summer of the last-mentioned year Brown moved his home to Farmington, Ontario County, and there was no reason for the inclusion of his name in later directories of Buffalo.

Before his removal from Cleveland, Brown had become a practicing as well as a practical abolitionist and was beginning to take just pride in the fact that he was losing none of his "cases." Soon after he began working on the lake steamers, he had begun to carry fugitive slaves to Canada by way of both Detroit and Buffalo. In his "lucrative situation on one of the lake steamboats" he found it convenient and often adventurous to hide fugitives from injustice, as they came to be called, and to convey them beyond the jurisdiction of the "person held to service or labor" clause in the United States Constitution, Article IV, Section 2, and the Federal fugitive slave law of 1793. Once, according to a tale Brown told long after he had left the region of the Great Lakes, a young fugitive of very dark complexion was trailed by his claimant to the home of an abolitionist in Cleveland. For ten days the claimant and his coadjutors watched so closely the abolitionist's home and also all steamboats departing from Cleveland, that it seemed impossible for the fugitive to avoid recapture. In this emergency Brown secured the help of a painter; and, "In an hour, by my directions, the black man was as white, and with as rosy cheeks, as any of the Anglo-Saxon race, and disguised in the dress of a woman, with a thick veil over her face." Thus disguised and with Brown as his guide, the fugitive embarked on the steamer *North America,* without being recognized by his claimant, and was carried to Buffalo, whence he proceeded to Canada.[4]

Here Brown seems to have adhered much closer to the

[4] William Wells Brown, *The Black Man, His Antecedents, His Genius, and His Achievements,* New York and Boston, 1863, p. 25. This story had been previously related by Brown's daughter Josephine in her *Biography of an American Bondman,* Boston, 1856, pp. 50-51.

spirit than to the letter of truth. Unless the painter was miraculously skillful and the pursuers of the fugitive were inconceivably naive, painting the fugitive as Brown said he had him painted would have been an ingenious way, not of concealing his identity, but of calling attention to him. It is true, of course, that in escaping from slavery fugitives often assumed various disguises; and in helping as many to escape as he did, Brown had to resort from time to time to various expediencies. Some of these might have seemed incredible, but to be useful all of them had to be probable as well as possible—which painting a fugitive hardly seems to have been.

Within a few weeks after his removal to Buffalo, Brown participated in what might have been called the clearing of a wreck on the Underground Railroad. About this time Bacon Tate, a slave-trader of Nashville, Tennessee, went to Buffalo to recapture some slaves who had escaped from Nashville and had settled in the Niagara area. Among these was a family whose surname was Stanford and who had established a home in Saint Catherines, Ontario. The family consisted of a man, his wife, and their child about six weeks old. With the assistance of "a profligate colored woman" who was a servant in the Eagle Tavern in Buffalo, Tate informed himself concerning the situation of the Stanfords, and late one Saturday night he sent four men to Saint Catherines to kidnap them. At sunrise the next morning, with their captives bound and gagged in a carriage the kidnappers crossed the Black Rock Ferry on the Niagara River. After stopping for a few minutes in Buffalo, where their number was reduced and their team was changed, the kidnappers proceeded southward to Hamburg, about eleven miles from Buffalo. There they stopped at an inn to change horses again.

Meanwhile, the kidnapping having been discovered in Saint Catherines, news of it had reached Buffalo before noon, and a group of Negroes from that city, including Brown, had gone in pursuit of the kidnappers and their captives. The group overtook them at an inn in Hamburg, where, encouraged by the innkeeper, they quickly rescued the Stanfords and took them northward again, followed by the kidnappers. When Tate, who was still in Buffalo, was informed about the turn of affairs, he appealed to the sheriff of Erie County for help. Late in the afternoon a group of about fifty persons, most of whom were Negroes, armed with pistols, knives, and clubs took the Stanfords to the Black Rock Ferry to send them back to Saint Catherines. They were intercepted near the ferry by a sheriff's posse of "some sixty or seventy men," and a free-for-all fight between the two groups ensued. Amid the confusion thus created, the Stanfords were put in a boat and rowed across the Niagara River to Canada, while the rescuers and their sympathizers cheered.

Now that their aim had been accomplished, about forty of the rescuers submitted to arrest by the sheriff's posse and were taken to Buffalo and imprisoned for the night. Whether Brown was one of the forty who were arrested is not altogether clear; but if he was, this seems to have been the only instance of his being in prison after he freed himself from slavery. On the following Monday morning those who had been arrested were taken before a justice named Grosvenor and charged with breaking the peace of the Sabbath and apparently with unlawful assembly. Twenty-five of them were bound for appearance in a higher court, by which they were eventually found guilty and fined from five to fifty dollars. No one had been killed in the melee at the ferry; but one man, who was an actor, had been so badly wounded that he died three months later. "Thus ended," said Brown, "one of the most fearful fights for human freedom that I ever witnessed." Freedom, he had found, was indeed more than a word. It involved fighting not only for one's own security but also for that of others; and paradoxically enough, it might mean imprisonment or even death for its defenders.

A search of the *Buffalo Commercial Advertiser* for September, October, and November, 1836, the principal newspaper then being published in Buffalo, revealed no information about the incident I have just synopsized. My authority for it is Brown's account, which seems to have been first published in his *Narrative,* Fourth Edition, Boston, 1849, pages 109-124.

In a lecture before a small audience in Corinthian Hall, Rochester, on October 4, 1854. Brown incidentally referred to his participation during his residence in Buffalo in another kind of rescue of a man who had been accused of being a fugitive slave. According to Brown, on one occasion he and other abolitionists retained Millard Fillmore as counsel "for an alleged fugitive" and that Fillmore served without accepting a fee, explaining that he considered it "his duty to help the poor fugitive." This was the same Fillmore, Brown observed, who as President of the United States had signed the Fugitive Slave Bill of 1850.[5]

Brown also did anti-slavery work in Buffalo in less dramatic but none the less effective ways. He welcomed anti-slavery agents and lecturers as guests in his home. He made his house a station on the Underground Railroad; and because many fugitive slaves passed through Buffalo en route to Canada, he frequently had stopover passengers to accommodate. Moreover, "As Niagara Falls were [sic] only twenty miles from Buffalo, slaveholders not unfrequently passed through the latter place attended by one or more slave servants. Mr. Brown was always on the lookout for such, to inform them they they were free by the laws of New York, and to give the necessary aid."[6]

Among the Negroes in Buffalo Brown discovered many who, like himself, had freed themselves from chattel slavery; but among them he also found many who were being victimized by another kind of servitude, namely, servitude

[5] *The Liberator,* October 27, 1854, p. 171.

[6] Josephine Brown, *Biography of an American Bondman,* Boston, 1856, pp. 52-53.

to intoxicating drinks. In order to abolish this evil, Brown organized a temperance society—one of the first to be organized in western New York—and served as president of it for three terms.[7] That the society became popular and made progress was evidenced by the fact that it grew rapidly. According to Brown's earliest published account of it, within three years its membership numbered more than five hundred of the total Negro population of less than seven hundred which Buffalo then had.[8] In 1843, however, after Brown had retired from the presidency of the organization, it had "upwards of 300 members," although the Negro population of the city had not decreased, even if it had not been noticeably increased.[9]

While this society flourished, it met periodically to discuss and promote temperance, but its meetings incidentally served other good purposes. They became forums in which members were afforded opportunities to learn the fundamentals of parliamentary procedure and public speaking. In these meetings Brown learned both and thereby further prepared himself, as he was doing by studying grammar, mathematics, history, and literature, for the work he was to begin doing as an anti-slavery lecturer within the next six or seven years. He did not then know, of course, exactly what work he was to do during the next twenty-five years, that temperance reform was not to be his primary interest for that period, nor that he would devote much time to it during the last twenty years of his life. Without losing interest in the cause of temperance, he became increasingly interested in the organized abolition movement and sought to translate his interest into action more extensive than his work as a conductor on the Underground Railroad

[7] William Wells Brown, *Three Years in Europe; Or, Places I Have Seen and People I Have Met*, London, 1852, p. xix.

[8] *Narrative of William W. Brown*, Second Edition, Boston, 1848, p. 108.

[9] *Minutes of the National Convention of Colored Citizens: Held at Buffalo, ... August, 1843*, New York, 1843, pp. 36 and 37.

had been. In the mean time other things beside temperance and abolitionism claimed some of his attention.

A daughter had been born to the Browns in 1835 and another in 1836, while they were still living in Cleveland. The first of these children had died when she was only a few months old. In the summer of 1839 a third daughter was born to the Browns and was named Josephine. This was the child who within twenty years was to make her father proud of her for many reasons. But now while she was a baby, although she filled her father's eyes with light, he was worried about her and her sister's future. Because of the pro-slavery power in the South and the anti-Negro sentiment in the North, he could hardly expect that there would ever be realized in America for either Josephine or her three-years-old sister the kind of future he wanted to be theirs. Could it be realized anywhere else? He wondered. Why not travel a little and try to find out?

In 1840 Brown visited Cuba and Haiti and possibly other islands in the West Indies. If the purpose of his trip was what I have conjectured in the preceding paragraph, probably Haiti was his principal objective. He had doubtless heard of the successful revolution of the Haitian Negroes and was interested in the possibilities of life unhampered by race prejudice in the Negro republic. On the contrary, knowing that slavery still existed in Cuba and that it had been only recently abolished in the British West Indies, he could scarcely have dreamed of finding better prospects in the former than in the United States or as good opportunities in the latter as in Canada. Brown probably was not favorably impressed by what he saw on his trip. Anyway, he said nothing about it in any of the editions of his *Narrative* or in any of his autobiographical sketches, nor did his daughter Josephine mention it in her biography of him.

In his *The Negro Author,* New York, 1931, page 168, Vernon Loggins said that possibly Brown made a trip to the West Indies between 1854 and 1863. Loggins's conjecture is based on Brown's statement in the "Preface" to his *The Black Man*, New York and Boston, 1863, page 6, that he had visited the West Indies. In this statement there is no specific reference to time. Apparently Loggins was unaware of Brown's remark in his *The Rising Son*, Boston, 1874 pages 80 and 140, that he had visited Havana in 1840 and Haiti about the same time. I have traced Brown's activities in the northern United States and Canada month by month from his return to America in September, 1854, after a sojourn of five years in Great Britain, to December, 1858, and from May, 1859, to December, 1862, when the first edition of *The Black Man*, including the "Preface," was actually published.[10] If Brown made a trip to the West Indies between the dates mentioned by Loggins, he must have done so during the first four months of 1859, and that trip should not be confused with the one he made in 1840.

After visiting the West Indies, which he might have done between navigation seasons on the Great Lakes, Brown returned to his work on one of the lake steamers and therewith to his conductorship on the Underground Railroad. As an officer on what might have been called the Lake Erie Division of this railroad, he was popular and busy. Between the first of May and the first of December, 1842, he carried sixty-nine fugitive slaves to Canada. In 1843 on a trip to southern Ontario, he renewed acquaintances with many Negroes whom he had helped to get there. In the village of Malden alone he saw seventeen who had been his passengers.[11]

During Brown's nine years of freedom his observations in Cleveland, Buffalo, and elsewhere had aroused in him a profound concern for the welfare and the future of Negroes in America; but he had not learned much about what Negroes beyond the communities with which he was

[10] See the brief reviews of this book in *The Liberator* for December 12, 1862, p. 198, and in the *National Anti-Slavery Standard* for December 20, 1862, p. [3].

[11] *Narrative of William W. Brown*, Boston, 1847, pp. 109-110.

familiar were doing as a group to improve their condition, nor had he become acquainted with the Negroes who might be correctly considered leaders beyond their respective communities. Before the end of the summer of 1843 he learned a great deal about what Negroes as a group were trying to do for themselves, and he came to know many of the Negroes who had achieved some prominence and whose names he had seen ocacsionally in anti-slavery newspapers. Early in August, with the Reverend George Bradburn of Massachusetts, Frederick Douglass arrived in Buffalo to hold anti-slavery meetings. These meetings had been scheduled as a part of the "Second Series" of the "One Hundred Anti-Slavery Conventions" which were to be held during the last six months of 1843 "chiefly in New York, Pennsylvania, Ohio, and Indiana."[12] Being displeased with both the place provided for the meetings and the first audience, which seemed to him to consist of "ragamuffins", Bradburn withdrew and took the next steamboat to Cleveland, where his brother Charles resided. The meetings were to be held in an old building at the intersection of Washington and Seneca Streets, because it was the best place available to the local abolitionists who had arranged for the meetings. This structure had once been a Baptist church, but more recently it had been the central post office.[13] There Douglass spoke daily for almost a week "to audiences constantly increasing in numbers and respectability," until a Baptist church "was thrown open" to him; and when the church became overcrowded, he "went on Sunday into the open Park and addressed an assembly of four or five thousand persons".[14]

If Brown attended these meetings, as presumably he

[12] See the notice concerning these conventions in the *National Anti-Slavery Standard* for July 20, 1843, p. 27. According to this notice meetings were to be held in Buffalo August 7th-9th.

[13] See H. Perry Smith (Editor), *op. cit.*, II, 527.

[14] *Life and Times of Frederick Douglass*, Written by Himself, New Revised Edition, Boston, 1895, p. 284.

did, they were probably the first occasions on which he saw Douglass and heard him speak; and as will be seen, he accredited Douglass with doing remarkable good for abolitionism in Buffalo. In November, 1842, the American Anti-Slavery Society had held a series of conventions in Rochester, Syracuse, and Utica mainly for the purpose of counteracting the influence of the Liberty Party in what might have been regarded as its headquarters in western and central New York.[15] Frederick Douglass, Charles Lenox Remond, and William Lloyd Garrison had been scheduled to participate in these conventions, but Garrison had been the only one of the three to get as far west as Rochester.[16] For all three of them this had been the first trip to central and western New York. Douglass and Remond made their second trip to the region and their first to Buffalo in the summer of 1843, while they were on their tour of the One Hundred Anti-Slavery Conventions to which I have referred.

While reading the *National Anti-Slavery Standard* for July 20, 1843, page 27, and *The Liberator* for July 21st, page 115, Brown must have seen an announcement saying that "A national convention of colored citizens of the United States" would be held in Buffalo on the third Tuesday in August, and expressing the hope "that all who can make it convenient to attend will be present to aid with their wisdom the deliberations of the meeting." The convention began "agreeably to the call", as was recorded in its official minutes, on Tuesday, August 15th, and continued for five days.[17] The "large public hall" in which the first session was held was the same building in which Douglass

[15] See the notices in the *National Anti-Slavery Standard* for October 27, 1842, p. 83, and in *The Liberator* for November 4, 1842, p. 175. See also Wendell P. and Francis J. Garrison, *William Lloyd Garrison, 1805-1879, The Story of His Life Told by His Children*, Boston, 1894, III, 63.

[16] Wendell P. and Francis J. Garrison, *op. cit.*, III, 65.

[17] *Minutes of the National Convention of Colored Citizens: Held at Buffalo, ... August, 1843*, New York, 1843, 39 pp.

had recently lectured against slavery. About forty persons were present for this session. The six representatives from Buffalo were William Wells Brown, Samuel H. Davis, Abner H. Francis, William Hall, Henry Thomas (one of the temporary secretaries), and George Weir. The Reverend Amos G. Beman of New Haven, Connecticut, was chosen president of the convention and was supported by a superabundance of vice-presidents—seven of them, one of whom was Douglass.

Brown served on the Committee on the Roll of Delegates, the Committee on Rules, and the Committee on Finance. The fifteen rules drawn up by the second of the committees just named, of which there were two members in addition to Brown, evinced a clear understanding on the part of the committee of parliamentary procedure. Brown spoke at several of the sessions but did not attract special attention as a speaker. Nothing he said and only extracts from other speeches were recorded in the minutes of the convention. *The Buffalo Daily Gazette* for Friday, August 18th, page [3], more or less favorably reported the convention and especially commended Henry Highland Garnet, then of Troy, and Douglass as speakers, but it did not mention the activities of Brown or any other representative from Buffalo. Apparently *The Buffalo Commercial Advertiser* carried no report of the convention.

At one of the sessions Garnet read his *An Address to the Slaves of the United States of America,* advising the bondmen to choose "Liberty or Death" and urging them to resort to violence if necessary to free themselves. The address provoked a considerable amount of discussion. A. M. Sumner of Cincinnati argued that adoption of it by the convention "would be fatal to the safety of the free people of color of the slave States, but especially so to those who lived on the borders of the free States; . . . . ." Others who spoke against adoption were Beman, Brown, Douglass, and Remond. After being considered and reconsidered at several sessions, a motion for the adoption of the address was lost by a vote of 9-14. On the third day of the convention a resolution proclaiming it "the duty of every lover of liberty to vote the Liberty [Party] ticket so long as they are consistent with their *principles*" was passed, with seven dissenting votes. Brown, Douglass, and Remond were among the dissenters. At a session the next day it was resolved that the conventions should "hail with pleasure the organization of the Freeman's Party, based upon the great principles contained in the Declaration of Independence, ..." Brown, Douglass, and Remond opposed this resolution, because they took it for granted that the Freeman's Party was the same as the Liberty Party, and they "neither believed in the party, nor in the leading men of the party, and as a matter of course could not and would not enroll themselves under its broad banner, nor encourage others to do so; . . . . . ." As Garrisonian abolitionists, who advocated immediate emancipation but did not expect to achieve it directly by means of partisan politics, Douglass, at that time, and Remond were naturally unsympathetic towards the Liberty Party. Whether Brown's vote was determined by their influence or by his knowledge of the brief history of the Liberty Party there is no telling. In spite of opposition the resolution was adopted; but for Garnet, who had supported both this one and the one referring directly to the Liberty Party, and Brown this was not the end of the matter.

On August 30th and 31st, less than two weeks after the adjournment of the National Convention of Colored Citizens, the Liberty Party held a national convention in Buffalo. Brown was not one of the one hundred and forty-eight delegates who attended this convention, but he was at one of its sessions at which Garnet spoke. The latter's remarks on that occasion gave impulse to what seems to have been Brown's first writing to appear in print. This was a letter which was published in the *National Anti-Slavery Standard* for October 5, 1843, page 70. In this letter Brown accused Garnet of erroneously reporting "in presence of one or two thousand people" that the National Convention of Colored Citizens had recently passed a resolution adopting the views of the Liberty Party, with only two dissenting votes, both of those having been cast by delegates "from Massachusetts'. From Garnet's reference to the residence of the two delegates, Brown identified them as Douglass and Remond; and after noting that "six or seven" had voted against the resolution, as he thought Garnet should have remembered, he confessed himself bewildered by Garnet's singularizing of these two individuals. The good anti-slavery work which Douglass and Remond had recently done in Buffalo as well as elsewhere, Brown thought, entitled them to much more credit than Garnet seemed willing to give them. "Who was it", Brown asked rhetorically, "that came to Buffalo, and by their eloquence and enthusiasm in behalf of bleeding humanity, called thousands to hear them, and greet them with thunders of applause? Who was it that tore the veil of prejudice from the eyes of the whites of this city? Who was it that came here when the doors of the churches were barred, and with their mighty voices caused them to open to the friends of the slave? Who [sic] are we mainly indebted to for the great change in public sentiment in this city? The unanimous voice of Buffalo will answer, Abby Kelley, George Bradburn, C. Lenox Remond, and Frederick Douglas [sic]. It was they that came here and prepared the ctizens of the city to receive friend Garnet, and the rest of those talented men that have visited Buffalo within the past summer; . . . . When I see such quibbling, by such men as Henry Highland Garnet, it makes me tremble for the fate of the slave at the hands of political parties".

From what I have said above on the basis of the official minutes of the National Convention of Colored Citizens, it appears that Garnet's account of the vote pertaining to the Liberty Party was erroneous, as Brown said it was.

Whether Garnet ever publicy acknowledged his error has not been ascertained. I have found no statement from him in the *National Anti-Slavery Standard* in reply to Brown's letter.

Meanwhile, late in the fall of 1843, probably not until after the navigation season on Lake Erie had ended for the year, Brown became a lecturing agent for the Western New York Anti-Slavery Society.[18] The details of the new agent's agreement with this society, which had been only recently organized, seem to have remained unrecorded. It is exceedingly probable, however, that he began working for no specified salary, but received a part of whatever collections were taken after his lectures, as he was still doing as late as the spring of 1846. In a notice in the *National Anti-Slavery Standard* for May 7th of that year, page 195, Joseph C. Hathaway of Farmington, who was then president of the society, appealed to the public for funds. In this notice Hathaway also said that Brown, "an eloquent and efficient laborer in the anti-slavery field", was the society's general agent and lecturer and that "While thus engaged, he is dependent for his sustenance on the aid of the philanthropist".

At first Brown limited his lecture trips to the towns and villages in Erie County or near it, for he was restricted no less by the want of experience than by the inconveniences which traveling in cold weather then entailed, especially for Negroes. But wherever he went, he found many who needed to be divested of race prejudice and converted to abolitionism. One of the first towns to which he went to lecture was Attica, about thirty-five miles east of Buffalo. After his meeting, which he held in the evening, he found that no tavern in the village would lodge him for the night. As a last resort he went back to the church in which he had lectured and spent the night there. Because it was ex-

---

[18] *Narrative of William W. Brown*, Second Edition, Boston, 1848, p. 108.

tremely cold, he had to walk around in the building most of the night to keep from freezing.[19]

If Brown was surprised by the indifference towards abolitionism which he found in some places, he had good reasons to be astonished by the antagonism towards it which he found in others. Early in the winter of 1844, probably in January, he went to East Aurora in Erie County and almost missed getting a hearing because of the anti-abolition spirit that prevailed there. In the autobiographical memoir in his *The Black Man,* published nineteen years later he related his experinece in East Aurora on this occasion; and afterwards his account was corroborated by Alonzo D. Moore a native of the town. At the time of Brown's visit Moore was a little boy, but his father was Brown's host and introduced him to the assembly in the church in which he had been scheduled to lecture. Thirty years later Moore wrote a "Memoir of the Author" for Brown's *The Rising Son* and in this he recounted some incidents connected with Brown's visit to East Aurora.[20]

Upon arriving at the church Moore's father and Brown found it already crowded—with what kind of audience they were not long discovering. As soon as Brown began his speech a mob consisting of the majority of the men present began coughing, whistling, and stamping their feet. During the barrage of noise thus created "unsalable eggs, peas, and other missiles were liberally thrown at the speaker". One of the eggs hit him in the face and spattered the bosom of his shirt, making him look somewhat ridiculous for a few moments. If this was his first time to be so unceremoniously received by an audience, it was certainly not to be his last. From the experiences of other anti-slavery agents he already knew that he must either learn to master situations like this one or give up as an anti-slavery lecturer.

[19] Josephine Brown, *Biography of an American Bondman,* Boston, 1856, p. 55.

[20] William Wells Brown, *The Rising Son; Or, The Antecedents and Advancement of the Colored Race,* Boston, 1874, pp. 9 and 33-35.

After half an hour of excitement Brown descended from the pulpit; and standing in front of the altar he told the rabble that he would not address them even if they wanted him to do so—and that it any of them had been held in slavery as he had been, they would not have had the courage to escape, for their actions of the last half-hour had shown them to be cowards. Then he told of his life as a slave and how he had escaped and concluded his narrative with an appeal for the abolition of race prejudice and slavery. In this speech of an hour and a half he won the support of an erstwhile antagonistic audience for the cause he represented.

Prior to the meeting some members of the mob had taken to the belfry over the main entrance to the church a bag of flour which they had intended to empty on Brown when he went out. But the man who had been designated to decoy Brown to the place in which he could be floured and to signal his cohorts at the opportune time had been so favorably impressed by Brown's speech, that instead of leading Brown into the trap, he warned him concerning it, even telling him what the signal for the pouring of the flour was to be. Taking the scheme for a hoax, Brown maneuvered to get the flour poured on others, who proved to be some of the best citizens of the town — and thereby caused the perpetrators of the prank to be arrested.

Within the next few months, having gained both self-confidence and experience as a lecturer, Brown began filling engagements throughout western New York. Although he kept his home in Buffalo more than a year longer, he was out of Erie County as well as the city as much as he was in either. He was now acquiring a statewide reputation as an anti-slavery crusader, a reputation which within the next ten years was to spread throughout the northern part of the United States and also over Great Britain.

WILLIAM E. FARRISON

North Carolina College
at Durham

BOOK REVIEWS

African Traditional Religion. By Geoffrey Parrinder. (London: Hutchinson's University Library 1954. Pp. 156. Price 8s. 6d.)

This little book is a general description and appraisal of indigenous beliefs and practices with reference to religion and magic in Africa south of the Sahara. That part of the continent, taken alone, is vast, and there is considerable diversification of physical type and cultural development including religion, among its inhabitants. Some generalized cultural characteristics nevertheless are recognizable as being widely diffused among the regional and local varieties and in this respect a degree of uniformity exists. According to Parrinder "This great comparative homogeneity of African society is apparent in the religious sphere," and he proposes "to treat African religion on a comparative basis, gathering material from various parts of the continent" (p. 11).

With the increase of international and colonial tensions in present-day life, there has been a growing awareness of the position of Africa; hence it is important to understand the African peoples. It would seem that one of the fundamental differences between African culture and that of what is called the West is that in the latter there is a manifest dichotomy between the world of sacred and sentimental values and that of secular and rational interests, while for the Africans these two worlds are continuous and often mutually interpenetrating. "To Africans," says Parrinder (p. 10), "the spiritual world is so real and near, its forces intertwining and inspiring the visible world that, whether pagan or Christian, man has to reckon with 'things invisible to mortal sight'." The significance of religion, of the Africans' entire "spiritual world," then, must be recognized in the attempts of westerners to establish and maintain harmonious relations with them.

In African pantheons, there appears to be universally a high god; in West Africa particularly there is a hierarchy of lesser gods, some of them associated with natural phenomena; and the ancestral spirits over the whole region have an important role in religious belief and behavior. Religion exercises a strong influence in social life, so that the chief's position is supported by sacred as well as secular sanctions and in some instances he is a "divine" or "semi-divine" ruler while the head of the family or

315

kin-group is also its priest and the mediator between the living and the ancestors. There are various specialized religious functionaries including priests and priestesses to the non-ancestral gods in West Africa, diviners, rain-makers, mediums, magicians, sorcerers, witches, and witch-doctors. Belief in witchcraft seems to be highly pervasive and tenacious in African societies, but it should not be evaluated as mere ''superstition.'' It must be studied in its own cultural milieu if its real social functions are to be understood.

The sacred world of the African shows great flexibility and toleration for various beliefs and practices. This multilateral approach to the problems of life is indicated by Parrinder when he says (p. 26), ''Magic, or dynamism, is a part of the belief in a spiritual world which is found all over Africa. It cannot be said that Africans are simply animists, believing in personal spirits and polytheistic pantheons. Nor are they merely animatists, thinking of unco-ordinated energies. A few writers would call them monotheists, since all powers are subject to the Supreme Being. But this again would over-simplify the picture.

''The fact is that we find mixed types of religious belief, in which different phases are found side by side: dynamism, spiritism and theism.''

Islam and Christianity have found varying degrees of acceptance in Africa but have not replaced the indigenous beliefs and practices. Their success in their mutual competition and in becoming more firmly established depends perhaps on their abilities to serve the African's needs and at the same time to respect his personality, and on the attitudes of the groups with which they respectively are associated. There are factors that favor both, although it is not clear which may be the stronger. ''Where these two world missionary religions meet there is rivalry, and it cannot yet be decided which will be the dominant religion. In East Africa the conversion of Uganda to Christianity has checked the southward spread of Islam. In many parts of West Africa Islam seems to be gaining the majority, since it takes over old customs more easily than Christianity, but the issue is still far from being decided'' (p. 142).

Africa is experiencing great social change in religion as in other respects. African religion has been a positive force in social cohesion, and one can appreciate the statement (p. 146) that "The greatest danger in African religious life is that the old should disappear, without some new religious force to take its place. Unchecked individualism, self-seeking, corruption and materialism are the great enemies of modern Africa. Yet the past has been so thoroughly impregnated with religion and its ethics that it is difficult to see how an ordered society can be established without them."

This book, taken as a somewhat general manual, is a useful introduction to the religious world of the African. It shows an appreciable amount of objectivity and sympathetic understanding.

MARK HANNA WATKINS

Howard University

Through Malan's Africa. By Robert St. John. (New York: Doubleday and Co., 1954. Pp. 317. Price $1.95.)

Mr. St. John's *Through Malan's Africa* is just what the title suggests, an account of his experiences and observations as he traveled through the Union of South Africa as it stands in the grip of the Malan National Government. The book cannot be placed, however, in the category of an ordinary travel book, for, no matter how horrible or unjust they might be, there are no interruptions of the vivid and detailed accounts of incidents, episodes, or relationships to record any reactions thereto. The accounts of District 6 in Capetown; the salary scale of white, Colored, and African teachers; a baton charge of South African policemen; the abominable conditions of Africans working in the mines; the transportation problem; the degradation of towns, villages, and reservations inhabited predominantly by Africans; the system of apartheid; and the utter disregard for any suggestion that the native African is a human being and should be respected as such—all attest to the author's objective approach.

It seems that Mr. St. John's purpose for writing this book is to give to the world a vivid and factual picture of conditions in the Union of South Africa and to determine through the Africans themselves where they feel that their greatest hope lies. This the author has achieved magnificently. Starting at Cape Town, he visits strategic cities and other points in all the states of the Union. He observes the economic, political, social, and religious life of the people and interviews their leaders in these areas. The results of his penetrating insight he gives in the clear-cut descriptions of the peculiar characteristics of all the peoples of the land—the half million whites made up of Dutch, French, German, and English and the ten million non-whites made up of Colored people, Africans, Indians, and Malays.

The climax of the book is Mr. St. John's recounting of the story of the few thousand Africans who he believes may hold in their hands the destiny of their people. A significant part of this story is that these Africans themselves believe that the only salavation of the Africans is in their own hands and that it lies in developing their own strength. It is the author's impression that these are "People going Somewhere, People on the March, People on the Way Up."

This book along with the succinct reports on the vital groups, institutions, and issues in South Africa today given in *The South African Way of Life* edited by G. H. Calpin can well serve as documentary evidence to the fictionized materials in Alan Paton's *Cry, The Beloved Country* and *Too Late the Phalarope*.

Finally, this reader cannot imagine one's remaining adamant, uninterested, and unconcerned about the problems in South Africa today after a reading of *Through Malan's Africa*.

GERTRUDE B. RIVERS

Howard University

The American People in the Twentieth Century. By Oscar Handlin. (Cambridge, Mass. Harvard University Press, 1954. Pp. 243. Price $3.75.)

This work tells who the people of the United States are, the sources of their origin, and the processes of adaptation which have made them what they are. The various changes in immigration restrictions and devious adjustments to environment and one another are comprehensively covered. Here are accounts and illustrations of the pressures and strains which immigrants have met as they fused themsleves into the American melting-pot. Cultural, ethnic, and social amalgamations appear to have proceeded systematically according to patterns which have not varied appreciably with restriction changes during the last thirty years. The author not only employs the techniques of social history in his explorations, but uses those of human geography as well in his analyses and interpretations. Such problems as mobility in response to industrial demands, urban-rural shifts of population, and the dustbowl displacements are described in the regional changes which have helped mightily in developing the composite Americans of 1954.

Negroes, Mexicans, and Asiatics are specific currents in the human streams which have flowed, and they receive special consideration which their importance warrants. Among others Jews occupy a singular position because, perhaps, of their unique genius in business and nearly anomalous position among the waves of immigrants who have come to the United States. The Negroes, Asiatics, and Mexicans are possibly the most disadvantaged with the exception of the Puerto Ricans who are in a different category as migrants from a dependency of the nation. Chapter II, "The Color Line," logically stems from the minority elements identified with color, but evidently the influence of this subtle factor has been far-reaching and out of proportion to the sheer numbers of natives and immigrants represented in the total population. Dr. Handlin's examination and interpretation of the color issue are in strict historical fashion, and this seems to shed new light on the entire treatment of immigration and its Americanization which are the central themes of the work.

Out of the complicated nexus of racial elements emerges a consciousness of Americanism and loyalties difficult to define. Immigrants and their descendants represent varying degrees of split-loyalties to the countries whence they and their ancestors came. That hate-groups should appear is quite understandable although the work does not indicate specifically all of the reasons. The dispassionate treatment of the "color line," however, may justify the conclusion that color has been the most fundamental. While the Civil War legally ended slavery, its ideology was perpetuated in segregation which most immigrants have gladly accepted in their adjustment and adaptation to American ways. Yet, the heterogeneous masses of immigrants and their descendants seem to have been molded with increasing degrees of modification and satisfaction into the America of the twentieth century. The testing fires of two World Wars, the hard experiences of alternating booms and depressions, and the difficulties of foreign relations at present have brought Americans of different ideologies and loyalties closer together.

The author probes not only the diverse immigrant elements, but he reviews their mobility and the motives which have brought the fusion which has taken place. The exoduses of Negroes, the importation of Mexicans, and the banning of orientals receive attention which their importance among American people today deserves. Especially interesting is the rise of restriction after World War I, and it is significant that a Protestant Christian missionary, Sidney L. Gulick with experience in Japan, led the way with suggestions! These were incorporated in the laws of 1924 which were based upon quotas that reduced arrivals to a minimum without precedent. The quotas were weighted in favor of what were believed the "superior peoples of Northern Europe," and the orientals were practically eliminated. How much these departures contributed to East-West tensions and explosions in World War II is not mentioned, but they were undoubtedly momentous.

Probably one of the most valuable revelations of this investigation is in the rise and decline of "native groups and societies." These have served many purposes of mutual aid and education in Americanization and have waned in response to new demands. Fundamental among immigrant aims has been the desire to belong and identify themselves with authority and power in the American community. Immigrant conformity to American customs and mores including, of course, antipathy to Negroes has generally been willing as any careful investigation of the records will show.

The values of the *American People* by a distinguished social historian are outstanding. While the author does not document his revelations, he has assembled them from personal contacts, many letters, and out of working familiarity with twelve languages. The style is so clear and moving that laymen and scholars will be fascinated by the running accounts of how many strains of blood, race, ideologies, and loyalties have fused in the twentieth century American. Dr. Handlin has made in this work one of the most vital historical contributions of 1954, and it may well be considered a charter of guidance, toleration, and sanity in safeguarding genuine Americanism.

W. M. BREWER

The Nature of Prejudice. By Gordon W. Allport. (Cambridge, Mass. Addison-Wesley Publishing Company, Inc., 1954. Pp. 537. Price $5.50.)

In his *Nature of Prejudice*, Gordon Allport has brought together into a unified scheme and in one volume most of the numerous theories, experiments, and researches accomplished in the field of the dynamics of group prejudice. It is a definitive work which embraces the entire range of the nature, extent, levels of causation, and characteristics of prejudice from both the psychological and social point of view. The author has admirably woven the data and approches of the various social disciplines into an overall conceptual framework. Thus apart from being a comprehensive analysis of the complex subject of prejudice, the work is also an outstanding example of the use of the interdisciplinary method in the social sciences—an approach which doubtless will be increasingly utilized in the applied spheres of the human sciences.

The book reports on much of the work which had been previously undertaken by others and by the author and his associates over a period of years. To this extent much of it is not new to the close followers of the literature in this field. This observation is not a negative criticism of the book, however, as the need for a unified, comprehensive, and extensive treatment of the subject from all of its various theoretical approaches has been recognized for a considerable period of time by students and practitioners alike.

The book is organized into eight sections each of which thoroughly analyzes major considerations of the problem of prejudice. It is excellently documented, clearly written and replete with descriptions, summaries of research, and experiments undertaken. Where issues are debatable, the author objectively presents the conflicting points of view but at the same time endeavors to resolve the issues.

The earlier sections are concerned with the phenomena of preferential thinking, group formation, group differences, and selected theories of prejudice as they relate to these basic human characteristics. The middle sections of the work examine the acquisition of prejudice and demonstrate the relationships of learning, inner psychological conflicts, the social structure, and social contacts to the development of prejudicial attitudes and behavior. Section VI entitled "The Dynamics of Prejudices" deals with what the author terms (p. 391) "the infantile, repressed, defensive, aggressive and projective portions of unconscious mental life." He indicates that important as these considerations are, however, they do not account for the whole weight of prejudice formation. Thus in later chapters, he examines "character structure" and shows how the entire social world of the individual is important in the development of his personality and attitude formation with respect to prejudice and behavior.

Part VIII, "Reducing Group Tensions," brings to focus all of the prior information which the author has presented in the attempt to bring data to bear on the problem of achieving improved human relations. An evaluation of the several methods of reducing tensions is presented including legislation. The author holds to an eclectic view regarding action programs and sees some merits in all approaches. "After all" he states on page 518, "the fundamental question is can citizens learn to seek their own welfare and growth not at the expense of their fellow men, but in concert with them?" The author states that the human family does not yet know the answer but hopes it will be in the affirmative. It is the opinion of this reviewer that Allport's *Nature of Prejudice* will definitely make a contribution to the accomplishment of this objective as students, teachers, and other citizens utilize its findings in coping with this fundamental problem of our times.

JOSEPH H. DOUGLASS

Washington, D. C.

Waitman Thomas Willey, Orator, Churchman, Humanitarian. By Charles H. Ambler. (Huntington, W. Va. Standard Printing & Publishing Co. Pp. 282. Price $3.50)

The only change in the map of the United States as a result of the Civil War was the inclusion of West Virginia, which was organized into a state from the Virginia lands west of the Alleghenies. The most significant figure to participate in the formation of the new state was Waitman T. Willey. A man of varied interests, Willey was the orator of separate statehood, temperance, internal improvement, abolition, and enfranchisement of the freedman. By his oratorical ability, political aptitude, and sound judgment, he was able to follow the movement to completion.

Dr. Charles H. Ambler, retired professor of history of West Virginia University, has devoted considerable care and study to revive interest in the almost forgotten man who did so much to make West Virginia a part of the Federal Union in 1863. In doing this the author has drawn heavily upon the diary kept by Senator Willey as well as available newspaper materials of his day.

In close contact with Ben Wade of Ohio, Waitman T. Willey was to guide the bill for West Virginia statehood through Congress, and even influenced President Lincoln in his decision to sign the bill. Though a conservative slaveholder, Willey through his influence was a potent factor in leading West Virginians to accept abolition and the Fifteenth Amendment. Professor Ambler states that, "Although Willey knew Negro suffrage was unpopular in West Virginia, he did not sidestep it. Instead, he repeated arguments made by him in the Senate and elsewhere in its behalf. His presentation was based on two fundamentals, viz: No representative government can stand and prosper that does not derive consent from the governed, and a citizen cannot be taxed without representation in a democratic society." (p. 158) Willey lost the election of 1870, but left far reaching influence by his position.

In discussing the later days of Senator Willey when he was attempting to develop an historical society in connection with the university, Professor Ambler states that, "In like manner, he may not have recalled that he himself was entering the dawn of a social and historical oblivion that would almost completely erase his memory from the Negro race, whose possibilities, rights, and interests he, more than any other West Virginian, had defended, secured, and popularized. But such is the irony of social and political trends." (p. 173) And such is the irony of history.

J. REUBEN SHEELER

Texas Southern University

Confederate Georgia. By T. Conn Bryan. (Athens, Georgia: University of Georgia Press, 1953. Pp. x, 299. Price $4.00.)

Bryan's *Confederate Georgia*, begun as a doctoral dissertation at Duke University, is the most comprehensive study of life in Georgia during the Civil War which has come to this reviewer's notice. Careful examination of the volume reveals that Professor Bryan has succeeded admirably in his announced aim: "to depict as completely as possible the scene within the state" during the critical years, 1861-1865. In fifteen chapters of which those on secession, Georgia-Confederate relations, and internal political problems are easily the best, the author treats every significant phase of the subject: production and distribution during the war, wartime finance, plantation life and slavery, state military campaigns, social diversions, the press, education, and religion. The account is clear, realistic, and intimate and is based upon the dominant theme of a people constantly making adjustments and adaptations to a new way of life occasioned by the War.

This work further documents the fact that in Georgia, as in other Confederate states and in the North, there existed considerably more than token opposition to secession and war. Many northern jurisdictions had to contend with "copperheads," and Georgia had to contend with a group branded as "co-operationists" who rejected the contention that the election of Lincoln was sufficient justification for secession. Opposition and defection were particularly evident in the mountainous regions of north Georgia where the economic pattern differed from that of the rest of the state in that there was little interest in plantation economy and slavery.

Georgia politics between 1861-1865 was dominated by Governor Joseph E. Brown who shattered state political precedent by winning election to four gubernatorial terms. The Governor "towered over the legislature and dominated the state almost as though he were the sovereign of an independent republic." Strongly supported by the common people of the state, he avidly protected Georgia's rights against invasion by Confederate authority and insisted upon "Georgia having her rights and wishes respected." War weariness and disillusionment, which became evident after Sherman's invasion, resulted in a proposal, initiated by Governor Brown, to depose President Davis and seek a negotiated peace with the Union.

Georgians were generally convinced after 1861 that state security required the establishment of effective measures to silence pro-Union sympathizers and to control the Negro population which numbered 462,198 slaves and 3500 free Negroes in 1860 and constituted approximately forty-four per cent of the population. Warnings, threats, and "vigilance committees" appear to have silenced the former, but efforts to control the Negro took the form of legislative enactments, more voluminous and repressive than those of any other Confederate state. This policy of control, only partially developed in *Confederate Georgia,* strengthened the slave code and imposed additional restraints upon free Negroes. The state was sealed against the entrance of free Negroes from other jurisdictions, provision was made for the enslavement of ''vicious'' free Negroes, and the employment and freedom of movement of slave and free Negro alike were further curtailed.

To some readers, among them this reviewer, the author's hesitancy in critically interpreting his sources sometimes results in the absence of those significant reflections and insights anticipated by the reader. Moreover, in light of the slight evidence presented, one might justifiably question the contention that the ''war had a salutary effect in arousing interest in the social and moral status of the Negro'' (p. 243). Certainly Reconstruction history of Georgia proves rather conclusively that such interest as might have been aroused failed to survive beyond the war years. A treatment of educational efforts of free Negroes during the War, e.g., those in Atlanta and Savannah carried on in contravention of the law would have enhanced the chapter on education.

But these are perhaps minor matters, for *Confederate Georgia* remains a distinct contribution to the growing historiography of the South. The format is attractive and the bibliography exhaustive.

B. H. NELSON

Miner Teachers College,
Washington, D. C.

The Journey. By Lillian Smith. (Cleveland: The World Publishing Company, 1954. Pp. 256. Price $3.50.)

The Journey re-affirms Lillian Smith as one of the most perceptive, liberal, and perhaps the most enduring of today's writers. Her self-imposed mammoth task was ''to find an image of the human being that I could feel proud of . . . to reassure myself of man's power not only to survive on this earth but to continue growing in stature . . . to believe that we can fulfill our role in this evolving universe of which we have been given such awesome glimpses.''

Her conclusion? ''To find the point where hypothesis and fact meet; the delicate equilibrium between dream and reality; the place where fantasy and earthly things are metamorphosed into a work of art; the hour when faith in the future becomes knowledge of the past; to lay down one's power for others in need; to shake off the old ordeal and get ready for the new; to question, knowing that never can the full answer be found; to accept uncertainties quietly, even our incomplete knowledge of God: this is what man's journey is about, I think.''

Between question and answer lies a rich harvest for the reader. Weaving together threads of passionately meaningful memories—childhood playmates—childhood playmates handicapped and neglected, a paraplegic struggling to walk, conversations of mothers whose children ''never grew,'' the churchyard graves of 6 children all under four, among countless other glimpses of human beings closing the gap between dream and reality, she forms, as every man must do, her own optimistic image of man. She sees the creative role death plays in life and the fulfillment gained by those who view it as a beginning of new relationships to themselves, to others, and to the dead. Childhood, unmasked by Freud, she explains, becomes not a place of shame and confusion but a ''green growing place'' to solace the sorely tried. She presents an inspiring picture of scientists treating not an isolated physical segment of man but the whole man (mind, emotions, skills), clearing childhood diseases, fighting anxiety and stress in human emotions—in short, using their knowledge for man's whole life.

The crucial experiences which the artist accepts for creativity produce masterpieces to quicken the hearts of men across centuries and forge an unending heritage of human experience joining every generation to preceding ones. ''Without art and God man can never come to terms with his past and relate himself to his future.'' With a paratrooper she searches for the meanings of ''courage,'' ''sacrifice,'' ''fortitude,'' and discovers ''honor.'' ''Honor is a word that could, if believed in by enough people, completely destroy totalitarianism. . . . For it gives dignity and value to man's personal and public relations; it makes means as important as ends; it confers equality on experience.''

Within the confines of a review one is hard put to point out the most poignant experiences and the most useful conclusions so rich, well knit and artistic is the whole. One must simply read for himself one of the most spiritually alive books of the year to gain the optimism with which she views our world. "I believe future generations will think of our times as the age of wholeness: . . . when man learned finally to esteem tenderness and reason and awareness and the word which set him apart forever from other living creatures; when he learned to realize his brokenness and his great talent for creating ties that bind him together again; . . . when he began to realize his infinite possibilities even as he sees more clearly his limitations; when he began to see that sameness and normality are not relevant to human beings but to machines and animals; when he learned to accept his need of God and the law that he cannot use Him, to accept his need of his fellow men and the law that he cannot use them, either; when he learned that 'what is impenetrable to us really exists,' and always there will be need of the dream, the belief, the wonder, the faith."

MARJORIE N. FELTON

Washington, D. C.

A BIBLIOGRAPHY OF RECENT PUBLICATIONS ON NEGRO HISTORY

BY HAROLD T. PINKETT

UNITED STATES

BOOKS

Ashmore, Harry S. *The Negro and the Schools.* Chapel Hill, N. C.: University of North Carolina Press. 1954. Pp. 228. $2.75.

Blackford, L. M. *Mine Eyes Have Seen the Glory* (story of Mary Berkeley Minor Blackford, anti-slavery Virginian). Cambridge: Harvard University Press. 1954. Pp. xix, 293. $5.00.

Brown, Ira V. *Lyman Abbott, Christian Evolutionist.* Cambridge: Harvard University Press. 1953. Pp. 303. $5.00.

Buckler, Helen. *Doctor Dan: Pioneer in American Surgery.* Boston: Atlantic-Little, Brown. 1954. Illus. Pp. 381. $5.00.

Donald, David (ed.). *Inside Lincoln's Cabinet: The Civil War Diaries of Salmon P. Chase.* New York: Longmans, Green and Company. 1954. Pp. 342. $6.50.

Du Bois, W. E. B. *The Souls of Black Folk.* New York: Blue Heron Press. 1953 (reprint). Pp. 264.

Eaton, Clement. *History of the Southern Confederacy.* New York: Macmillan Company. 1954. Pp. 351. $5.50.

Ellison, Rhoda C. *History and Bibliography of Alabama News-papers in the Ninteenth Century.* University, Ala.: University of Alabama Press. 1954. Pp. 209. $4.00.

Handlin, Oscar. *The American People in the Twentieth Century.* Cambridge: Harvard University Press. 1954. Pp. 244. $3.75.

La Farge, John. *The Manner is Ordinary.* New York: Harcourt, Brace and Company. 1954. Pp. viii, 408. $4.75.

Morison, Elting E. (ed.) *The Letters of Theodore Roosevelt.* Vols. VII and VIII. Cambridge: Harvard University Press. 1954. $20.00.

Nicholas, Alice. *Bleeding Kansas.* New York: Oxford University Press. 1954. Pp. 307. $4.50.

Pressly, Thomas J. *Americans Interpret their Civil War.* Princeton: Princeton University Press. 1954. Pp. 347. $5.00.

Shannon, A. H. *The Racial Integrity of the American Negro.* Washington: Public Affairs Press. 1953. Pp. 262. $3.25.

Wesley, Charles H. *The History of Alpha Phi Alpha: A Development in College Life.* Washington: Foundation Publishers. 1953. Pp. 526. $5.00.

ARTICLES

Abram, M. B. Racial Picture in the Southern States of the U.S.A. *International Affairs,* Jan., 1954.

Applewhite, Marjorie M. Sharecropper and Tenant in the Courts of North Carolina. *North Carolina Historical Review,* Apr., 1954.

Daw, Roma Baker. Colored Yeast (story of Thomas Cross, religious leader in Michigan). *Michigan History,* Mar., 1954.

Durden, Robert F. The Prostrate State Revisited: James S. Pike and South Carolina Reconstruction. *Journal of Negro History,* Apr., 1954.

Futch, Ovid L. Salmon P. Chase and Civil War Politics in Florida. *Florida Historical Journal,* Jan., 1954.

Hill, Herbert. Southern Negroes at the Ballot Box. *Crisis,* May, 1954.

James, Josef C. Sherman at Savannah. *Journal of Negro History,* Apr., 1954.

Kendrick, Ruby M. They Also Serve: The National Association of Colored Women. *Negro History Bulletin,* May, 1954.

Mendelson, Wallace. Dred Scott's Case—Reconsidered. *Minnesota Law Review,* Dec., 1953.

Rutland, Robert. The Copperheads of Iowa: A Reexamination. *Iowa Journal of History*, Jan., 1954.

Shoemaker, Floyd C. Missouri's Proslavery Fight for Kansas. *Missouri Historical Review*, Apr., 1954.

Taylor, Alrutheus A. Fisk University and the Nashville Community. *Journal of Negro History*, Apr., 1954.

Taylor, Joseph H. The Great Migration from North Carolina in 1879. *North Carolina Historical Review*, Jan., 1954.

Thrun, Caroline W. School Segregation in Michigan. *Michigan History*, Mar., 1954.

DOCUMENT

Foran, William A. The Attempted Conversion of James L. Orr. *Journal of Negro History*, Apr., 1954.

LATIN AMERICA AND THE WEST INDIES

BOOKS

Entralgo, Elias José. *La liberación étnica cubana*. Habana. 1953. Pp. 272.

Pressoir, Catts. *Haiti: Monuments historiques et archéologiques*. Mexico City: Pan American Institute of Geography and History, Commission on History. 1952. Pp. 32. Plates. Paper.

Schurz, William L. *This New World: The Civilization of Latin America*. Illustrations by Carl Folke Sahlin. New York: E. P. Dutton and Company. $6.00.

Vidal y Saura, Fulgencio. *Haiti: Primer Estado Negro*. Madrid: Morata. 1953. Pp. 210. Ptas. 100.

Williams, Gertrude. *The Economics of Everyday Life in the West Indies*. University of the West Indies. 1953. Pp. 52.

ARTICLES

Bastide, Roger. Relações racais entre negros e brancos en São Paulo (cont.). *Anhembi* (São Paulo), July, 1953.

Ganzert, F. British West Indies Federation. *World Affairs*, Winter, 1953.

Manley, N. W. Rural Work. *Farmer* (Kingston, Jamaica), Nov.-Dec., 1953.

Markoe, William M. Faded Glory at St. Croix. *Interracial Review*, June, 1954.

Moore, W. R. Jamaica: Hub of the Caribbean. *National Geographical Magazine*, Mar., 1954.

Plata, Horacio Rodriguez. Primer centenario de la libertad de
los esclavos. *Boletín hist. antiguedades* (Bogotá), Feb.-Mar.,
1953.

MICROFILM

United States. National Archives and Records Service. *Despatches
from the United States Ministers to Brazil, 1809-1906.* Microcopy No. 121. Washington: National Archives and Records
Service. 1954.

AFRICA

BOOKS

Abrahams, Peter. *Tell Freedom.* New York: Alfred A. Knopf.
1954. Pp. 370. $4.00.

Antor, S. G. and Ecker, Paul. *"Most Secret" Politics in Togo-
land.* New York: Contemporary Press. 1953. Pp. 27.

Campbell, Alexander. *The Heart of Africa.* New York: Alfred A.
Knopf. 1954. Illus. Pp. 487. $5.00.

Cookson, John. *Before the African Storm.* Indianapolis: Bobbs-
Merrill Company. 1954. Pp. 279. $3.50.

Goris, Jan-Albert (ed.). *Belgian Congo-American Survey.* New
York: Belgian Chamber of Commerce in the United States.
1954. Pp. 169.

Hickmann, Ernst. *Belgisch-Kongo: Structure and Entwicklung
einer Kolonialwirtschaft.* Bremen: F. Trüjen. 1952. Illus.
Pp. 132.

Maclean, Joan C. *Africa: The Racial Issue.* New York: H. W.
Wilson Company. 1954. Pp. 198. $1.75.

Meeker, Oden. *Report on Africa.* New York: Charles Scribner's
Sons. 1954. Pp. 410. $5.00.

St. John, Robert. *Through Malan's Africa.* New York: Doubleday and Company. 1954. Pp. 317. $3.95.

Taylor, Don. *Rainbow on the Zambezi.* London: Museum Press.
1953. Illus. Pp. 224.

Upthegrove, Campbell L. *Empire by Mandate: A History of the
Relations of Great Britain with the Permanent Mandates Commission of the League of Nations.* New York: Bookman Associates. 1954. Pp. 239. $3.50.

ARTICLES

Christensen, James B. African Political Systems. *Phylon,* First
Quarter, 1954.

Coleman, James S. Nationalism in Tropical Africa. *American Political Science Review*, June, 1954.

Gunther, John. Inside Africa's Gold Coast. *Collier's*, May 28, 1954.

Haviland, W. E. The Use and Efficiency of African Labour in Tobacco Farming in Southern Rhodesia. *Canadian Journal of Economics and Political Science*, Feb., 1954.

Hinden, Rita. Self-Government in Africa: Problems of Status in Divided Societies. *Phylon*, First Quarter, 1954.

Hodgkin, T. Panafrica, Eurafrica, Malanafrica. *Spectator*, Mar. 26, 1954.

Jackson, Barbara W. The Gold Coast: An Experiment in Partnership. *Foreign Affairs*, July, 1954.

Martin, K. From Colony to Nation. *New Statesman*, Jan. and Feb., 1954.

Moss, John. Native Welfare in South Africa. *Fortnightly*, Aug., 1954.

Padmore, George. British Parliamentary Delegation Reports on Kenya. *Crisis*, May, 1954.

Ward, B. The Gold Coast as a Dominion. *New Commonwealth*, Dec. 21, 1953.

CANADA AND EUROPE

ARTICLES

Banton, Michael. The Economic and Social Position of Negro Immigrants in Britain. *American Sociological Review*, Dec., 1953.

Fleming, Roy F. Negro Slaves with the United Empire Loyalists in Upper Canada. *Ontario History*, Winter, 1953.

Landon, Fred. Abolitionist Interest in Upper Canada. *Ontario History*, Oct., 1952.

Little, Kenneth. The Position of Colored People in Britain. *Phylon*, First Quarter, 1954.

Pool, Rosey E. The Negro Actor in Europe. *Phylon*, Third Quarter, 1953.

PERSONAL

ALAIN LeROY LOCKE

Alain LeRoy Locke died in New York City June 9, 1954. He was born in Philadelphia, Pa., September 13, 1886 and his parents were Pliny I. and Mary (Hawkins) Locke. He attended the public schools and prepared for college at the Central High School and the Philadelphia School of Pedagogy. Entering Harvard, he graduated in the class of 1907 with Phi Beta Kappa honors, and he was the first and only colored American Rhodes Scholar. This scholarship he won from Pennsylvania to Oxford University where he studied three years and received the B.Lit. degree in 1910 before studying at the University of Berlin 1910-1911. Later he returned to Harvard 1915-1916 and received the doctorate there in 1918 with a dissertation on the *Theory of Values* which was never published.

Coming to Howard University, Washington, D. C. in 1912, Locke remained there until 1953 when he retired after forty years of service. On leaves of absence he was Inter-American Exchange Professor to Haiti 1943; visiting professor at Wisconsin 1945-1946; the New School of Social Research 1947; and New York City College 1948. During his long tenure at Howard, he was identified with the modern development of that institution and participated in the progressive changes there during his time. While his courses in philosophy usually had small enrollments, the introduction of orientation offerings afforded some contact and opportunity for acquaintance with nearly all entering college freshmen. Moreover, after the elimination of the College of Education at Howard, Locke helped in the development of the present Liberal Arts College and its community of scholars. He worked many years to establish a chapter of Phi Beta Kappa at Howard and lived to participate in the initial exercises there in April of 1953.

Locke's training abroad in philosophy and belles-lettres was unequaled by that of any colored scholar in his time and he, likewise, spent longer continuous periods in formal study abroad than any colored person of record. He was not, however, trained in history and never manifested any interest in the Negro History Movement. Yet, it may be said that practically all of Locke's writings and lectures were in the bounds (some perhaps peripheral) of cultural, intellectual, and social Negro history. There is doubt that he made any original contribution to philosophical knowledge after his doctoral dissertation. His chosen vineyards, nevertheless, were carefully cultivated and he ranged very widely in sharing his knowledge. Howard University was his headquarters, but few scholars lectured as extensively as Locke did and his themes always dealt with some aspects of philosophy, art, aesthetics, and their applications in human and cultural relations with particular reference to Negroes. It was his custom to go abroad nearly every year until his health, which was never robust, precluded these sojourns in Europe where he kept in touch with his cultural and philosophical interests. These were varied rather than concentrated in specific areas as may be observed from his published works and a final volume which he presumably finished and this should appear in time.

Dr. Locke published: *Race Contacts and Interracial Relations,* 1916; *The New Negro,* 1925; *The Negro in America,* 1933; *Frederick Douglass, a Biography of Anti-Slavery,* 1935; *The Negro and His Music,* 1936; *Negro Art—Past and Present,* 1937; *The Negro in Art,* 1941; (With Bernard Stern) *When People Meet: A Study in Race and Culture Contact,* 1941; Editor of *Plays of Negro Life,* 1927; and *Bronze Booklet Series—Associates in Negro Folk Education,* 1927. He served also as contributing editor to "Survey Graphic," "The Board of the American Scholar," and was a contributor to "Phylon." These do not include all of Locke's literary contributions which were widely distributed and dealt with subjects on Negro life and culture.

Locke has generally been credited with originating the "so-called New Negro of the 1920's," and he encouraged the "Negro Renaissance." There is uncertainty that the former ever existed because the Negro is fundamentally American and in oppression, persecution, and suffering, the most American of all! The Negro Renaissance was a complex of many facets—cultural, ethnic, and literary. Locke's knowledge of many of these was comprehensive, and he labored arduously in the interpretation of their finer aspects. There has been considerable exploitation of the renaissance to the credit and discredit of American Negroes. The "white racists and segregationists" seized the Negro Renaissance to emphasize false vaunted innate differences between Negroes and other

Americans with stress chiefly on the "sensational and sordid." Publishers found in the glorified shortcomings of Negroes an avid market with some best-sellers and several Negroes of ability responded for the rewards of publicity and dubious profit. Even Negro dialect was extensively employed (almost anything which had potentialities of portraying the Negro as a different species of humanity) and the authors knew (or should have known) that Negro dialect was anathema to correct English usage. On the other hand, there was opportunity for righteous protest and many writers found outlets for their ability and competence in writing. The result was probably positive for Negro literary progress although Negro dialect threatens now to kill the movie, "Carmen Jones." The use of Negro-dialect is passing into its proper locus of folklore to which it should be restricted in scholarly fashion like the folklore of other people. In so far as the Negro Renaissanse employed dialect as a popular medium of expression it was a cultural disservice.

Dr. Locke's contribution was in the dissemination of culture, goodwill, and the improvement of human relations. In these and many other rôles he was a statesman-philosopher who devoted his knowledge in the common cause of sharing what he had learned with over a generation of his students and the thousands of other people to whom he lectured. He was a rarely cultured gentleman whose refinement was contagious. To meet and know him was a pleasure because he was the personification of modesty in spite of his academic training. Students, scholars, and ordinary people found him easy to approach and generously sympathetic in all endeavors to help propagate culture and understanding. Nothing made him happier than to pass the light of his learning at Harvard, Oxford, and Berlin to others as great teachers have always done. Dr. Locke wore the mantle of his unique knowledge with dignity, humility, and grace, like the sages of all time, and he will be remembered as a disseminator of culture, refinement, and graciousness among those who most needed it.

MARY CHURCH TERRELL

On July 24, 1954 Mary Church Terrell in her ninety-first year passed away at Annapolis, Maryland. She was born in Memphis, Tennessee, September 23, 1863, and her parents were Robert R.

and Louise (Ayers) Church. They sent their young daughter at an early age to Yellow Springs, Ohio for elementary training after which she entered Oberlin Academy then attached to Oberlin College. This enabled her to spend nine years in the Oberlin abolitionist community and the first college in America to admit women. There she completed the classical course and graduated in the class of 1884 as one of the earliest college-bred American colored women. At the Oberlin College Centenary 1933 she was included in the one hundred outstanding graduates, and her alma mater bestowed upon her the Doctorate of Humane Letters in 1948. After graduation and against her father's wishes, she accepted a position at Wilberforce University and taught there two years before she came to M Street High School, Washington, D. C., where she taught one year. Having been trained in Greek and Latin, she early developed a yearning for modern language study. In 1887 her father took her on a trip to Europe where she remained the next two years studying French, German, and Italian which she learned fluently to speak in systematic programs of study under natives in France, Germany, Italy, and Switzerland. On returning to America, she was possibly the most highly trained colored woman in the United States, but she did not choose teaching as a career and only taught romance languages occasionally as sometime instructor at Howard University.

Some men and women ardently seek leadership; professionals are selected, blessed, and protected to lead as they are directed; and others rise to leadership through their ability and the choice of those who are to be led. Mary Church Terrell belonged to the last group from whom all "genuine leaders" have come almost invariably without effort on their part. At her death she was one of the most distinguished women in America and had been the peerless dean of colored women over sixty years. If "Ye shall know them by their fruits," her stewardship was abundantly accounted for in labors for many causes during her active and crusading years in the nation's capital. Although Mrs. Terrell toiled in many efforts for civic and social betterment, she devoted her great ability, consecration, and devotion chiefly to colored women in behalf of whom she always served as "a watchman on the wall." The colored woman in the United States has been doubly disadvantaged because of race and sex while colored men bore only the burden of race—quite enough alone.

Mary Church Terrell was one of the founders of the National Association of Colored Women at the Nineteenth Street Baptist Church, Washington, D. C., July 21, 1896, and she was elected its first president. She helped to insert there and then in its constitution the rule that no president should serve more than two consecutive terms, and she loyally worked in the organization ever afterwards. In 1904 she represented colored women at the Quinquennial International Congress of Women in Berlin, Germany, and addressed them in French and German on the "Progress and Problems of Colored Women." She again represented her sisters at the International Congress of Women for Permanent Peace at Zurich, Switzerland in 1919 and at the World Fellowship of Faith in London, England in 1937. Her activities at home were equally significant as she was a charter member of the *N.A.A.C.P.* and helped to organize it in 1909. Two years later in 1911 she directed the one hundredth anniversary of Harriet Beecher Stowe in Washington, D. C. Indeed, her leadership activities were far-flung, and the causes in which she served were numerous.

During her nearly seventy years in Washington, D. C. Mary Church Terrell was one of the community's outstanding women, and she served on the Board of Education with distinction at different times eleven years. Her training, experience, and judgment enabled her there to contribute invaluable advice on issues, policies, and problems which were often difficult. Though a civic and social leader of the highest stature, she as willingly led picket-lines as she fearlessly presented petitions to Theodore Roosevelt and William Taft on behalf of the summarily discharged Brownville, Texas Negro soldiers in 1907. Unselfishly and courageously she joyously led in such ventures without ever seeking honors or publicity although many honors were gladly bestowed upon her. She was a shining example of the possibilities of a colored woman of "exceptional advantage," and she had no heroine story ever to tell about her "accomplishments in spite of handicaps" as many Negroes have truthfully but too often told. Here was a colored woman of rare culture, dignity, experience, training, and world travel whose attainments had no racial standards of measurement.

As a club woman and lecturer, Mary Church Terrell had an

unusually full life. Few women were called upon to lecture on as many subjects and over as long period as she did. Colored women in particular and colored people in general were always dominant in her platform and conference appearances. Although never a writer, she wrote articles occasionally and they were published in such publications as the "North American Review," "The Nineteenth Century and After," and the leading newspapers. Her autobiography, *A Colored Women in a White World* 1940, contains accounts of her many-sided activities and life. Some of her most militant and noble adventures, however, were in the years after the publication of that work. The American Association of University Women and Washington, D. C. Restaurant cases and the Ingrahm Imprisonment case in Georgia, for example, were among her final efforts. Likewise, the tribute to her at the Statler Hotel October 10, 1953, in Washington, D. C. was the highest honor in the record of this remarkable woman and it would be a crowning chapter. Throughout her long life colored people in America have had no more staunch and uncompromising defender at home or abroad. She allowed no defamer or maligner of Negro honor—especially that of Negro women—ever to escape the logic of her excoriation. It is significant that she cited occasions at home and abroad in her autobiography where she might easily have kept silent, but she retaliated racial affronts instantly. Mary Church Terrell walked with the lowly and exalted, the illiterate and highly trained, and all admired and held her in high esteem. Among them her crusades and pioneer adventures will inspire others to carry on, and there also will remain for her a crown that will not fade away.

HISTORICAL NEWS

"The Negro in America Today" by Alan Paton in *Collier's* pp. 52-66 for October 15, 1954 is the most dispassionate, hopeful, and significant interpretation of School Segregation which has been published since Mr. Chief Justice Warren delivered the momentous decision of the United States Supreme Court May 17, 1954.

Howard University will be the temporary headquarters of the recently formed International Society for the Scientific Study of Race Relations, and E. F. Frazier is President with W. O. Brown of Boston University Secretary-Treasurer. George Belandier of L'Ecole Practique des Hautes Etudes, J. A. Barnes of the London

School of Economics, A. A. Hourani of Oxford University, and A. W. Lind of the University of Hawaii are the Executive Committee.

The School of Advanced International Studies of Johns Hopkins University held a conference on "Contemporary Africa" at the Sheraton Park Hotel, Washington, D. C. August 9-13, 1954. Lorenzo D. Turner, an authority on linguistics of Roosevelt University, read a paper on "Western Culture in Africa and its Effects upon the African." H. M. Bond, E. F. Frazier, and R. W. Logan participated as discussion leaders, and Ralph Bunche presided as chairman at the closing banquet.

The World Council of Churches met at Evanston, Illinois August 15-31, 1954. D. W. Nichols, Bishop of the A.M.E. Church, J. H. Jackson, President of the National Baptist Convention, Inc., and P. K. Dagadu of the Gold Coast African Church Council were elected to the ninety-member Policymaking Central Committee.

Benjamin E. Mays addressed the Second Plenary Assembly of the World Council of Churches at Evanston, Illinois August 21, 1954 on "The Church and Racial Tensions." This challenging arraignment of Christian practices on segregation was extended to wider audiences by its publication in the "Christian Century" September 8, 1954.

Fisk University has become the first colored institution to secure membership in the Rhodes Scholarship Trust. The Fisk student who receives the scholarship will be the first Negro to study at Oxford University on one of the Rhodes grants since Alain L. Locke 1907-1910.

Simeon L. Carson, the eminent surgeon of Washington, D. C., died September 8, 1954. He practiced among the Indians of the West five years after graduation in medicine from the University of Michigan in 1903. Coming to Washington, D. C. in 1908 as Assistant Surgeon-in-Chief of Freedmen's Hospital, he also served as professor of Surgery in Howard University Medical School until 1919 when he opened the Carson Hospital. There he attained a national reputation as a very skillful surgeon before he partially retired in 1939. He was admired as the "beloved physician", and he held life membership in the Association for the Study of Negro Life and History.

Leon A. Ransom died August 24, 1954 in his fifty-seventh year.

He was a member of the widely known and acclaimed quartette of constitutional lawyers, Houston, Marshall, Nabrit, and Ransom, who were the architects of civil rights strategy for the N.A.A.C.P. in the great cases since 1932. Ransom was a brilliant legal scholar of the highest training and was dean of the Howard University Law School at its zenith when he resigned in 1949.

Theodore K. Lawless was recipient of the thirty-ninth Spingarn Medal which was awarded at the annual meeting of the N.A.A.C.P. in Dallas, Texas June 29, 1954. In addition to his distinguished medical record, he has been very active in church, civic, philanthropic, educational, and civil liberties work.

Richard C. Jones has been appointed successor to John W. Davis as director of the United States Foreign Operations Mission to Liberia. Jones is a retired high army officer, and he has had banking experience in Louisville, Kentucky and business connections in Chicago, Illinois.

Joseph H. Douglass has received an appointment as Representative of the United States Secretary of the Department of Health, Education, and Welfare. This position is especially significant because it has no label of ''specialist or assistant advisor on Negro affairs!'' The appointee has distinguished himself in his own right in training at Harvard, as Fulbright Lecturer in the University of Egypt 1952-1953, and as dean of the State College, Fayetteville, North Carolina. His name derives directly from Frederick Douglass whose fame incidentally has honor in this splendid achievement.

Integration of the Public Schools of Baltimore, Maryland, St. Louis, Missouri, and the nation's capital is proceeding satisfactorily. Hence the prophets of calamity and doom are seeing against their wills that democracy and the American way of life need no steel curtain of segregation.

J. Reuben Sheeler, formerly head of the History Department at West Virginia State College, has been promoted at the end of his first semester there to the headship of History and Geography at Texas Southern University at Houston, Texas.

INDEX OF VOLUME XXXIX

J

Jack, Homer A., 6
Jackson, J. H., 338
Jackson, Lena Terrell, 125
Jackson, William Andrew, 40
Jacksonville Ministerial Alliance, 276
Jacobin Club, Paris, 292
James, Josef C., article by, 127-137
Jay, William, 188
Jews, 319
Joachim, John, 293
Johns Hopkins University, School of Advanced Studies, 338
Johnson C. Smith College, 86
Johnson, Andrew, 11, 15, 26
Johnson, Charles S., 6
Johnson, H. W., 204
Johnson, John, 129
Jones, Richard C., 339
Jones, Thomas Jesse, 159
Journal of Negro History, 163, 217, 245, 257
The Journey, reviewed, 325-327
Judd, Norman, 17

K

Kansas-Nebraska Act, 88
Kelley, William D., 16
Kesselman, Louis C., 147
King, Mary E., 35
King, Primus E., 274

Labor unions, 230
Lafayette, 294-295
Langston, John, 11
Latimer's Law, 199-200
Latimer, George, 199-200
Latin America, work on, 82-83, 156-157, 237-238, 329-330
Lawson, Warner, 142-144
League of Women Voters, Jacksonville, Fla., 276
Leeds Young Men's Anti-Slavery Society, 27
Lewis, Albert O., review written by, 232-233
Lewis, Hylan, 162
Lewis, Israel, 53, 56
Lewis, William H., 164
The Liberator, 308
Liberian Centennial, 154
Liberty Hall, 49
Lincoln, Abraham, 130, 225, 231
Lincoln University, 86, 246
Lind, A. W., 338

Lindsay, Arnett G., 4-5
Lindsley, J. B., 113
Liston, Hardy, 86
The Literary World, 95
Locke, Alain, 216-217, 246; biographical sketch, 332-334; 338
Logan, R. W., 338
Loggins, Vernon, 305-306
London Emancipation Society, 41
London *Daily News*, 29-30
London *Times*, 37
Longworth, Nicholas, 53
Louis, Joe, 152
Lyman Abbott, Christian Evolutionist, 149-151
Lynch, James, 129, 136-137

M

Malan, Daniel, 317-318
Malvan, John, 43
Manley, Norman W., 154
Marshall, Thurgood, 85, 339
Martin, Gaston, 291
Martin, J. Sella, 39-40
Martineau, Harriet, 41
Maryland, Colonial era in, 67-69; fugitive slavery and Prigg case, 185-205
Marx, Karl, 231
Massachusetts, fugitive slavery law in, 199
Mason, James Y., 196
Mathews, John E., 273-274, 275, 276, 281
Mays, Benjamin E., 338
McCloy, Shelby T., article by, 284-297
McElwee, Samuel A., 125
Meigs, Montgomery C., 127
Merrill, James G., 121
Mexicans, 319, 320
Meyer, Agnes E., book by, reviewed, 233-235
Michigan, Negro suffrage in, 18, 20, 25
Michigan, Negro suffrage in, 1865-1870, 14, 25, 26
Middleton, Arthur Pierce, book by, reviewed, 67-69
Miles, Theodore G., review written by, 153-154
Miller, Kelly, 215
Millin, Sarah Gertrude, book by, reviewed, 221-223
Mills, James, 128
"Ministers without Portfolio," 3, 27-42

Russell, Lord John, 41
Russell, Richard, 146
Russwurm, John B., 209, 210
Ruth Sloan Associates, Inc., 163

S

Sanchez, G. Warren, 273-274, 278, 279
Saunders, Prince, 211
Savannah Herald, 135
Savannah Republican, 93
Saxton, R., 135
Schlesinger, Sr., A. M., 150, 245
School of Advanced International Studies, Johns Hopkins University, 338
Schurz, Carl
Schweitzer, Albert, 7
Scottsboro case, 153
Scribner, Dora Anna, 86
Selassie, Haile, 246
Seward, William, 188, 196
Shackelford, Jane D., 255
Sheeler, J. Reuben, 144-145, 163, 339; review written by, 322-323
Sheiner, Leo, 278-279
"Sherman Savannah," 127-137
Siriboe, Kwasi
Slave songs, 142-144
Smalls, Robert, 96
Smedley, Robert, 204
Smith vs. Allwright, 270, 271, 272, 274-275, 283
Smith, E. P., 112
Smith, Frank Gatewood, 125
Smith, Gerrit, 11
Smith, James McCune, 208
Smith, Lillian, book by, reviewed, 325-327
The Social Politics of FEPC, 147
Socialist Party, 215
Souls of Black Folk, 85, 140-142, 150
South Africa, 221-223
The South African Way of Life, 318
Southall, Sara E., 147
Southern Baptist Convention, 245
Southern nationalism, 223-225
Southern Presbyterian General Assembly, 245
Southern Regional Council, 246
Sphinx, 153
Sprague, William, 90-91
Springfield Republican, 15
Squatter Sovereignty, 197
Stanton, Edwin M., 127
States' rights, the Prigg case, 185-205
St. Domingo, slave trade in, 169-172, 174

St. John, Robert, book by, reviewed, 317-318
Stevens, Thaddeus, 13, 15, 16
Stewart, Ferdinand A., 125
Still, Peter, 204
Still, William, 204
Story, Joseph, 193, 194, 197
Story, William, 194
Stowe, Harriet Beecher, 336
Struggle for Africa, 74-75
Suffrage, Negro, 1865-1870, 8-26
Sumner, A. M., 309
Sumner, Charles, 11, 13, 14, 24, 91
Sun, 94
Supreme Court, action in Prigg case, 185-205
Sweat, Edward F., review written by, 229-232

T

Taft, William Howard, 164
Tallien, Madame, 294
Tallmadge Amendment, 66
Tarbox, Increase, 11
Tate, Bacon, 301-302
Tate, Merze, review written by, 220-221; 245
Taylor, Alrutheus A., 2; article by, 111-126, biographical sketch, 240-242
Taylor, Glasgow, 128
Taylor, Robert N., 129
"Teaching the History of the Negro in Secondary Schools," 4
"Teaching Negro History to Adults, with Emphasis on the History of the Negro in California," 4
Terrell, Mary Church, 255, 334-337
Terry, Emma Jane, 125
Texas College, 159
Thirteen against the Odds, 152
Thirteenth Amendment, 23
Thirty-Ninth Congress, 15
Thomas, Henry, 309
Thomas, Jesse B., 66-67
Thompson, George, 39, 40
Through Molan's Africa, review of, 317-318
Tillman, Ben, 231
Tilton, Theodore, 8-9, 11, 22, 23
Tobacco Coast: A Maritime History of Chesapeake Bay in the Colonial Era, 67-69
Too Late the Phalarope, 318
Toombs, Robert, 29
Trenholm, H. Council, 252
Truman, Harry, 232